YOUNG AMERICA

A Nation Divided: Studies in the Civil War Era

ORVILLE VERNON BURTON AND ELIZABETH R. VARON, EDITORS

YOUNG AMERICA

*The Transformation of Nationalism
before the Civil War*

MARK POWER SMITH

UNIVERSITY OF VIRGINIA PRESS

Charlottesville and London

University of Virginia Press
© 2022 by the Rector and Visitors of the University of Virginia
All rights reserved
Printed in the United States of America on acid-free paper

First published 2022

1 3 5 7 9 8 6 4 2

Library of Congress Cataloging-in-Publication Data
Names: Smith, Mark Power, author.
Title: Young America : the transformation of nationalism
before the Civil War / Mark Power Smith.
Description: Charlottesville : University of Virginia Press, 2022. | Series: A nation
divided: studies in the civil war era | Includes bibliographical references and index.
Identifiers: LCCN 2022016239 (print) | LCCN 2022016240 (ebook) |
ISBN 9780813948539 (hardcover) | ISBN 9780813948546 (ebook)
Subjects: LCSH: Democratic Party (U.S.)—History—19th century. | Nationalism—
United States—History—19th century. | United States—History—Civil
War, 1861–1865. | United States—Politics and government—1815–1861.
Classification: LCC JK2316 .S62 2022 (print) | LCC JK2316
(ebook) | DDC 324.2736/09—dc23/eng/20220427
LC record available at https://lccn.loc.gov/2022016239
LC ebook record available at https://lccn.loc.gov/2022016240

Cover art: "Young America Polka." (Library of Congress,
Prints and Photographs Division [LC-USZ62-89318])

Contents

Acknowledgments

When I began the research for this project at University College London, I could not have imagined I would be finishing a book, seven years later, in Arizona, on a postdoctoral fellowship. In this time, so many wonderful people have had an enormous impact on my work, whether they know it or not. Perhaps most of all, I would like to thank Adam Smith. Ever since taking his course on modern America as an undergraduate, I have been hooked on the history of the United States. Adam has showed me what a good historian can do, guided me through the field, and given me the freedom to find what I want to say. Without him, I simply would not have been able to begin this book, let alone see it through to the end. I would also like to thank David Sim, Richard Carwardine, Alex Goodall, and Matthew Mason for their readiness to offer incisive comments on early drafts and to probe me to think about new ideas in unfamiliar ways. Mara Keire and Iain McDaniel both inspired me to draw on cultural and intellectual history by showing me the exciting avenues these disciplines can take.

I would like to thank the University of Oxford, particularly Mansfield College and the Rothermere American Institute, for their warm welcome in my most recent role as a Junior Research Fellow. I could not have asked for better colleagues than Daniel Rowe, Alice Kelly, Helen Lacey, and Steve Tuffnell. I also thank the whole of the School of Historical, Philosophical and Religious Studies at Arizona State University, especially the Political History and Leadership Program, for making me feel at home in their academic community after finishing my doctoral work. Donald Critchlow and Jonathan Barth were invaluable mentors, taking me through the publication process and inspiring me with their scholarship, teaching styles, and work ethics. Catherine O'Donnell offered me a standard of intellectual history that I could strive for, as well as invaluable advice for finding my feet in the classroom. James and Courtney Hrdlicka were generous with both their ideas and books when hosting at their various Arizona residences, while Adrian Brettle never failed to pique my curiosity with the beguiling range of his historical knowledge. I also thank Roxane Barwick and Amy Shepard for their witty and warm company.

Particularly in the later stages of this project, my work has benefited from a number of scholars who have shown great generosity in sharing their thoughts, namely Joshua Lynn, Michael Woods, Yonatan Eyal, Andrew Shankman, Daniel

Peart, Billy Coleman, Alys Beverton, Craig Bruce Smith, and Jon Grinspan. These scholars showed me what an academic community can be at its best. I am also grateful to the anonymous reviewers for the University of Virginia Press for providing such detailed, encouraging, and thoughtful feedback. Their comments challenged me to think harder about the project while distilling what my work was about with clarity and precision. I thank Nadine Zimmerli at the University of Virginia Press for her invaluable guidance and lively conversations about the world of academia. I never expected the process of publishing my first book to be as smooth and enjoyable as she made it. I am also grateful to Leslie Tingle for precise and constructive copyediting.

I would not have been able to undertake the research for this book without the generous support of a number of funding bodies that do so much to sustain humanities research in the UK. I am grateful to the Wolfson Foundation for a Postgraduate Scholarship in the Humanities, as well as the British Association of Nineteenth-Century Americanists for a travel award. The annual meetings for BrANCH, BAAS, SHEAR, and S-USIH have provided stimulating audiences for papers derived from many sections of this book.

At University College London, I was fortunate enough to meet a tightknit group of colleagues and friends with whom I spent long evenings talking history at the Birkbeck Bar: Matt Griffin, David Tiedemann, Andrew Short, Gareth H. Davies, Jack Sergeant, Agata Zielinska, Shane Horwell, and Grace Redhead all deserve thanks for keeping my spirits up and academic passions alight. At Arizona State University I was lucky to enjoy the company of another circle that usually gathered after work on Friday afternoons at Casey Moore's Oyster House: Henry Thompson, Helen Baxendale, Scott Scheall, Matt Simonton, Trevor Shelley, Adam Scales, Patrick Bingham, and, most especially, Adria Laborin. I would also like to thank the many students I taught at ASU. Once they had got past the shock of listening to US history lectures in a British accent, these young people were a constant source of inspiration. Seeing my students pursue history with such purpose and enthusiasm constantly renewed my passion for studying the past. I also thank my schoolteachers for stimulating my curiosity long before I chose to study history at university. In particular, I thank Andrew Swarbrick, whose literature classes on American fiction were a huge part of why I came to focus on the history of the United States in the first place.

My family and friends have been a welcome source of support throughout this project. My mother and father, Theresa and JP, have always encouraged me to pursue my interests, while I have benefited from my sister's reading recommendations since I was a teenager. I am grateful to my late grandfather John for fostering my desire to ask questions about history and to explore where the answers might lead. I thank my grandfather Alan for his companionship in California after long spells either at ASU or in the American archives. Finally, my friends have provided great strength and inspiration throughout the process of writing and research. Everyone who helped to make 20 Sutherland Square such a wonderful home between 2014 and 2018, especially Katie Lines, deserves huge thanks, not least for reminding me there is life outside the library.

YOUNG AMERICA

Young America Democrats—
The Post-Jacksonian Generation

By the time Andrew Jackson died in 1845, the party antebellum Americans termed "the Democracy" had undergone a subtle but significant ideological shift. Having settled many domestic disputes of the 1830s in the party's favor, a new generation of Democrats, known as the Young America movement, emerged in the following decade. Still pursuing the contours mapped out by the great patriarchs of the party, these Democrats nonetheless sought to renew the Jacksonian agenda. At the center of their worldview was a desire to reshape the international order according to the same "Democratic principles" of state sovereignty, racial homogeneity, and self-government that had proved so popular within the United States. To fulfil these ends, the Young America Democrats pushed for territorial expansion on the American continent; the promotion of democratic, independent nation-states in Europe; the spread of free trade around the world; and the advancement of a "Democratic" intellectual culture. When slavery became an intractable issue during the 1850s, Young Americans remained a coherent faction within the party.[1] Although some peeled off to join the Republican ranks, a shared commitment to Jacksonian ideology framed the political choices of these former allies who had previously united under the Democratic banner. Of course, the interrelated concerns that informed the Young America movement had shaped Democratic ideology since the administration of Thomas Jefferson. Nevertheless, two factors—one domestic and one foreign—heightened the cosmopolitan character of both the policies and the ideology of the Democrats from 1837 to 1861: the success of their agenda within the United States and the influence of liberal nationalism in Europe.[2]

In some respects, the very success of Andrew Jackson's Democratic Party made a change in orientation unavoidable. Since Jackson's election to the presidency in 1828, the Democrats had waged an unrelenting war against the Second Bank of the United States. Preserving the sovereignty of individual states against federal encroachment was a central component of the Jacksonian political tradition.

Because one fifth of the bank's deposits were owned by the federal government, Jackson's followers believed the dominance of the bank by centralized authorities was economically unstable and politically unconstitutional. After a protracted political struggle known as the Bank War, Jackson vetoed a bill for the bank's recharter in 1832 and withdrew federal funds in 1833, destroying its character as a mixed corporation. Jackson's heavy-handed economic strategy and liberal use of the executive order contributed to economic downturn in 1837 and earned him the name "King Andrew" among his political opponents. Nevertheless, by the end of the decade, the Democrats had been largely successful in turning the public against a national bank. As Pennsylvania Democrat George Dallas pointed out in 1847, "the Bank of the United States" had "intellectually descended to the Tomb of the Capulets." It was no longer necessary "to conjure up its ghost."[3] Similarly, in 1852 Illinois's James Shields counted "the great struggle against a national bank" as one of the Democrats' victories against the "impediments" to national progress.[4] Having severed the link between finance and the federal government, Democrats sought new avenues for the melioration of the struggling masses—by which they meant white working men. While jealously guarding the independence of the states at home, Democrats set about extending self-government in the American hemisphere and beyond.

In addition to the shifting priorities of domestic politics, huge transformations in the global order shaped the Democrats' more internationalist worldview. Across Europe calls for reform among the middle and working classes reached their apex in the 1840s, with liberal and radical groups demanding political representation, increased freedoms, and economic opportunities. In February 1848 the French overthrew their constitutional monarch, King Louis Philippe, and established the short-lived Second Republic. That same year uprisings followed in Ireland, Hungary, and Prussia. Closer to American shores, Cuban creoles chafed under Spanish rule, and Latin American revolutionaries like Narciso López attempted to instigate uprisings during the 1850s. These revolutions in Europe and Latin America mostly ended in failure: none managed to establish the social stability necessary to maintain a republican government. As the late Victorian historian G. M. Trevelyan pointed out, "1848 was the turning point at which modern history failed to turn."[5] But despite the evanescent nature of these uprisings, the revolutionary agitation that marked European politics during the 1840s and 50s gave new impetus to American political culture. Just as democracy became a real prospect in Europe, technological innovations such as the telegraph and the steamship drew Americans into a closer union with the transatlantic world. During the 1840s newspapers and periodicals detailed events in Europe with incredible precision and distributed new issues to a larger readership in the United States with alarming rapidity. This flow of ideas was matched by the movement of people. Steamships carried dispossessed political refugees to American shores, of which many had been exiled for their incendiary political ideas and writings. Between 1841 and 1850 the rate of immigration was almost triple that of the previous decade.[6] Safe in the United States but marked by their tumultuous experiences at home, immigrants from Ireland, Germany, and Hungary began to shape public life in the United States by entering journalism and the universities as well as by serving in both chambers of Congress.

In this context, it was almost impossible for Americans to ignore the tumultuous state of European affairs. The Democrats, in particular, turned their attention to an international order fizzing with possibilities. A movement emerged within their ranks that took its very name from the revolutionary groups transforming Europe. Joining Young Ireland and Young Italy, Young America stepped onto the political scene. This group of Democratic politicians and writers pushed to reform the international order through America's political, cultural, and intellectual influence. After fighting for decades to promote state sovereignty, free trade, and universal suffrage for white men in the United States, Jackson's ideological heirs looked to do the same beyond the nation's borders. At the same time, they wanted the United States to have its own revolution to promote a more "democratic" intellectual life no longer enthralled to European standards. As we shall see, the Young Americans shaped the Democratic Party as a whole, but they also remained more internationalist, self-consciously intellectual, and insistently "progressive" than both their more moderate and explicitly proslavery colleagues.

The ideological foundations for this new Democratic movement were laid out in the pages of a periodical that was—from 1840—based in New York City, the *Democratic Review*. From its establishment in 1837 until 1846, the publication was edited by its founder, John O'Sullivan, who was a leading Young American of Irish descent allied to congressmen like Stephen Douglas—at least until the outbreak of the Civil War. In the spring of 1846 O'Sullivan ran into financial difficulties and sold the magazine to political economist Thomas P. Kettell and the diplomat Henry Wikoff. During the period from 1846 to 1851, Kettell was credited as editor. Nevertheless, O'Sullivan was still connected to the periodical and continued to advocate for the same version of American nationalism as the *Review*. In 1852 the Kentuckian George Sanders assumed the editorship until the periodical disbanded in 1859, while sources also credit the Irish revolutionary Thomas D. Reilly as editor from 1852–53.[7] As well as covering politics, the *Review* published more broadly on intellectual culture, commenting on fields such as literature, political economy, history, and international law. During its two-decade existence the periodical published numerous articles by Democratic political thinkers, politicians, and literary critics such as William A. Jones, Henry Gilpin, and Alexander Everett, as well as European revolutionaries such as Victor Hugo and Thomas F. Meagher.[8] The *Review* was the most widely circulated Democratic periodical in the country; its reach was truly national and extended into both the Northern and Southern sections of the Union. Fellow Democrats at the *New York Evening Post* estimated that the number of subscribers exceeded five thousand after the first issue in 1837, although this is almost certainly an exaggeration.[9] Subsequent historians have estimated the total to be somewhere between two and three thousand. During the 1840s the *Review*'s readers increased still further. One hyperbolic article from January 1840 claimed that 140,000 copies had been distributed (an average of 6,000 per issue), although O'Sullivan privately estimated the figure at 3,500.[10] Other Jacksonian papers certainly approved. The *Boston Post* said of the publication that "no review in the country is conducted with so much ability."[11]

John O'Sullivan and his brother-in-law Samuel Langtree founded the *Democratic Review* to counter British influence in American intellectual life. Although the nation had declared political independence in 1776, O'Sullivan still believed the Union suffered from Britain's overbearing influence in culture and thought as well as from its geopolitical dominance over the international order. In an introduction to the first edition in 1837, he wrote, "All history has to be re-written; political science and the whole scope of all moral truth . . . considered and illustrated in the light of the Democratic principle."[12] Always disparaging of the past, he claimed, "We have no interest in the scenes of antiquity, only as lessons of avoidance of nearly all their examples."[13] The *Review* set out to reform international law, political theory, and political economy according to the "Democratic principle" of local self-government for white men and in opposition to federal interference. Similarly, the magazine believed literature could promote democratic mentalities in America and Europe. Books with sympathetic depictions of the struggling masses were important vehicles for democratic reform at home and abroad. Fundamentally, the Democrats could only promote their political agenda of popular sovereignty, localism, and free trade by transforming the different components of American thought to conform to their party's fundamental principles.

However, literary elites within the United States presented a huge obstacle to Democratic reforms. From their heartland in New England, former Federalists—and later Whigs—dominated literary culture in the United States during the early nineteenth century through a publication called the *North American Review*. As historian Marshall Foletta has demonstrated, after the demise of the Federalist

Party, conservatives in New England sought to sustain their political influence through the magazine's cultural and political output.[14] The *North American Review* published a mixture of literary, philosophical, and political articles that opposed Democratic ideology. In the political realm, the publication wanted to strengthen the federal government, protect the national bank, and preserve neutrality in foreign policy, as outlined in Washington's Farewell Address. Culturally, it argued that Protestant values would steadily promote social progress through discipline and self-restraint. Mindful of the nation's historical lineage, it celebrated the Union's intellectual ties with Great Britain, praising England's literature and common law even as it championed American authors. Lastly, as I shall explore below, the publication upheld a Burkean vision of the Union as an interrelated "organism" mediated by an interventionist federal government. Taking aim at this worldview, O'Sullivan complained in 1839: "Why cannot our literati comprehend the matchless sublimity of our position amongst the nations of the world—our high destiny—and cease bending the knee to foreign idolatry, false tastes, false doctrines, false principles?" He bemoaned the "tendency to imitativeness, prevailing amongst our professional and literary men, subversive of originality of thought, and wholly unfavorable to progress."[15]

The *Democratic Review* matched this nationalism in intellectual culture by advocating for a more assertive foreign policy both in Europe and on the American continent. After the Revolutions of 1848, Democratic writers were eager for Congress to offer congratulations and official recognition to the struggling nations of Europe. The Continent was a particular concern, the reasoning went, because imperial dynasties subjugated white populations who—on account of their race—had the capacity to establish independent nations. When these empires suppressed the revolts of 1848, the *Review* argued that America had a responsibility to intervene. Just as the despots of Europe banded together in the Holy Alliance, it proposed that the Union should adopt a policy of "intervention for non-intervention" to ensure the success of democratic nation states against their better organized and more powerful oppressors. This might involve suspending diplomatic relations, enjoining economic sanctions, providing political asylum, and even sending arms, money, and troops across the Atlantic. Even as they turned their sights to Europe, Young America Democrats also sought to build on the territorial gains the United States had acquired during the Mexican War. When the conflict came to an end, one writer anticipated further territorial expansion on the continent: "The eagle has scarcely spread his wings over California and Oregon, yet already Canada on the north, and Cuba on the south, seek the shelter of his plumage."[16] This interventionist foreign policy and internationalist ideology, combined with a strategy to revolutionize intellectual culture, formed the core of the *Democratic Review*'s political agenda.

As well as providing ideological heft for Democratic administrations, the periodical was associated with several high-ranking politicians within the party. Personal associations and shared political convictions drew Democratic politicians and writers connected to the *Review* into a common project. In addition to publishing articles and speeches by significant Democratic politicians, the *Review* singled out allies through a regular column that outlined the lives of contemporary statesmen. In 1847 the publication lauded New Hampshire's Edmund Burke not only for his commitment to popular sovereignty and free trade but also for the intellectual labor he performed on behalf of the Democracy. The *Review* described the congressman as a "progressive democrat" and a much-needed political theorist for this later period. Notably, the congressman's work on the Rhode Island revolt established, for the first time, a "link in the chain of finished essays on the theory of the American government, in all its parts, which may be said to have been forged by Jefferson." Moreover, "Very few private libraries in New England" could apparently "compare in usefulness" with Burke's writing because of its "uncompromising hostility to everything aristocratic or un-American."[17] In its "Political Portrait" of George Dallas in 1842, the *Review* also emphasized the Pennsylvania Democrat's potential to produce something of enduring intellectual value. The publication first praised Dallas's qualities as a statesman, holding up his "brilliancy of genius" and "spotless personal life." Ultimately, however, it hoped he would withdraw from "participation in public affairs" so that "literature may yet receive from his pen many of those contributions, in which genius and taste are brought to illustrate the dictates of a judgement always enlightened, and the honest sentiments of a generous heart."[18] Of course, the publication dedicated space to overtly proslavery Democrats and more moderate figures within the party, too. Nevertheless, praise was only offered insofar as these statesmen conformed to the periodical's radical political program. John C. Calhoun's support for nullification, for example, meant his early political career had seen "right and wrong . . . intermingled," while James Buchanan was "more prone to moderate views and measures . . . than always, we confess, harmonizes exactly with the inclination of our own mind."[19]

In turn, political figures associated with the *Review* praised its efforts to articulate and popularize Democratic ideology. California's Edward C. Marshall, for example, boasted of his loyalty to Young America and proudly and publicly allied himself with the *Democratic Review*. In 1853 Marshall told the House of Representatives he supported the annexation of Cuba "in behalf of Young America and the progressives with whose opinion I sympathize."[20] In another speech that year, he explicitly defended the *Democratic Review* against the charges of more conservative Democrats like John C. Breckenridge, who denounced the radicalism of the periodical's politics.[21] Marshall's loyalty did not go unnoticed by the editor. According to his wife's diary, George Sanders was "delayed" in returning home "for . . . Marshall of California's speech in reply to Breckenridge of Kentucky," which sought to "to defend Mr. Sanders and the *Review.*"[22]

This book defines Young Americans as both the regular contributors to the *Democratic Review* and the politicians associated with it—who were united by a more cosmopolitan, and self-consciously progressive, iteration of Jacksonian ideology. Although these figures did not always define as a movement, they did share the same political project: to defend and extend the principles of state sovereignty, local self-government, and free trade for white men around the world. Moreover, these Democrats formed a loose political network that centered around the *Review.* In Congress Senator Stephen Douglas of Illinois, who the *New York Herald* called the "embodiment and representative of Young America," was the figurehead of the movement.[23] His allies included Ohio's Samuel S. Cox, Philadelphia's John Forney, and Illinois's William Richardson in the House, and Mississippi's Robert J. Walker and Louisiana's Pierre Soulé in the Senate. Douglas maintained an active correspondence with editors George Sanders and John O'Sullivan as well as the historian George Bancroft. Newspapers and political figures would often use the terms "Young America" or "young Democracy" to describe these figures, which I have replicated as much as possible.[24] Critics of the movement who invoked the term are especially useful in demonstrating Young America's influence on the larger political culture. Furthermore, there were instances when political figures were associated only with specific tenants within the Young America program, or they drifted in and out of these circles. As with any set of political ideas, people embraced them to varying degrees, while their influence extended beyond a core group of supporters.[25] Understanding Young America's influence in the latter half of the 1850s requires a wider view of the network around the movement, as several key figures gravitated to the Republican Party. Although in some cases they shed the label, these former Democrats maintained some of the alliances, and many of the ideas, that had characterized their allegiance to Young America.

Furthermore, a surprisingly tight network did remain loyal to Stephen Douglas throughout the 1850s, advocating a set of policies and ideas they had developed in the previous decade. In this tumultuous period of political reorganization, the term Young America can be an especially useful way to track intra- (as well as inter-) party loyalties. Referring to "Democrats" and "Republicans" is limited in its usefulness when the parties were being transformed beyond recognition. They were plagued with truly profound factional disputes within their own ranks as well as defections and strategic alliances with other organizations. The Democracy, for example, contained Cotton Whigs and Fire-Eaters who never saw eye-to eye-with Young Americans, while the Republicans laid claim to radical abolitionists, former Democrats, and conservative Whigs. At the same time, the loyalties conveyed by the tags "Northern" and "Southern" came with a host of their own problems and failed to convey the extent to which the ideologies of the "second party system" continued to shape the political climate. In this context, a term like "Young America" is particularly effective at capturing a faction cohering around Stephen Douglas that cannot be understood purely in terms of either sectional loyalties or political parties that were, more than ever, a composite of different ideological groups. Finally, Douglas himself remains, in some senses, an understudied figure. Although there are illuminating biographies of his life and political career, no scholar has examined Douglas as part of a wider faction that found its home *within* the Democratic Party.[26]

At times I will refer to Young America Democrats as Jacksonians, since their politics were—self-consciously—derived from Andrew Jackson and his supporters. Free trade, federal nonintervention in the states, territorial expansion, and popular sovereignty were all staples of the Young America program. Furthermore, like the descriptor "Young America," the label "Jacksonian" allows historians to describe a political tradition that—increasingly—was not tethered to a particular party. Nevertheless, as historian Leslie Butler acknowledges, the term "Jacksonian" has distinctively domestic connotations: therefore, it will not be the primary lens through which I study the Young Americans, a group whose ideology and cultural identity was so closely modeled on the European revolutions.[27] Furthermore, scholars successfully deploy the term "Young America" to subtly distinguish between different generations of Democrats. Although Jackson remained a towering political and cultural influence for Stephen Douglas's generation, the latter had an even stronger internationalist consciousness and were readier to embrace the market revolution, while they hoped to extend Jackson's political victories to the broader realm of cultural life. As historian Stewart Winger writes, "By the 1850s, Young America had replaced the Jacksonians as Lincoln's chief ideological opponents."[28]

In the period from 1844 to 1861, Young Americans did not view their main antagonists as the more conservative factions within their own party, although tensions between the two groups did flare up at crucial junctures. As chapter 1 explores, Young Americans primarily defined themselves in opposition to their Whig opponents from 1844 to 1854, particularly those associated with the conservative periodicals the *North American Review* and *American Whig Review.*

And, as chapter 6 explains, Republicans became their main rivals after 1854. But there were intraparty distinctions between Young Americans and more conservative Democrats as well as more avidly proslavery figures within the South. The latter generally did not accept either the political ideas or the policy prescriptions of this radical new movement. Democrat John C. Calhoun, for example, disdained both the notion of "natural rights" and the idea that the United States should intervene in faraway revolutions.[29] Although some South-erners such as George Sanders, Robert J. Walker, and Pierre Soulé supported Young America, it was often proslavery Democrats who took the dimmest view of the prospects of republicanism in Europe, fearing the consequences a cru-sade for liberty abroad would have on the security of slavery at home. Even in the case of Cuban annexation, which seemed so beneficial to the South, many Southerners did not support the policy as proposed by the Young Americans. Kentucky's John Breckenridge, for example, might have wanted to strengthen slavery in the tropics, but he also was more sympathetic to the imperial proj-ects of proslavery European powers and disparaged the emancipatory rhetoric of the Young Americans.[30] More moderate Democrats from the North, such as William Marcy and James Buchanan, were more sympathetic to Young America, but they did not advocate the program of territorial expansion force-fully enough. For example, they called for the annexation of Cuba to be done gradually, so as not to inflame European powers.

Moments of heightened tension saw these fissures within the party flare up. As Democrats jostled for party control before a presidential nomination, Young Americans often lashed out at older members for not embracing their progres-sive ethos and for truckling to their Whig opponents. In the run-up to the pres-idential nomination of 1852, for example, George Sanders published a series of articles denouncing the candidates Lewis Cass and James Buchanan in favor of the nominee who most vociferously supported the Young America program, Stephen Douglas.[31] In 1856 many Young Americans expressed their frustration with Buchanan's nomination for the presidency. John Geiss, for example, wrote to Douglas that "it was a great error" because "his name adds no strength to the Democratic Party, but rather diminishes it." He worried that Buchanan's opposition to the annexation of Oregon would be made public before the elec-tion, while he told Douglas "the true democracy hope, if he is elected, you will be the power behind the throne."[32] However, these flashpoints of intraparty conflict were not the only battlegrounds for Young America throughout this period. Most often, ideological temperaments and political priorities—rather than intractable differences in political belief—distinguished Young Americans from their Democratic colleagues. Furthermore, Young Americans portrayed the

Whig Party as such a stark antagonist that this division frequently overshadowed fairly significant differences *within* the party. During the late 1850s further complications arose (explored in chapters 6 and 7), when Cotton Whigs joined the Democracy, while the Fire-Eaters became more overtly proslavery. Former enemies became political allies as the main parties reorganized along sectional lines. In this context, a faction like Young America offers a window into older political identities that persisted as sectional ideologies reshaped the second party system.

In contrast to the one, full-length study of the politics of Young America, this book contends that the real significance of the movement does not lie solely in their break with a previous generation of Democratic politicians or with other Democrats within the party.[33] By examining Young America within the context of antebellum political culture at large, I argue that the movement advanced a novel conception of American nationalism: one that combined politics and intellectual culture by drawing on the liberal tradition of natural law. This book certainly focuses on the politics of Young America. It does not primarily analyze the better-known literary side of the movement, led by the critics Cornelius Matthews and Evert Duyckinck.[34] However, I do examine how political figures drew on intellectual and literary culture to articulate a distinctive ideological orientation that transcended more conventional sources of political authority.[35]

Young Americans transformed politics from a struggle between different parties, sections, and even nations into a debate over the liberal political tradition itself. For most of the early republic period, the tradition of natural rights was distinct from the nation, with its specific political institutions, culture, and history.[36] But Young America elided the two, creating a new form of liberal nationalism that merged political and natural rights. In the words of historian Dorothy Ross, "While theorists had long distinguished between natural and political rights, the increasing democracy of the antebellum decades had blurred the distinction."[37] The different aspects of the Democratic program, including popular and state sovereignty as well as free trade, became synonymous with natural rights for white men and formed the basis of an imagined international order.[38] Democracy itself, which constituted the bedrock of American nationality, increasingly became a natural right that predated political institutions, rather than a national inheritance designed to safeguard more fundamental rights.[39] This transformation in the American experience has implications for theories of nationalism more broadly. European scholars like Benedict Anderson have drawn attention to nationalisms rooted in an imagined past. According to Anderson, elites constructed memories of a particular people and place in the forums of popular culture. But the liberal nationalists of the Young America movement popularized a different model: an idea of humanity based on fictitious rationalizations of the future, which were tied to the present through the working of providential laws.[40]

Natural law was an idea developed in the philosophy of seventeenth-century liberal thinkers such as John Locke.[41] It asserts that certain rights are inherent in human beings irrespective of time and place; rights inscribed in the transcendent authority of nature, as it was created by God, and comprehensible by reason. Historians of American political thought have explored this concept as it appeared in the early republic, particularly in relation to the drafting of the Constitution and the Declaration of Independence.[42] But very few scholars have noted its significance in antebellum political culture outside of abolitionist and antislavery circles.[43] Yet it was in precisely this period of Atlantic history that natural rights were fiercely contested and reevaluated in light of new ideas about the nation. Although still concerned with the rights contained within the Declaration of Independence, nineteenth-century Americans departed from the social contract theory, which shaped the political philosophy of John Locke and Thomas Jefferson, in favor of new theories of national development.[44]

During the revolutionary era Jeffersonians had defined natural rights in relation to an abstract notion of humanity's presocial past, which they termed a "state of nature." To safeguard these rights, communities entered into a social contract that could be dissolved if the government infringed upon their liberties without consent. While social contract theory provided a general way to understand the formation of political society, it was not alive to the individual differences between nations or to historical change. More dangerously, the contractualism of the founding generation remained vulnerable to rupture. The Romantic nationalists of the early nineteenth century, particularly Germans like John Gottfried Herder, offered a solution to this problem.[45] They rejected the universalism of the Enlightenment in favor of a historicist understanding of national development. Although their supporters went in many different directions, the Romantics stressed the individual spirit of particular peoples, manifested in specific geographical locations. Rather than entering into a political compact on the basis of rational calculation, the Romantics argued that unspoken traditions and customs cemented social bonds over time. The Romantics, then, sought to explore not only how national characteristics manifested themselves in specific forms but also how nations changed in different historical circumstances.

Like the Romantics in Europe, mid-nineteenth-century Americans tended to reject the social contract as fictitious. More concerned with the nation as a whole, the *North American* and *Whig Reviews* wrote about the nature of man *within* society—a state they saw as the only natural and eternal one. As one periodical noted, "The 'social compact' was made only in the imagination of the philosophers"; society was not "made" but "grew . . . that the first social bond was kinship, and not contract."[46] During the 1840s the more conservative Whig Party conceived of the Union as an "organic" entity that rested on positive laws, historical traditions, and a common culture built up over time. Strictly speaking, this was a historicist product of human ingenuity.[47] But the nation's historical lineage and common culture concealed the artifice through a web of social bonds. Whigs opposed social contract theory because they were horrified at the idea that society could be dissolved by the will of the majority, even if the government infringed upon natural rights. Nonetheless, because of America's exceptionalist political culture and strong Enlightenment tradition, this corporatist vision was fused with a Lockean respect for private property rights.[48] Moreover, the premium on social stability facilitated social progress, which took shape in the moral reform of the individual.

The Young Americans, who came to dominate the Democratic Party during the 1840s, went further in fusing the nation with the tradition of natural rights. For them, the Union should not merely appear organic so as to conceal—and thereby strengthen—its own artifice. Instead, the social, economic, and political relations of the nation were, themselves, governed by natural law. Like the Whigs, Young Americans departed from social contract theory, but they did so for different reasons. They disdained the notion that people surrendered their natural rights upon entering society. Rather, these same rights came to fruition, and enjoyed practical manifestation, within the social order itself.[49] The nation, therefore, was neither a product of positive laws designed to safeguard its members nor a historicist account of a particular people. Instead, the social, political, and economic order was inscribed with all the divine authority of nature. Sovereignty ultimately lay with a unified and morally righteous popular will, which existed independent of and prior to formal political institutions. Certainly, radicals in the early republic had referred to the inherent right of the people to revise constitutions, even if their natural rights had not been infringed. But Young Americans believed the natural rights of white majorities not only applied at moments of constitutional revision but in the governing of political communities at all times.[50] Suffrage was thus refashioned as a natural right for white men, even as it became only one of many ways to express the people's will. Throughout the book, I refer to the natural right to popular sovereignty in the same way Young Americans understood it throughout the 1840s and 50s: to apply to white communities exercising democratic power over all aspects of life, not exclusively at moments of revolution or constitutional revision.

This view of the Union had significant implications for the Young American political program. As democracy became a natural right, the voice of the people could find expression outside conventional arenas: for example, in literary and intellectual culture. The economic order required no federal intervention but functioned according to the natural laws of supply and demand.[51] Chapter 1 explores the movement's wide-ranging intellectual ambitions as well as the opposition they faced from conservative Whigs, from 1844–54. Instead of needing protection from majoritarian rule, Young Americans believed universal rights were wholly consistent with popular government. O'Sullivan wrote that "though the majority is not always right probability is in its favor." Although he admitted "men may be deceived, mislead, prejudiced, corrupted by flattery, inflamed by eloquence," ultimately "in the conflict of free thought and free discussion, the evil will cure itself."[52] As such, democracy generated political progress on its own accord, tending toward neither majority tyranny nor social stagnation. More dangerously, restrictions on voting did not simply exclude "underdeveloped" races from an electoral system that depended on moral and intellectual development and loyalty to the nation. Instead, these boundaries reflected the immutable and "natural" laws of race, thereby carving political divisions into humanity itself.[53]

Chapters 3, 4, and 5 look at the ways Young America's nationalist vision shaped the Union's role in the world. Chapter 4 explores how this view of democracy as a transcendent principle informed Young America's optimistic attitude toward the Revolutions of 1848. Even when the revolutions faltered in the early 1850s, Young Americans saw democracy in Europe as eminently attainable, particularly with the inspiration of America's increasingly democratic culture. Young Americans also advocated "intervention for nonintervention"—a more interventionist foreign policy designed to guarantee the natural right of European nations to exist as independent states. Although there was some irony to this claim, federal intervention was justified to *create* a harmonious system of independent nations but not to meddle within their jurisdictions. Chapters 3 and 5 examine how the idea of natural law shaped the policy of US territorial expansion, particularly the annexation of parts of Mexico and Cuba. In particular, the Young Americans' view of democracy as a universal principle for white men made them optimistic about bringing self-government to these regions and ridding the mainland United States of its slave population. Blinded by ideology, none acknowledged the Union was trampling on the sovereignty of independent states like Mexico, which had *themselves* only recently overthrown European rule; none acknowledged that federal power and bound labor were instrumental in clearing Indian territories and creating the legal and commercial institutions that propped up their imagined social order.

That is not to say Young Americans lacked historical consciousness or respect for national characteristics. One of their chief spokesmen was the historian

George Bancroft, who wrote the first multivolume history of the United States while also fulfilling a diplomatic mission and maintaining an active correspondence with Illinois's Stephen Douglas. Other Young Americans talked explicitly about the unique characteristics of the Union during the mid-nineteenth century. As I explore in chapter 4, those who urged intervention in Europe did so precisely because the world had changed dramatically since George Washington warned against "entangling alliances" in his Farewell Address. Moreover, Young Americans were sensitive to what they perceived to be unique aspects of national character. Pierre Soulé, for instance, urged the voluntary annexation of Cuba to the United States because of the Spaniards' "Castilian pride."[54] Similarly, Young Americans advocated nonintervention in the states as well as foreign nations because of endlessly diverse characteristics that resisted homogenization.

But underlying these geographical and historical distinctions was the idea that democracy constituted a natural law for white men. History was not to be studied for its own sake, or even for the sake of preserving valuable traditions and institutions; history should be studied in order to throw off the shackles of the past. Epochs might vary but the impulse toward democracy existed across time and space. It was no coincidence that George Bancroft saw himself as a poet as well as a historian and concerned himself as much with art as with history; these disciplines he believed could uncover the timeless principles underlying historical change.[55] The purpose of historical consciousness was not to remain faithful to the past but to measure the extent to which the Union had progressed beyond previous eras and to capture principles underlying the contingencies of a given moment.[56] Certainly, fundamental material facts changed. Technological innovations like the telegraph and the railroad altered what the Union was capable of.[57] The very term "Young America" denoted the nation's coming of age and the arrival of a new epoch. But this obsession with historical change concealed a blatant disrespect for historicism. The "Democratic principle" would soon make national and historical distinctions obsolete, propelling the Union into an ideal state.

The conservative *Whig Review*, edited by George Colton, traced Young America's egregious view of popular sovereignty to a generation of Democrats who rose to prominence in the 1840s. Although "the Democracy of 1844 makes great pretensions to antiquity," Colton said, they are emphatically *"modern."* It was this group that "exclusively appropriate[d]" for themselves "the title of Democrat."[58] The *Whig Review* called these Democrats the "Dorr and Dallas calibre" and linked them to a rival publication called the *Democratic Review.*[59] These Democrats had misinterpreted the principles at the heart of national existence: "To talk . . . of an inalienable, indefeasible, not-to-be-surrendered, absolute right of suffrage, is, in itself, absolute nonsense; just as absurd as when the equally insane ranters, on the other extreme, talk of the natural, inalienable and inde-feasible rights of the Crown."[60] Like the older social contract theorists, Whigs valued their nation's history precisely because its political system was artificial, while nature could be cruel and disorderly. For Young America, the only state of nature was an idealized future, free from history itself.

During the 1840s and early 50s, the association of the Young Americans with youth, speed, and progress was explicitly contrasted with the conservatism of the Whigs. Like many other political identities, the term "conservative" in the ante-bellum period described very different modes of thought because it was a multi-faceted concept. Before the advent of a coherent "conservative movement" in the United States after World War II, the term was used by a variety of different groups to denote very different programs. Nonetheless, as historian Adam I. P. Smith has demonstrated, it held a talismanic appeal in mid-nineteenth-century America.[61] Moreover, despite the very different contexts in which it was used, the term generally denoted a cautious attitude to politics that was respectful of the past. It was considered a spur—not a drag—on progress. Conservatism provided stability and salvaged the most valuable aspects of human history on which to build a better future. Like Smith, I would argue that conservatism more often complemented, rather than contradicted, the liberal tradition in the United States—although some figures like Sidney George Fischer and Rufus Choate remained suspicious of the universalist aspects of Enlightenment thought. In general, both parties embraced the liberal tenants of progress and universalism, even as they claimed to be conservative. Democrats argued that natural rights and majoritarianism could be conservative principles conducive to social order, while Whigs made the case that their historicist understanding of the nation was also a catalyst for progress. In the ultimate hybrid of the two traditions, universalism could be legitimated through a conservative appeal to "ancient rights." Moreover, both parties had more conservative factions within them. The old-line Whigs, for example, might criticize Young America Democrats for their commitment to unbridled majoritarianism and natural rights. But a Democrat like Nathaniel Hawthorne could take aim at Whig reformers for ignoring man's inherent limita-tions, which were rooted in original sin.[62]

That said, overall, Whigs employed the term "conservative" in a more posi-tive way in their political discourse. Moreover, Whigs rooted their liberal—or universalist—program of social progress and individual rights in a preliberal idea of the nation as a particularist community—a view indebted to the Irish philosopher Edmund Burke.[63] The preliberal program of positive laws, alle-giance to precedent, and cultural continuity provided essential prerequisites for the liberal values of individual rights and social improvement. Without them the nation would simply disintegrate, taking any higher ideals down with it. Conversely, Young Americans argued that the nation and its political system were merely a great conglomeration of natural rights. In this vision there was no trade-off between different freedoms that could be mediated through democratic decision-making. Instead, democracy played a fundamentally different role, joining the ranks of these universal values and facilitating their exercise.

But the Whig Party did not remain the chief opposition to the Democracy during the 1850s. After the Mexican War ended in 1848, a burgeoning antislavery movement took shape in the Northern states and displaced the Whigs as a political force. Historians of Jacksonian Democracy frequently end their narratives here.[64] Historiographical disagreements about the Whigs and Democrats give way to debates about the sectional crisis and the causes of the Civil War. The fundamentalists argue that the rise of Northern and Southern ideologies destroyed the second party system and polarized politics around irreconcilable visions of the nation. The revisionists contend that the breakdown of the party system was already underway before these sectional ideologies emerged. In this reading, the main parties had become indistinguishable on key issues, while the nativist movement, which was hostile to immigration from Europe, dragged voters away from the Whig machine. It was only the ensuing political vacuum that facilitated the rise of the antislavery Republican Party. Unlike the fundamentalist accounts, the revisionist view presents the breakdown of the second party system and the sectionalizing of American politics as discrete moments with different causes. But both interpretations still locate the main ideological divide as standing between North and South.[65] These readings leave little room for the Democrats' nationalist aspirations in our understanding of the coming of the Civil War.[66] To conform to a sectional narrative, Democrats are usually dismissed as "doughfaces" secretly in league with the Slave Power or as rootless pragmatists desperate to compromise at any cost.[67] But the Young America movement brings a group of Democrats back into focus who never conformed to the Northern and Southern versions of nationalism that dominate our understanding of this crucial decade. In this context, the Civil War was caused less by the strength of sectional ideologies than it was by the failure of the center ground: first in creating, and then failing to control, these conflicts.

Despite their national scope, Young Americans were primarily a force for instability and polarization.[68] The movement destroyed an older conception of democracy as a means of compromise and reconciliation and forced Americans to stake out sectional positions. Eager to develop the territories of Kansas and Nebraska, Illinois's Stephen Douglas legislated for their swift incorporation as states under the principle of popular sovereignty, first proposed by Democrats George Dallas and Daniel Dickinson. This was a process by which white men in the territories would decide the future of slavery through a democratic vote. Douglas hoped the act would have sufficient appeal to both Northern and Southern politicians to break the congressional stalemate delaying the territories' entry into the Union. But the Young Americans also believed that slavery, like any other issue, should be subject to the self-government of white men because this was a natural right that resisted congressional dictation, except on issues that directly contravened the Constitution. As popular and state sovereignty were universal rights, these Democrats believed they would produce inherently moral outcomes, even on this fraught issue. For Young Americans, withdrawing federal intervention was its own moral test: whatever local communities decreed would spontaneously drive social progress. If this was a compromise, it was compromise of a very peculiar kind. The Kansas-Nebraska Act was based on the consistent application of a universal principle rather than the balance of competing interests. Moreover, there was no diluting of Democratic principles in confining the principle of popular sovereignty to white men. In Jacksonian circles, slavery was a source of controversy, but the notion of the racial inferiority of nonwhites was not. Many critics of the Kansas-Nebraska Act acted in the Whig tradition when they rallied against the new and dangerous principle that it introduced. Young America's critics denied that white majoritarianism was an inherent right and predicted that instability and polarization would replace the national settlement built around the Missouri Compromise of 1820, which Douglas and his allies had destroyed.

Moreover, even as they preached the virtues of free labor, Young Americans enlarged the influence of slavery in the Union. Their white majoritarianism shielded the Slave Power from the antislavery movement and renewed planters' hopes for exporting slavery to Kansas and Cuba. Crucially, the act overturned the Missouri Compromise, which prohibited slavery north of the 36°30' parallel. Since popular sovereignty did not guarantee the exclusion of slavery in Kansas and Nebraska, the act potentially facilitated its extension into areas in which it had previously been excluded. Many Northerners—both Democrats and Whigs—considered the Missouri Compromise sacrosanct and despaired at what they saw as a Southern plot to extend the power and influence of their section. Of course, this did not mean Douglas and his supporters were mere saggy agents of the master class or pragmatists desperate to compromise at any cost. Rather, their racial ideology was closely aligned with the Southern wing of the party, and their ambitions dovetailed, to a great extent, with the planter elite, while they showed a naïve faith that settlers in the western territories would surely vote against slavery in the end. Young Americans had thus created a new and dangerous national settlement, while strengthening the dominance of the master class. Opposition proved fiercer than even Douglas expected, and it did not dissipate as many of his supporters predicted. Several Whigs and a good number of Democrats joined the rising Republican Party, which proposed to exclude slavery from the territories outright.

As Young Americans advocated for natural law and the Slave Power encroached on the territories, Northerners found it increasingly difficult to fall back on the Whiggish nationalism of the previous decade. In effect, the preliberal aspects of the Whiggish worldview were marginalized in the political upheavals that convulsed Europe and North America after 1848. The revolution and war on these two continents created the conditions in which nations were being forged anew. Whether in the imagined wilderness of the western territories or the postimperial regimes of Europe, it became increasingly difficult to rely on legal precedent, cultural cohesiveness, or historical traditions, which all required time to develop. In the territories slavery could not be protected out of respect for positive law, the historical lineage of the American Union, or the existing realities of social relations. Moreover, the Young Americans had dispensed with an older vision of Burkean nationalism. They did not wish to balance competing interests, mediate conflicts through representative institutions, or submerge questions of natural justice under the weight of history and tradition. Rather, they smuggled a distinctly radical solution into the center ground: that a mere majority vote of white men should settle the contentious moral issue of slavery for all time. This shifted the meaning of the natural rights contained within the Declaration of Independence and the very foundations of national existence—while enlarging the Slave Power.

Plunged back into a state of nature, previously conservative figures were forced to stake out radical positions. Compromise for the sake of stability was acceptable in the existing states, but the violation of new territories—or the acceptance of the Young Americans' perversion of natural rights—would rob the Union of its moral force. The commitment to social progress, which absolved the American nation of the relativism that distinguished European Romantics, hung in the balance. The Republicans, therefore, subscribed to their own vision of liberal nationalism, which tied the Union to a different idea of the transcendent authority of nature. In the process the Lockean respect for natural rights, which was previously concealed by the Whigs' organic conception of the Union, came to the fore. Where they had adhered to Whiggish compromise, now men like Lincoln and William Seward argued that the "higher law" and natural rights should determine the status of slavery. It mattered little that Douglas and his allies did not expect slavery to go into the West or that they brandished their Free-Soil credentials. For Republicans, the *natural* right to the fruits of labor, which transcended racial divisions, was absolute and eternal and distinct from the *political* right to popular sovereignty.

Faced with this rival interpretation of the tradition of natural law, the Young America movement did undergo a real discursive shift. In the 1840s it was common for Young America Democrats to justify their political project as an essentially radical one. Democrats took a favorable view of the previous century's most polarizing event, the French Revolution, including the Jacobins.[69] Furthermore, they frequently used the term "philanthropy" in a positive context.[70] Up against the conservative Whig Party, this stance was an appropriate one. The Republicans, however, presented a very different threat. Explicitly an antislavery party, they often attacked the Democrats for not extending their conception of natural rights beyond the white race. In this context the Democratic Party as a whole became the party of the "common good" as it tried to preserve racially homogeneous communities and maintain the stability of the Union. Where they had previously championed individual freedoms against the claims of the collective, the Democrats now sought to preserve the stability of white communities against a push for Black rights. Although they continued to use the phrase "natural law," Democrats also used terms like "patriotism" and "conservatism" more frequently in their political discourse.[71] After 1854, then, their political rhetoric shifted to accommodate the demands of common life, a transformation I will explore in more detail in chapter 6 on Young America's role in the sectional crisis. As Young Americans stubbornly struggled to implement a universalist program in the midst of anarchy and disorder, they nonetheless adopted the language of conservativism—if not the preliberal outlook—to legitimize their actions.

Indeed, although Young Americans drew on increasingly conservative language, the natural right to popular sovereignty as a solution to the slavery crisis—even when restricted to white men—had unmistakably radical origins, and many longstanding conservatives in this decade certainly recognized it as such. Furthermore, supporters of the movement detested abolitionists and Southern Fire-Eaters for the same reason they had fought against Whigs, and the influence of the British Empire, in the previous decade. While Whigs made majoritarian democracy contingent on culture, custom, and positive law, abolitionists insisted on rights that preceded political participation and applied them to races that most Americans excluded from the polity. Moreover, both Whigs and abolitionists compromised the right to labor as much as the right to vote. Whigs expropriated white communities to fund federal programs, while abolitionists extracted surplus value from white men by forcing communities to accept Black peoples who could not support themselves. Similarly, the planter elite undercut the wages of white workers and degraded their labor through proximity to Black workers while extracting surplus value without effort and exercising disproportionate political influence at the local and federal levels. Ultimately, the sectionalists of the 1850s resembled the Whigs of the 1840s insomuch as they undermined the white man's independence and challenged the natural basis upon which his supposed inherent right to popular rule rested. Young Americans subscribed to a Democratic nationalism—free labor and popular sovereignty for white men—that saw both the Slave Power and the abolitionists as a threat to the natural order. After 1854 the ideologies common to the second party system still shaped antebellum politics.

As the decade drew on, Young America continued to exacerbate ideological polarization, and denied the nation a workable solution based on an older conception of nationhood. The movement forced previously conservative figures to stake out radical positions in the free states, while aiding and abetting the Slave Power. Indeed, both Northern and Southern coalitions forged sectional visions crafted in Young America's own image.[72] But Young Americans also replaced the Whigs in the center of US politics. Thus, the only genuinely bisectional solution was a radical version of democracy rooted in natural rights: one that further inflamed debates about natural justice and broke down territorial loyalties. Without much compromise to offer, Young Americans were forced to wage a war on two fronts. On the one hand, they increasingly chafed under the proslavery wing that dominated the Democratic Party. As soon as the Kansas-Nebraska Act was passed in 1854, it became clear that Southerners would use every weapon in their arsenal to institute slavery in new territories. For the Fire-Eaters of the South, slavery was the principle that lay at the foundation of the nation—it was the "cornerstone" on which the entire republic, and the rest of the world, should rest. Just as Young Americans used the federal government to guarantee states' rights at home and national sovereignty abroad, proslavery ideologues actively intervened to protect their natural right to slave labor. It became increasingly clear the South would not relinquish its grip on the federal government and let Young America's political order thrive. Concessions were given on the workings of the Kansas-Nebraska Act and the Fugitive Slave Law, but at critical moments the Young Americans turned against the Fire-Eaters and Cotton Whigs who dominated their own party. Compromise for its own sake had never been a priority for Young America, and this was as true in 1857 as it was in 1846. A battle of principles raged on, one that frequently descended into physical violence and threatened to destroy the Union itself. On the other hand, Young Americans resisted the encroachments of the Republican Party. At times strategic alliances were formed (and defections made), but many Young Americans remained intensely suspicious of the party's racial politics and perceived federalism. Douglas and his allies dragged votes away from the antislavery movement whenever their principles did not win out.

Facing a polarized political climate largely of its own making, the Young America movement did fray under the weight of its own contradictions. Although popular sovereignty and racial homogeneity were perfectly compatible, local majoritarianism could not function easily as a natural right. Democracy had worked perfectly well in American history as a process, but it was not an absolute value. Young Americans themselves began to disagree about the workings of particular elections. These conflicts took on undue significance because voting was held up as a hallowed process that would determine the most fundamental moral questions for all time. Democrats previously sympathetic to Young America could not stomach their old allies' interpretation of the political process and defected to the Republican fold. For them, temporary federal intervention was justified because slavery had become so closely entwined with the federal government—to an extent that required active uncoupling. Although popular sovereignty and nonintervention remained natural rights for white men, some intervention was necessary to correct years of federal overreach. Other Young Americans remained Democrats but rallied against the Buchanan administration's alliance with the Slave Power. They reached out to Republicans, asking them to accept popular sovereignty as a more just, moderate, and effective means to create a Union dedicated to free labor. Democrats warned their old colleagues in the Republican ranks that antislavery activists would infringe on other areas of life once the size and scope of the federal government had expanded, while Republicans cautioned Democrats that the Slave Power constituted federalism in disguise.

As politics increasingly divided along sectional lines, many Young Americans found themselves politically homeless or split among rival parties. But their Unionist vision held sway. Many still believed the "intractable conflict" over slavery was less important than the fight for white men's natural rights against the power of federal and imperial authority. Always anxious that Whigs were reorganizing in new forms, Young Americans continued to see each other as kindred spirits, even across party lines.[73] This was not just paranoia. As the parties became unrecognizable in the great realignment of this decade, distinctly Whiggish ideas did infiltrate the Republican, Constitutional Unionist, and even Democratic ranks. In this maelstrom, Young Americans clung to the ideology of Herrenvolk democracy and states' rights even as they disagreed over their practical application. But in the end, even those who remained loyal to Stephen

Douglas struggled to unify around this set of ideas. The hybrid of natural rights and nationalism was now mainstream, forcing Douglas's dwindling band of supporters to do battle with rival interpretations of his millenarian national story. Douglas's presidential run as a Northern Democrat in 1860 marked the last gasp of a flailing worldview. When secession began, what was left of Douglas's faction broke rank and camped out behind opposing sides of the Mason-Dixon line. Even then, though, commonalities persisted: former allies fought over what constituted the proper political process and legacy of Andrew Jackson.[74]

Perhaps the most significant reason for the failure of the Young America movement was its inability to offer a compelling solution to the problem of race. Rather than an intractable ideological divide, the issue of slavery was a practical problem for many Democratic nationalists. Much more significant to them was the threat of racial integration and amalgamation. In this context, slavery was just one of many ways to deal with a population that should never have been brought to North America in the first place. Democratic historian George Bancroft summarized the prevailing view when he argued that the slave trade was a product of European imperialism.[75] If popular sovereignty had prevailed in the eighteenth century, he wrote, then slavery would never have taken root in the United States, nor would a Black population exist within the Union. In the Jacksonian imagination, imperial power, slavery, and racial mixing were three components of the same political project.

Young Americans disapproved of slavery but thought that the alternatives were often worse. If slaves were emancipated and permitted to settle in white communities, they would not be able to compete for wages or participate in political debate. In this scenario Blacks would either die out as they struggled for subsistence wages among a superior population, or they would undermine the stability of the community. Racial miscegenation was also a constant fear. The steady degeneration of the white race through mixing with an "inferior" people plagued the Democratic imagination. As such, slavery was a largely inadequate answer to the question of what to do with the Union's Black population.[76] The tropical climates were seen as more desirable locations for enslaved laborers, although even there the institution was seen as the best of a range of imperfect options. Others believed slavery would not expand another inch under the American flag and would be meliorated, and eventually abolished, under the Union's control. For many Young Americans, retaining slavery where it already existed or expanding it to the tropics prevented free Blacks from plaguing white communities on the American mainland, especially in the western territories.

The only other futures Young Americans frequently envisaged for enslaved Blacks were either colonization or extinction, sometimes labelled "extermination."

In the case of colonization, some writers drew on a vision of "manifest destiny" for the Black race. These Democrats believed that in parts of Africa close to the equator, Blacks would outcompete whites, creating their own free-labor communities.[77] Others looked forward to the total extinction of the Black race, a destiny comparable to that of the Native Americans who were supposedly receding before white civilization.[78] This group thought that Blacks would fare no better in Africa than they did the United States. Left to themselves, Blacks would die out on the African continent just as they would in America; war and famine would inevitably plague a race that lacked the intelligence required for sustainable agriculture and a stable political process. These different visions of the future constituted solutions to the illusory problem of Black inferiority for Democrats of all stripes: from Southerners to Free-Soilers in the North. The racism and antiabolitionism so present in Democratic discourse cannot be readily categorized as either anti- or proslavery. Rather, slavery was just one idea, within a range of ideas, about how to confront a much larger issue of racial inferiority. It was this problem that posed a profound threat to the natural rights of white men.

There was nothing inconsistent between these racial politics and Young America's larger program. As historians of the British Empire have long understood, phrenology and racial science fit snugly within the mid-nineteenth-century liberal worldview—one that Young America certainly subscribed to.[79] Just like liberals in Britain, the Democratic Party—and especially Young America—drew universal distinctions based on natural law rather than culture or custom; they trusted empirical or scientific observation over scriptural authority; and, finally, they believed in social and economic progress over outdated notions of the inherent dignity of individuals created in God's image. Indeed, it was precisely Young America's universalism that condemned as less than fully human those who did not see the virtues of its political system. The predominance of natural law over more particularist ethical theories based on culture or history left Young Americans utterly incapable of seeing the humanity of people who lacked their cultural and political traditions. Young Americans simply could not explain human distinctions without recourse to innate divisions between species rather than reference to custom. Races perceived to be innately unsuited to self-government were assigned no inherent rights as human beings nor given any hope of incorporation within the polity.

Despite the movement's enormous influence in the early 1850s, Young America's ambitions were largely frustrated by secession and the outbreak of war. Split not only between two sections but between rival parties in the North, Young Americans found their vision of progress undermined by the course of events. Unbeknownst to them, this form of Democratic nationalism had reached its height in 1854, only to be undermined by an economic policy that included high tariffs and the consolidation of the federal apparatus during wartime. But this division had not been brought about merely because Southerners and Northerners, ultimately, did harbor divergent views about the nature and morality of slavery, or even because Jacksonians began to disagree about the practical workings of democracy. At every stage Young Americans forced these debates into being by inaugurating a process of constant referenda across the nation. By mixing procedural and abstract values, they denied Americans a peaceful solution to this conflict and destroyed the only form of nationalism that might have preserved peace. Nonetheless, after the Civil War many Jacksonians who had gravitated toward the Republican Party returned to the Democratic fold. Conscious of the ideological currency that Democratic nationalism had carried all along, the Democracy now used their liberal worldview for ever-more-reactionary ends: most significantly, to row back the hard-won freedom that Black people had seized during the confusion and horror of civil war.

1

The Intellectual Culture of the Young America Movement, 1844–1854

Before the emergence of the *Democratic Review*, democracy was not, strictly speaking, considered a natural right. Americans generally believed their democratic regime, at least in part, emerged from laws, customs, and institutions peculiar to the Union. There were, of course, universal rights to life, liberty and property—applicable to white men, in particular. However, most Americans distinguished these from the democratic political system that made the nation distinct. Rather than being a transcendent ideal, self-government was, in the very early republic, rooted in an artificial social contract that was designed to protect against the abuse of more fundamental rights. Or—according to a view that became increasingly popular after the Revolution—democratic government had emerged organically through the historical development of the nation. Indeed, for many Americans, natural rights of any kind had given way to particularist sources of national belonging. As historian Frank Towers argues, "By the 1820s . . . officials in most post-revolutionary states had de-emphasized natural rights as the distinguishing marker of their respective national values in favor of cultural markers like folklore."[1] Either way, democracy—and the nation itself— was a product of human ingenuity. Specifically, it rested on customs, laws, and institutions that had grown up in the United States.

Within the political system, Americans certainly disagreed. But the mediating force of representative government combined with competition between the main parties served to contain these conflicts.[2] Parties gave voice to different factions without resort to open hostility, while congressional representatives weighed the competing interests within the Union. This respect for parties and congressional compromise had its roots in the Federalists' view of "faction" and was especially popular in the Federalist Party and later with the Whigs. But it also had its adherents among antebellum Democrats. Andrew Jackson's political strategist, Martin Van Buren, who earned the nickname the "Little Magician," argued the two-party system was essential to create stability in a democratic society. Certainly, after 1824 Americans embraced parties to a much greater extent than they had during the years of the early republic or the Era of Good Feelings, when a culture of deference to political superiors was more pronounced. But during the entire period from the revolution to the 1830s, political figures were keen to mediate majority rule through representative institutions and to balance competing interests within the republic.[3] For many, the specific cultural and historical lineage of the Union would also keep these political antagonisms in check and promote unity.[4] Thus, American politics primarily operated on two levels: citizens were divided around partisan competition while being united around allegiance to the nation as a particular cultural and historical community. Whatever different views Americans might take on issues like the national bank, they could unite around the Union's common history and cultural output. With the advent of Young America, a new narrative of national development came to prominence: one that argued the nation (and its political system) was not a distinct entity based on specific cultural and historical circumstances but a universal system based on natural laws. Young Americans' political discourse did not treat the Democratic Party as one component of a larger political community. Rather, the Democratic program would overcome the different interests within the nation and rule according to "Democratic principles." This political outlook was inherently internationalist, as these principles applied across the world, with little concern for geographical boundaries.

There was, of course, a broad consensus in American politics that sovereignty, at a fundamental level, resided in "the people." As historian Christian Fritz makes clear, popular sovereignty was the dominant principle in American constitution-making from the Revolution to the Civil War.[5] Americans from across the political spectrum believed that power was *fundamentally* vested in the people and required their consent to function. As the Revolution taught, the people had the right to revolt and form a new government when a regime unduly and arbitrarily infringed upon their natural rights without their consent. But this appeal to *natural* rights constituted a discrete revolutionary moment, while the practice of democracy, including suffrage, rested on *political* rights. By the 1840s both conservative and progressive figures in the Whig Party continued to distinguish between the political privileges of democracy and suffrage and the natural rights of property and the fruits of one's labor. Furthermore, even at the constitutional stage, more conservative Whigs appealed to self-government as a political inheritance rather than a natural right. These figures argued that constitutions could only be reformed according to the provisions contained within them. The American Revolution was not a revolt in favor of natural rights but one to defend historic privileges guaranteed by the existing colonial legislatures under English constitutional law—privileges that had nonetheless been sub-verted by the British monarchy.[6] This line of reasoning was popular among the conservative sections of the Whig Party, particularly in the *American* and *Whig Reviews,* discussed in this chapter.

Certainly, a more expansive view of popular sovereignty had been widespread in arguments for constitutional revision since the American Revolution as well. More radical figures, particularly in the Jeffersonian tradition, proposed that "the people" possessed an inherent right to alter constitutions to make these docu-ments better conform to their happiness and aspirations, even if their natural rights were not infringed.[7] Constitutional revisions did not need to abide by an existing constitution's amendment provisions, while constitutional conventions did not require the approval of state legislatures. Nevertheless, although it could be invoked at any time, this inherent right to alter and abolish governments only applied at the constitutional stage—and here it was practically limited through the conditions required for a "sovereign people" to emerge. Moreover, these fig-ures were aware that this "sovereign people" could only *practice* democracy (rather than governing as a mere mob) once some combination of cultural cohesion, historical traditions, and legal precedents had bound them into a political com-munity. Although the majority could act outside of political institutions and laws at times of constitutional revision, in the regular course of government, they were required to give form to the power of political communities and distil the people's will amid conflicting interests.

Conversely, Young Americans incorporated the day-to-day functioning of democracy within their cannon of natural rights, even as it was simultaneously limited by race and gender. White men possessed an inherent right to the fran-chise and formed political communities irrespective of traditions or conven-tions. Most significantly for the fate of slavery in the United States, white men would make inherently just decisions—the voice of people was the voice of God. This was a total elision of natural and political rights.

But the rejection of federal power, positive law, and cultural and historical traditions presented Young Americans with a problem that spoke to some of the tensions within the idea of liberal nationalism itself: What sources of political authority could legitimize and guide the nation in the absence of these older restraints? The answer for Young America lay in intellectual culture. In the ante-bellum United States, a naïve scientism was widespread. In radical circles, many Americans believed social, political, and moral life followed the same natural laws as the physical world. Just as scientists could discover the laws of matter and motion, political scientists and even literary figures could identify forms of activity that conformed to human nature. These same people could supposedly provide the blueprint for a harmonious and progressive political system and promote loyalty once one emerged. The many authors and political economists who supported the Democrats therefore proved to Young Americans that the party's political program conformed to rights found in nature. As well as acting as political guides, poets and novelists could express the voice of the people through their work. As a natural right, popular sovereignty did not depend on representative institutions or geopolitical boundaries. Instead, the people generated an authentic expression of popular sovereignty that preceded these factors and merely required the absence of restraint to thrive. Artists and intellectuals thus replaced external coercion as a means of commanding loyalty to the nation and distilling the people's will.

But there was also a darker side to the Young Americans' use of intellectual culture. If political science and literature naturalized popular sovereignty for white men, then so-called sciences (e.g., phrenology) constructed an idea of humanity that permanently excluded "inferior" races. While abolitionists used the natural law tradition to attack slavery, Young Americans defined it in opposition to federal interference and used it to naturalize their own political program of states' rights, popular sovereignty, and white supremacy, while also pushing for territorial expansion and free trade, as later chapters will explore.

Political Science: The *Democratic Review* and Its Rivals

Although the antebellum Democracy has earned a reputation for parochialism, Young America Democrats combined politics and intellectual culture in order to articulate a self-consciously progressive worldview.[8] From its inception, the *Democratic Review* distanced itself from an older tradition of political science, popular in the seventeenth and eighteenth centuries, that subscribed to the social contract theory. For the *Review*, these thinkers established an unnecessary dichotomy between the "natural" and "social" state: between the state of nature and civil society. Writers at the magazine criticized, in particular, the idea that men voluntarily yield any of their natural rights in return for the order and stability enjoyed in civic life. Furthermore, they attacked the prepolitical idea of the state of nature for being fictitious since white men were inherently political beings. Political scientists in the mid-nineteenth century, the *Review* insisted, should examine society and politics in the real world to deduce the natural rights of humankind, in the same way that other human and physical sciences approached their subjects as empirical phenomena subject to natural law.[9] In the absence of external intervention and arbitrary power, social and political orders would emerge that were enshrined in nature rather than the laws and institutions of a specific state or nation. Many of the political privileges of national belonging could thus be reimagined as universal rights discernable through reason. For Young Americans, this meant that democracy no longer depended on particular traditions, legal precedents, and/or political institutions; indeed, it could, in fact, be held back by them.

As historian Dorothy Ross argues, the projection of scientific assumptions onto social questions was at the heart of nineteenth-century social science, and buttressed the ideology of American exceptionalism, more broadly, in the antebellum United States. Since the nation should rest on a set of harmonious principles, rooted in nature, the trade-offs and competing interests that defined European statecraft would become increasingly irrelevant to political life. Ross makes clear that a range of progressive thinkers came to embrace this perspective.[10] But Young Americans, in particular, expanded the remit of natural rights to include the political right to democracy for white men. Moreover, during the 1840s, the more conservative Whig Party still maintained a sharp division between nature, on the one hand, and society and politics on the other. As we shall see, the Young Americans not only undermined an older view of the social contract but also a historicist view of nationalism popular among the Whigs: one that argued the Union was an amalgamation of competing interests held together by common traditions, positive laws, and political and civic institutions that had developed over time.

Young Americans believed white men were inherently prone to majoritarianism in all times and places, once the arbitrary powers of society and the state were stripped away, whether these were legal precedents, cultural and historical customs, or political institutions. One of John O'Sullivan's articles—"Democracy" (1840)—rejected the idea of the social contract as well as the Whigs' historicist view of national development. In this reading, democracy was not an artificial system of government separate from more fundamental rights; it was, *in itself*, a natural right for white men, requiring only the absence of federal interference to thrive. The editor argued, "So far from demanding, in order to its enjoyment, the sacrifice of any natural right, it is itself but a great natural right, serving to secure and strengthen others, while it reveals the only limitation the Deity has imposed on unrestricted freedom." O'Sullivan used the discourse of natural law to legitimize the liberal social order he envisaged in the United States: "Man's only truly *natural state* is, when he conforms to all those natural laws which the Creator has instituted in that physical, intellectual and moral economy in which he is placed."[11] According to this view, the positive laws of the federal government were not a necessary means of ensuring social stability. In a decentralized republic the divine order of nature would replace the arbitrary

legislation laid down by federal elites. The people formed a political unit independent of the state, one with a unified moral will. These units only needed to
be left alone to facilitate the creation of democratic communities. As the *Review*
summarized, the people will "grow, and flourish, and expand, from causes as
powerful and irresistible as the law of nature."[12]

Since democracy did not depend on the institutions of government, Young
Americans did not see voting as the sum total of democratic activity. These
political thinkers believed that the "people's will" existed independent of systems of representation and beyond the drawing up of election districts through
positive law. The only essential foundation for a democratic society was the
absence of external interference. Wherever federal or imperial authority did not
intervene, popular sovereignty could be found. As such, the voice of the masses
was not solely articulated through political institutions at the national or state
level. For example, the laws of supply and demand also expressed the people's
will and formed as important a part of democratic life as voting. O'Sullivan
wrote that "we may rest assured that labor will be put forth . . . and capital will
be applied where it shall command the best return. The agency of government
is obviously not required here. . . . It is an infringement of natural right."[13] Since
tariffs interfered with the most efficient distribution of labor and capital and
favored one branch of industry at the expense of another, they curbed peoples'
inherent rights. Conversely, free trade allocated resources according to popular
demand and therefore conformed to the publication's view of the natural order.
Similarly, literary figures could express a unified popular will independent of
representative bodies. As the literary critic at the *Democratic Review,* William
Jones, put it, "It is in poetry especially that we must look for the purest expression of the popular feeling. It is in poetry that . . . the national spirit is most
faithfully evolved."[14] Thus, the idea that self-government was a natural right for
white men allowed the *Review* to remake different aspects of national life in the
party's image: to Democratize not just the political system but the nation itself.

Other writers in the orbit of the *Democratic Review* often argued that scientific inquiries could discover universal moral, social and political relations for
national life, rather than falling back on an abstract "state of nature," or rely-
ing on historicist accounts of national development. They followed O'Sullivan's
lead when he wrote, "The inquiry into human rights is the fundamental pre-
liminary question of political science" because "it embraces the great doctrines
of science, the first truths of government," while tariffs were "an infringement
of the first principles of social union, perversion of the clearest doctrines of
science."[15] Philadelphia Democrat Henry Gilpin, who had written brief articles
for the *Review* shortly after its inception in 1837, supported its efforts to expand

the remit of the sciences to moral, social, and political questions.[16] In one of his many addresses before university audiences and literary societies, Gilpin praised Newton for applying his mind not just to the study of "the laws of physical nature" but to religion "by means so purely abstract and scientific." Ultimately, "there is no one science—there is no one range of inquiry or of thought—that does not aid and illustrate every other."[17] Similarly, the Young American Charles Goepp, who was a German American and ally of Stephen Douglas, championed "the discovery of a new principle . . . aiming at political institutions based upon science." Like many Young Americans, he believed the Democratic program was inherently internationalist, contrasting its universalist agenda with "nationalities, which are political institutions based on accident."[18] Although scholars have focused on the literary ambitions of Young Americans, the science of politics was also an important component of their intellectual ambitions.[19]

In the *Democratic Review,* the political theorist and phrenologist from Boston Nahum Capen was singled out as a champion of Young America's work in this field. In one issue of the periodical, New Hampshire's Edmund Burke praised Capen for his labor on behalf of "moral science." In 1849 Capen published his most famous work, *The History of Democracy,* which, according to Burke, was devoured by "eminent Democrats," including Robert J. Walker, George Dallas, and Isaac Toucey.[20] In a number of seemingly diverse works of political theory, history, and phrenology, which were nonetheless united in their enthusiasm for popular sovereignty, Capen offered up his work as a science of society. In an account of the late Mexican War published in 1848, he explained, "It is become the true province of science to investigate not only the laws of inanimate matter, of the unmeasured regions of space, but of the immortal soul itself, in the recesses of its intellectual, moral and religious nature."[21] Steeped in naïve scientism, Capen believed he could discover the universal principles that shaped human activity, much as they did "inanimate matter." Adopting the role of social engineer, he could discover those "eternal laws of right which in the process of moral change will give equal freedom to the prince and to the slave."[22] In his *History of Democracy* Capen acknowledged his debt to scientific method, explaining, "It is only by the aid of science that knowledge is made useful."[23] Knowledge might be acquired, but only science could interpret the progressive or providential dynamics in social life. According to Capen, "Science not only comprehends the knowledge of things and principles,—but the supreme skill of the understanding in discovering the natural system of their development."[24] Certainly, some Whig political economists, such as Henry Carey, came to speak of social science and "natural law," particularly in the late 1840s and 50s.[25] But they focused on labor systems rather than the political right to popular sovereignty. As we shall see, Whigs remained profoundly uncomfortable with the idea that democracy was a natural right, even for white men.

Indeed, the more conservative Whig periodicals, which were O'Sullivan's chief ideological rivals, rejected the scientism of the *Democratic Review*. First founded in Boston in 1815, the *North American Review* had long dominated intellectual life in the United States. Although historians of Young America tend to focus exclusively on the *Democratic Review*, the ideological contours of Jacksonian nationalism become clearer in relation to rival publications.[26] Provoking accusations of "literary Toryism" from Democratic writers, the *North American Review* took a firm stance against the influence of intellectuals in the political sphere.[27]

The *Review* was particularly uncomfortable with men of letters who justified their political outlook according to universal principles. After the French revolution of 1848, the periodical's editor, Francis Bowen, wrote an article titled "French Ideas about Democracy and the Community of Goods" that blamed the failures of the revolution on the prominent role intellectuals played in the political process. Bowen pointed out that "literary men" had exercised "disproportionate" influence in the provisional government established in 1848: Marrat, Flocon, and Louis Blanc were newspaper editors; Lamartine was a poet and historian; and Arago a prominent scientist. The secretary of this "remarkable association of men of letters" was Pagnerre, a bookseller, and the epicene novelist George Sand wrote the dispatches for the secretary of the interior. The article conceded that these talents flourished in the political environment of the republic because it recognized talent "wherever it is found," in contrast to the monarchical policy of suppressing subversive scholarship. However, the *Review* cautioned against giving these figures a significant role in government, since the "sanctity of letters" was "profaned by false gods." Just as Demosthenes made a "sorry figure" as a general, Lamartine failed "behind the barricades" in June, and Louis Blanc became a terrible foreign minister: by attempting to "reduce their utopian theories to practice" these scholarly figures soon "excited the scorn of Parisians."[28] In contrast, England was not blighted by this pernicious tendency to glorify abstract ideals. In the United Kingdom, Macaulay and Lord Brougham were the only two cabinet ministers hailing from the literary world.

Bowen went on to exempt the American Revolution from the abstractions that marred European politics in 1848. Unlike the French Revolution that began in 1789, history and tradition laid the foundations of the new order in 1776, meaning intellectuals played a more modest political role. The American Revolution was not a "Quixotic crusade in favor of human rights in general, nor a war undertaken only to show that all men are free and equal" but a fight to restore old privileges.[29] Thus, it refrained from glorifying those "phantoms" that had inspired the French poet and politician Alphonse de Lamartine to proclaim, "The French revolution was the only practical attempt a nation ever made to realize the doctrines of Christianity."[30] The article finished by appealing to intellectuals to adopt a more measured role in political life, to explain the "truths of political economy and civil polity" with some "higher purpose than the hope of affecting the party politics of the hour." Instead of following the changing winds of public opinion, they should take the lead in educating the masses and so encourage gradual progress within a stable political order. Thus, the educated "ought not to wait, as the members of the French academy did, till they are reminded by the thunder of the cannon directed against the barricades . . . that they also have a work to do for the preservation of society and the interests of truth."[31]

Francis Bowen also took a very different view of natural rights than did John O'Sullivan. Unlike the Democratic editor, Bowen rejected the idea that the natural order was a desirable model for political life. Without the "wheels of government," he wrote, men must "go back to a state of nature, to reside in caverns and forests."[32] While Young America politicians drew on liberal political thinkers like Emer de Vattel and Adam Smith, Bowen turned to Thomas Hobbes, writing there would be "no arts, no letters, no society, and, which is worst of all, continual fear and danger of violent death, and the life of man, solitary, poor, nasty, brutish and short." Francis Bowen denied that the Founding Fathers had broken ties with Great Britain only to turn back to the state of nature. "When the connexion between Great Britain and her American colonies was broken by the Declaration of Independence," he wrote, "the people of this country did not at once abandon all their civil institutions, and fall back into a state of nature." Implicitly criticizing the Jacksonians for being *too* intellectual, he pointed out that American institutions "were not made by philosophers and theorists, but by practical men."[33]

By the mid-1850s conservative periodicals continued to argue that political and social traditions exerted a more beneficial influence over the national mind than scholars, literary figures, and political scientists. In a review of a work of political science entitled "The Theory of Human Progression," the *North American Review* said, "We have begun to despair of man's social regeneration by any system of political truth superimposed *ab extra* and not developed by himself."[34] The publication dismissed the claim that "the multitude are moved in *mind*" because they "imbibed the theories of former speculators," taking instead a more dour view of human nature and political change. Accordingly, "the axioms of equity" were "invaluable as goals of political progress," but "men with flesh and blood" prove that "certain nations must be, and ought to be, more restrained in the enjoyment of their natural rights than others." Although

Democrats and radical Whigs might appeal to natural rights, the publication argued that "the real nature" will have her way in due course.[35]

Another conservative literary periodical, the *American Whig Review*, was equally critical of the role of intellectuals in political life. Whig writer George H. Colton established the *Review* in October 1844 to counter the influence of O'Sullivan's Democratic periodical, particularly in the upcoming presidential election between James K. Polk and Henry Clay. Historian Robert Scholnick has argued that, together with the *Democratic Review*, the publications "served as the competing ideological centers for the parties," which "engaged in an ongoing dialogue."[36] Like Francis Bowen's *North American Review*, the *Whig Review* criticized a form of politics based on intellectual abstractions. In particular, it provided a coherent critique of the Democrats' notion that popular sovereignty was a natural right that should provide the foundation of a new international order.

In 1849 a *Whig Review* article on "The Presidential Veto" lamented that because "the greater number of questions are determined by the will of the majority" in America, "a large class of our politicians, seldom accustomed to look beneath the surface . . . conclude that the majority have a *natural* right to govern."[37] For these Democrats, "whatever tends to hinder the free and full expression" of the will of the majority "is contrary to natural law, and smells of usurpation." The article caustically noted that "these sage politicians would do well to remember, that the right of the majority to rule is a *civil*, not a *natural* right, and exists only by virtue of positive law." The problem for this writer lay in the fact that the abstract notion of a "majority" had no meaning on its own. Without civil law, political institutions, and territorial boundaries, there could be no popular will. As the article explained, "Civil society must be constituted before you can even conceive the existence of a political majority." Positive law must prevail over the majority's fictitious "natural right" to govern: "If . . . a given constitutional provision should restrain the majority, prevent them from making their will prevail, that is no just cause of complaint; for no law is broken, no right is violated."[38] Another article in 1848, "The Future Policy of the Whigs," outlined the difference between the main parties as follows: "The one side holds, that this very decision by majorities is not established by any merely natural law but by a constitutional regulation; while the other side contends, that the majority, assembling when and where they please can assume power over individuals—to govern the few by the many."[39]

The *Whig Review* fundamentally disagreed with attempts to make popular sovereignty an abstract right rather than a privilege for those capable of exercising it properly. In "Human Rights," the magazine argued that "suffrage is no indefeasible or abstract right, independent of a wise expediency, but a question of

fact to be decided by all the lights of reason and experience." The article saw this
new conception of the right of suffrage as proof of the corrupt intellectual culture
of the American nation, complaining that "the public mind, in our country, has
been utterly perverted by this doctrine of natural right."[40] It contrasted Thomas
Dorr and George Dallas with conservative thinkers "Burke, Johnson, Coleridge
and Arnold": "Did not these men know something of the art and power of reasoning? . . . Was a light withheld from their minds, which has revealed itself to
Dorr and Dallas?"[41] The Whig writer went on to blame natural rights nationalism
for the policy of national expansion advanced by the *Democratic Review,* tying
the publication's "perverted" political philosophy to its wrongheaded program of
territorial aggrandizement. By claiming the "inalienable rights of man, in nul-
lifying all its existing institutions," Americans could emigrate to foreign lands,
form political communities, and outvote the existing population on issues as mo-
mentous as annexation to the United States. If this seemed farfetched, the *Review*
advised its readers to study how some Democrats "proposed to obtain California
and even all Mexico."[42] As we shall explore in chapters 3, 4, and 5, Young Americans' conception of natural rights did shape their confidence about the prospects
of democracy in Europe and Latin America.

Given their different interpretations of political science, it is unsurprising
that the *Whig* and *Democratic Reviews* clashed over the merits of works in this
discipline. The two publications disagreed most vociferously over a book by
Jacksonian political theorist Elisha P. Hurlbut published in 1844: *On Human
Rights and their Political Guarantees.* Hurlbut's book was Jacksonian to the core,
forcefully advocating self-government as a natural right, denying the nation
was an "organic community," and rallying against the government's authority
to intervene in matters of trade. Hurlburt emphatically rejected the idea that
human beings "depart" with any of their "natural rights" upon entry into society,
dismissing this notion as an "apology to tyrants." He argued it was wrong to
look up to written constitutions with the kind of "profound reverence" that
Americans were used to. Instead, "the first exhortation should be to bring the
written constitution to the test of natural laws." Drawing on the work of Swiss
theorist of international law Emer de Vattel, who, as we shall see, was very
popular among Democrats, Hurlbut wrote that "no engagement can oblige, or
even authorize, man to violate the laws of nature."[43] Thus, popular sovereignty
might be excluded by virtue of local law, but it should be preserved in places
where it already existed. Intervention by federal or imperial authorities in politics or economics would "obstruct the true course of humanity": "Man," Hurlbut wrote, "comes into society with the capital which God has given him, and
he demands 'free trade.'"[44]

The *Democratic Review* praised Hurlbut's publication as one of the first works of the "new" "American" political science for which it had so long advocated. In an article from 1845 entitled "Hurlbut's Essays on Government," the *Review* lauded him for writing "boldly" about man's "capacity for self-government."[45] Ever aware of what foreign observers thought about the United States, the *Review* hoped that a copy of Hurlbut's *Human Rights* would find its way to the French political theorist Alexis de Tocqueville. Tocqueville had praised the "conservative" elements of American society in his recent work, *Democracy in America,* and the *Review* believed Hurlbut could remind him of the Union's radical promise. The periodical was particularly troubled by Tocqueville's praise for American lawyers. According to the Frenchman, they performed the same function as the European aristocracy, providing examples of responsible and moral behavior in an otherwise fickle and restless nation. By contrast, the *Review* labelled these lawyers "worshippers of precedent" who "quoted bad Latin." Fortunately, Hurlbut's work proved that not all legal minds were apologists for the status quo. The *Review* told its readers: "There hath not been seen, no, not in America, such bold championship of the largest political liberty as the ten essays of Mr. Hurlbut exhibit." Yet "he is a lawyer in full practice at the New York bar." The publication tentatively suggested, "Perhaps an accomplished lawyer can be a philosophical democrat."[46]

The one aspect of Hurlbut's work that was met with ambivalence in the *Democratic Review* was his argument that the franchise should be extended to women. One Democratic critic reported that "the principle is boldly asserted that women are unjustly and unwisely excluded from its enjoyment, more particularly those who have not yet been called to share their social and political responsibilities with the sterner sex by marriage." In an otherwise unequivocally positive assessment, the *Review* struck an uncertain note: "Of this view we can only say at present that the argument both for and against" is "stated with great force and fairness."[47] The *Review's* ambivalence about this aspect of Hurlbut's politics taps into a wider tension between Young America Democrats associated with O'Sullivan's periodical and some of the more radical figures who moved in their orbit, among whom were socialists, abolitionists, and campaigners for women's rights. As I shall explore, Young America Democrats were only too happy to exclude women and African Americans from the natural right to popular sovereignty.

However, we should be careful not to label Young America Democrats "conservative" for this reason. They drew political hierarchies on the basis of cutting-edge phrenological theories about white man's "superior nature"—according to the very same scientific standard of natural law that they used to justify democracy. Although it goes against the grain of contemporary morality, the exclusion of women and nonwhites was an intrinsic, and wholly consistent, component of the most "progressive" Democratic thought.[48] Indeed, the ideologies of progressive democracy and racial hierarchy were often found in the same texts and were promoted by the same people. Just as political scientists believed society was governed by universal laws, they were drawn to pseudoscientific theories that explained political behavior with reference to the innate qualities of different races. The Jacksonian political theorists Nahum Capen and Elisha Hurlbut were both vocal advocates of phrenology and subscribed to deeply racist worldviews.

George H. Colton's *Whig Review* took for granted the fact that phrenology and radical democracy were two components of a broader progressive ideology that rooted politics in the innate and universal authority of nature rather than the moral development of the individual within society. The periodical published a particularly unfavorable assessment of Hurlbut's book, classing it with an entire field of erroneous social science that had emerged in the nineteenth century. One writer mocked "this famous modern doctrine of the inalienable and indefensible right of majorities to rule minorities" that "so utterly escaped the notice of all philosophers, legislators, and theologians" of a previous era. This was an earlier, ignorant time, the publication said sarcastically, when "phrenology had not been discovered—Combe and Fowler had not lectured—Dorr had not fought for human rights, and Counseller Hulbert had not written." Like many critics of Young America, the *Whig Review* rejected the idea that "nature" should become the highest arbiter of political affairs. The article was profoundly uncomfortable with what it saw as Hurlbut's view that "'the duty of the legislator is most plain'" "'*it is simply to conform to natural truth.*'" Or, as Hurlbut pointed out elsewhere, the legislator "'is but the minister and expositor of nature.'"[49]

As a substitute for religion, Hurlbut could only offer the unreliable science of phrenology as the foundation of political authority. But as the *Whig Review* pointed out, this secular vision left no theological guide to political progress, nor a moral ideal to strive toward: "Should, any, however ask—what do you mean by natural truth? How is the great question which Christ left unanswered, when interrogated by Pilate, rendered more easy by the insertion of the word, natural? In reply to all such queries, the simple inquirer is referred at once to the map of the skull. There you have it—all marked out in black and white, and as plain as the boundaries of Texas. There you may see . . . *the whole of man*, in this *democratic* collection of patterns and desires."[50] The periodical criticized Hurlbut's argument that the psychology of the white man made him uniquely suited to democratic government, just as the black man was inherently unsuited to it. Both perspectives ignored the fact that the moral development of the individual was a prerequisite for majority rule, not to mention institutions and legal precedents that had emerged over time. The *Whig Review* did not believe popular sovereignty was necessarily a moral good, in and of itself. The periodical pointed out that the voice of the majority was based on nothing more than a collection of wants and desires contained in the brain. Without religious authority, the unrestrained exercise of these impulses through majoritarian decision-making would not produce social progress. A political order based purely on the secular authority of nature would indulge the worst appetites of the community, resulting in military conquest and material acquisition. For Whigs, the Young Americans' idealization of an unrestrained "natural order" that treated the wants and desires of local communities as inherent moral goods was already turning the Union into an imperial power. As the *Whig Review* pointed out, "If it desire the instant occupation of Oregon, or the annexation of Texas, or California, then the national combativeness . . . is will, and law and constitution, and the very soul of the body politic."[51]

Literary Culture: The *Democratic Review* and Its Rivals

Political scientists and natural law theorists were not the only class of intellectuals that shaped the political ideology of Young America. Writers at the *Democratic Review* also argued that authors and literary figures should use their role as "interpreters of nature" to exert political influence. Like political science, Young Americans exploited literary culture to present their partisan agenda as a set of universal values. In the process, they transformed the meaning of nationalism from loyalty to a particular place to a set of transcendent natural laws. This section will explore the movement's relationship with literary culture by analyzing the reception of Nathaniel Hawthorne's campaign biography of Franklin Pierce in the *Democratic Review*. But first I will explore the role of literary figures in the politics of Young America.

The *Democratic Review* frequently argued that more literary figures should enter political life. One writer claimed, "The remark is often heard that poets should never become politicians, because politics is a business . . . , yet we find the greatest poets have uniformly been the warmest partizans."[52] But, at the same time, the *Review* maintained that literary figures were "unlike ordinary political hacks" since they almost uniformly supported the Democrats.[53] This rhetorical strategy was designed to universalize Democratic ideology by making it synonymous with enlightened thought. Just as democracy was a scientific principle, literary figures were "necessarily . . . republican" because they recognized the ideology conformed to human nature itself. Similarly, within the United States, an author's "constitution of . . . intellect" and "conscious moral sense" meant that they tended to support the antebellum Democracy.[54] Young Americans allied themselves with literary culture for the same reason they had political science: to argue that their policies were based on innate human qualities. Authors who understood the workings of man would therefore gravitate toward the Democrats, while Democratic values could find their expression in great literature.

Other publications described the literary culture of the Democratic Party in similar terms. James Gordon Greene's *Boston Post,* for example, said the party was "made up of two parts"—"hard working farmers and laborers" and "intellectuals"—and claimed that with "few exceptions . . . our first class literary men belong to the Democratic Party." Like the *Review,* the paper drew on the status of literary culture to make the clam that the Democratic Party embodied universal laws. Being "deeper reader(s) in human nature than others," and familiar with the "vast resources of the human soul," authors and poets were supposedly natural democrats. They had "more confidence in the capacity of man for self-government" because they were more perceptive readers of human nature. The important support literary figures lent to the Democracy, therefore, testified to the universalism of the party's political program. The *Post* argued, "It is no small evidence of the truth of democratic principles that men of the highest order of talent generally embrace them."[55]

For Young Americans, the role of the literary figure was to articulate the voice of the masses and the "spirit" of self-government. In Democratic literary culture, the author or artist depicted universal values to audiences irrespective of social status or the formal trappings of social hierarchy. As the Democratic historian George Bancroft pointed out, art appealed to a universal aesthetic sense that made people conscious of abstract rights, existing outside time "in every age and every country."[56] Bancroft wrote that we cannot perceive what is "just and right without feeling within ourselves a consciousness that there exists something in the abstract as right" through intellectual or aesthetic attainment.[57] Bancroft believed literature and art were so well suited to democratic society precisely because they communicated universal values irrespective of rank or position. And for Young Americans like Bancroft, it was democracy itself, embodied in the people's unified moral will, that constituted the highest moral law. Indeed, Bancroft himself was a strident Young American, beloved by both the *Democratic Review* and the movement's congressional leader, Stephen Douglas.[58] In the words of the

Review, Bancroft could "stir the heart of man" through his histories because they expressed "the spirit of free institutions and of human progress."[59]

The *Democratic Review* drew attention to other novelists, historians, and poets who supported the Democrats to reinforce the party's image as the true representative of universal values. After Henry Wikoff assumed ownership in 1846, the magazine dedicated a regular column to American drama. As a former theatre promoter in Europe, Wikoff had an interest in proselytizing national culture across the Atlantic. It is perhaps unsurprising, then, that he gravitated towards America's most famous tragedian, Edwin Forrest. Americans—but particularly Democrats—believed Forrest's very style of acting was a rebuke to British standards. Forrest was muscular and forceful in contrast to the supposedly effete style of Britain's tragedians, such as his great rival, William Charles Macready. Even before Wikoff became owner, the *Review* claimed Forrest's performances expressed the voice of the masses and palpably embodied the national spirit. During his theatre tours of England, the periodical believed, the actor promoted self-government by showing that "the people" had the intelligence and character to rule themselves.[60] Evidence suggests Wikoff even stirred up the rivalry between Edwin Forrest and Macready that led to the Astor Place Riot in 1849: a protest against one of Macready's performances in New York that caused dozens of deaths on the streets of the city.[61] In September 1846 Wikoff penned an article in the *Review* that accused Macready of turning British critics against Forrest.[62] Wikoff alleged that Macready encouraged journalists to make scathing attacks on Forrest's performances during his tours of Britain. American audiences then retaliated against Macready when he visited the United States, culminating in a furious protest against his appearance in Macbeth at the Astor Place Opera House in 1849. Embroiled in international literary feuds, Forrest was not only a national hero but a great figure in world history. Despite the venom it later came to attach to the term, the *Review* labelled the actor "philanthropic": he could liberate men's minds from the "mysterious influence of caste," even in the "remotest corners of the earth."[63] These cultural icons were closely associated with Young America's political wing in the popular press. One newspaper, for example, published a cartoon of Illinois Democrat Stephen Douglas in the guise of a "gladiator" with the recognizably muscular legs of Edwin Forrest.[64]

Literary critics at the *Review* were also keen to single out Nathaniel Hawthorne for hyperbolic praise, saying the nation's "prose poet" could be "paralleled only in Germany."[65] Hawthorne's role in elevating the party from the political into the national sphere is apparent in several pieces. One contrasted the timeless nature of his political essays with the "political speeches" by "little men" who are "laid up for the most part in oblivion in fat, spongy volumes of the

Congressional Globe."⁶⁶ Hawthorne's essays, in contrast, were truly national in character, rooted on the firm foundation of the democratic principle. This view of democracy was typical of Young America: that there was a unified "people's will" that existed prior to systems of political representation. And that this could be best expressed not by congressmen or politicians but by intellectuals and literary figures.

The *Democratic Review* praised Hawthorne's biography of Democratic president Franklin Pierce as proof that the author recognized the universalism of the party's political program. Most scholars assume that Hawthorne wrote Pierce's biography as a favor to a friend, since the two men had been college friends at Bowdoin. Bereft of money, he was also undoubtedly holding out for a political appointment. It was not uncommon for writers to receive diplomatic posts—a useful source income in the absence of a steady salary from writing. Nevertheless, I would add that Hawthorne's campaign biography also enabled the party to stake a claim to the universal ideals portrayed in literature. As Hawthorne himself acknowledged in the *Scarlet Letter,* he could often be "inactive in political affairs" due to a tendency to "roam at will in that broad and quiet land where all mankind may meet."⁶⁷ By employing Hawthorne to write Pierce's biography, the Democrats claimed to encapsulate these broader, innate aspects of human nature. Indeed, in its reception of Hawthorne's *Life of Franklin Pierce,* the *Democratic Review* suggested this was no ordinary campaign biography: it offered voters not just specific policy proposals but also a larger vision of the American nation as a "progressive democracy," above party politics.

After the work's publication in September 1852, the *Democratic Review* praised the *Life of Pierce* for promoting principles over partisanship. One reviewer saw it as a welcome departure from the current state of "the biographies of our great men," which "have all been thrown into the hands of lawyers, disposed of as goods and chattels to an executioner." Instead, the *Life of Pierce* signaled a "new era" in which authors would begin to address political subjects. Since the "termination of the contests" between the "Federal" and "Democratic" parties, the *Review* noted that "the chief minds of our country" have "abstained from the field of political writing." Hawthorne's biography indicated that, once again, authors sympathetic to the Democratic cause would promote the "broad principles" that characterized American nationality. While "selfish vanity" motivated the "feeders" who contributed to the *Congressional Globe,* Hawthorne could write about Pierce more accurately, the *Review* argued, with the "power of giving that exact and full representation of a great man."⁶⁸

Since it was written by an eminent American author, the *Review* also claimed the biography should satisfy a bipartisan audience. It insisted that "not even the most envious Whig critic" could possibly class Hawthorne's work among the "campaign lives" and other "ephemeral publications" of bygone ages.[69] However, unsurprisingly, the Democratic writer praised the parts of the book that portrayed Pierce in the image of Young America. He noted, for example, that "in his very blood," Pierce was a "progressive Democrat"—a positive characteristic, since the "broader and more enduring conservatism of Democratic principle in all things" could protect the republic without "adding thereto the immobility of brain which constitutes the characteristic of men of old ideas."[70] In its analysis of Hawthorne's campaign biography, then, the *Review* argued that a new era was at hand, in which literary figures would play a more active role in political life, especially by promoting the "Democratic principles" that characterized the nation. The magazine's review of the *Life of Pierce* proceeded to explain how these same principles would drive the administration's more expansive foreign policy. It predicted that Pierce would dedicate himself to "the extension of the American Democratic system wherever possible," to "form and maintain an American, and Republican, and Democratic law of nations," and also to "enlarge its diplomatic force, and to place in diplomatic position men . . . of Republican principles."[71]

The interpretation of the *Whig Review* was, of course, very different. Colton's periodical was outraged that a "national" author, whom they claimed had conservative inclinations, could lower himself to the status of a political hack. One critic accused Hawthorne of becoming a "mere party tool," no doubt responding to the "vivid inspiration of some promised office." Apparently, the author had brought forth a book which will "bring him neither fame nor credit." Rather than bolstering national principles, the *Life of Pierce* merely showed the depths to which intellectuals could fall in the present age: it was "doubly disgusting . . . in an age of freedom to see a man of ability voluntarily prostitute his pen, for the paltry object of some government salary. . . . There are 'hacks' enough, Heaven knows, infesting every city."[72] Here, the *Whig Review* deliberately tried to break Hawthorne's ties to the Democratic Party by reestablishing the author's role as a figure above party politics. Instead of Hawthorne enhancing the Democrats' reputation, the Whigs argued the Democratic Party had debased that of the author. In trying to raise their political program above partisan concerns, Young America had ground down the proper role of literary culture in the antebellum republic.

Furthermore, Whig writers made the case that the Democrats had coopted the author's reputation unfairly. In fact, they claimed, Hawthorne disdained the very universal outlook the Democratic Party represented. The *Whig Review* maintained that, in truth, Hawthorne did not belong to a political party. He was "national—national in subject, treatment and manner. . . . He has never damned himself to the obese body of party. . . . He belongs to all of them!"

Indeed, the writer went further, arguing that the conservative aspects of Haw-thorne's fiction proved that he was—if anything—a natural Whig. Apparently, Hawthorne's short story "Earth's Holocaust," published in 1844, "embodied . . . the fundamental thought of that Higher Conservatism upon the eternal base of which all wise and true Whigs have planted their feet."[73]

It is not difficult to see why this story appealed to conservative literary critics at the *Whig Review*. Indeed, the narrative might be read as an elaborate satire on the Young America nationalists who were so eager to appropriate the author's legacy. In it, Hawthorne describes an attempt to build a vast bonfire to burn "the accumulation of worn-out trumpery" consisting of sinful pleasures and outdated forms of knowledge.[74] The hallmarks of monarchical society, including "coates of arms, badges of knighthood, crowns and scepters" as well as vices like liquor, tobacco, and weapons of war are thrown into the flames in the name of social progress. When everything has been incinerated, a group of bystanders, including an executioner, some criminals, and a mysterious visitor, strikes up a conversation. Unhappy that there are no evils left for the executioner to pun-ish, or for the criminals to indulge in, the executioner offers to help them to a "comfortable end on the nearest tree." But the "dark-complexioned" visitor tells them not to worry since there is one last thing the people forgot to throw onto the fire—the human heart itself. "Unless they hit upon some method of purifying that foul cavern," the stranger says, "it will be the old world yet."[75] In this satire of antebellum reform, the *Whig Review* saw the same profoundly conservative message that they believed was at the center of their party's ide-ology. Moreover, by reasserting the primacy of original sin, Hawthorne's story reminded readers that "political creeds" cannot be "separated" from the "Ethical and Religious"—"one always has and always will grow out of the other."[76]

The equally conservative *North American Review* also chose to emphasize the aspects of Hawthorne's literary work that were skeptical of social progress. In this case the publication championed "The Celestial Railroad," a satire of antebellum reform movements. The short story depicts a vainglorious attempt to build a railroad to heaven, which is accidently directed straight to hell. The story has similar implications to "Earth's Holocaust," with most critics, then and now, reading it as a comment on the futility of elaborate schemes aimed at human melioration. The *North American Review* praised Hawthorne's final image, where "onward the car rolls over the Slough of Despond, on a shaky causeway built of books of German rationalism and Transcendental Divinity."[77] As an assault on the notion that moral progress would inevitably accompany technological change, the *Review* believed the story ridiculed the type of Young America nationalism that the *Democratic Review* stood for. For both conservative publications and the *Democratic Review*, then, Hawthorne's work contained a political message that transcended partisanship. But while Whigs argued his stories reaffirmed conservative principles, Democrats claimed he was one of their own, well-versed in the laws of nature.

Far from being backward or anti-intellectual, Democratic theorists saw literary culture and political science as important components of Democratic political thought. The *Democratic Review* drew on both disciplines to emphasize the inalienable and universal character of their political program. However, there was a more sinister side to Young America's liberal worldview: the very same natural law that made democracy an inherent right for white men also permanently excluded nonwhites from the social order.

Race: The *Democratic Review* and Its Rivals

Traditional explanations for the racism in Democratic political culture have come to very different conclusions. One explanation offers a more positive assessment of the party, arguing the exclusion of Blacks and Native Americans was an "inconsistency" in an otherwise liberal worldview.[78] Another is far bleaker, arguing the party's liberal rhetoric was a mere "fig leaf" for Southern interests.[79] But these apparently opposite conclusions in fact share the same pitfall: both separate the racial ideology of the Democrats from the party's broader program. The first explanation assumes the racist aspects of Jacksonian culture were at odds with liberal assumptions, while the second absolves the Northern states of their own role in cultivating racism alongside the South. Rather, we need to recognize that Herrenvolk democracy—self-government for the master race—was a core aspect of Democratic nationalism, which fitted neatly inside its larger ideology.[80]

It is true the *Democratic Review* had a broad Southern readership. Just like the Democratic Party at large, the periodical had to satisfy slave owners in the South as well as supporters of free labor in the North. As O'Sullivan pointed out in 1845, the *Review* was "national in its character and aims." As such, the editor explained that it "abstains from the discussion of a topic . . . necessarily excluded from a work circulating equally in the South as in the North."[81] Furthermore, the periodical received contributions from both Northern and Southern writers. The Southerner Thomas P. Kettell, who assumed the editorship in 1846, had a clear opinion on the inferiority of the Black race: "It is sufficiently proved by the world's experience," he wrote, that a Black person "will not work at all if he can help it . . . the *vis inertia* of the black blood is so great, that even a large mixture of white blood will overcome it only so far as to induce the individual to perform menial offices, clinging to the skirts of white society."[82] However, it was not pressure from the Southern states that primarily encouraged white supremacy in the pages of the *Review*. As O'Sullivan's article highlighted, slavery was a contentious topic in the nation at large, but the inherent inferiority of nonwhite races was certainly not.

To understand how the racism of the Young America movement fitted within their broader worldview, we need to examine how the prospect of racial equality challenged these Democrats' core beliefs. For Young Americans on both sides of the Mason-Dixon line, the prospect of free Blacks within the United States posed a threat similar to Whiggish conservatism—and the legacy of British rule from whence it came. Namely, both implicitly acknowledged the contingency of democratic government. Whigs taught that democracy rested on federal authority as well as history, culture, and positive law. Similarly, the antislavery movement acknowledged natural rights to labor, which preceded democratic government and extended to a group that almost all Americans excluded from the political order. Indeed, Whigs found it easier to salvage the essential humanity of nonwhites from their failure to exercise popular sovereignty. Furthermore, the Whigs' contingent view of democracy, which rested on belief in human improvement, did frequently open up the possibility of admitting Blacks into the political process. The fact that Black people resided within the Union, contributed to its development, and imbibed its culture and traditions gave them more potential to exercise political rights. Conversely, Young Americans drew racial distinctions that were inherent and cut across geopolitical boundaries: Black peoples' presence within the Union did not even have the potential to confer political authority on that community.[83] At the same time, white men could penetrate the borders of nonwhite nations with impunity, spontaneously establishing democratic communities irrespective of their ties to the land. Moreover, Young Americans had no conception of natural rights distinct from popular sovereignty. Deemed unable to practice democracy, nonwhite people were doomed to anarchy and extinction or to be propped up "artificially" through the use of federal power. In terms of labor, too, both Whiggish conservatism and abolitionism threatened the natural rights of white men in the same way. Whigs might extract surplus value from white communities for the federal government's internal improvements program. But as individuals who could not support themselves, Blacks would do the same through the burdens placed on white communities. We might say, then, that Democrats had their own free-labor ideology that often worked against the forces of antislavery.

Moreover, the racism that underpinned these arguments was rooted in the same assumptions as Young America's broader liberal tradition. The doctrine of racial inferiority, for example, cut across geographical boundaries, rejected over-bearing religious authority in favor of science and nature, and worked toward progress and economic efficiency. The very same liberals who rebelled against the patrician Whig class used the same intellectual authorities to permanently exclude nonwhites from even the most basic of rights. Once we appreciate racism as a complementary facet of Jacksonian political culture, what might look like inconsistencies on the issue of slavery begin to add up to a more coherent ideology. While slavery could be tolerated for fear of free Blacks in the polity, many Democrats favored deportation to the tropics, or even extinction, in order to rid white communities of Black labor in any form. Moreover, slavery could be supported in order to ward off the abolitionist threat but had to be vociferously attacked once the Slave Power started to override white majorities. Ultimately, what was decided mattered less than the fact that white men made the choice.

Just as it used political science and literature to justify democracy for white men, the *Democratic Review* drew on both disciplines to exclude "inferior" races from the body politic. In terms of science, the publication lauded works of phrenology, a pseudoscience that permanently barred "inferior" races from the benefits of democracy. In terms of literature, they argued that nonwhites were incapable of producing great work and encouraged white authors to portray "inferior" races according to their debased natures. One of the most cited writers in the *Democratic Review* was the New York physician John Van Evrie, who argued for the exclusion of Blacks because of their innate qualities. Van Evrie made the case for the "natural" inferiority of nonwhite races and the inherent democratic nature of white communities in the same text. In an 1853 pamphlet called *Negroes and Negro "Slavery,"* Van Evrie argued that the presence of Blacks in America had made the first European settlers in the United States conscious of their own "natural equality," thereby helping to discredit the artificial distinctions of the Old World. He wrote, "The presence of the negro was and always must be a test that shows the insignificance and indeed nothingness of those artificial distinctions which elsewhere govern the world and constitute the basis of the social as well as the political order."[84] Van Evrie tried to make racial exclusion compatible with the universal nature of American democracy by arguing that the social hierarchy in America was based on natural divisions rather than the artificial distinctions of Europe.

The *Democratic Review* also used literature to construct an idea of humanity that excluded nonwhites from the benefits of democracy. As we have seen, the *Review* argued that the prevalence of literary figures among the Democratic ranks proved the inherent worth of the party's principles. Similarly, it claimed that the supposed lack of culture among nonwhite races revealed the absence of true humanity among these groups. For example, in an 1846 issue, the *Review* declared that African nations had "never possessed any literature, even an alphabet, however rude," and that this would "always be the case in Africa."[85] Just as George Bancroft celebrated "man's" innate capacity for democracy, the *Democratic Review* portrayed Native Americans as an inferior species, bereft of this essential trait. In an 1846 poem entitled "The Indian Love," the *Review* presented Native Americans as bloodthirsty and savage: "I am a wild Lennape chief, / And love the game of life; / See yonder sumach's crimson leaf! / 'Tis paler than my scalping knife."[86] Similarly, in 1838 the periodical complained about the "sickly sentimentality" of most writing on Indians.[87] It is evident that the *Review* excluded Blacks and native peoples from even the most basic civil or political rights on the same grounds that they asserted the white man's right to democracy. Even in creating hierarchies, then, Young Americans maintained that democracy was an essential human trait, rooted in the universal authority of scientific and literary culture rather than social or moral development.

In contrast to its Jacksonian counterpart, the *Whig Review* targeted racial theorists as part of its broader attacks on political "science" and critiqued the Democrats' view of the relationship between literature and race. The publication singled out *Vestiges of a Natural History of Creation,* by the Scottish evolutionary scientist and phrenologist Robert Chambers, for criticism, not only for its scientific racism but for its larger thesis that political progress could be reduced to innate, or natural, laws.[88] *Vestiges* was a speculative natural history that argued for an evolutionary view of human development. It ended with an account of how the natural laws that improved the human species would inevitably lead to political progress: a theory that proved popular among political radicals on both sides of the Atlantic. In 1845 the *Whig Review* attacked Chambers for basing a theory of social development on the secular authority of nature rather than religious scripture. The writer bemoaned the "supereminent [*sic*] degree" to which works of its kind peddled "traits of impudence, arrogance and profound ignorance of Revelation." The publication criticized Chambers's assertion that the "natural" quality of race had driven both the political advancement of whites and the degradation of nonwhite peoples. The periodical complained that every social development was reduced to the operation of general laws, rooted in the secular authority of nature, rather than Protestant faith: "Individual men and individual nations, and even races have suffered and perished in those backward cycles which the scheme admits to be necessary to the general progress."[89] Indeed, it was common for other Whig thinkers to complain that Roberts Chambers overemphasized the innate characteristics of man rather than exploring the moral development of the individual.

In line with its broader theory of democracy as a contingent rather than natural political system, the *Whig Review* stressed the capacity for social improvement among nonwhite peoples, thereby avoiding the dichotomy common to Jacksonian thought between degraded and superior races and nondemocratic and democratic peoples. In 1845, for example, the *Review* published an article entitled "The Past and Present of the Indian Tribes," which took an optimistic view of the prospects of the Cherokees within the United States. The article stressed environmental explanations for the differences between white and nonwhite populations, sometimes contrasting the behavior of "civilized" Indians with the behavior of crude and uneducated white Americans. The writer, for example, wrote that he had heard of a "young daughter of a Cherokee chief" who "laugh[ed] at a visit she had received from a storekeeper of some wealth, who lived near the line of the United States, because the vulgar man did not know how to use a silver fork."[90]

The *Whig Review* lay responsibility for the Indians' tragic fate at the hands of those Jacksonian heroes on the frontier and their flagship policy of Texas annexation. These attacks are significant because they reveal the Whigs' ideological assumption that the destruction of Indian communities was more a product of circumstance than inherent defects. Moreover, they rejected the Democrats' idealization of the frontier as well as the supposed inherent morality of self-governing white communities. The *Review* took aim at "the villainy of the frontier desperado" and the "unprincipled men whom the rumor of gold mines, in all ages, has sufficed to entice from their settled homes." If Texas was annexed to the Union, the *Review* complained that it would become even more difficult for native people to preserve their sovereignty, as they would be squeezed onto increasingly small patches of territory. The Whig writer blamed this land grab on the "idlers who infest every frontier city of our land as the Eldorado, the possession of which is to realize the dreams of their vagabond cupidity."[91]

One of the most contentious racial theories of the 1850s starkly illustrates the different attitudes to race between Whig and Democrat: that of polygenesis, which was the idea that races had different origins rather than constituting one human species. In the nineteenth century it was sometimes fused with Christian thought through the idea of separate creation myths. Although the *Democratic Review* had initially remained wary, the periodical had always subscribed to more fixed racial hierarchies than its Whig counterpart. Certainly, in 1842 one writer at the *Democratic Review* defended the idea that all the races were descended from Adam and Eve in response to the publication of *Crania America*, by Samuel Morton, a text that made the case for separate creation stories. The article, however, still maintained the inferiority of nonwhite races and highlighted inherent differences in the construction of the brain.[92] Furthermore, when polygenesis became more popular during the late 1840s, the *Democratic Review* came to embrace the theory and began to argue passionately in its favor.[93] This more rigid form of racial hierarchy appealed to the *Review* because it made natural factors the only criteria for democratic government—a belief that chimed with their broader view that popular sovereignty was an innate characteristic of the white race. When Young Americans constructed political hierarchies, they did so according to the widest and most impenetrable authorities: namely, the making of separate human species.

If the *Democratic Review* held fast to the notion that whiteness was the only criteria for democratic participation, the *Whig Review* argued that contingent factors, such as evangelical culture, custom, and education, made people more suited to self-government. Indeed, critics of polygenesis often hailed from a Whig background. The Christian preacher Thomas Smyth, for example, became a favorite at the *Whig Review* for arguing that the new theory of polygenesis was incompatible with the account of man's creation found in the Bible. On top of this, Smyth argued that polygenesis was wrong to attribute social success to inherent racial categories found in nature, rather than to Christian civilization and moral uplift. In this account we find not only an assault on the faulty science of separate creation myths but also a critique of Young America's broader theory of political progress. If Blacks' failure to establish self-government was due to their social, religious, and natural environment, then whites' successful implementation of popular sovereignty might be reduced to these factors, too, rather than the doctrine of natural rights. The *Democratic Review* was therefore unsparing in its denunciation of Smyth's work. In particular, it was at pains to point out that Smyth's biblical account of political progress could not account for those "Pagan whites" who "recovered from barbarism to a high degree of civilization without external aid." In attacking Smyth, the *Democratic Review* was shutting down an argument that had the potential to undermine their entire worldview: that man's moral development—rather than inherent qualities—made him suited to democratic government.[94]

These different portrayals of race in the *Whig* and *Democratic Reviews* suggest the parties' respective "natural" and historical explanations for democracy partly account for their distinct racial politics. The *Democratic Review* should therefore be considered neither a Northern nor Southern periodical but a Jacksonian one. Ultimately, the racial ideology it advocated can be characterized as a combination of white supremacy, free labor, and popular sovereignty that had traction across the nation. Indeed, despite its faith in inherent racial characteristics, the *Democratic Review* did not make the case that slavery was a positive good. The magazine, as well as many of its contributors and readers, came from the Northern states and abided by free-labor ideology. As I will explore in chapter 7, even during the height of the sectional crisis, editor John O'Sullivan maintained that slavery degraded both white masters and workers. Although the periodical entertained the idea that slavery could be perpetuated in the tropics, it did not see a future for slavery on the American continent. Instead, the publication advocated a kind of free-labor ideology based on the principles of white supremacy, frequently advocating a process of either colonization or extermination as the path to a free society for white men. One article asserted that "the very decided superiority of an entire free population over a mixed population of freemen and slaves" was "shown too clearly in the progress of the United States to be in any way questionable." The article predicted that the essential superiority of free labor would mean free states would gradually replace slave states within the Union. However, this would not be achieved through the enfranchisement of the Black population but by their extermination "in an operation as unerring though somewhat slower than that which substitutes the white population in place of the Indians."[95] Another article published in 1846, during Young America's supposed "liberal phase," looked forward to the eventual extinction of the Black race: "When the blacks shall have been thrown upon their own resources, the increase in their numbers will stop, and ultimately they must become extinct as a race on this continent."[96]

Overall, these Democrats were eager to define nationality in universalist terms. Young Americans looked to the natural laws of political and racial science to replace more traditional authorities, such as government intervention and cultural and historical cohesion, as guarantors of stability and progress within the republic. The Whigs had a very different idea of what nationhood meant in practice. These more conservative figures argued that a feeling of disinterested patriotism, based around sharper territorial boundaries, could temper fierce partisan debate. Irreconcilable interests were unavoidable but could be balanced within a harmonious Union. By shifting political debate into the realm of intellectual culture, Young America Democrats, both in Congress and the pages of the *Democratic Review,* fused the political rights, belonging to the nation, with natural rights, belonging to a racialized view of mankind. The principles contained within the Declaration of Independence, which should have provided shared foundations for the international order, were remade in the Democratic image. Rather than mere disagreement over policy, O'Sullivan and his allies began a debate over the meaning of the liberal tradition itself. This nationalist vision was not parochial or backward-looking—characteristics that historians tend to ascribe both to Jacksonian politics and to the idea of the "nation" itself. These Democrats certainly worked to construct an "imagined community" in the pages of their periodical. However, this ideal was not based on images of a fictitious past, as Benedict Anderson has suggested of European nationalism.[97] Rather, Young Americans subscribed to a very different conception of the nation: a Jacksonian image that looked to an image of a future that was connected to the present through the working of natural laws.

2

The Dorr Rebellion

DEMOCRACY, NATURAL RIGHTS AND
THE DOMESTIC POLITICS OF THE 1840S

In 1840 Rhode Island was the only remaining state in the Union that had neither created a new constitution after the American Revolution nor instituted
universal white male suffrage. Unlike the rest of the nation, the state continued
to operate under its old colonial charter, passed in 1663 during the reign of King
Charles II. Instead of granting unconditional voting rights for white males over
the age of twenty-one, the charter, like many of its time, contained a property
qualification of $134. When it was first instituted, the constitution was deemed
sufficiently democratic. Since Rhode Island had a largely rural population in the
seventeenth century, most farmers owned enough land to meet the requirement.
But rapid industrialization and unprecedented levels of immigration during the
mid-nineteenth century saw the state fill with the poor and disenfranchised. By
1840 the majority of the state's population lived and worked in urban areas and
earned wages that gave them no hope of qualifying for a ballot on election day.
Other states had suffered similar changes during the nineteenth century but had
altered their constitutions accordingly. In Rhode Island almost two-thirds of the
white male population over the age of twenty-one could not vote. Still laboring
under an outdated political settlement that not only predated but appeared
to contradict the values at the heart of the nation's founding, the situation in
Rhode Island was ripe for revolution.

After every formal effort to alter the state charter failed during the 1830s,
Thomas W. Dorr held an extralegal convention in October 1841. His supporters
drafted a new People's Constitution that granted the vote to all free white men
after one month's residence. Although he had—at first—proposed giving the
vote to Blacks, Dorr backed down in 1840 under pressure from the state's immigrant community. Irish laborers formed a disproportionate part of the disenfranchised urban population, and many saw themselves in conflict with African
Americans for political rights. Insecure about their status, these new arrivals
argued that whiteness alone entitled them to vote. To quell the groundswell of

democratic agitation, the general assembly in Rhode Island issued a rival Free-men's Constitution, which conceded to some of Dorr's demands. But conservatives remained especially opposed to the expansion of voting rights for Irish Catholics, whom they believed constituted the "floating masses, often turbulent and always irresponsible, which make great cities great sores."[1] The Protestant editor of the conservative *Providence Journal,* Henry B. Anthony, chastised nearby New York for allowing European migrants to vote before they obtained citizenship.[2] Anti-Dorrites also feared that an Irish Democrat from New York, such as Mike Walsh, would rouse the people against the colonial charter—a fear that did, in fact, materialize when Walsh lent his support to the revolt that eventually broke out.[3] Unfortunately for the conservatives, when the two constitutions were later subjected to a popular vote in 1841, the Freemen's Constitution was overwhelmingly rejected. The People's Constitution was accepted not only by all white males over the age of twenty-one, but—Dorr claimed—also by the residents who could already legally vote in the state.

Faced with an intractable conflict in early 1842, these rival conventions elected governors of their own—Dorr for the Suffrage Party, and Samuel Ward King for the so-called Law and Order faction. Presided over by two rival governors, the state was teetering on the brink of a civil conflict. Unable to implement either of the two new constitutions and clinging on to the formal apparatus of power, Samuel King clamped down on the supporters of the Suffrage Party and declared martial law. But President John Tyler appeared reluctant to offer the state federal support. Seizing the moment, Dorr launched a futile attack on an arsenal in Providence to better arm his growing band of supporters. Unfortunately for the Dorrites, King's superior numbers crushed the uprising. Dorr fled to New York, where he was forced to disband his followers—despite receiving some aid from the Democratic Party machine at Tammany Hall. Conscious of the scale of anger in the state, King recognized the need to liberalize the constitution and issued a new one in September 1842. This extended the vote to any white male who could pay the poll tax of $1 for the upkeep of the state's schools but retained the property qualification for new immigrants—to the horror of many Democrats. Even more horrifying, the Law and Order Party enfranchised the state's Black population. This was the sole instance in the entire history of the pre–Civil War era United States of a state enfranchising African Americans after their voting rights had previously been revoked. Strange, then, that it should come from the self-consciously conservative and nativist forces in Rhode Island. Undoubtedly, this was a pragmatic move and hardly reflected King's deep affinity for Black rights. After Dorr denied them suffrage, Blacks had deserted his movement and actively assisted the Law and Order faction in suppressing the rebellion. In return, King extended the right to vote, rightly predicting that the Black community would support Rhode Island's Whig Party. But, as we shall see, it was also the Whiggish conception of political rights as contingent that opened up a space for the Black residents to seize power in the first place.

In some respects, King's counterrevolution returned Rhode Island to a more fortunate time. Indeed, before an 1822 law denied Blacks the right to vote, a great number had met the requirements enshrined in the colonial charter. Although conservative critics of Dorr were hardly racial egalitarians, they did create a constitution at odds with the racial politics of the time. After Dorr's failure, Rhode Island's Black population participated in the state's Fourth of July parade, carrying instruments that the government had confiscated from Dorr and the rebels.[4] As for Dorr, with a bounty of $5,000 over his head, he was finally arrested in 1843. Although his friend John O'Sullivan had been arguing for over a year that Dorr should be allowed to vindicate himself in a court of law, events did not unfold in quite the way O'Sullivan hoped. The trial was purposefully located in the conservative town of Newport, Rhode Island, where an unsympathetic jury agreed on a sentence of life imprisonment and hard labor. Dorr earned the dubious distinction of being the first American to be convicted of treason by an individual state. The second would be a man who put similar ideas in the service of a very different cause: John Brown, sentenced in Virginia in 1859, on the eve of the Civil War.[5]

Despite being an isolated and anomalous event, the Dorr Rebellion sparked a ferocious debate in Congress over values at the heart of America's founding. Perhaps more than any other incident in this period, it crystallized what historian Adam I. P. Smith has termed the fundamental "philosophical and constitutional dispositions" between the main parties.[6] Or, in the words of historian Erik Chaput: "The Dorr Rebellion is more than a limited, local event, two decades removed from the grand drama of the Civil War; rather events in the Union's smallest state reverberated throughout the halls and backrooms of Congress as the nation's politicians tried to sort out the meaning of freedom. Like the issue of the status of slavery in the territories it raised profound questions about the location of sovereignty that only war could ultimately solve."[7]

In its immediate aftermath, American congressmen fell silent on the Dorr Rebellion. Eager to make it onto the Democratic ticket in the upcoming election of 1844, many of the more radical Democrats based in New York—Dorr's natural allies—avoided public support for the People's Constitution to avoid alienating the more conservative wing of the party. Ohio's William Allen and Democratic historian George Bancroft were among the only voices to lend support to Dorr's actions. This all changed after New Hampshire's Edmund Burke published his extensive congressional report on the rebellion in 1844. As Burke wrote to George Bancroft that year, "The full report will contain every authentic paper connected with the suffrage movement from its first inception to the noble speech of Dorr before his sentence."[8] With some of it ghostwritten by Dorr himself, Burke's report threw its unconditional support behind universal white male suffrage.

Particularly striking about Burke's report, and the reason it triggered such widespread disagreement in Congress, were the philosophical justifications for Dorr's conduct. It made intricate arguments that tapped into deep-seated ideological divisions about how the two major parties conceived of the American nation, the very same schisms reflected in the *Whig* and *Democratic Reviews*. Indeed, these fundamental divisions, which emerged in the aftermath of this civil conflict in Rhode Island, continued to define politics in the antebellum North until the outbreak of the Civil War in 1861. While analyses of sectional divisions have frequently dominated this period, the disagreement over democracy at the heart of the debates raged just below the surface of national politics.

Furthermore, the network of writers and congressmen who were prepared to defend Burke's report offers an insight into the composition of the Young America movement as a particular constituency of the Democratic Party. As I have discussed, the writers and politicians who supported Young America did not organize regular meetings or rallies but did form a loose network around the *Democratic Review*. Certainly, the relationship between the writers at the periodical and the congressional wing of Young America could be fraught with tension. However, there was a distinct network of more "progressive" Democrats who revolved around the publication and enjoyed close relationships with its two main editors: John O'Sullivan and, after 1852, George Sanders.[9] Within Congress, these politicians tended to cluster around the rising star of the Democracy, Stephen Douglas, popularly known as the "Little Giant" on account of his physical and political stature respectively. Some of Douglas's key allies put themselves forward to defend Burke's report, such as John A. McClernand, a representative from Douglas's home state of Illinois. Another friend and close adviser to Douglas who became vocal in the debate was the eminent American historian and staunch Democrat George Bancroft. Looking at how these men defended Dorr, we can see that the network that constituted Young America also had a specific ideological orientation rooted in the idea of natural rights.

One of the primary reasons the Democrat from New Hampshire, Edmund Burke, penned his defense of the rebellion was to justify the revolt with the aim of eventually acquitting Dorr of his lifetime sentence. To this end, the report contained a series of excerpts from pamphlets and conventions protesting Dorr's innocence from 1841 onwards, as well as a statement from the congressional committee Burke had assembled to create the document. A variety of different arguments for Dorr's innocence emerge, but one thread runs throughout: that democracy was a natural right for white men contained within the Declaration of Independence. For Burke and his associates, democracy was not merely a system of government, still less one of "virtual representation," whereby intelligent citizens would balance the competing interests of the citizenry. Rather, ultimate authority resided in the people, whose voice preceded and stood independent of government itself. Dorr's People's Convention therefore "proclaimed that the people in their political capacity are above all laws, and all constituted forms of government, which were their own creations, and they could mould and reform at pleasure. Such is the principle which the committee believes was intended to be asserted by the Signers of the Declaration of Independence."[10] Going further, this natural right to self-government applied not only at the moment when constitutions were revised, but before and after their implementation. The people therefore had a natural right not only to revise the constitution but also to adjudicate every other issue pertaining to the community. This was a novel view that went further than previous constitutional theories and manifested itself in arguments for white men to be granted suffrage as a natural right. In contrast, the more conservative Whig Party conceded that the outdated colonial charter required reform but argued that an expansion of the suffrage should be made according to the constitution's existing authority. The Whigs maintained that the people had no inherent right to alter the charter at will nor the authority to do so in the name of an inalienable right to suffrage, since democracy was not a natural right.

Despite their reputation as a backward and "folkloric" party, this group of antebellum Democrats rooted their ideology in liberal political philosophy, or—as they often termed it—the "science of politics."[11] In particular, Burke repeatedly turned to the authority of nature to justify Dorr's new constitution. "It is not reasonable," he argued, "to suppose that the majority, by whose consent the compact was originally formed, would yield up the powers to which they were by nature entitled, to the minority." It was not reactionary populism but "the voice of nature, of reason, of true philosophy" that dictated that sovereignty should lie with the people, manifested in the will of the majority.[12]

Defending democracy as a natural right also required an assault on the more conservative form of nationalism advocated by the Whig Party. Burke attacked the Whiggish notion that the nation constituted an organic entity that preceded the political rights of individual citizens—one that protected past and future generations as much as the present one. Flying directly in the face of his namesake, Burke declared, "The dead cannot bind the living; and, therefore, when any compacts or institutions of the dead become burdensome or oppressive to the living, the latter may alter or abolish such compacts or institutions and form others that will secure to them the enjoyment of the rights to which they are, by nature, entitled." The committee believed that "the right of suffrage is a natural, [not] a conventional right."[13]

Burke's report also rejected the idea that people lacked the virtue required for Dorr's brand of direct democracy—that the people were "unstable, fickle and fond of change . . . [and would] unsettle the foundations of all governments."[14] As we shall see, such arguments were common in discussions of the Dorr Rebellion as well as in later debates over slavery in the next decade. In both cases, more conservative commentators argued that the people were liable to mob rule. Since the days of Socrates, majorities supposedly made decisions motivated more by passion, jealousy, and rage, rather than with calm or deliberate reason. A whole lineage of Whig thought warned that majorities were liable to suasion by charismatic dictators: the modern-day Caesar was truly "King Andrew" of the Democratic Party.[15] In the 1850s former Whigs charged that slavery should not be left to settlers in the territories since their views were liable to corruption, especially if they shared presses and pulpits with the Slave Power.

But Burke took a very different view of political majorities, arguing that the voice of the people was tantamount to "the voice of God."[16] No conflict existed between democracy and individual rights, since the former was an inherently virtuous system, uniquely suited to human nature. Free from the forceful restraint of the state, the people were perfectly capable of exercising good judgement in a sober and considered way. Anticipating an argument that assumed even greater significance after the failures of the 1848 Revolutions in Europe, Burke claimed that the masses were, in fact, a conservative force. "So far from the people desiring change and instability," Burke wrote, "history proves that they are in favor of stability and permanency; and that they long bear the abuses, oppressions and tyranny of government before they resort to their ultimate right which is *revolution*—by force in despotic governments."[17] The 1848 revolution in France, which had so terrified conservatives in Europe and the United States, was, for the New Hampshire Democrat, the product of "unfeeling, heartless and ruthless oppression."[18] While conservatives believed the aftermath of the French revolution exposed the folly of majoritarian politics, Burke lay blame solely on the overbearing power of the state.

In the report Burke also reprinted the proceedings of several pro-Dorr meetings that took place from 1841 to 1844. These texts only reinforced his central argument that democracy was a natural right. One convention, which had assembled at Providence on February 22, 1841, turned to the authority of nature to promote a "state constitution." "We contend," they declared, "that a participation in the choice of those who make and administer the laws, is a natural right, which cannot be abridged, nor suspended any further then the greatest good of the greatest number imperatively requires." Conservatives, who would argue otherwise, made the "radical error" of assuming that "political rights" exist by virtue of the "political compact." Moreover, "The reasoners will tell you about rights created by society," the convention declared, whilst "we wish to ask . . . what those rights were which existed before political society itself."[19]

Many congressional Democrats met Burke's report with enthusiasm, while Whigs furiously disputed the notion that popular sovereignty should constitute a natural right. As a coauthor of the report, prominent Democrat and Douglas ally John A. McClernand sprang to its defense in the House of Representatives, although not before registering his anguish at seeing the report turned into a point of disagreement in the first place. These were great national principles, McClernand insisted, that should have never been up for political debate. The report "grasps not only the fundamental principles of civil government," he argued, "but also those great and inestimable rights which constitute the title to man's divinity—which verify the fact of his creation in the image of God."[20] Instead of presenting the rebellion as a contest between different factions, McClernand linked it to a much longer, age-old struggle between different ideological perspectives: one belonging to enlightened reason, the other to an age of despotism. The struggle was as much for control of universities and publishing houses as it was for the halls of Congress. McClernand reminded his audience that when seventeenth-century natural rights theorist Algernon Sydney was beheaded on suspicion of plotting against Charles II, the "learned" scholars of Oxford University declared "every principle by which a free constitution can be maintained 'impious' and 'heretical.'" While Thomas Dorr sat alone in his jail cell, the "learned" Federalists denounced him the same way. McClernand urged his fellow representatives to heed Jefferson's words to keep pace with "the progress of knowledge, the light of science and the amelioration of the condition of society."[21]

Significantly, McClernand viewed the contest over Dorr's rights as an intellectual dispute as much as a political one. Young Americans drew on intellectual culture, including philosophy, political economy, and literature, to legitimize their vision of society. As guides to natural (or transcendent) truth, Young Americans believed these disciplines should provide the foundation for a political order that would cut across geographical boundaries. Conversely, many Americans, especially on the conservative side, continued to view politics as a struggle between different factions that provided checks and balances on each other, ensuring no one group became dominant. Best exemplified by the antebellum Whig Party, these political thinkers saw the nation as the primary site of political loyalty as it emerged over time. The transcendent rights derived from liberal philosophy certainly existed, but they stood outside the confines of political communities based on compromise and tradition. The more conservative vision of the nation was best exemplified by the eighteenth-century Irish political theorist Edmund Burke, who viewed society as an "organic entity" that evolved over time. Sure enough, McClernand signaled out Burke for "advance[ing] the same doctrine" as the Federalists who criticized Dorr, leading McClernand to wonder if "the opposition have borrowed the idea of *sovereignty* and *immutability* of government" from him. Indeed, McClernand claimed the anti-Dorrite faction was even more reactionary than Burke. The Irishman had at least admitted that the people should make the "original compact" that would form their constitution, while the Federalists wanted Dorr to submit to a colonial charter that their ancestors had no hand in drafting. In their backwardness the Whigs surpassed even Burke: they had "out-Heroded Herod."[22]

Democrat William A. Kennedy reinforced McClernand's arguments in the House of Representatives. Another supporter of Stephen Douglas, and a self-proclaimed "western man," Kennedy endorsed the interpretation of the Declaration of the Independence put forward in the report on Rhode Island. He condemned those congressmen who were not prepared to implement the natural rights outlined in that immortal document and who denied the right of suffrage was contained within it at all. He lamented that the American people "had heard it declared on this floor, that the right of suffrage was not a natural right; and that the doctrine of Thomas Jefferson, which was incorporated in the Declaration of Independence, was a 'mere abstraction' which might, or might not, be reduced to practice." Kennedy countered that "in the West, they were accustomed to believe that their fathers meant what they said when they asserted that the people had the power and the ability to govern themselves."[23]

In the House of Representatives, Democrat Henry Williams made perhaps the most eloquent summary of democracy as being something more than a mere political system. Williams contended that democracy was not a system of representation but an attribute of humanity, one that preceded the institutions of government. "If inherent," popular sovereignty "is not a right derived from an organization of state, but must be before and above human government—a right that belongs to man as a member of the human family," he argued. "If inalienable, it cannot be chartered away, relinquished or parted with. It becomes an attribute of humanity, distinct from and superior to government that attaches to the people at all times."[24] Williams singled out for praise the prominent

Democrat George M. Dallas, who later became vice president under James K. Polk in 1846, noting his idea that democracy was a form of peaceful revolution. Williams quoted Dallas favorably: "A convention is the provided machinery of peaceful revolution. It is the civilized substitute for intestine war; the American mode of carrying out the will of the majority, the inalienable and indefeasible right to alter, reform or abolish their government."[25] What is significant here is that Williams was not just expressing his admiration for Dallas's policies or political outlook. Rather, he believed Dallas had interpreted American nationality in the right way—according to the universal principles that made the Union a model for the international order.

Conversely, the anti-Dorrites were not just an opposite political faction but a separate nation within the United States, abiding by fundamentally different political principles. Using language unimaginable in Whig discourse, Williams said, "The principle thus promulgated by the despots of Europe, to uphold the arbitrary governments of the Old World, is the same . . . now advocated by the opponents of the Rhode Island suffrage party." They subscribed not to "the American but the European theory of government"—not the "doctrine of popular liberty but the one concocted by the Holy Alliance."[26] Like many Young Americans, Williams tied the struggle against Dorr's opponents to a broader battle against a pantheon of conservative thought that had its origins on the other side of the Atlantic. Just as the growth of revolutionary societies in Europe, such as Young Italy, would eventually culminate in the uprisings of 1848, the movement to liberate Dorr was part of a broader struggle for America's intellectual independence from the Old World.

Whigs in Congress met the Democrats' justifications for the Dorr Rebellion head-on. Indiana's Caleb Blood Smith was adamant that these radicals had conflated political and natural rights in a way that dramatically misread the Declaration of Independence. He complained that "in modern times, there had been manifested by a large portion of the community a disposition to flatter the people."[27] Democrats would talk "at great length" about "what they were pleased to term the natural rights of the people—the right of suffrage, the right of self-government, and the right of the people to do as they pleased at all times and under all circumstances." Conversely, Smith had "never subscribed to the doctrine of *vox populi, vox dei*—that the voice of the people is the voice of a God," because it was merely the monarchical doctrine of undivided and absolute sovereignty applied to the masses. He especially chastised those Democrats who argued that "the people of Rhode Island had exercised only the right which the God of nature gave them." Smith criticized Kennedy for saying "he regarded the right of suffrage as a natural right"—that "the God of nature had conferred the rights of suffrage on the whites."[28]

In order to separate political rights from those that were natural, Smith pointed out that participation in the electoral process was contingent on a number of factors. He reminded the House that large groups of human beings were excluded from political rights. Not only were African Americans and women barred from suffrage, but white men before the age of twenty-one were as well. With these caveats, Smith did more than just point out the dangerous implications of Democratic ideology for racial and gender hierarchies. He also demonstrated the fundamental inconsistency in the belief that democracy was a universal good. Humans were—self-evidently—not born political beings, if twenty-one years had to pass before the exercise of suffrage. Smith saw democracy as one political system among many, not a law that was true in all places and at all times. He did believe in natural rights, but these were "life, liberty and the pursuit of happiness."[29] Self-government was designed to safeguard these fundamental liberties but was not—in itself—part of the natural law tradition. This was not a purely theoretical point. If democracy was not a natural right, it relied instead on a common culture and set of religious beliefs to survive. For the conservatives of Rhode Island, Protestantism provided this foundation, while the hierarchical system of Catholicism threatened only to undermine it. In a typical nativist move, one popular broadside warned that deferring to the authority of bishops would only create a culture sympathetic to kingship, advocating "Church without Bishop: a State without a King."[30] The decision to maintain a property requirement for naturalized citizens was, therefore, more than an afterthought. It was possible for the Law and Order Party to enfranchise the native born—including African Americans—based on their theory of popular sovereignty. But the property requirement aimed at Catholic migrants remained essential.

For their part, Young America Democrats did not accept the notion that Black people were entitled to the same rights as white Americans, since they believed that the races had fundamentally different natures. However inconsistent this might appear to Whigs like Caleb Smith, these racial distinctions, like the rest of the Young America program, were based on the presumed universal authority of nature rather than the paternalistic rhetoric of "civilization" or moral improvement. Democrat William Kennedy argued that abolitionists tried "to keep the free citizens of this country from the exercise of their rights by attempting to drag within the circle of the American people a class . . . that were not a part or parcel of them."[31] Kennedy and others like him saw the presence of Black people as synonymous with the destruction of white communities; they believed Blacks were temperamentally incapable of popular sovereignty on the same basis as whites. Moreover, Kennedy had no conception of individual rights outside democratic communities, meaning he could not conceive of free Blacks flourishing within white society. Dorr himself dealt with race in a similar fashion. If the problem of Black "inferiority" sat uneasily alongside the notion that democracy was a human right, Dorr could respond in one of two ways: he could either enfranchise the Black population or deny their humanity altogether. In no uncertain terms, Dorr chose the latter. In February 1844 Edmund Burke warned Dorr that some Southern Democrats "do not hold so absolutely to the doctrine of popular sovereignty as we do in the North." From prison, Dorr responded that the slave was "not actually a man," since he could not "partake of the sovereign power."[32] Even in this exclusionary moment, the equation of democracy with humanity remained strong.

Outside the halls of Congress, the debate over the Dorr Rebellion raged on between prominent intellectuals attached to the two main parties. Another Douglas supporter, George Bancroft, stepped in to defend the natural right of political majorities to alter their governments at will. The first scholar to undertake a comprehensive history of the United States, Bancroft completed his national story in ten volumes from 1834–74. Bancroft had studied in Europe during the early nineteenth century, and his epic narrative was heavily influenced by the teleological stories of national development popular among German historians at that time. The Democrat hoped to show how the United States had achieved what he believed to be the highest state of moral progress in humanity's quest for perfection. Invited to a convention protesting Thomas Dorr's imprisonment in September 1844, the historian apologized that he could not attend. Instead, he wrote a letter to the convention explaining his views on the rebellion and the subsequent imprisonment of Thomas W. Dorr. The letter expressed similar opinions to Democrats in the House like John McClernand, referring to the "late efforts of the majority in Rhode Island" to "obtain their inalienable rights"—a design that "commends itself to humanity and justice." Bancroft was particularly incensed at what he saw as Dorr's fraudulent trial in the conservative district of Newport and the jury's decision to sentence him to lifetime imprisonment. During Dorr's trial the prosecution tried to portray the "inalienable rights" upheld by the Dorrites as "belligerent' rights" that would thus "give legal perpetuity to despotic authority throughout the world."[33]

More conservative intellectuals were fundamentally opposed to Bancroft's position. Boston Whig George T. Curtis responded that a political majority was not in itself a sign of moral virtue and that the very idea of a natural right to majority rule made no sense. Without political organization—the implementation of positive law, the drawing of state boundaries—the majority had no character, let alone political power. Curtis rejected Bancroft's appeal to "natural rights" outright. When the Jacksonian historian cried, "Shall a man in the nineteenth century, and in an American land . . . be locked up to labor in absolute solitude?" Curtis replied that he should as soon as he disobeyed society's positive laws—"Whenever he commits a crime against society."[34] Bancroft might have written frequently of a new democratic age in which the federal government would not be required to quell expressions of majority rule. But Curtis believed the federal government would always have a role in controlling civil society, either to preserve justice or keep order: "So says the law of most countries, in this century; so it has said in former times, and so it will say to the end of time, unless a better mode of checking crime is discovered."[35]

The debate over the Dorr Rebellion divided the major periodicals of the day, too. Among writers at the *Democratic Review*, even concessions to Dorr's demands did very little to appease their anger. After Dorr's failed attempt to capture the arsenal in Rhode Island, Samuel W. King's government knew constitutional change was inevitable and drew up a more liberal constitution that appeared to satisfy many of Dorr's complaints. Although it fulfilled several of their practical aims, the *Democratic Review* chastised this response for not adequately addressing the underlying principles at stake. One writer complained that Rhode Island was "about to receive" an extension of suffrage "as a boon from the sovereign grace of her rulers, instead of taking it by her own voluntary action, as her just and natural right."[36] Elsewhere, the *Review* held fast to this notion of popular sovereignty. "Let alone" and "untrammeled" by positive law, the states "will grow and expand from causes as powerful and irresistible as the law of nature." The writer argued, "If the free voice of a great people is the voice of god, so is their united energies a type of omnipotence."[37]

Like their Democratic opponents, conservative writers believed the principles were more important than the practical consequences of the case. The editor of the *North American Review*, Francis Bowen, did not take issue with Samuel King's decision to appease the movement to reform the outdated colonial charter. Bowen acknowledged the similarities between the Freemen's Constitution and the Peoples' Constitution originally drafted by the Dorrites (except—one might add—that it retained the property qualification for recent immigrants).[38] In fact, Bowen was convinced that the colonial charter should have been reformed long ago, like comparable constitutions in other states of the Union. In common with a dynamic conservative tradition that began with the philosopher Edmund Burke, Bowen knew that to stubbornly maintain the status quo—for its own sake—was as dangerous as quixotic change. He acknowledged that "reform had become *expedient,* and it was unwise to withstand it so long," but Bowen was very clear that "we do not say, that the Assembly should have made this concession *as a matter of right.*"³⁹ This was not a mere matter of linguistic pedantry: Dorr's doctrine that democracy was a natural right had its parallel "only . . . in the detestable ravings of Danton or Marat."⁴⁰ Just as Democrats connected their reform movement to a wider transatlantic struggle, conservatives compared their enemies in the United States to radicals in the French revolution of 1848. Indeed, Whigs made common cause with European conservatives who were fighting against a similar theory of natural rights.

Four years later, in 1848, Bowen's conservative view of the European revolutions cost him his chair at Harvard. In a series of articles in the *North American Review,* the editor argued the revolutions were not born out of a universal struggle for democratic rule but were an extension of the Hungarians' pursuit of ethnic nationalism, based on the slaughter of Slav minorities. The editor's rejection of the idea of a democratic brotherhood of man led to his dismissal and clearly alienated him from his intellectual circle.⁴¹

The leading Whig intellectual from New York City, Daniel D. Barnard, shared Bowen's desire to anchor the nation in positive law. As he explained to the Phi Betta Kappa Society at Yale College, "Each man shall . . . observe the positive laws of the state religiously"; this is the foundation of "national morality" and "national wisdom." Outside the nation, there was "no other natural state . . . except . . . a mere animal one." Furthermore, "Those who are looking after the 'natural rights' of men, if they mean to look after any thing higher and better than the mere immunities which belong to an animal and brute nature, must turn their regards to Society . . . or they will find them nowhere."⁴² This was an assault not only on the idea that constitutions could be reformed in the name of a natural right to suffrage but also on an older argument, which dated back to the American Revolution, that the people could alter a constitution without appealing to the authorities contained within it.

Taking aim at the "science of politics" popular in antebellum Democracy, Barnard refused to reduce politics to natural laws for the same reason he detested phrenological accounts of the natural history of creation: both recognized science as the true foundation of human knowledge instead of a higher or divine authority separate from mere political, or animal, existence. Thus, Daniel Barnard told his Yale audience, "Just as we would appeal from the conceited and atheistical doctrines of a modern sciolist in his 'Vestiges of the Natural History of Creation' to the better philosophy of the Bible in regard to the origin and the character of the individual man; so we would appeal from the . . . shallow doctrines of the whole school of political materialists."⁴³ Here, Barnard focused his ire on an early work of evolutionary theory by the phrenologist Robert Chambers. This "natural history of creation" was regularly chastised in conservative periodicals like the *Whig Review* for reducing human history, including political developments, to natural laws rather than the embrace of Protestant religion.[44]

One thinker managed to smuggle this distinctly Whiggish conception of nationalism into the pages of the *Democratic Review.* Orestes Brownson began his political life sympathetic to socialist politics, transcendentalism, and the sort of direct democracy advocated by the Young Americans. In 1838 he established the *Boston Quarterly Review,* which published eminent Democratic thinkers like George Bancroft and eventually merged with O'Sullivan's publication in 1842. But in 1843 the former Democrat began flirting with Roman Catholicism and converted the following year. One might expect this newfound faith to turn Brownson against the Law and Order Party, on account of their nativism. But, as is so often the case, Brownson's religious conversion was accompanied by a shift towards more conservative politics. Now a committed Catholic, Brownson had acquired a better awareness of the inherent sinfulness of humanity, turning him away from the politics of human perfection. Reflecting on the Dorr Rebellion in 1843, he penned a long essay entitled "Origin and Ground of Government," in which he proved that self-government was the result of positive rather than natural law. Brownson criticized the Suffrage Party for being "obliged, then, to proceed without law, without government, till they could get their new government into operation."[45]

As one might expect, the intellectual vanguard of the Whig Party was delighted by Brownson's conversion. Whig Calvin Colton, the writer of the *Junius Tracts,* praised the fact that "when the Dorr insurrection broke out in Rhode Island, Mr. Brownson's bravely attacked the *principle* of that rebellion in the *Democratic Review,* with which he was then connected." Apparently, this was a "good service to the country, though [Brownson] had the misfortune to offend his readers, the patrons of that magazine." The political philosophy Colton admired in Brownson's writing was the idea that "changes in the fundamental law of a State, must be made according to the *provisions* of that law. Else, it is a revolution." This article—so offensive to O'Sullivan's *Review*—was a "manifest condemnation of the Dorr Party and movement."[46] These Whig protests against Dorr were widely distributed and strongly argued. In the end, the constitution drafted by Dorr's opponents was allowed to stand. Indeed, the property qualification for immigrants was not reversed until 1888. Furthermore, in 1849 the US Supreme Court declined to pass judgement on the legality of the People's Convention on the grounds that it was a political question, best left to other branches of government.

But the tides were turning in Dorr's direction. In 1845 his cheerleaders in the Young America movement managed to secure their hero's release from prison, and in 1851 his civil rights were restored. Most importantly, the state legislature annulled the judgement of the Rhode Island Supreme Court against Dorr in 1854, declaring that the colonial charter had authorized a despotic and un-American form of government. With this final vindication, many Democrats looked out at the United States as their model republic. Similarly, on the international stage, by the end of the 1840s the natural rights that Dorr and his supporters had forced onto the domestic agenda in the United States were gaining ground. In Europe and Latin America a new generation of revolutionaries declared their inalienable right to institute democratic governments. As we shall see, the Young Americans and their opponents moved their debate over the meaning of natural rights from a domestic to a global context. Would the Revolutions of 1848 prove that democracy was a universal principle? Or would it turn out to be a fragile set of institutions and customs based on specific historical and cultural circumstances? The next decade and a half put these questions to the test both within the United States and around the world. Unfortunately, Dorr would never see his ideas played out in practice. He died just one year after his pardon in 1854, following ill health caused partly by his harsh imprisonment during the previous decade.

3

Global Transformations

TERRITORIAL EXPANSION
AND DEMOCRATIC POLITICS

After Rhode Island became the final US state to implement universal white male suffrage, the Democracy had achieved many of its domestic objectives. In search of new horizons, Young Americans turned to the Western Hemisphere to extend the principle of popular sovereignty for white men. Territorial expansion had calamitous consequences. In the pursuit of a white republic, Young Americans openly advocated the extermination of indigenous people, including Native Americans and Mexicans. Similarly, the annexation of new territory in Latin America promoted the expansion of slavery, while new slave states bolstered the South's representation in Congress. Even as Young Americans based their arguments for annexation on principles of free labor, these were steeped in racial ideology. Nonwhites were to be either segregated or play no part in the expanding nation. Nevertheless, just as the problem of slavery was one response to a wider, "scientific," problem of presumed racial inferiority, territorial expansion fitted squarely into Young America's liberal worldview. This ideology was based around universal principles rather than geographical boundaries; it was rooted in nature rather than culture; it endorsed the democratization of knowledge rather than scriptural authority; and it promoted the maximization of economic gains rather than outdated ideas about the sanctity of the individual. Territorial expansion was not a southern phenomenon but a Democratic and a national one, specifically centering around the most self-consciously progressive liberals within the party.[1] Rather than a mere smokescreen, the liberal culture of Young America also catalyzed the Democrats' program of dispossession.

The issue of territorial expansion was certainly inextricably linked to the problem of slavery, but in complex and conflicting ways. For the powerful planter class, who held so much sway over the federal government in the first half of the nineteenth century, territorial acquisitions were a means of enlarging their own power. Through the annexation of new slave states, the South could increase the number of enslaved people within the Union, bolster the region's representation in Congress, and shore up the influence of slavery in the Western Hemisphere more broadly. But from the perspective of Young Americans—many of whom hailed from the North or had ties to both regions—the tropics served a different purpose. These Democrats thought that equatorial regions could neutralize the slavery issue by placing it on a national footing. Young Americans argued that expansion southward would provide new homes for enslaved laborers. This took Black workers, whether enslaved or free, out of white communities on the mainland while maximizing profits in tropical regions where whites would supposedly not work as efficiently. At the same time, Americans would practice a more Christianized version of slavery than other European powers and outlaw the international slave trade. As more Jacksonians defected from the Democrats to the Republicans, these political figures took a concern for territorial expansion into their new party. An exploration of the liberal and antislavery case for expansion does not involve special pleading: the Young Americans instrumentally worked to prop up slavery, while the consequences of their program were abjectly illiberal. But it is more unsettling, and perhaps more useful, to consider how Americans with abstract antislavery beliefs and liberal commitments became embroiled in the perpetuation of a profoundly violent and destructive system.

Territorial Expansion and Natural Law

Slavery had always been at the heart of Texas's struggle for independence. After becoming part of Mexico in 1821 following that country's War of Independence against Spain, Texas had a small population of around three thousand residents. Sparsely populated and situated on Mexico's external border, the territory was vulnerable to raids by neighboring Indian tribes, particularly the powerful Comanche empire.[2] In the hope of defending its new territory, Mexico liberalized immigration laws to bolster Texas's population, leading to a huge influx of American settlers, mostly made up of slave owners from the Southern states. Soon these new arrivals outnumbered the Tejanos and began to bristle under a distant and inflexible Mexican government. Predominantly Protestant, they resented, for example, the residency requirement to adopt the state religion of Catholicism. But it was only after Mexico abolished slavery in 1829 that the settlers truly stood on the brink of revolt. Bound labor provided the foundation for their economy, and abolition by Mexico further convinced the settlers their future was only secure as an independent nation. After winning independence in 1836, an overwhelming majority desired annexation to the United States, eager for the federal government to protect their property against outside interference by their western neighbor, Mexico, or an antislavery power like Britain. The problem for Texas, however, was that people in the northern United States recognized that slave owners were leading the calls for annexation.

Despite being a staunch supporter of Texas's independence from Mexico, Andrew Jackson delayed US diplomatic recognition of the new Republic of Texas, fearing that antislavery Northerners would punish the Democrats in the 1836 election. After the Democrats proved victorious, newly elected president Martin Van Buren continued to reject calls for Texas's annexation on the grounds that it would heighten sectional tensions and empower antislavery Northerners in the Whig Party. When expansionist John Tyler assumed the presidency in 1841 after Whig William H. Harrison passed away just weeks into his term of office, Northerners voted down his proposal for annexation in Congress.

As the presidential election of 1844 neared, then, Democrats desirous of Texas's annexation needed to galvanize popular opinion in the Northern states behind their expansionist program. Mississippi Democrat Robert J. Walker made the most important contribution to this agenda with his *Letter Relative to the Annexation of Texas,* published in the *Washington Globe* on February 3, 1844.[3] Subsidized by a secret "Texas fund" established in Washington by wealthy Southerners, particularly speculators in Texas landholdings, it is easy to dismiss the document as a cynical ploy by Northern doughfaces. Eager to see the extension of slavery, Southern elites clearly did enlist Walker to convince a Northern populace to bolster the interests of the plantation elite. However, this is not how the letter was seen by most Americans in the antebellum North, or by Walker himself. Widely reprinted in papers like the *New York Herald* and the *Philadelphia Pennsylvanian* and distributed in pamphlet form as well, it proved to be a media sensation. As historian William Freehling points out, no one came forward to refute the letter, suggesting Northerners accepted the legitimacy of Walker's political vision.[4] Furthermore, Walker was not a straightforward doughface, or "Northern man with Southern sympathies." Originally from Philadelphia, his closest political and personal connections were with Northern and western Democrats like Stephen Douglas and George Dallas, whose niece Walker married. Like Douglas, Walker broke with Buchanan over the Lecompton Constitution in 1857 and supported the Union during the Civil War.

Rather than being mere Southern propaganda, the popularity and authority of Robert J. Walker's letter can be best understood as an expression of the sort of Young America nationalism long promoted in the pages of the *Democratic Review:* one that drew on the authority of intellectual culture to naturalize a set of Democratic political relations. In particular, Walker drew on recent theories put forward in the natural sciences to make the case that Texas annexation would lead to the disappearance of slavery in the Upper South. Studies of so-called isothermal lines posited that climates closer to the equator were more habitable for Black populations, and Walker argued that both slaves and free Blacks would gravitate southward toward the newly annexed territories, leaving free labor communities behind them. In conjunction with this infamous line of reasoning, he proposed a larger case for territorial expansion based on geographical science. He argued that Texas "naturally" belonged to the Union, since it was bound into one entity by the same river valley. By citing recent pseudoscientific discoveries about climate and race, Walker appealed to "universal laws," supposedly discernible through reason and rooted in the transcendent authority of nature. He argued that because Texas was a "large and indisputable portion of the Valley of the West," joined to the interior of the continent by the Mississippi River, nothing could justify their separation. Indeed, Walker claimed that he was merely advocating the "re-annexation" of Texas, since it had been naturally entwined with the Union prior to the passage of political legislation. "Our boundary and limits will always be *incomplete*," Walker insisted, "without the possession of Texas; and without it the great valley and its mighty streams will remain dismembered and mutilated." A western nationalist to the core, he claimed the unity of the valley had been destroyed by eastern federalists—dismembered at a time when "the west" was "wholly unrepresented in the Cabinet at Washington."[5]

O'Sullivan's *Democratic Review* was enthusiastic about Walker's argument. "What do you think of annexation?" O'Sullivan asked Henry Gilpin in 1844. "In my April Number I have gone for it though coupling with it the indispensable condition of the consent of Mexico."[6] For the *Review,* the issue of Texas became mere "physical geography," not politics: all the territory to the north of the Gulf of Mexico would one day "come together in one homogeneous unity of political system."[7] To deny this was not just bad politics but a rejection of enlightened thought. The Union imagined by Walker was a "simple geographical fact which can only be questioned, as it appears to us, by one equally blind in mental and physical vision." Similarly, forces much "deeper" than politics would solve the controversy over slavery.[8] Neither South nor North should be concerned with the "balance of power" between the states, because this was to prioritize power over principle. In the absence of federal intervention, natural laws would prevail: "Free states will be made faster than slave ones,—to say nothing of the probable decay of that institution in some of the more northern of the Southern States, in proportion to its southward growth over Texas."[9]

Robert J. Walker's "laws" of climate and race formed an integral part of Young America's broader conflation of natural and political rights. The white man's natural right to popular sovereignty in the political realm, as he conceived it, found a worthy counterpart in the natural laws of climate: both used the authority of nature to legitimate a universal system of democracy for white men, coupled with racial segregation and the eventual extinction of slavery. Massachusetts Democrat Alexander Everett confronted those slave owners in the Upper South who feared that annexation would lead to the loss of their slaves. For Everett, this merely delayed the inevitable. He quoted approvingly a Southern congressman who feared that "slaves [would] be carried to Texas by a law as great and certain as that by which water finds its level," leaving North Carolina, Tennessee, Virginia, and Maryland with homogenous white populations.[10] Moreover, with Texas under US control, Americans could better police the international slave trade there, which was tacitly maintained by the large numbers of plantation owners. Chesdon Ellis viewed the shift in slave populations as merely a "change which depends on natural laws, where obstructions to progress are removed." Even Robert D. Owen, who was more ardently antislavery than most Democrats, argued that "the institutions" that "recognize the equal rights of (the slave's) color" were to be found in Mexico and further south. Owen asked whether shutting slaves out was "by that very act, virtually prolonging [their] bondage?"[11] The same environmental laws that dictated the movement of Black laborers would destroy Indians. Herschel Johnson cited the phrenologist Orson Fowler's maxim that "nature has so ordained it that the Indian shall recede before the march of civilization."[12] The natural right to political sovereignty went hand-in-hand with laws of racial segregation and degradation shaped by the environment; all were written in the great volume of nature and governed by "scientific" principles.

Having struck a chord with Young America's broader ideology, Walker's letter was successful in galvanizing support for the Democratic candidate James K. Polk in the election of 1844. Thrusting expansion onto the national agenda, Polk's candidacy solidified Young America as a political network. But unity did not come easily. At the Democratic convention that year, just months prior to the national election, the political figures who came to rally behind expansion were bitterly divided. Originally, John O'Sullivan backed Martin Van Buren and tried to engineer his nomination behind the scenes. Both were New York Democrats committed to Free Soil. And, at this point, O'Sullivan, like Van Buren, was prepared to delay the acquisition of Texas. But Robert J. Walker, whose expansionist arguments had already caught O'Sullivan's eye, pushed for a candidate who would support immediate annexation. Despite his popularity, this would not be Martin Van Buren. On the same day that President John Tyler saw his proposal for annexation rejected in the Senate, both Van Buren and Whig frontrunner Henry Clay published letters denouncing immediate acquisition. Alarmed, Walker and his allies swung into action. They insisted that any Democratic nominee pick up two-thirds of the convention vote, a policy that effectively sank a divisive candidate with little support from the South like Van Buren. Instead, the party settled on a relatively unknown man who would become the first president under the age of fifty: James K. Polk, or, as his supporters named him, "Young Hickory."

Polk's nomination marked the arrival of the post-Jacksonian generation. The political coalition that made up the Young America movement now pushed for territorial expansion to enthusiastic supporters on both sides of the Maxon-Dixon line. With Polk as their party's candidate, O'Sullivan and many of his allies in the North quickly moved into line (although Van Buren remained bitter). Always receptive to Walker's argument for antislavery expansion, O'Sullivan advocated immediate annexation. Even when O'Sullivan bolted in 1848 to join the Free-Soil Party—partly to avenge Van Buren's defeat—he never abandoned this worldview. Indeed, that same year he visited Polk in the White House with Illinois's Stephen Douglas to press for the annexation of Cuba. Starting in 1844, then, O'Sullivan and his allies in New York and Massachusetts worked tirelessly for the agenda of Young America, in alliance with Southerners like Mississippi's Robert J. Walker. Together with Samuel Tilden, O'Sullivan established a short-lived newspaper in New York called the *Morning News* so he could "support Mr. Polk's administration as I did jealously and effectively in its election."[13] And it paid off in a significant election win.

Polk was undoubtedly able to attract support in Northern cities like New York because he connected the issue of Texas annexation with the dispute over Oregon. While some Northerners might have been reluctant to annex slave territory, many nonetheless desired to expand into British North America. But the prospect of moving slaves from the Upper South toward the Southwest was also attractive to Democrats in the free states, and doing so would not involve a costly war with the world's largest empire. Ultimately, many wanted to see slavery extinguished from mainland America through further migration southward.

Making good on the nationalist tenor of his campaign, Polk formally annexed Texas in December 1845—a move ratified by the Lone Star State the following year. But this legislation did not formally settle Texas' boundaries: Exactly where were her borders to be drawn? Since independence had been declared in 1836, Mexico had been locked in a dispute with the Republic of Texas over its very existence. Mexico did not recognize Texas's decision to declare independence and, in any case, insisted that the contested territory extended only as far south and west as the Nueces River. Conversely, the Democratic administration under Polk argued that Texas encompassed all territory north and

east of the Rio Grande. Polk sent Louisiana's John Slidell to make secret negotiations with Mexico in the vain hope that these ambitious boundaries would be
accepted. When the insulting offer was rebuffed, Polk sent troops under General
Zachary Taylor to the border of the Rio Grande in a deliberate act of provoca-
tion, setting the stage for armed confrontation.

In the end, this border dispute was settled by a conflict that cost thousands of
Mexican lives from 1846 to 1848. The brutal reality of Young Americans' foreign
policy makes it easy to write off their liberal values and intellectual concerns as
mere smokescreens concealing a sincere desire for war. But the reality was much
darker. Many Young Americans displayed a deep aversion to armed conflict.
During the Oregon boundary dispute, for example, expansionist Democrats like
President Polk might have threatened Britain with war if she did not concede
a disputed section of territory in the Pacific Northwest to the United States—
one that had been under joint occupancy since 1818. But O'Sullivan called for
the government to "secure us the whole, and THE WHOLE WITHOUT A
WAR." Further south, O'Sullivan fully expected Mexico to peacefully concede
the entirety of Texas to the United States. He suggested conflict might only be
necessary if the Mexican government pursued armed resistance to annexation
after the fact. When Mexico issued verbal objections to annexation, O'Sullivan
still refused to believe the government would take action. The Mexicans were, he
argued, "holding out for a better price." When war finally broke out, O'Sullivan
wavered due to his long-standing commitment to pacifism.[14] The combination
of O'Sullivan's misguided belief in the inherent justice of his vast territorial
ambitions coupled with his naïve faith in Mexico's willingness to accept them
meant he instigated a conflict without a thought to its human costs.

Moreover, the particular form of liberal nationalism to which Young America
subscribed was a contributing factor to the Union's violent foreign policy, rather
than merely obscuring it. The political culture of Young America certainly provided a justification of violence for wavering Democrats to plug in to. But, more
broadly, it also popularized a series of assumptions that encouraged support
for war. A millenarian view of the global order as divided between the principles of democracy and despotism made foreign conflicts—in this case, over the
fate of an independent Texas—of the most immediate concern. Furthermore,
the Young Americans' racialized view of universal democracy meant that white
men could penetrate the borders of nonwhite nations with impunity in order
to establish their own political system: ties to the land among the inhabitants
of Mexico meant nothing. Finally, a war between rival ideologies, rather than
powers, fostered the idea that violence was a fleeting trial that would lead to a
more just global order rather than a permanent reality of international relations.

Although many liberals and proponents of natural law did not support the war, Young Americans provided one interpretation of where these values could lead. In the end, the larger purpose of extending liberal principles rendered war an incidental evil. The war with Mexico, which the Young Americans had actively instigated, was—for these naïve Democrats—qualitatively different from those that had gone before.

As the Mexican War raged on, Young Americans were particularly keen to appeal to the prominent natural scientist and Romantic thinker Alexander von Humboldt. As a scientist globally revered for interpreting the workings of the natural world, Humboldt appealed to Young Americans' particular vision of the national community. The historian George Bancroft met Humboldt during his diplomatic mission in Europe, reporting to Polk that the German polymath "gave me leave to say to you how greatly pleased he was" with America's "position in Mexico." According to Bancroft, Humboldt deemed the territory east of the Rio Grande "legitimately due to us," as he praised the "moderation" of Polk's presidential message on the subject, which won his "cordial, unhesitating adhesion."[15] Although Bancroft did not explicitly refer to Humboldt's scientific research during this exchange, it was significant that Bancroft asked the prominent scientist's opinion on territorial questions, particularly in light of Walker's writings on Texas affairs. Bancroft was especially pleased with Humboldt's response, since he believed the scientist's honorary Mexican citizenship made him a penetrating observer of this particular conflict. In 1847 Bancroft mentioned Humboldt in a similar way when writing to his wife. He reported that the scientist believed it was "impossible" and "unwise" to "come down and take all Mexico," but he thought that all north of the 35th latitude the United States "ought certainly to have."[16] After a string of American victories on the battlefield, Bancroft wrote to Polk that America's military success in the war had "changed entirely the complexion of European opinion" from opposition to support. The King of Prussia, "with Alexander von Humboldt for his companion," now "views our progress as the cause of civilization."[17]

It is unclear whether these were mere fabrications on Bancroft's part, since Humboldt had, at other times, been a fierce critic of American expansionism.[18] On several occasions the scientist argued against the war with Mexico and the annexation of Cuba on the grounds these "conquests" would expand slavery.[19] If he was acting in bad faith, Bancroft would not be the first to appropriate Humboldt's intellectual authority for his own purposes. In the 1850s Humboldt entered into a widely publicized dispute with the Southerner J. S. Thrasher for using his work to justify the annexation of Cuba. Thrasher translated

Humboldt's book on the natural history of the island but purposely omitted an entire chapter in which the scientist denounced slavery. Aiming to increase the appetite for annexation in the United States, this was a strategic effort on Thrasher's part to place Cuba before an American audience without fanning the flames of antislavery agitation. Nevertheless, American Democrats still looked to natural science to legitimize their vision of the Union. With their expert knowledge of the natural world, public intellectuals were perfectly placed to arbitrate questions of national expansion in mid-nineteenth-century America.

Scientific discoveries were part of a larger appetite for intellectual culture by which Young Americans rooted the political and social relations of the Union in natural law. The Declaration of Independence might have singled out the natural rights to "life, liberty and the pursuit of happiness," but Young Americans argued the entire development of the nation rested on the laws of nature. Democracy, free trade, and state sovereignty were natural relations, rather than the products of positive law or of historical, cultural, and religious traditions. Furthermore, the progress of the nation was linear, just like the discoveries in the arts and sciences on which it was based. Herschel Johnson, who would be Stephen Douglas's running mate in 1860, claimed that it was "the achievements of scientific discovery" that had triumphed over the "obstacles to the unlimited enlargement of our borders," referring to the feats of engineering that had enabled the development of railroads and steamships. He pointed out that "political economy" had made Americans familiar with the "source of national wealth," while "international law" had "unfolded the duties of nations."[20]

Johnson's reference to the law of nations was part of a much wider view of the international order. Throughout the period from 1844 to 1861, Young Americans tried to reshape the global order according to the principles of international law rather than the balance of power. From the Mexican War onward, they were quick to single out the eighteenth-century Swiss theorist, Emer de Vattel, to sanction the Union's more assertive international role. Although the Young Americans took his ideas to greater lengths than he could have ever imagined, Vattel was a useful model because he created a theory of international relations grounded in the idea of natural justice. Although mediated by custom, he argued that natural law should govern the relations between states.[21] In Vattel's thought, natural law certainly did not mean popular sovereignty for white men. In fact, it referred to the ability of the sovereign state to act in its self-interest, which included the formation of a political regime adapted to its own needs. But Vattel worked within a tradition of thinkers who had tried to systemize the law of nations to elicit general rules that would govern the international community. One article in the

Democratic Review distinguished between the global order of the ancient world, which was mostly governed by "power," and that which came after the Protestant Reformation. "After the introduction of Protestantism, at the beginning of the sixteenth century," the writer declared, "we find, for the first time, that princes and people subjected themselves to certain notions of public ethics, derived from the law of nature," even though "the absolute idea of *equality of rights*" was yet to be established.[22]

Writing in the mid-eighteenth century, Vattel also made a specific innovation that Young Americans were quick to seize upon: namely, he outlined a special circumstance in which one power should be permitted to intervene to preserve the sovereignty of another. As historian David Armitage notes, "Vattel's crucial innovation was to argue that rebels against a sovereign or 'public power' could legitimately be recognized as belligerents."[23] This was a significant departure from his predecessor, Hugo Grotius, a sixteenth- and seventeenth-century Dutch thinker who maintained that the right of revolution was forbidden for the sake of peace and good order. To make such a shift, Vattel reclassified legitimate rebellions as civil wars. During a civil war, Vattel argued, the two sides stood "in precisely the same predicament as two nations," meaning conflict should be allowed to occur.[24] This also opened up space for outside intervention. Legal theorists generally acknowledged that it was wrong to interfere in other countries' legal affairs—for example, to come to the aid of one side or another in an internal rebellion. But Vattel turned war *within* nations into one *between* nations, meaning that international, rather than domestic, law applied. Under the law of nations, foreign states were permitted to intervene to aid one of the two warring parties.

In the eighteenth century these ideas were put to use by a broad spectrum of thinkers and statesmen, some of whom Young Americans would have despised. The conservative Irish philosopher Edmund Burke, for example, cited Vattel to justify intervening on behalf of the Bourbon monarchy in the aftermath of the French Revolution. Disparate interpretations flourished because of the vague criteria Vattel used to determine when a revolution had become a civil war: namely, that the "insurgent party" needed to have "justice on their side."[25] What Young Americans meant by "justice" was very different, of course, from both Vattel's meaning and what Burke had inferred half a century before. As the more moderate Democrat Lewis Cass noted in 1852, even Vattel's law of nations was "the law of sovereigns. It is principally for them and their ministers that it should be written," while the Democrats believed in the "right and capacity of man for self-government."[26] But Vattel still provided a theory of international relations based on universal principles rather than pure custom that Young Americans could put to work. Rather than providing a smokescreen for violence, these ideas pushed Young Americans toward armed conflict. As disputes within states were reimagined as revolutions and civil wars, Young America Democrats looked to defend their principles beyond the borders of the Union. Conversely, a nation whose foreign policy focused on power rather than principle would more likely intervene in foreign struggles when it faced threats to the stability of the international order, or threats to itself.

During the Mexican War, Young Americans used Vattel's ideas in pursuit of their territorial ambitions. In 1844 Boston Democrat Alexander Everett, brother of the famous Whig statesman Edward, published an article in the *Democratic Review* examining the validity of Texan independence under international law. The article acknowledged Mexico's claim that the Texas revolution was an illegitimate rebellion and that the territory was still technically under Mexico's jurisdiction. Everett admitted that—if this were true—US intervention in the internal affairs of Mexico could not be justified. Just like the Revolutions of 1848, most Young Americans denied they were actively involving themselves in the political affairs of other nation-states. However, once Texas's status as an "independent nation" was "a fact," then "this being assumed, we knew that we were authorized by the laws of nations to deal with her, in every respect, by word and by deed, as an independent nation."[27] Everett argued the Union was policing the relations *between* states—a doctrine of "intervention for non-intervention" that ensured that states could act independently on the international stage. Robert Dale Owen, whose father was the eminent Welsh utopian, agreed the Union had a duty to protect Texas's independence in order to uphold international law. For the Democrat Owen, the entire international order would be under threat if powerful monarchies were permitted to undermine the sovereignty of nations. According to Vattel, Owen said, "the laws of natural society are of such importance to the safety of all the states" because "if the custom once prevailed of trampling them under foot, no nation could flatter herself with the hope of preserving her national independence." It was this concern for international stability that meant "all nations . . . have a right to resort to forcible means for the purpose of repressing any one particular nation who openly violates the laws of the society which nature has established between them."[28] Far from supporting a war of national aggression, Owen believed Texas annexation was compatible with the natural right to national sovereignty, as prefigured by Vattel.

The Young Americans understood international law in relation to an idea that had a long history in European political thought: the balance of power. This concept originated in the Treaty of Westphalia in 1648, which ended Europe's wars of religion, and persisted through the seventeenth and eighteenth centuries. But from the late 1700s onwards, it took on a particular salience. In the revolutionary wars at the turn of the nineteenth century, France had tried to reshape Europe according to the principles of the Revolution. After Napoleon's defeat at Waterloo in 1815, the five victorious major European powers met at the Congress of Vienna to draw up a conservative plan for peace. Under the influence of Austrian diplomat Klemens von Metternich, they established the Concert of Europe to preserve equilibrium on the continent. Furthermore, the three more conservative powers in this coalition, Austria, Prussia, and Russia, formed the Holy Alliance for the explicit purpose of suppressing revolutionary movements. To challenge this new order, an age of popular revolts began. Nationalist movements turned against the hegemons of Europe, hoping to make the continent more responsive to the will of the people. As an American counterpart to the European revolutionaries, Young Americans also rallied against Metternich's influence.

Young America Democrats were adamant that the practice of the balance of power was fundamentally opposed to international law. Furthermore, this was not just a problem for Europe. When the French statesmen François Guizot suggested intervention against the Union in the Mexican War, Young Americans were outraged. New York Democrat John A. Dix told his fellow senators they were "doubtless aware," that the "'right of intervention' was asserted by Guizot, Minister of Foreign Affairs in 1845 in the French Chamber of Deputies, to 'protect the independent states and the equilibrium of the great political forces in America.'" Dix countered with a denial that the "balance of power" derives "any authority from international law"; thus it had no "applicability to the political condition of this continent." Under the pretense of creating a system of balances "artificial in its structure," he told the Senate, the monarchs of Europe had kept their own people in subjugation. "From a mere right to combine for self-preservation," he said, European powers had suppressed revolutionary movements, making "it in practice a right to divide, dismember and partition states at their pleasure." Dix set his sights on destroying a theory of international relations that had dominated European politics "from the Treaty of Westphalia to the Ottoman dispute of 1840" and replacing it with one ruled by "moral, if not physical agencies."[29]

From their viewpoint in the mid-nineteenth century, Young Americans argued that Vattel alone was not sufficient to combat the balance of power. Rather, America should produce a new conception of international law to counteract the prevailing dogma in Europe. Democrat David Dudley Field is perhaps most famous for his attempts to codify common law in America, but he was also an advocate for this new conception of the law of nations. In an article in O'Sullivan's *Review,* Field highlighted Britain's erroneous attitudes toward the international order. He fumed at a claim made by the *Edinburgh Review* that "ignorance of international law" was the "glaring defect of American statesmen." The Democrat pointed out that America had produced some of the finest legal scholars to date, such as Jefferson, Jay, and "the best living writer on international law," Henry Wheaton, while Britain could not claim a single one. This disagreement over international law, Field argued, came down to a fundamental difference in the interpretation of the rules of international conduct. "There is one subject above all others on which there can never be a difference of opinions among Americans," and "that is the introduction into the new world of the European system of intervention." According to Field, the "balance of power is an idea purely European," and "it has no place in the relation of other states."[30] Similarly, an article from 1851 on "Lopez and his companions" complained that Britain, fearful of American expansion, exercised too much influence over "doughy" Whig statesmen on the question of Cuban annexation. Regrettably, it explained, all information on both European and Latin American revolutions continued to be gleaned from British periodicals. "The 'Edinburgh and Quarterly,' the 'London Times,' and the 'London Morning Chronicle' are our instructors in the law of nations, the principles of liberty and the duties of philanthropy." The article concluded, "The truth is, that there is, at this moment, no nation or government so completely under foreign influence, as that of the United States"[31]

What an American theory of international law would look like remained vague, as the discipline was very much in its infancy. The American scholar Henry Wheaton had only just produced his seminal volume, *Elements of International Law* in 1836, which constituted the first major American work on the subject. The *Democratic Review* argued, "Mr. Wheaton set forth . . . the general proposition that the foreign policy . . . of European nations, has been guided by their monarchs," and that "intermarriages have connected them by ties of consanguinity and affinity; which constitute them one family scattered over the different thrones of Europe."[32] By contrast, Young Americans recognized the sovereignty of democratic nations and states as a natural right for communities of white men. This had obvious implications for these Democrats concerning intervention in Mexico. Robert Dale Owen argued that it would not be "the spirit of 'Young America'" to let the Texans perish at the hands of Mexico, while we "turn over here the leaves of musty volumes" and tolerate an "outrage . . . upon the law of nature and of nations." At the same time, Owen hinted that new law would need to be written to justify American annexation, since "there never was, in the history of the world before, so far as my reading extends, an offer made by one of the independent nations of the earth to merge her sovereignty in that of another."[33] These were unprecedented times, and Young America would rise to the occasion.

The Whigs, by contrast, still seemed indebted to European notions of the balance of power, arguing the United States could not intervene in Mexico because she was a sovereign power, despite Texas's rival claim to independence. Robert J. Walker rallied against Henry Clay for denying the "sovereignty of Texas" and "her right to incorporate herself into the American Union without the consent of Mexico."[34] "If this be so," Walker pointed out, "then our Declaration of Independence unfurls, the sovereignty of the people is a fiction [as is] their right to resist tyranny and establish an independent government." This was not just a defense of Texas's fundamental right to revolution but also a bid for the state's natural right to merge its sovereignty with the Union and share the same political regime. This conflation of Texas's natural and political rights, so typical of Young America, made war a competition between principles rather than powers. In the process Democrats took on new allies beyond the bounds of the Union and established more fundamental divisions with their rivals at home. They became embroiled in foreign conflicts and justified war as an incidental evil with the power to generate a spontaneous moral order at the global level. At the same time, politicians within the Young America movement drew on the cultural and intellectual nationalism of the 1840s and 50s to make their case for violent expansion.[35]

4

Nature and the Political Order

YOUNG AMERICA AND THE EUROPEAN
REVOLUTIONS OF 1848

Perhaps more than any single event, the immediate aftermath of the Revolutions of 1848 strengthened the radical cosmopolitanism of Young America Democrats. During a diplomatic mission to Britain, historian George Bancroft took time out of his schedule to visit France during the spring of 1848. Bancroft was a prodigious scholar, whose magnum opus, the *History of the United States,* was one of the first multivolume histories of the founding of the American nation. In his scholarship Bancroft advocated democracy as a natural law, presenting democracy as a transcendent principle that shaped the development of human history. It was exactly this worldview that influenced Bancroft's response, and that of the Young America movement more broadly, to the Revolutions of 1848. In March, when the French revolution had just broken out, Bancroft wrote home to Secretary of State James Buchanan: "Has the echo of American democracy which you now hear from France no power to stir the hearts of the American people to new achievements?" Far from being at the vanguard of worldwide revolution, the United States would need to study events closely and learn from their development. Bancroft ultimately believed that the Union constituted an ethical ideal—its very existence was tied up with the fate of nations across the Atlantic. He "love[d] the Union" because "the principle of popular power lies at the bottom of our institutions."[1] The *Democratic Review* responded in similar terms. Despite its reputation as an organ of strident American exceptionalism and militant nationalism, the periodical urged the Union to take heed from changes in European society. It declared that "patriotism is a false-bond" because "each should feel himself a citizen of the world—a friend of man everywhere." Before the term assumed more negative connotations for Democrats during the late 1850s, the *Review* relished the "universal recognition of expanded philanthropy."[2]

True, Americans across the political spectrum expressed their upmost enthusiasm and support for these great uprisings. Some grew beards in the style of the Hungarian nationalist Louis Kossuth, a man christened the George Washington

of Hungary. Others attended plays that celebrated the overthrow of constitutional monarch Louis Philippe in France. But when the revolutions faltered,
many Americans began to see their own government as an "exceptional" one.[3]
The Union, according to this view, rested on unique historical and social conditions that facilitated a thriving democracy. As the 1850s unspooled, Americans
grew gloomier. With sectional tensions on the rise, people began to fear for
the prospects of self-government within the United States itself. By 1854 most
political figures had turned away from international issues to focus on domestic
tensions centered on the crisis over slavery—but not Young America. The view
that democracy constituted a natural right sustained their confidence in the
revolutionary cause throughout the 1850s. Democracy was always an imminent
prospect, as long as Americans cared to promote it and to assist their European compatriots against the Holy Alliance. At the same time, Young Americans' racial exclusivity blinded them to sectional tensions. Their political order
rested on the principle of popular sovereignty for white men, not concern for
slaves and other nonwhite groups. Thus the widening gulf between North and
South was not a conflict with which to engage but a mere distraction: the real
battleground was for the rights of white men against the centralizing forces of
imperial or federal power.[4]

   Two broad attitudes characterized Young America's response to the Revolutions of 1848: first, optimism about the success of the uprisings; and second,
support for American intervention. Unlike their Whig counterparts, Young
Americans were unwavering in their commitment to the revolutions, assured
of their success if only Europe's imperial powers could be held in check. Most
Young America Democrats regarded the failures of 1848 as temporary setbacks
within a providential transition towards democracy, a movement that was as
inevitable as changes in the natural world.[5] Conversely, the Whigs were skeptical that military intervention could create democratic nation-states. Without
the necessary historical and cultural conditions, Europeans were not capable of
creating democratic societies and might not even desire them. Secondly, Young
Americans maintained that the Union should make its presence felt through
cultural, political, and even military intervention. Cultural pressure and congressional declarations were vital weapons in the fight against European despotism. Many advocated official recognition of republican governments in the
wake of the uprisings and urged Congress to condemn imperial powers that
compromised national sovereignty. Going further, they recommended America
suspend diplomatic relations with the offending parties. Most controversially,
Young Americans made the case for military intervention. They argued America
should abandon George Washington's plea in his Farewell Address of 1796 to

avoid "entangling alliances" with foreign powers. The international system had been transformed since the late-eighteenth-century world of the Founding Fathers. Foreign policy must change accordingly.

Despite apparent contradictions, these two attitudes were compatible and fit within the Young Americans' broader political program. First, an activist foreign policy might seem to belie the idea that these democratic revolutions were imminent or were the product of natural laws. Nevertheless, intervention was necessary—not because European nations were not ready for independence but precisely because they were. The only forces holding back national sovereignty and democracy were the imperial powers of Europe, and every day wasted was one in which the natural right to democracy might have been achieved. Conversely, many Whigs revealed a more pessimistic outlook. Even after a successful foreign intervention, European nations would flounder because their communities lacked the historical and cultural conditions required for self-government to function. As was the case for territorial expansion, the issue of time thus revealed an ideological divide (albeit one that existed on a continuum) rather than being merely a matter of emphasis: the question of whether intervention was required now, or later, reflected different accounts of how democracy emerged. Second, the use of federal power in foreign policy was compatible with its absence in domestic affairs. The government should not meddle *within* states, or favor one at the expense of another, because these were issues of positive law and local custom best left to individual communities. But it could promote natural rights—namely by upholding the political order in which sovereign democracies could thrive.[6]

By presenting this particular view of American nationalism, Young Americans created a new "imagined community" in American political culture: one that rested not on the territorial boundaries of the American nation but on a democratic international order. Without this development, their enthusiasm for democracy in Europe is much harder to imagine. It was the Young Americans who first began to think of the Union as what David Hendrickson has termed an "international system."[7] As well as expanding west into the North American continent, Democrats turned east to conflicts beyond the bounds of the Atlantic Ocean.

European Politics and the Election of 1852

In the spring of 1848, revolution erupted on the streets of Paris. Decades of overpopulation in rural areas had led to urbanization and overcrowding in the major French cities. Conditions were dire among the urban poor, and disease ran rampant through the growing number of slums. Artisans and master craftsmen felt the pressures of an enlarged urban proletariat. Guilds had been formally abolished, and the burgeoning workforce became a source of fierce competition. The situation became critical after the economic panic of 1847, which contributed to shortages of bread. At the same time, the middle classes were suffering under the July Monarchy. King Louis Philippe had ruled France as a constitutional monarch since the July Revolution of 1830. Although some observers hoped he would make important reforms, the king did not go far enough, and in 1835 he placed a ban on public meetings. Facing urban unrest in 1847, foreign minister François Guizot prohibited liberal opponents of the king from meeting. In protest, reformers began a banquet club in the summer to discuss the widening of the franchise and to debate new political ideas like liberalism, republicanism, and democracy. The first event took place in Paris, but the meetings quickly spread throughout the French provinces. As these complaints became more acute, liberal Orleanists, who had traditionally supported Louis Philippe, joined forces with republicans and urban workers to overthrow the king. On February 22, 1848, the monarchy suppressed a banquet being held in honor of George Washington's birthday. As a potent symbol of republican government, this rebuke to Washington was shortly followed by an uprising in Paris.

The revolution in France was accompanied by revolts across Europe, including in Ireland, the German and Italian states, Denmark, Hungary, and Sweden. Many of these were nationalist revolutions as well as being liberal and republican in character, which challenged the great empires of mid-nineteenth-century Europe. In Ireland a movement for social reform had grown in the 1830s among dispossessed Irish Catholics who resented the rule of Protestant landlords and their imperial allies in Britain. In 1839 these rebels took on a new name, calling themselves Young Ireland. Although it initially attracted modest support, the movement soon gained a broad following when the potato famine of the 1840s devastated the rural population. Tensions came to a head in 1848 with a failed uprising in the county of Tipperary. Many republicans fled to the United States, where they carried on their revolutionary activities through the Fenian Brotherhood.[8] Others gravitated toward Young America and the Democratic Party, among them Thomas Devin Reilly, who for a brief period edited the *Democratic Review* alongside George Sanders. Reilly's biographer, Jon Savage, was also forced to flee to the United States after a failed attempt to take control of an army barracks. In the United States the massive influx of Irish immigrants found a natural counterpart in America's strong tradition of resentment towards the British establishment.[9]

As the Irish struggled against the wealthiest and most far-reaching empire in the world, liberal nationalists on the Continent faced the combined weight of the Holy Alliance. The German states revolted against Prussia, while Italy and Hungary took on the Hapsburg Empire. The Italian nationalist Giuseppe Mazzini began the first of the "young" movements in 1831; it evolved into a secret society committed to the unification of the Italian peninsula. Just as the Union on the American continent became a means to resist British oppression, the Italian nationalists sought to unify a patchwork of independent states against the might of the Austrian monarchy. This process, known as the Risorgimento, was initially unsuccessful and was only completed in 1861—the year the American Civil War broke out. The Italian nationalist Giuseppe Garibaldi even made an offer to Abraham Lincoln to take command of the Union forces. France also faced counterrevolution in the early 1850s. Napoleon I's nephew, Louis Napoleon, was elected president of the Second Republic in 1848; in 1851 he appointed himself emperor. He took some liberal actions, including countering the Austrian invasion of Italy in 1859 and making a free-trade treaty with Britain in 1860. But he ruled as an absolute monarch and made good on France's long-standing threat to intervene in North America in 1861 when the United States was distracted by civil war.

Perhaps the most famous of the Revolutions of 1848 among Americans was the Hungarian uprising, which probably offered people in the Union the best cause for optimism. Nationalist leader Louis Kossuth took power in Buda and Pest. He demanded the Hapsburgs respect civil liberties, withdraw Austrian troops from Hungary, and recognize the national parliament. This prompted the resignation of the Austrian foreign minister, Klemens von Metternich, sending shockwaves around the world. As the architect of the Holy Alliance established at the Congress of Vienna (1814–15), Metternich's departure seemed to mark an end to imperial hegemony. When the Hapsburg Empire tried to reassert its authority, the Hungarians fought valiantly and won key victories against the Austrian forces. But the Holy Alliance was not over yet. After one and a half years of fighting, Tsar Nicholas I marched into Hungary with three hundred thousand troops and made light work of the fledgling Hungarian nation. Austria declared martial law, and Kossuth was forced to flee, first to England and then the United States. In America he embarked on a speaking tour, appealing to the people to send arms and money to the Hungarian rebels.

These appeals were, in some respects, well received in the United States. Thousands turned up to hear Kossuth speak. Associations of Americans and recent immigrants waxed lyrical in his honor and made toasts to the Hungarian nation.

Theatres dramatized the war of independence against Austria, while Kossuth was christened the George Washington of Hungary and his style of beard adopted by fashionable men on the streets of New York. In the halls of Congress, American representatives tried to pass more concrete measures of support. Michigan Democrat Lewis Cass and the modernizing Whig William Seward introduced resolutions that condemned Russia's brazen subversion of the principle of national self-determination.[10] Although neither politician believed America had a right to interfere with another country's domestic institutions, both thought it could condemn the interference of one state with the affairs of another. Young America Democrats like Stephen Douglas and his allies in Congress argued that the United States should not only condemn but actively police the relations between different European nations, giving rise to the doctrine of "intervention for nonintervention."

Isaac Walker was one Young America Democrat who called for the United States to abandon her policy of neutrality and assume a more assertive role in combatting Russia's autocratic influence in European politics. Walker noted that although Washington had cautioned against "entangling alliances" in his Farewell Address, the words of the nation's first president were no longer relevant. The country had grown in prosperity and was ready to assume a new role as a more assertive power on the world stage. Apparently, Washington had never intended his words to "become an established principle" to govern the country in its "maturity and power." Although "in its infancy," it could only look to Poland's failed uprising of 1830 with "manifest commiseration"; now the United States was ready to throw its weight behind the democratic cause. The Wisconsin politician declared he was "for the cause of liberty and free government against slavery and despotism throughout the globe and this without disguise." Certainly, it was wrong to meddle in "internal concerns," but the Union could police the relations "between nations" since it had a responsibility to help uphold international law. Against "such interference" as Russia practiced in Hungary, Walker would have America "interpose both her moral and physical power."[11] Young Americans stressed the Union did not have to intervene in Europe to rectify each and every injustice. Nevertheless, the nation should act when circumstances were favorable. With the United States open to the idea of intervention, monarchical regimes would think twice before infringing upon national sovereignty. Ohio's David T. Disney pointed out the United States was not "bound to intervene with armed force on all occasions," but only "if the particular case does indeed require." Stephen Douglas proclaimed, "I cannot say that I would not interfere under any circumstances," worrying that complete nonintervention would give carte blanche to European empires.[12]

Young America Democrat Pierre Soulé agreed, making perhaps the most famous case for American intervention in this period. Like Walker, the Louisiana
senator proposed that Washington's Farewell Address was not applicable to the
new circumstances in which the country found itself. When Washington spoke
in 1793, "we were just emerging from a sea of agitation," Soulé declared; the
treasury was "exhausted," and the "fate of democracy was uncertain." He went
further, declaring that no man, however great, had the authority to bind future
ages with worn-out precedents: "It is not in the power of man" to impart "immutability to any of his works." This code originated not in dusty tomes but
in the "moral order of the universe"—those laws that bound mankind in "one
harmonious whole."[13] Outside Congress, Young Americans made a similar case.
In a lecture on international law in front of an audience in Ohio, Samuel S. Cox
elucidated "the generalizations from history" that "have been connected with the
laws of human nature." But he cautioned against being "fixed in the past and def-
erential to forms."[14] What had been appropriate for one age might be irrelevant to
the mid-nineteenth century with its superior transportation and communication
methods. The same fundamental laws existed throughout time but became more
fully appreciated and practically realized as human beings threw off the shackles
of the past.

Even older and more conservative Democrats like Lewis Cass argued that
America should issue a condemnation of Russian foreign policy. For all their
prescience, old ideas about international law were not sufficiently progressive
for the present age. "Why even Vattel, enlightened as he was," said Cass, "tells
us that 'the law of nations is the law of sovereigns.' It is principally for them and
their ministers that it should be written." Democrats did not want international
disputes arbitrated among the existing sovereign powers. Instead, Cass told
Congress, "We believe in the right and capacity of man for self-government. . . .
We believe he is everywhere fitted, even now, for taking part in the administration of political affairs."[15] Similarly, at one rally for Louis Kossuth at the Jackson
Democratic Association, Lewis Cass promoted "the advancement of human
rights throughout the world," while the "young and vigorous" Stephen Douglas claimed, "I think it is time America had a foreign policy—a foreign policy
predicated on a true interpretation of the law of nations—a foreign policy in
accordance with the spirit of the age."[16]

Of course, some progressive Whigs joined the Young America Democrats in
taking an unequivocal moral stance on European politics—most notably William Seward. Like Walker and Soulé, Seward believed there was a common morality, rooted in the laws of nature, that should regulate the international order.
In search of this universal code, he turned to writers on the law of nations. They

"teach us that States are free, independent and equal moral persons, existing for the objects of happiness and usefulness, and possessing rights and subject to duties defined by the law of nature, which is a system of politics and morals founded in right reason."[17] Furthermore, Seward contended that Washington only intended Americans to use his words as a guide, not as a prescription. But here Seward was defending the right of revolution when natural rights had been infringed. Unlike the Young Americans, he did not propose white men had a natural right to democracy before and after constitutions were made, or that white men possessed a natural right to suffrage. These remained political rights. Moreover, Seward was one of the most bellicose Whigs on foreign policy, and the party at large mostly took a different view.

More influential for the party's platform were conservative figures like Tennessee Whig John Bell, who argued that rather than requiring outside intervention, the failures of 1848 undermined the ideas about democracy at the heart of the Young America movement. He described a particular group of radical Democrats, active in both Europe and the United States, who had been the most assured of the revolutions' success. He told the Senate there was a party "widely diffused over the country" that had its origins in quixotic European theorists and that "denounce[d]" our institutions "as oppressive and unjust to the natural rights of mankind." "We are told," Bell said, that "reform lingers far in the rear of the advancing spirit of the age . . . that too much of the old anti-democratic levean still lurks and ferments in our constitutional forms and in our legislation." He saw that both the American and European variants of this school of thought "proceeded from the same error. . . . They all proceed upon abstractions." He added, "From the complexion of recent transactions in Europe, it would unfortunately seem that . . . public opinion . . . has rejected popular intervention as an unsafe basis of government." After the disappointment following the European revolutions, democrats "must come to understand that the competency of man for self-government is not a simple or universal truth; but that it is a complex and conditional proposition."[18] Bell acknowledged there was "an equality which is agreeable to nature—a liberty and equality resting on a basis that will stand." But, he maintained, "all else" was "spurious, delusive and mischievous," including the idea that direct democracy was the harbinger of liberal values in each and every case.[19] Bell chastised the "thousand presses in this country" that insist that "the spirit of Democracy is necessarily progressive." While undoubtedly all men had a "passion for civil liberty," this was only one among many competing desires to be balanced against the love of novelty, the influence of fashion, the passion for national glory, the sentiment of loyalty, and "the servile worship of eminent men."[20]

By the time the nationalist leader finished his tour of the United States in July 1852, some of the mania for Kossuth that had gripped the nation just a year earlier had waned. Abolitionists and antislavery activists were exasperated and disappointed with his failure to condemn the South's peculiar institution. Whigs like Bell, for their part, remained suspicious of foreign intervention. Despite the justice of their cause, the Hungarians would need to wait for democracy to be fully realized. Practical assistance, even in the form of diplomatic resolutions, risked incurring the ire of monarchical powers and departed from Washington's Farewell Address. But the Young America movement retained close ties to the Magyar and nourished high-hopes for the cause of liberal nationalism in Europe. Indeed, Young America forced this issue to the forefront of the national conversation in the election of 1852.

Before the Democratic Convention, the figurehead of Young America, Stephen A. Douglas, hoped to gain the presidential nomination. As the rising star within the Democratic Party, he had every reason to be confident. The Democrats were gravitating toward a program of international intervention for which Douglas had long been the champion. One supporter wrote to Douglas: "I naturally in common with my brethren of the Democratic Party styled 'young Democracy' wish to have a candidate" who is "a living example as to what eminence, genius, intellect and untiring industry, can arrive at under our institutions."[21] Douglas was well placed to capitalize on the influx of European immigrants during the late 1840s who popularized Young America's cosmopolitan vision. In a pamphlet on Louis Kossuth, Pennsylvania Democrat Charles Goepp wrote that "the mission of the American Union, since its foundation," had been the amalgamation of the "multiplicity of states" into one. This was not merely a continental mission: "An ideal state, established by reflection and choice" must consist in the "Union of all men."[22] Although such bombastic sentiments aided Douglas in the nation at large, the men who uttered them proved his undoing in the cut-throat world of Washington politics. The idea that democracy was a transcendent right rather than a political prerogative could not offer much comfort during the demands of a presidential campaign.

Unfortunately for Douglas, George Sanders assumed editorial duties at the *Democratic Review* in 1852 and shifted the publication in an even more radical direction. Kentucky congressman John Breckenridge remarked that the *Review* had not "been hitherto a partisan paper but a periodical that was supposed to represent the whole Democratic Party." Commenting on its increasingly radical tone, he told the House of Representatives, "Recently I have noticed a very great change."[23] Breckenridge was particularly critical of the relationship between Stephen Douglas and Sanders's periodical. Ahead of their party's nominating convention in 1852, the Kentucky politician accused Douglas of collaborating with the *Review* for a series of articles that denounced his opponents as conservative has-beens. In leading articles the *Review* did indeed criticize "old fogy" candidates such as Lewis Cass and William Marcy, as well as the Democrats' official organ—the *Washington Union*—for hostility to political progress. But this had certainly not been done at the behest of Douglas, who recognized the articles were alienating the more moderate Democrats he needed to win over. In the House, Douglas's staunch ally, fellow Illinois Democrat William Richardson, denied collaboration. Still, Breckenridge accused the Young America movement of arrogantly dismissing the principles of the revolutionary generation. Although in favor of social progress, he wanted "to progress in line with the principles of our fathers"; not to abide by different values altogether.[24]

Conscious that his own political ambitions were slipping through his fingers, Douglas became increasingly desperate. He wrote to Sanders, pleading with the editor to adjust the *Review's* tone accordingly. Sanders published a riposte, claiming his magazine did not take orders from a mere congressman.[25] Despite the *Review's* support for Douglas, it seemed the organ could not resist this opportunity to denounce professional politicians. Other supporters of the Democracy urged Douglas to embrace the *Review's* support. Businessman William Grandin advised Douglas, "Were I in your place I would allow my friends to take their own course, and not 'repudiate' (as such is your rumored intention) anything based on truth, reason and promise."[26]

Nevertheless, the *Democratic Review* ultimately helped to cost Stephen Douglas the nomination. As Douglas himself observed, the attacks against his opponents had done him great harm. Although the *Review* did not explicitly endorse Douglas until March 1852, the senator's ties to the publication were common knowledge. Moreover, Douglas's image had not helped him build a reputation as a consensus candidate or a dignified statesman. The senator's scruffy dress sense, his relative youth at age thirty-nine, and his fondness for cigars, whiskey, and chewing tobacco alienated several Democrats, especially those Southerners with pretensions to gentility. Making matters worse, the Little Giant was no stranger to backroom deals. The image of Douglas discussing reckless schemes for territorial annexation in some dingy oyster cellar over a box of cigars appeared to voters a new and undignified way for a statesman to behave. Politically, Douglas's bisectional stance alienated figures on both sides of the Mason-Dixon line. Southerners suspected that he was not, in the end, prepared to protect slavery, while some Northerners feared that his territorial ambitions disproportionately favored the South. As often happens to idiosyncratic candidates, Douglas found that for every one of his dedicated followers, there was a Democrat who would rather see almost anyone else gain the nomination. Two years after the convention, George Sanders wrote to Douglas in an effort to put this incident behind them. Sanders compared the situation to Louis Kossuth's "spontaneous expression of sentiment" in his own favor, which had supposedly damaged his reputation. The editor claimed that he nonetheless sought "earnest friends, even though their enthusiasm should sometimes lead them into indiscretions" on his behalf. "The chief cause of complaint on my part," Sanders wrote, was the culture of Washington, DC, which sought to "hold a man responsible for everything that his friends may say or do." Sanders lamented that Douglas had "lent" himself to "this policy," thus sacrificing two men's independent character for mere political clout.[27]

Ahead of the 1852 election, then, who did the Democrats choose? After a deadlocked convention in which various candidates saw their fortunes rise and fall, the party settled on a dark horse—the handsome nonentity Franklin Pierce. This selection did not particularly displease anyone. Although no particular faction had succeeded, Democrats of various stripes had, at least, the satisfaction of seeing their rivals fail. Furthermore, Piece's inability to articulate meaningful policies allowed everyone to project their own positions and prejudices onto his candidacy. Although the nomination had eluded Douglas, Young Americans nonetheless believed Pierce was an adequate vessel for their political ambitions.

Propped up by more powerful men, the uninspiring Franklin Pierce was able to pull off an astonishing reunification of the antebellum Democracy in 1852. Just four years prior, internal divisions had cost the Democrats the presidential election. The antislavery Barnburner faction bolted from the Democratic fold after Lewis Cass was named as the party's presidential candidate. This was partly because the Barnburners were committed to Free Soil, while Cass's policy of popular sovereignty opened the Mexican Cession to the expansion of slavery. But it was also because the Barnburners harbored a personal grudge. Cass was believed to have denied their leader, Martin Van Buren, the Democratic nomination in favor of James K. Polk in 1844. By refusing Cass their support in the election of 1848, the Barnburners could exact a timely revenge. Although many "conscience Whigs" also joined the Free-Soil Party, the Democrats suffered a higher number of defections. The choice of Democrat Van Buren as the Free-Soil Party's presidential candidate alienated potential Whig voters, who chose to stand by their party in large numbers. In the end, Van Buren picked up a surprisingly high proportion of votes in the North—around 15 percent. Since large numbers of Free-Soil supporters came from the Democratic Party, this was sufficient to deny Cass victory. Interminably divided, the Democrats lost traditional strongholds, such as New York, to the Whig machine.

The situation under Franklin Pierce in 1852 was fundamentally different. Both pro- and antislavery Democrats rallied around their party. In part, this was because the Compromise of 1850, guided through Congress by Stephen Douglas himself, had (for the moment) put an end to agitation over the slavery question. Former Free-Soilers were happy to rejoin the Democrats because of the Compromise. Although many fumed over the Fugitive Slave Law, the Compromise consecrated free labor in California and looked like it would do the same in the New Mexico and Utah Territories. To the horror of many Southerners, who wanted to extend the Missouri Compromise line, it looked like the Democratic principle of popular sovereignty had reserved large swathes of the Mexican Cession for free labor. But political calculation was also at work. With the problem of slavery in remission, Free-Soilers saw an opportunity for the Democrats to win another election victory. Terrified at the prospect of another Democratic defeat, many former Free-Soilers hoped to unite the party in order to win the election and promote its principles abroad. Indeed, the issues at stake in the election appeared to favor the Democrats, particularly the Young America faction.

Certainly, some sectionalists still refused to make peace with the Democrats' official policy. On the one hand, Fire-Eaters like Alabama's William L. Yancey were unhappy with the Compromise of 1850. These extremists would only be content with measures that guaranteed Southerners protection for their human "property" within the territories. According to this reasoning, the territories were the common property of the states, meaning the legal protection the South afforded to slavery applied to these areas as well. On the other hand, antislavery Democrats like John P. Hale remained loyal to the Free-Soil Party and the principles of the Wilmot Proviso. But, in the main, Democrats reunited under a platform that owed its principle objectives to the Young America movement. It had certainly not been Franklin Pierce's personal qualities that had won the election. Compared to a war hero with genuine credentials like Winfield Scott, Franklin Pierce did not see much action in the Mexican War. He was chiefly remembered for fainting during the Battle of Churubusco after suffering intense pain brought on by a wound from a previous battle.

Kossuth himself was certainly prepared to look past Pierce's personal failings in the hope that a reunited Democracy would implement Young America's foreign policy. Disappointed by the Union's reluctance to offer any practical assistance in 1852, the Hungarian hoped Pierce might do more and endorsed his presidential run. Although we sometimes associate European liberalism with the antislavery movement in the United States, the presidential campaign of Franklin Pierce was the highpoint for transatlantic nationalists in the orbit of Young America. Throughout the 1850s George Sanders continued to warn Kossuth against "sectionalism" as "music and luxury to the enemies of Democracy."[28] That said, other liberals on both sides of the Atlantic rejected Sanders's characterization of the antislavery movement as antithetical to the cause of national independence in Europe. The British campaigner against slavery, Joseph Barker, published a letter denouncing George Sanders in London newspapers. He rejected Sanders's idea that "interfering in any way with the question of American slavery" would "injure the cause of freedom on both sides of the Atlantic," pointing out that "if the Democrats of Europe were in the hands of American slaveholders, they would be gagged before tomorrow." The leaders of the antislavery movement in America would come to the aid of Europe, Barker insisted, when they saw the "*Leaders* of democracy in Europe espousing the cause, not of a nation, but of a Man."[29]

Nevertheless, different attitudes toward European politics were apparent in the conventions of the Democratic and Whig Parties ahead of the Election of 1852. The Whig platform took pains to express caution about intervention in European affairs. It stated, "While struggling freedom everywhere . . . enlists our warmest sympathy . . . , we still adhere to the doctrines of the father of this country, as announced in his Farewell Address, of keeping ourselves free from all entangling alliances with foreign countries, and of never quitting our own to stand on foreign ground." "Our mission," the platform declared, "is not to propagate our opinions."[30] This reflected the Whiggish view that the transition to democracy would be a slow process. To be sure, some were unhappy with this stance. John Wells declared that it was only a "narrow patriotism" that could "reach no further than the limits of its own territory" and admitted that he was ashamed of the platform that recommitted the party to Washington's Farewell Address.[31] But many obliged. James Cooper argued that top-down reform was necessary to prepare the ground for self-government. The revolutions would soon "compel kings to concede to their subjects' natural rights," which "belong to all men," but the monarchs would need to stay in power to prevent "excess in their exercise."[32]

While Whigs wavered on the issue, the European Revolutions of 1848 became a decisive theme in the Democratic campaign. Thomas D. Reilly was one Young American who believed the imminent success of European nationalism would find its parallel in a Democratic election victory. Before he had come to the United States, Reilly was a prominent activist in the Young Ireland movement. After the failed uprising at Tipperary, he fled to the United States and began

editing the *Democratic Review* alongside Sanders. He was recruited precisely because he supported its progressive agenda. As his biographer and fellow Irish nationalist Jon Savage wrote, Reilly was one of the "new generation" of writers "not
trammeled with the ideas of an anterior era—men who would bring not only
young blood but young ideas to the councils of the Republic."[33] Similarly, when
recommending Reilly for a political appointment in the 1850s, Stephen Douglas
described him to President Pierce as "one of the ablest political writers of the
age," who had "devoted his life to the cause of liberal principles and progressive
ideas." Douglas alluded to Reilly's support for Young America, saying, "His appointment would be esteemed a compliment to a large class of our people who
sympathize with the efforts of free institutions throughout the world."[34]

Although he conceded that the Revolutions of 1848 had experienced setbacks, Reilly still retained his faith in the cause of European nationalism. Like
many Young Americans, he argued the failures in Hungary and Ireland were
only temporary and were comparable to the situation in the United States. In
one article endorsing Pierce for the presidency, Reilly argued that the counterrevolution that Europe had endured from 1848 to 1852 had its parallel in
the United States in four years of Whig rule. The election victory of Millard
Fillmore in 1848 thus "united the fate of Europe's conquered nations with that
of hitherto triumphant democracies" like the United States. The Union, like
France, had been "duped into the worship of a name merely victorious on the
battlefield"—in the case of France, Louis Napoleon, and in America the war
hero Zachary Taylor. Consequently, the Americans had "yielded, contempo-
raneously with the French people, the power of American Republic, and the
control and use of its government, into the hands of a party-colored faction."[35]
Similarly, Philadelphia Democrat Thomas L. Kane claimed the lull in support
for Kossuth at the end of his national tour had, in Philadelphia, given way to
a renewed sense of enthusiasm. Kane admitted, "At one time we were so low
that we could count, all told, five men in Philadelphia, faithful to Kossuth."
But "now we have secured the five districts of our city and county . . . from
Wayne to Greene" and—"in both houses"—"probably have a majority of our
Democratic delegation in congress" who were in support. According to Kane,
the Hungarian, whom he called the "apostle," would have a "welcome when he
returns to us that will make his heart choke with satisfaction." Anticipating its
importance for the coming presidential contest in 1852, Kane said, "I must see
the Kossuth organization perfected before there is holiday for me," and he admitted that "the campaign of 1852 will be the vilest in our history."[36]

Part of the reason such "distant revolutions" infiltrated American political
discourse was that large numbers of European immigrants flocked to the

United States following the uprisings.³⁷ In the presidential campaign of 1852, Young Americans felt they were perfectly placed to attract these new arrivals. Democratic congressman Edmund Burke wrote to Pierce in 1852: "The grand ideas which are the most potent in the election are sympathy for the liberals of Europe, the expansion of the American republican westward and the grasping of the magnificent purse of the commerce of the pacific, in short, ideas for which the term Young America is the symbol."³⁸ The Pierce administration's internationalist agenda did not go unnoticed in the Whig press. The *True American* lamented that "had Washington been among us in 1851 or 52," he would have been aghast at the "Pierce Democracy promising war with Austria, France and Spain" to "please" "foreign adventures from Cuba, Hungary or Italy."³⁹

The influence of Young America certainly paid off in the election: the Democratic Party won an extraordinary victory. Picking up twenty-seven out of thirty-one states, Pierce achieved the highest share of the electoral vote since James Monroe ran unopposed in 1820. Because Pierce is consistently voted one of the worst American presidents based on the failure of his administration, we can sometimes lose sight of the hope and optimism that accompanied his election.⁴⁰ The twin issues of popular sovereignty and European politics that were at the heart of Young America's worldview had proved astonishingly successful. Reflecting on the Democrats' lull in support before the 1856 election, George Dallas asked, "Can anyone tell me what has become of the mighty avalanche of democracy that . . . tumbled Franklin Pierce into the White House?"⁴¹

Just as Young America's influence within the Democratic Party reached a highpoint, some newspapers anticipated a realignment in party politics. *Cooper's Clarksberg Register* wrote, "The only re-modification of parties that we can foresee is that which may possibly grow out of the differences in sentiment between the 'Old Fogies' and 'Young America.'" A reorganization of the parties around the polarized attitudes to Young America nationalism did not seem unlikely in the early 1850s. As the *Clarksberg Register* pointed out, "Conservatism and progress are again brought into collision and *may* be made the basis of a new party organization but even in this case we will be much surprised if the Democratic party does not maintain its identity as the Progressive or Young America party, shorn perhaps of many of its ultraisms."⁴² Similarly, the *Baltimore Sun* proclaimed that there would soon be a new party dedicated to intervention in Europe, to Free Soil, and to land reform headed by two Douglas allies, Robert J. Walker and Isaac Walker. Kossuth had, apparently, "brought into action elements already existing in this country" that would "overwhelm and obliterate all that sixty years of prudent statesmanship has established as a barrier against intervention in the wars and quarrels of the Old World."⁴³

For some Young Americans, this realignment was the culmination of ideas they had popularized in the *Democratic Review* for quite some time. Jane Cazneau, a regular contributor, wrote to George Bancroft in 1848 that "the Whigs are broken, their party disbanded and their old organization only available as the nucleus" for reforming their ranks. "The Whigs, or rather conservatism," Cazneau insisted, is "preparing for the creation of the new party. It may take the old name for it is the old soul but the robes and motto are new."[44] This new party of "conservatism" would include all those opposed to unbridled expansion, including Whigs, moderate Democrats like Lewis Cass, and Barnburners.[45] In opposition would be a more "progressive" Democratic Party, committed to an interventionist role in the world. A realignment of this sort did not occur. But in 1852 the Democratic Party did present itself as the harbinger of radical cosmopolitanism and made interventionism a new focal point in party politics.

Many believed the election of Franklin Pierce in 1852 meant Young America's ideas could have practical application. Democrats Charles Goepp and Samuel S. Cox gleefully expected the Pierce administration to take a more vigorous role in Europe. Goepp dedicated his work *The New Rome* (1853, cowritten with fellow German émigré Theodore Porsche) to the incoming Democratic administration. He wrote, "This work is respectfully dedicated to Franklin Pierce . . . being a guess at the spirit in which he was elected."[46] Similarly, Samuel Cox served in the Pierce administration as secretary of the legation at Lima in 1853, a move into the diplomatic service typical of Young Americans. United in their enthusiasm for Pierce in 1852, both men also supported Stephen Douglas throughout the 1850s. After campaigning for Pierce in the Midwest, the Little Giant himself toured Europe, where his supporters at home watched his every move. Springfield postmaster Isaac Diller praised Douglas for "upholding the honor and glory of [his] country in the midst of crowns and coronets, the same as at home, among the true sovereigns." Douglas was, Diller insisted, the perfect man to visit the continent, as he would learn more in a matter of months about the Europeans' "fervent aspirations for liberty" than most Americans would in several years.[47]

One of the ways Pierce sought to influence European politics was to send prominent Young Americans to Europe on diplomatic missions. These included appointments of Samuel Cox to Lima, John O'Sullivan to Lisbon, George Sanders and George Dallas to London, August Belmont to the Hague, and Pierre Soulé to Spain. Less significant figures were also sent abroad, such as New York Democrat Daniel Sickles, who was appointed secretary of the US legation in London under Buchanan. A decade earlier, in the 1840s, historian George Bancroft had been appointed as US consul to London, and in 1852 Nathaniel Hawthorne was sent to Liverpool after writing his campaign biography of Franklin Pierce, which was widely celebrated in the *Democratic Review*. Lucrative diplomatic positions were, of course, a fitting reward for Young America's support in the presidential election, especially for writers who would have otherwise struggled to make ends meet. But Young Americans also hoped to propagandize American values in Europe and believed the artists and writers among them were best placed to do so. In 1853 the *Spirit of the Times* wrote, "We must have diplomats . . . not only well versed in the law of nations but who are thoroughly imbued with the idea of Young Europe and Young America." The paper singled out the historian George Bancroft as someone who "exemplified" "the beauty and sublimity of the institutions of freedom."[48] Similarly, August Belmont hoped that American diplomats would "carry a moral influence with them which will be of more real benefit to the cause of freedom in Europe than all the material aid we can at least for the present give them."[49] Finally, the *Democratic Review* complained of the consular service under Taylor and Fillmore's Whig administrations: "So admirably had our Fogy diplomatists and representatives kept our light under a bushel . . . our institutions and our very existence out of sight, that popular astonishment" is expressed on the continent that "we were even white."[50] The *Review*'s remarks perfectly encapsulated the noxious combination of racial superiority and postcolonial anxiety that was typical of Young Americans. The independent exercise of political rights was based solely on the natural attributes of race and gender. The servility of American diplomats compromised their independence and therefore the racial purity that formed the basis of their inherent rights.

The anxieties about American diplomats extended beyond the circle of Young American appointees. The conservative secretary of state William Marcy issued a famous dress circular to American minister abroad, instructing them to wear modest "American" dress in foreign courts. Instead of elaborate diplomatic attire, the consuls would don a plain black uniform with a sword by their side. This was not only taken seriously by ministers abroad but widely documented in the American press.[51] As minister to Holland, August Belmont recommended to Stephen Douglas in 1853 a broader overhaul of the diplomatic service. He complained that "we send full ministers to . . . the most absolute governments of Europe," like Prussia, Russia, and Spain (which was yet to have its own revolution in 1854).[52] But the Union sent "only charges to Belgium, Sardinia, Sweden, Denmark," which were all countries "where thus far constitutional guarantees have withstood the reactionary pressure bearing down upon them all in 1849."[53] Belmont argued, "We pay therefore a mark of respect and deference to absolutism while it is not only our duty but the stern necessity of our foreign policy to countenance and encourage constitutional liberty in every country."[54] He believed giving Americans ministers the same rank would provide "further evidence" that the Union rejected the old-fashioned hierarchies of European diplomacy.

Other Young Americans wanted to propagandize their views more directly. George Sanders, as ever, went the furthest, issuing direct public appeals to the powers of Europe. He wrote to the Swiss Confederation protesting their decision to abridge the right of asylum for political refugees, and to Louis Kossuth urging him to resist the lure of "sectionalism" in US politics.[55] Finally, he appealed to the French people, defending the Revolution of 1789 for being less violent than the Bourbon Monarchy and detailing America's plan to colonize her free Black population in Africa.[56] These pronouncements attracted the ire of monarchical powers and quickly became controversial in the United States. William Marcy warned Buchanan that he had received four copies of Sanders's letter to the Swiss Federal Council, translated into French, Italian, German, and Spanish, which had passed through the US legation under Buchanan's supervision. Marcy was sure that Buchanan would "as readily and severely condemn as anyone" these "uses of the Legation" in London.[57] A year into his diplomatic career, the Senate refused to confirm Sanders's appointment, forcing him to return to the United States. The Kentuckian protested, claiming he had pioneered a new style of public diplomacy that appealed directly to the people in dealing with monarchical powers. He hoped this would prevent the kind of secret negotiations that had characterized European diplomacy under the Holy Alliance.

Despite his dismissal, Sanders did not drift too far outside the Democratic mainstream. Many prominent Democrats stood by his decisions. Belmont praised Sanders's "generous and patriotic heart," claiming that "the republican spirit in Europe is subdued but not revoked" and that interventions like Sanders's letter "never fail to exercise the most beneficial influence on its dormant power."[58] Both men would go on to campaign for Stephen Douglas in the election of 1860. Louis Kossuth also expressed his support for Sanders in a letter to the *New York Times*. Owing to the "'manly independence of his character,'" Kossuth pointed out that Sanders would never have asked for his backing.[59] Nonetheless, the Hungarian felt the need to point out that Sanders "remains dear to the Democracy of Europe" because he proved himself "deliberately jealous of the independent exercise of the rights of a free citizen and of a member of the sovereign people."[60] In the end, even the most independent republican required the services of influential friends.

It was not just George Sanders who ran into trouble. Pierre Soulé was arrested for passing through France on route to his diplomatic mission in Spain. This was partly because of Soulé's reputation as a fiery revolutionary figure.[61] But it was also because of two other factors that made France suspicious of the United

States. The first was Sanders's letter to the French people, which fell into the hands of Jerome Bonaparte and reached his cousin, the Emperor Louis Napoleon.[62] The second was the Dillon Affair, in which the French consul stationed in San Francisco, Patrice Dillon, was arrested for ignoring a subpoena to testify in an ongoing case against a Mexican diplomat accused of violating the 1818 Neutrality Law.[63] Dillon was freed within an hour, but he took offence when the order for his arrest was not withdrawn. After Dillon returned to his consular residence, he took down his flag to protest the dishonor shown to the French nation. The Union could only make amends, he insisted, by saluting the French tricolor. Marcy believed this was too much and refused. But eventually both nations agreed to resolve the dispute, exchanging salutes in the harbor of San Francisco. With honor restored, the French reopened their consulate. As for Soulé, the French foreign minister apologized and clarified that he would be able to pass through France but not reside there.

Prominent Democrats sprang to Soulé's defense. Hardly a proponent of Young America, Secretary of State William Marcy nevertheless wrote to John Mason, US minister to France, asking, "If the French government should insist upon having more done in regard to the affair of M. Dillon, would not the United States be bound in honor to ask for something more in the way of satisfaction in the case of Mr. Soulé?"[64] The *Daily Pennsylvanian* claimed to be no supporter of Soulé's politics but argued his treatment could not be neglected because of "personal rancor."[65] George Dallas lamented the "painful and perplexing" situation Soulé found himself in, complaining that "the entire press of Europe seems to have made him a target," while "the gulled and prostitute papers of this country, as usual, swell the cry." Soulé's treatment was an "affair of honor," and he would "rather overlook a kick from the mayor of Greytown than the Emperor of France."[66] Soulé did act in reckless ways in Spain, challenging members of high society to duels, appearing in ostentatious dress at bullfights, and offering the Queen Mother money to sell the island of Cuba.[67] But despite some critics, the slights he suffered under Spanish and French rule were reported sympathetically in the Democratic press.

As recent historians have pointed out, Young Americans like George Sanders and Pierre Soulé fitted squarely within the political traditions of the antebellum Democracy.[68] The radicalism of these men's exploits was symptomatic of the increasingly progressive tone of the party at large—particularly its sympathy for the European revolutions. Although Soulé and Sanders always tried to be one step ahead of their party, plenty of Democrats within the administration supported their radical political agenda. Soulé was ultimately brought down through his involvement in writing the Ostend Manifesto alongside James

Buchanan and John Mason. While Soulé's treatment in Europe had previously united Democrats from both North and South, this ignited controversy in the free states over the expansion of slavery, as discussed in chapter 5.[69] In 1855 Soulé was recalled from Europe, and his efforts were focused instead on territorial expansion southward, particularly into Central America.[70]

If American diplomats faced indignities in Europe, one incident in 1853 became a great success story for Pierce's expansionist foreign policy. This involved Martin Koszta, a lesser-known Hungarian revolutionary.[71] As Alabama's William R. Smith complained to the Senate, "I remember that two years ago this whole country was wild with enthusiasm about Kossuth: and now it seems to be wild about Koszta."[72] Like Kossuth, Martin Koszta had participated in the failed uprising against the Hapsburg Empire and then had fled to the United States after Austrian and Russian forces suppressed the revolution and implemented martial law. In the United States he declared his intention to become an American citizen in the summer of 1852. But before the naturalization process was complete, Koszta returned to Europe on a business trip. Just outside Smyrna, a small city under Turkish jurisdiction, three Austrian warships encircled the Hungarian, and he was placed under arrest. Fortunately, a captain in the United States navy, Duncan Ingraham, was sailing nearby in a small sloop of war. When the Austrians threatened to leave the port, Ingraham aimed his guns on the larger Austrian vessels and demanded Koszta's safe return. New York Democrat Caleb Lyon, an adventurer sympathetic to Young America, was travelling through Smyrna at the time. He encouraged Ingraham to "take the exile Koszta by force. . . . The eyes of nations are upon the little St. Louis and her Commander."[73] Unwilling to escalate the situation, the Austrians relented and agreed to dispatch Koszta to France while William Marcy negotiated with Hapsburg chargé d'affaires Baron Hulsemann over Koszta's safe return to the United States. Marcy mounted a precise and spirited defense of Koszta's right to expatriation as well as his natural right to liberty in a neutral port under Turkish jurisdiction. He also defended the Union's right to intervene on behalf of people domiciled within the United States, even if they had not yet completed the process of naturalization.

Captain Duncan Ingraham became a national hero who was widely celebrated across the United States. In 1854 Congress commissioned a medal to commemorate his actions. But beneath a superficial consensus, partisan affiliation did shape how people responded to the incident. Whigs agreed that Ingraham had acted gallantly in protecting Koszta's natural right to expatriation in a neutral jurisdiction where no positive law existed to the contrary. The Democrats, by contrast, tried to extract political advantage from the situation:

Ingraham's actions had been a great practical vindication of Franklin Pierce's inaugural address and the spirit with which he had tried to invigorate the diplomatic service. Louis Kossuth certainly agreed, writing that the captain "did more to raise the honor, dignity and reputation of the United States in the opinion of the world than all your unrepublican foreign diplomacy has done for years and years past."[74] Young Americans also argued that Koszta was *entitled* to protection from the United States, meaning Ingraham had not only a general right but a national obligation to intervene. Thomas D. Reilly observed, "The ballot box and so forth are reserved" for new arrivals who intended to become citizens, but "the right to protection from outrage is not reserved." If such rights existed at home, "why, therefore, not abroad?"[75]

Conversely, Whigs resisted this logic that threatened to collapse the boundary between natural and citizenship rights. The former Whig president Millard Fillmore complained that Koszta's status in the United States had "nothing to do with that sacred tie . . . which binds a naturalized citizen to his government and creates the corresponding duty of protection." Treating him as such, Fillmore insisted, would "destroy all distinction between a citizen and resident alien."[76] These discussions found their parallel in Congress, where the House debated whether the medal commissioned for Ingraham should be given in the name of humanity or for services to the nation. Despite a superficial national consensus on foreign policy, and growing sectional divisions during this period, partisan disputes still raged on. Whigs tried to preserve the distinction between the natural right to expatriation and the rights of the citizen to protection, while Young Americans collapsed not only political and natural rights but citizenship ones as well.

Despite the partisan nature of these disputes, sectional tensions did polarize the debate after the passage of the Kansas-Nebraska Act, which is discussed in chapter 6. Many Democrats defected to the nascent Republican Party, arguing the Union could only assume its proper role in the international order after slavery had been confined to its present limits.[77] For Republicans, questions about intervention in Europe gave way to an overriding concern for antislavery politics at home.[78] Nevertheless, several Young Americans deplored these "distractions" and championed the Democratic Party as the best hope for the Old World. These Democrats reached out to former colleagues to renew their focus on white Europeans. In the aftermath of the Koszta Affair in 1853, thousands of immigrants had formed the Ingraham Testimonial Committee in New York City to commemorate the captain and commission the medal that was subsequently debated in Congress.[79] This organization quickly morphed into the Society for Universal Democratic Republicanism, which met regularly until 1855, after the passage of the Kansas-Nebraska Act. Along with smaller Polish, French, and Hungarian immigrant societies, the meetings attracted prominent Young Americans such as Robert J. Walker, George Bancroft, and George Sanders, as well as transatlantic revolutionary figures who were admired by Young Americans.[80] For example, Charles Henningsen wrote letters to the society; this English adventurer had fought in the Hungarian revolution and alongside William Walker in the conquest of Nicaragua.[81] The racialized liberalism of these revolutionary figures nonetheless sat uncomfortably with others who took a more inclusive view of the natural right to the fruits of one's labor.

Indeed, the president of the society, the English liberal Hugh Forbes, supported the efforts of the antislavery movement to constrain slavery to its present limits in the United States.[82] When Forbes came to call on Sanders at his house, the Kentuckian blamed him for the rise of the "black Republican Party." Sanders despaired that Forbes would "sacrifice Europe . . . for the sake of the negroes," when "but for the southern state of Virginia you foreigners would have been murdered in the streets."[83] Sanders found himself in even more trouble when he gave a lecture at one society meeting in which he defended the use of the steam-powered guillotine for those who opposed the overthrow of Louis Napoleon in France. Ivor Gollovin wrote articles in the *Tribune* and *Times* attacking this position, claiming that Ledru-Rollin would have opposed it. Sanders, for his part, admitted that he "cannot say . . . whether he is of opinion that the friends who destroyed the republic will be sufficiently numerous and dangerous to require the establishment of a steam guillotine in the Tuileries," but that it was a "quick and comprehensive mode of getting through a horrible necessity."[84] There were evidently significant ideological differences between the liberals associated with Young America and the *Democratic Review* and those associated with the *Tribune*. The focal point of the disagreement was whether individual rights should be extended to nonwhites and perhaps to what degree violence could serve the revolutionary cause.[85]

As Franklin Pierce's popularity became more apparent in the aftermath of the Koszta Affair, some Whiggish intellectuals engaged the movement head-on— both at literary societies and on lecture tours. Even moderate Whig figures were no longer content to retreat into the safe conservative circles of the *North American Review*. Moving with the times, Whigs such as Edward Everett offered qualified praise, at least crediting Young America with good intentions. At a July 4 lecture in Boston entitled "Stability and Progress," the Whig statesman argued that both "conservative" and "Young America" politicians had valuable insights into the American republic but that "practical wisdom and plain common sense" were found "half-way between the two extremes." On the one hand, Everett argued, there were a class of men dubbed "conservatives" by the English, who had recently acquired the name "old fogies" in the United States. They possessed the appropriate respect for family, national traditions, and institutions, seeing "great, undoubted principles of right and wrong" in "constitutions," "laws," and "maxims." "Then there is the opposite side," Everett told his audience, "the 'men of progress' or as they sometimes call themselves in imitation of similar designations in most countries of Europe, 'Young America.'" Rejecting the concern for stability that came naturally to conservatives, Young America "get to think that everything, which has existed for a considerable time, is an abuse." Despite his Whig background, Everett even acknowledged the successful expansion of the American Union and anticipated more to come.[86] Nevertheless, the speed with which Young Americans wanted to reform the international order was reckless in the extreme. A Whig like Edward Everett could express his admiration for the goals of the movement while reminding his audience that a conservative disposition was also a prerequisite for progress.

Local newspapers denounced those speakers who were too critical of the Young America movement. The Whiggish intellectual (and later abolitionist) George William Curtis expressed his skepticism toward the idea during a speaking tour of Ohio. At the "Young Man's Lyceum" in 1853, he gave a lecture entitled "Young America" that mocked the movement's disregard for tradition. Curtis told his audience that "Young America . . . is secretly convinced that all these works of antiquity are only partial and incomplete affairs, not to be compared with what can be done in our day." Some of the papers in Ohio were heavily critical. Although it admitted there was some truth in Curtis' interpretation, one local newspaper said, "Young America is not an unmeaning word. It is a term which is fast assuming a national character." The paper cautioned its readers against too readily accepting the criticisms of Young America made by Bostonian intellectuals like George W. Curtis: "Be not too easily led by the nose," it said, by men with "an Eastern reputation for learning." Rather, "think for yourselves, judge for yourselves . . . bring down their teachings to the test of your own experience—make it practical, and if true, adopt it; and if not, reject it."[87]

If the Whigs were becoming more amenable to Young America, some global trends appeared to be moving in the movement's favor, too. The Revolutions of 1848 might have faltered on the continent, but free trade had been gaining ground in Britain for some time. This change was partly due to John Bright and Richard Cobden, who had successfully shaped the economic policy of mid-nineteenth-century Britain. For most of the nineteenth century, Britain had imposed high duties on imports of corn from the rest of the world. The country's mercantilist system was designed to protect domestic agricultural producers from foreign competition. Nevertheless, liberals in Britain argued these tariffs unfairly benefited landowners at the expense of urban workers. Laborers in the cities required cheap imports, the liberals claimed, as it would amount to a rise in real wages, which could be spent on food and clothing. The situation in Britain turned critical after the Irish famine that began in 1845. Struggling to feed the Irish population, the British needed to increase food imports as a matter of urgency. In 1846 Parliament repealed the Corn Laws, lowering tariffs and ushering in an era of free trade.

That summer, during the highpoint of Anglo-American tensions over the Texas and Oregon disputes, the *Democratic Review* found time to celebrate Britain's achievement. Using the language of territorial expansion, the writer called for the "practical annexation" of the manufacturing interests of England to the agricultural interests of the United States.[88] That same year the *Review*'s owner, Henry Wikoff, credited "the power of the Zollverin" (a German customs union originating in the 1830s) and the "Free Trade Party springing up in France" for undermining outdated ideas about international relations. "Now nations realize," Wikoff argued, "power does not come from taking citizens from their labors and making them fight for the 'balance of power,'" but is best achieved through citizens working to their "best advantage."[89] The domestic situation in the United States also gave Young Americans every reason to be confident. Coinciding with Britain's repeal of the Corn Laws in 1846, the Polk administration passed the Walker Tariff of 1846, based on a report made by Robert Walker, who was secretary of the treasury. This lowered the tariff from 32 percent to 25 percent: one of the lowest in American history.

The success of free trade became glaringly apparent to Young America five years later, in 1851, at London's Great Exhibition to showcase the "industry of all the world." During their trips across the Atlantic during the early 1850s, both Charles Goepp and Samuel Cox took the Great Exhibition as a sign that Europeans were beginning to adopt the Union as a model of international order, drawing the nations of the world together in an ever-greater commercial union. By gathering as a collection of independent states to celebrate the virtues of free trade, the fair showed European powers were starting to follow the American example. In *The New Rome*, Goepp wrote that in 1851 "the ocean world . . . held its first Olympic festival." With "all mankind assembled in union . . . who shall tell when the wonders of the world's fair shall have an end?"[90] Similarly, in *A Buckeye Abroad*, Cox wrote that the Great Exhibition had brought mankind together under the banner of political progress: "How is it with this Crystal Palace, wherein is really seen, not fantastically imagined, the fruits of human progress, resulting from the common labor of all men, springing from the germs implanted in our common nature by our Creator."[91]

These victories continued throughout the 1850s, even as domestic politics took a turn for the worse. Many Young Americans seemed to have a greater affinity for British liberals than the Democrats' Whig and Republican opponents within the United States. Pennsylvania Democrat George Dallas maintained the role to which he was appointed at the tail end of the Pierce administration, Minister to Britain, until 1861; the position alerted him to the transformations taking place in the country. As late as October 1858, Dallas wrote that the liberal MP John Bright "made a stirring speech on Reform" in front of his Birmingham constituencies that was "almost sufficiently Democratic for a 4th of July at Tammany Hall."[92] In another letter just five days later, he compared Bright to Tiberius and Gaius Gracchi, the two Roman tribunes who advocated land reform for the common people. Dallas asked fellow Philadelphia Democrat Henry Gilpin if Bright did not have a "claim to rank with these jewels of the Cornelia": "the two Gracchi," "as a diamond of the first water."[93] In December 1858 he wrote to Cass again, saying that if he were to "maintain his attitude in the House of Commons . . . it will be difficult to assign a limit to (Bright's) progress."[94]

Free trade had resulted in growing political and cultural ties between the United States and Great Britain. In 1856 Dallas explained to Secretary of State William Marcy that the Americanization of British politics had increased support for the Democratic Party in the upcoming presidential election. "The total disappearance of the Whig Party, their old allies," Dallas claimed, had "left" the British "very suspicious of the new factions."[95] According to Dallas, the British had no sympathy for nativist politics or the doctrine of "America for the Americans." A full eight years after the outbreak of the European revolutions, he told Marcy that it was "our steady adherence to republican doctrines, accompanied by the constantly augmenting prosperity and power of the country" that were "visibly undermining their former prejudices, and letting in upon their thoughts, their manners, and even their conversation, a great deal more democracy than they themselves are conscious of."[96] In another letter that same year, he singled out the hopeful aspects of European politics underneath the dispiriting spectacle of counterrevolution: Although "the end is not perceptible at first glance," he said, "I am much mistaken if the principle of rapid decay be not seated at the very heart of that league" of European monarchs. Its "rotten fragments" will be "shaken to the earth by popular convulsions, and that at no distant day."[97]

Fellow Democrats agreed that the success of British liberalism indicated the American Revolution had come full circle. In 1859 Democratic congressman Samuel S. Cox proclaimed, "England shakes with a new reform movement— John Bright trying to Americanize her by popular sovereignty"; while Robert J. Walker wrote to a friend from Britain in the 1850s to suggest that Britain should annex herself to the American Union and incorporate her colonies on an equal footing.[98] Thomas Kane confessed in a private letter that he was "impressed by the many signs appearing of the will of Providence that the two countries shall be drawn together and their ancient ties renewed again," although he made clear that he "despised the whole system of check and balance doctrines" and lamented that Britain's "social influence upon America must in every respect act prejudicially."[99] In *The New Rome,* Charles Goepp argued that "the political and social forces" in America must "take the lead"—"England, with her colonies, must be annexed to the American Union."[100]

But this would only happen insofar as Britain embraced the American ideals of popular sovereignty and free trade. Tensions between Young Americans and the British elite remained high. In 1856 relations almost broke down after a British diplomat, John Crampton, was found breaching the neutrality law by attempting to recruit soldiers in the United States to fight against the Russians in the Crimean War. With Secretary of State William Marcy about to dismiss Crampton from his post, George Dallas predicted a further rise in hostilities between the two powers. In May 1856 he warned that "we may look out for a series of retaliatory and recriminating acts between the two countries, which must lead, at no distant day, to the final trial of strength." He concluded, "When we are driven to that, we must throw the scabbard away, and tie the hilt to the hand."[101] Dallas saw abolitionist literature as one of the primary tools in Britain's arsenal. Behind so-called "British philanthropy" was ideological opposition to the democratic ideals of the United States. Dallas argued that the British displayed a "profound incapacity to understand the federative structure of our government." Fearful of America's growing influence, its former colonial master "keenly set on their Press, their Pulpits, their lecturers, their speakers, their novelists, their poets, and their historians to provide an overpowering chorus for the subversion" of the Constitution.[102] The Pennsylvania Democrat proclaimed, "Our Constitutional democracy, if *unsectionalized,* is our only means of baffling them."[103] As internal divisions flared, Dallas continued to see domestic politics through the lens of Britain's imperial designs.[104] Anti-abolitionism was a moral duty, since it preserved the American nation. Even with slavery intact, the Union proved that white men were naturally suited to self-government.

The Pennsylvanian also argued that monarchical powers were abusing international law to undermine the United States. At the end of the Crimean War in 1856, European powers, headed by Britain and France, issued the Paris Declaration to abolish privateering. Dallas marked this as an attempt to curb the growing power of the United States. The motion to abolish privateering would in particular hamper American filibustering in the tropics. Dallas observed that "out of the conference at Paris, and especially out of the alliance of France and England, has emerged a more formidable league of sovereign powers against sovereign peoples than has yet been witnessed by modern times."[105] Similarly, he wrote to the former editor of the *Democratic Review,* John O'Sullivan, that "these combined potentes of Europe" were trying to "force their international code upon us."[106] With the "joint condemnatory standard of 'Abolition of Slavery and Privateering,' they may put us on our mettle."[107] Although he suggested that filibustering efforts could be counterproductive, Dallas certainly perceived British opposition to the United States' involvement in the tropics as a plot to undermine American power.

Another diplomat in the Pierce administration, August Belmont, wrote to the editor of the *Democratic Review,* George Sanders, about his fear of a European invasion. He argued, "The day is not so far distant, when self-preservation will dictate to the United States the necessity of throwing her moral and physical force into the scale of European republicanism." He proposed that "reorganizing" and augmenting the navy was one way the United States could protect itself against "the jealousy of European powers."[108] Indeed, this was a common theme for Young Americans, with the likes of Galusha Grow, an interventionist representative from Pennsylvania, urging the House to dispense with "old fogy commanders" in the naval forces.[109] But Belmont's fear of European monarchs was not based on a pessimistic reading of the prospects of republican government. Like Dallas, Belmont remained hopeful that the setbacks after 1848 were temporary. He told Sanders, for example, that the Crimean War might offer the distraction necessary for a renewal of democratic agitation. In another letter he praised Sanders for writing to the president of the Swiss Confederation and criticizing his decision to abridge the rights of asylum in that country. Belmont told the Democratic editor, "The republican spirit in Europe is subdued but not crushed, and manifestos like yours cannot fail to exercise the most beneficial influence on its dormant powers."[110] Like Dallas, then, Belmont saw America's fate as inextricably bound to Europe.

Democrat Samuel S. Cox predicted a more general war between the United States and Europe, with the American scholars "armed only with the teaching of 'abstract truth.'"[111] Later, while serving in Congress in 1859, Cox only reneged on this earlier position because he believed Britain would not risk upsetting the balance of power in its absence. The nation dared not "pursue us to a fatal end," since—with its back to events in Europe—the "balance of power" might be "overwhelmed by a popular breath."[112] Walker was unequivocal in telling his British audience that the United States would assist them when the final trial of strength occurred: "Should the frantic despots of Europe bring on such a crisis, the American people, however distant they might be from the scene of the sanguinary conflict, however guarded apparently by the wide Atlantic, yet well they knew, that if despotism should establish itself throughout the continent of Europe, and England be involved in the contest, they must fight."[113] Moreover, "the present alliance of the tyrants of Europe" was not "partial or geographical" but a "rebellion" against the "rights of man, and the liberties of the world."[114] As long as democratic principles gained ground in Britain, it would be a vital ally of the United States.

With our hindsight that Civil War broke out in 1861, it is perhaps tempting to examine the period from the end of the Mexican War in 1848 to Abraham Lincoln's election in 1860 in terms of the emergence of Northern and Southern sectionalism. But Young Americans believed that the primary threat to their worldview came from Great Britain and the monarchical powers of Europe.[115] Whig and Democratic forms of Unionism persisted long into the 1850s, with fundamentally different political theories informing each one. As the argument over Hungarian intervention in 1852 shows, Young America Democrats disagreed with conservative Whigs over the theory of how democracy emerged. While Isaac Walker and Pierre Soulé believed white men were "naturally" suited to democratic rule, John Bell and others argued that history and moral virtue determined the stability of self-government in specific places. As we saw in chapter 1, behind this disagreement was a debate over the Declaration of Independence itself—whether democracy was included in the set of natural rights for white men, alongside "life, liberty and pursuit of happiness." Once we look at Young America's international ambitions in this context, we begin to see the United States' global reach extended east as well as west. Furthermore, we come to appreciate the enormity of the Young Americans' global visions. As well as looking for more territory on the North American continent, they foresaw war between the United States and the Holy Alliance and fantasized about the annexation of Europe. The Union was not just a nation but a model for the international order, a vehicle for liberal philosophy that would replace the balance of power with the rule of natural law. Moreover, it was Young America's particular conception of the Union that sustained these visions of the global order, through the 1852 election and beyond.

5

Cuban Annexation and
the Problem of Slavery

As Europe convulsed in violent upheavals, Young Americans were emboldened
to annex new territory, particularly the Caribbean island of Cuba.[1] Other territories fell within their sights during the decade before the Civil War, such as
Nicaragua, the Sandwich Islands, and parts of British North America. But after
the Oregon dispute of the 1840s, serious consideration of expansion northward
was chiefly limited to rhetoric in the newspapers. Influential slave owners were
uninterested in these regions, and it was far riskier to antagonize Great Britain
than more decrepit monarchical powers to the south. The Sandwich Islands
were certainly desirable, and Nicaragua even more so, but Young Americans
were most focused on the annexation of Cuba. In 1848, a mere three months
after the ratification of the Treaty of Guadalupe Hidalgo, which concluded the
Mexican War, John O'Sullivan and Stephen Douglas met with President James
Polk asking him to make an offer for the island.

Young Americans generally pursued two paths in their negotiations with
Spain, often concurrently. Some went through official channels by pressuring
Democratic administrations to threaten Spain with force if the country would
not sell Cuba to the United States. Others also encouraged—and sometimes
directly funded—filibustering expeditions. These were quasi-piratical raids to
overthrow Spanish rule in Cuba with assistance from the island's creole population. The Venezuelan émigré Narciso López, who was a friend of O'Sullivan's,
led one in 1851, funded by the Mississippi senator John Quitman.[2] With the
tacit support of Democratic President Pierce, Quitman prepared his own raid
in 1854. But the action was called off after the Kansas-Nebraska Act (passed that
same year) caused outrage about a proslavery conspiracy in the highest echelons
of the US government. Other filibusters set their sights on Central America.
William Walker launched a successful expedition to Nicaragua in 1856. He became president of the country until a coalition of other Central American states
combined to overthrow him in 1857. In the end, all of these privateers were

unsuccessful and attracted significant criticism in the United States. Antislavery activists were outraged by Southern land grabs, while many Whigs and Democrats saw these nonstate actors as a destabilizing force that brought disgrace and dishonor on the American government.

Like other aspects of the Young America program, attitudes toward these forms of expansionism existed on a continuum. For their part, Stephen Douglas, Pierre Soulé, John O'Sullivan, and George Sanders sympathized with filibusters. Indeed, the prominent nineteenth-century adventurer and leading accomplice in William Walker's invasion of Nicaragua, Parker H. French, asked Stephen Douglas in 1856 to repeal the Neutrality Act of 1818, legislation that prohibited the launching of unauthorized invasions from the shores of the Union into foreign countries that were at peace with the United States.[3] One of French's associates praised Douglas for "endeavoring to infuse young and vigorous blood into the councils of our hoary and feeble government" and hoped Douglas would become president in 1856.[4] By contrast, George M. Dallas, who was a prominent ally of these men, even if he remained suspicious of Sanders, outlined a slightly more moderate course. He would not repeal laws designed to "repress marauding and freebooting" but would take a "more ostensible attitude" than Secretary of State William Marcy on Cuban annexation. Dallas recommended the Pierce administration offer Spain a fair price for Cuba but take the island regardless. "There is the money. Take it or not as you please," Dallas imagined them saying, "but we take the island, openly, and, if needs be, in defiance of all Europe."[5]

What united these Democrats behind Young America's program of territorial expansion was their conflation of natural rights with the political rights of white men to rule themselves. All agreed the Democratic principle mandated the imminent expansion of self-government into the tropics, regardless of the balance of power between rival nations. Following the election of Franklin Pierce and beyond, the case for expansion was especially urgent, since the Whigs had ruled for the previous four years, suppressing filibuster expeditions and striking deals with European powers. In his inaugural address Pierce declared that he would not be deterred by these "timid forebodings of evil from expansion." Young Americans took particular aim at the Whigs' Clayton-Bulwer Treaty of 1850; this joint resolution between America and Britain committed both powers to cease expansion into Central America. Young Americans viewed this as an outdated and un-American form of diplomacy that preserved the balance of power to promote peace. Robert Walker wrote to Douglas in 1850, asking, "What would now be thought if a treaty had been made with England never to annex the Floridas, Louisiana, Texas, California, the Canadas or Cuba and who can say we will never desire to annex Central America?"[6] Walker and his allies believed the Whigs' undue concern for the balance of power had also hindered American expansion in the Pacific. Word reached Congress in 1852 that Kamehameha III, King of Hawaii, desired a closer alliance with the United States. Democrats feared the timid Whig administration had missed an opportunity to annex the Sandwich Islands. Expansionists in the Senate twice demanded information from Millard Fillmore, only to have the president deny the requests. California congressman Joseph McCorckle equated Fillmore's suspicion of entangling alliances with the outdated doctrine of the balance of power. It was therefore up to "enlightened minds" to resist "the hatred and terror of free government on both sides of the Atlantic" that had followed "the failure of Hungary, the overthrow of the French Republic and the suppression of liberty in Italy and the German states."[7]

This desire to expand America's political system resulted in a bellicose nationalism that chafed under slights from the Spanish government. Outrage peaked in 1854 when Cuban authorities seized a ship that had docked in Havana on route from Alabama to New York City. The ostensible reason was that the captain had not formally accounted for the shipment of cotton on board, but these rules were routinely ignored at the time. In fact, Spain was on guard against filibustering expeditions and suspected foul play. Although the matter was eventually resolved in 1855, Pierre Soulé, the US consul to Spain, issued an ultimatum to the Spanish government to redress the situation, which might have ended in war. With pressure mounting to annex the island, William Marcy instructed diplomats John Mason, James Buchanan, and Pierre Soulé to meet in Ostend, Belgium, to discuss negotiations with Spain. Failing that, Marcy issued the vague instruction to seek "the next desirable object, which is to detach that island from the Spanish dominion."[8] Although this did not necessarily mean threatening war, the incendiary Young American Pierre Soulé interpreted it as such.

Soulé, Mason, and Buchanan made no secret of their meeting at Ostend, which was widely reported in the European and American press. But when, through a possible leak, the *New York Herald* circulated the men's intention to declare war, the public was outraged. As Southern influence within the Democratic Party was becoming more assured, many Northerners saw this as yet another attempt to extend slavery, while others complained about the ad hoc nature of the negotiations, characteristic of an administration thought to be tacitly encouraging filibusters. Under congressional pressure, Pierce released the Ostend Manifesto in full to a braying Northern audience. With a presidential election in sight, Soulé was ordered to cease any discussion of Cuba, which he felt justified his immediate resignation. Despite this backlash against the Ostend Manifesto, the national Democracy maintained in its 1856 platform that "there are questions connected with the foreign policy of this country, which are inferior to no domestic question whatsoever."[9] Both before and after, Young Americans on both sides of the Mason-Dixon line continued to push for their expansionist agenda.

What lay behind the strength of expansionist sentiment was a conflation of natural and political rights. Young Americans connected the expansion of white men's democracy to the cause of natural rights around the world, grounding the extension of the Union in the nation's intellectual and moral development through time. A close ally of Sanders and the *Review*, California's Edward Marshall linked Young America's expansionist agenda to its efforts to develop intellectual culture during the early 1850s.[10] The Californian complained that the same people who opposed territorial growth also tried to thwart progress in political theory, literature, and science. In a speech before the House of Representatives in March 1852, he declared, "Every reform, every advance the nation has made, has been opposed by the same conservatism, which would now paralyze the national energy." For Marshall, the Louisiana Purchase of 1803 and the Texas annexation went hand-in-hand with the intellectual development of the nation. The "progress . . . of the kind that Young America contend[ed] for" was both "physical advancement" and that which "enlarged and liberated the American mind." The latter included the abolition of debtor prisons as well as the reform of property qualifications for the franchise, which had emerged from revolts such as the one in Rhode Island in 1841. Like territorial expansion, this intellectual advancement was inevitable since it was rooted in natural laws: "You cannot put down what is natural and ought to exist; and whatever abuses ought to be overthrown will be overthrown." The history of the United States was told as a gradual process of melioration brought about by Jacksonian principles. "Once men begin to think upon subjects like this," Marshall insisted, "you might as well attempt to control the human conscience."[11]

In another speech on the acquisition of Cuba given in January 1853—"on behalf of Young America and the progressives with whom I sympathize"—Marshall attacked Southern opponents of expansion, as well as Americans in the free states, for their "general reprobation of the doctrines of progress" and the "assertion of general principles." Rebutting the idea that the Union "could not with safety embrace any additional territory," he explained that expansion could only strengthen republican governments. If incorporating Cuba did, however, dismember the Union, then it would still teach the world a valuable lesson. "The experiment is worth trying," Marshall argued, as "good would result even from the temporary union." Even in failure "we would have introduced new ideas": "We would have taught lessons of self-government . . . of the equality of men in the eye of the law, of the dignity of the individual, without which . . . man had better not be." According to Marshall, "Whether we continued to exist as one union or broke into fifty free republics, the world would be improved by the diffusion of knowledge, which alone makes life tolerable."[12] Of course, this idealism about the inevitability of American expansion concealed the active role the federal government would play in these schemes. Marshall, for example, proposed giving the president an emergency fund of $10 million to use for the annexation of Cuba should Britain obtain the island while Congress was not in session.[13] Although Young Americans did not want to intervene in the internal affairs of independent states and nations, they were happy to use federal power to create the conditions in which these political communities could thrive.

Young America Democrat Samuel Cox shared Marshall's conviction that the nation could expand indefinitely because it was the embodiment of liberal principles. Cox saw the growth of the Union reflected in the laws of historical development that were driving democratic revolutions on both sides of the Atlantic. Even at the height of the sectional crisis, Cox was convinced that the Union would continue to gain power and influence. With an eye on developments in Europe, he said, "The disquieting aspect of cisatlantic politics signifies the consummation of territorial changes on this continent, long predicted, long delayed, but as certain as the logic of history." Just as the *Democratic Review* justified the Union according to the natural laws of social and biological science, Cox argued that "the law which commands this is higher than congressional enactment. If we do not work with it, it will work in spite of us."[14] Similarly, one writer in the *Review* said in 1859: "The geographical, commercial, moral and political relations formed by nature" between "that island and this country" were "gathering in the progress of time." Cuba had formed an "unnatural connection with Spain" and would "gravitate towards the North American Union" by the "law of nature."[15] Drawing on the liberal tradition of natural law, Cox advocated the annexation of the Mexican states of Sonora and Chihuahua as well as Cuba. First, he wanted to see the United States change its policy toward Mexico in order to "stabilize" the liberal factions there that were struggling for survival against centralizing, conservative forces during the Reform War—a civil conflict that raged from 1858 to 1860. Opening up free trade would improve the Liberals' chances by facilitating the *natural laws* of political development.[16] As with Cuban affairs, there was also a case for direct intervention, given the crimes Mexico had committed against American citizens. Such acts of aggression demonstrated that Catholic monarchists presented an existential threat to the American republic. Among the "wrongs" Mexico had wrought was the

surveillance of the post office, particularly the refusal to deliver consular correspondence unless it was first inspected by government authorities.

Other Democrats recognized that a younger generation within the party was
driving the case for annexation. A close ally of Stephen Douglas's from California, George E. Pugh, argued the Union's expansionist policy was led by a
generation of younger, more liberal Americans. As late as 1859 he declared that
those congressmen opposed to the expansion of the Union were "in antagonism
to the generation which with pulses warmer and quicker inspire us, with genius
more exalted than we can boast." He called for his fellow senators "to adapt . . .
our general policy . . . to the necessities of our children." Pugh's case for Cuban
annexation was steeped in the liberal universalism of the *Democratic Review.* He
was particularly critical of the view that creoles were not yet fit for independence,
a theory that not only ignored the history of the country but denied the Spanish
"all the characteristics of manhood." Drawing on the innate qualities of "man,"
Pugh conflated the notion of political and natural rights. Rather than assessing
the creoles' political development or examining their cultural traditions, Pugh
deemed them fit for self-government based on their "manhood" alone. Pugh's
vision totally rejected historical markers of national identity in favor of gender
and race. "Neither in Cuba nor anywhere else on this or the other side of the
Atlantic can there be found an individual of the Caucasian race, who does not
aspire, in his heart of hearts, to . . . participation in the government in which he
lives." Indeed, Pugh downplayed national characteristics in order to justify the
expansion of the Union. Although the creoles did share Spanish blood, this "did
not prove sufficient" to maintain relationships between Mexico, Central America,
or South America and their former imperial ruler. Hence, blood ties offered no
argument to prevent Cuba from coming into the Union. "There is no more di-
versity of race," he said, "between us and Cuba than all the states in the Union
have with each other."[17]

Suffrage was rooted in race and gender because these were inherent characteristics. White men were natural sovereigns whose political rights were not
contingent on external factors. In contrast, the principle of European statecraft
developed at the Congress of Vienna sought to bind rival powers in a web of
interdependence to stabilize the international order. George Pugh hoped America
was not "so corrupted by wealth—so effete" as to "extend to this continent . . . the
European system of the dictation of sovereigns to each other."[18] Pugh feared that
European powers wanted to prevent the advance of the United States after the
nation's victory in the Mexican War. Drawn together through their alliance in
the Crimea, France and Britain would now intervene in America's backyard.

Despite his stance against slavery, Democrat Thomas L. Kane echoed Pugh's gendered language when he imagined expansion into the tropics. During a visit to the West Indies in 1853, Kane said he saw that "fair land" as an "American annexationist" and gazed upon it "as a man looks upon a woman for the first time when he knows he is going to obtain her."[19] As Kane biographer Matthew Grow points out, "The following year, he supported a war to obtain Cuba from Spain, a cause normally associated with southerners looking to expand slavery's empire."[20] Many other "progressive" Democrats blamed the Whigs for sharing an ideological affinity with European powers. According to Thomas D. Reilly, the election of Millard Fillmore in 1848 saw America fall under the sway of the European notion of statecraft. Fillmore's truckling diplomacy was "protecting a despotic queen in Cuba" just as France "protected the Pope in Rome."[21]

Like other Young Americans, Reilly's frequent calls for Cuba to be "Americanized" suggest he thought the Spanish were capable of living within the Union.[22] Reilly also compared the plight of Cuba under Spanish rule to India under British control, bemoaning the fact that India has "not yet seen the glory of our flag." Keen to replicate the Union in South Asia, Reilly urged "sympathy with the Indian peoples for the overthrow of both English monopoly and Russian arms, and for the establishment from Cape Comorin to the Himalayah, of free trade and free governments in amity and commerce with our Pacific States . . . dictated by natural justice."[23] The Boston Democrat Maturin M. Ballou, who edited the prominent Jacksonian newspaper the *Bay State Democrat* during the 1840s, joined Reilly in championing the creoles' cause. Ballou published *A History of Cuba, or Notes of a Traveller in the Tropics*, which the *Star of the North* favorably reviewed in 1856.[24] After a long account detailing the history and climate of the island, Ballou's volume forcefully advocated creole revolution and the annexation of Cuba as a US state. However, he paused for a second to consider whether this would benefit the Cubans themselves. Although the iniquities of colonial rule were "forced upon the mind of the citizen of the United States in Cuba," Ballou wondered whether these "reflections . . . occur in the minds of the creoles?"[25] He noted, "We are told that they are willing slaves. Spain tells us so, and she extols to the world with complacent mendacity the loyalty of her *'siempre fielissima isla de Cuba.'* But why does she have a soldier under arms for every four white adults? We were about to say, white male citizens, but there are no citizens in Cuba."[26] The racial categorization of the creoles was, of course, significant. By stressing their whiteness, Ballou insinuated that Cubans were entitled to self-government. He chose to emphasize both their age and race because these were signs of distinction in Jacksonian culture—qualities that justified inclusion within the political community. The image of these "adults"—naturally suited to democratic government—being shackled under the yoke of military rule was carefully designed to produce outrage. By calling them "white male citizens," Ballou evoked the creoles' natural political condition before contrasting it with the sad state of an island where "there are no citizens." He even went so far as to argue that Cuba could have achieved the same illustrious fate as the United States had her imperial oppressor been as easy to topple as Great Britain. Ballou believed there was nothing unique about the Union, either as a people or a place, that made it any more suited to democracy than its tropical neighbor.[27]

Similarly, several Democratic newspapers saw creole resistance as a continuation of the recent European uprisings of 1848. The *Democratic Sentinel and Harrison County Farmer,* based in Ohio, proclaimed: "Americans will sympathize for the victims of oppression everywhere, whether in Hungary or Cuba, whether at home or abroad, and when we talk of enforcing our neutrality laws, or any other laws to prevent material aid to the oppressed, it would be as well to remember that we are but attempting to prevent action which arises from the noblest sympathies of the human heart."[28] As late as 1855, the *Indiana State Sentinel* declared that "Cuba has long been struggling for freedom but, like Poland and Hungary, she has been unfortunate." Similarly, the paper declared later that month: "English and French vessels insultingly flaunt their colors in sight of the coast of Florida; and they are there as Nicholas was in Hungary, to crush by the strong hand all revolutionary movements."[29] While Mexicans were imagined as nonwhites who would be exterminated in the process of expansion, the creoles in Cuba were included in the racial community entitled to political and natural rights.

For Young America Democrats, the Revolutions of 1848 and the politics of expansion in the Western Hemisphere had often been two sides of the same coin. Democrats had long predicted that monarchical intervention in North America would inspire a second wave of democratic revolutions in Europe. Before the Mexican War, Massachusetts' Caleb Cushing wrote in the *Democratic Review* that British "interference" in the conflict would be the signal of a general war, "calamitous to us" but "more so to them." It would be the "war of opinion" that Canning predicted long ago, "shaking to their foundations the . . . thrones of Europe."[30] Likewise, Philadelphia Democrat John A. Dix said, "Any attempt by a European power to interpose in the affairs of Mexico, either to establish a monarchy, or to maintain, in the language of M. Guizot, 'the equilibrium of the great political forces of America,' would be the signal for a war far more important in its consequences . . . than this."[31]

Similar hopes for a coordinated uprising persisted through the 1850s. In 1848 George Sanders and the New York steamship magnate George Law had shipped muskets left over from the Mexican War to Paris to provide practical support for the revolutions. Six years later, newspapers speculated that it was not "George Law's muskets" but an uprising by Kossuth that would thwart the efforts of England and France to interfere with the Union's attempts to acquire Cuba from Spain.[32] Some European revolutionaries did seriously entertain the idea of assisting the Union's southward expansion. For example, French democrat Alexandre Ledru-Rollin wrote to George Sanders in 1854 that the United States should pledge support to the Spanish republicans. He argued that a republican regime in Spain would transfer Cuba to the United States as a reward for supporting their revolution.[33] The same year, George Dallas predicted—incorrectly—that the military coup by centrist general Leopoldo O'Donnell against the Spanish queen would lead to a democratic uprising. Dallas was confident that "the consciousness of degradation has probably reached the masses of Spain, and that no people bear long." "Wait a while," he told his cousin Francis Markoe, "and I should not be amazed if a gallant outbreak of purifying democracy not only secures to us Cuba but offers Spain herself for annexation."[34] In the end O'Donnell made an alliance with his historic rivals in the progressive movement but stopped short of inviting Spanish democrats to form a government. Two years later, in 1856, he launched a second coup, consolidating the power of his centrist faction in Spain.

After many Americans lost hope in European politics, Young Americans continued to believe that an uprising in Cuba would be accompanied by upheavals across the Atlantic. In 1857 Ohio Democrat William Corry told the House that if "England, Spain, Russia and Austria dare to meddle" with Cuban annexation, "their own people will rise and rend them." And if this dramatic mass uprising did not occur, "we only want the amity of France," Corry exclaimed, "to sweep them all out of the ocean and to free Canada as well as Cuba, and then advance into the Baltic and the Mediterranean and the era of the people will begin to dawn for all mankind."[35] In 1859 Samuel Cox similarly depicted Europe on the brink of revolution, with England "trembling as the one hundred thousand soldiers across the channel" began to "build coastal defences" while "Mazzini issue[d] his rescript to the secret societies and open republicans of Italy" to be ready.[36] Because England "shakes with a new reform movement," Cox insisted that Britain would not dare intervene in America. If it did, "the balance of power might be overwhelmed by a popular breath."[37] Young America saw events in the American hemisphere as intimately connected to Europe, as they fought for the Democratic principle against the international networks of European monarchy.

The Problem of Slavery

In their tropical ambitions, the Unionists within the Young America movement allied with explicitly proslavery Fire-Eaters—men who would go on to secede from the United States, confident in their ability to perpetuate a slave empire in Latin America. The ideologies of these two groups were similar. Their racial taxonomy was built around white supremacy, and their economic interests dovetailed around the extraction of economic value in the tropics and the trade of commodities, whether cotton or corn, on the international market. But the two groups were subtly distinct, both in ideology and interests. While Fire-Eaters sought to perpetuate a system built around the permanent enslavement of the Black race, Young Americans (including their Southern supporters) more often wanted to eradicate Black labor of any kind from the bounds of the Union. A shared program of territorial expansion and racial politics kept these groups aligned for much of the mid-nineteenth century. But cracks appeared in the coalition that prefigured divisions in the Democratic Party and in the nation as a whole. While the prospect of tropical acquisitions gave slave owners a divine confidence in their labor system, it offered Young Americans a means to drive Black labor from the mainland United States, prevent free Blacks from menacing their Southern border, and expand the natural rights of white men to rule themselves. This was a Unionist vision. It instrumentally favored the expansion of slavery and attracted Southerners like Robert J. Walker, Pierre Soulé, and George Sanders, but it was also distinct from the "vast southern empire" that many Fire-Eaters wanted to build in Latin America.[38]

Both groups experienced flare-ups of racial anxieties in 1853 when Spain appointed a new captain-general of Cuba, Marquis Juan de la Pezuela, who harbored a well-known opposition to slavery. The decision terrified planters in Cuba and the southern United States as well as many observers in the free states. Ironically, Pezuela was instructed to end the importation of slaves, which was a goal many Young Americans professed to desire. In December 1853 he declared that slave traders would be fined and banished from the island for two years, while governors would be stripped of office for failing to inform him of illegal landings in the areas under their control. There was a British blockade already in place, but it proved ineffective because of the sheer expanse of Cuba's coastline. Fearful of their power and position, planters in Cuba increased pressure on President Pierce to annex the island. The following year the president offered $130 million, which Spain promptly declined. And, in April, prominent slave owners met with US ambassador William H. Robertson, imploring him to send in troops. Many planters in both the United States and Cuba clearly did want to strengthen slavery and sought to continue the importation of slave laborers.

Young Americans argued that Pezuela was not really interested in suppressing the slave trade. Rather, his real aim was to emancipate the Black population, stirring up what one writer called a "war of the races" that would make Cuban independence and annexation impossible, while threatening the very stability of the United States.[39] Failing that, Spain would sell the island to the British, who would carry out the same plan. In this context, slavery was a price worth paying to avoid a free Black population. George Dallas reported that Pierre Soulé, now the American consul to Spain, "writhes in anguish" that "the time of emancipation is ready for explosion," while Dallas himself confessed that there was "nothing attractive and annexable in a population of seven hundred thousand free negroes."[40] Worse still, emancipation in Cuba would prompt slave rebellions in the southern United States and increase the migration of free Black laborers. This fear of racial disorder encouraged more moderate Democrats to support Cuban annexation, too. James Buchanan, for example, was alarmed at rumors that the Mexican government had given a Cuban trading company the right to import Mexicans from the Yucatán to work as apprentice laborers. These workers would be bound to a supervisor for a number of years before being granted their freedom. According to Buchanan, this influx of free nonwhite labor would "barbarize the island" and make it an "unwholesome neighbor."[41]

In the end, these anxieties over race formed a core part of the Ostend Manifesto, which threatened Spain with force if she did not sell Cuba to the United States. Probably written by Soulé and edited by Buchanan and Mason, it declared that the Union "must not permit Cuba to be Africanized and become a second St. Domingo with all its attendant horrors to the white race."[42] Both Young Americans and Fire-Eaters (not to mention moderate Democrats) would have agreed with this statement, even as they disagreed subtly as to the precise cause of their fears. On the one hand, Fire-Eaters and Cuban planters were actively hostile to the eradication of the slave trade on the island. On the other, Young Americans feared an end to the importation of slaves only insofar as it would lead to free Blacks taking control of the Caribbean, thereby threatening the Union and interfering with the white man's natural right to self-rule. For Young America, the temporary evil of slavery was worth preserving to avoid this fate, especially as annexation would drain Blacks from the mainland and allow Americans to suppress the slave trade once the island was under their control. These concerns allowed some Young Americans to square the idea of annexing Cuba as one or more slave states with their abstract opposition to slavery. John O'Sullivan was not lying when he declared that there was a consensus "almost unanimous" in the northern states that slavery should not be extended into free territory, while in the same breath saying that Cuba would "of course" become a slave state.[43] Since the island already contained enslaved people, the government would be bringing the system under American control, thereby ameliorating the institution and controlling the traffic in human beings while preventing the island from being controlled by free Blacks.

Going further, Young Americans frequently made the case that Cuban annexation would temper the worst aspects of slavery under Spanish rule—particularly in hastening the demise of the slave trade, which Spain continued in the face of international condemnation. As early as 1848, when he defected from the Democracy to block the extension of slavery to new territories, O'Sullivan wrote, "We Barnburners will be as much pleased at [the admission of Cuba] as the Southerners themselves," on the grounds that it would help Americans police the international slave trade.[44] Trying to make an antislavery case for Cuban annexation, he told Douglas that he wrote a few "pro-Cuba articles" for the antislavery *Evening Post* to "prepare Northern opinion" for "acquisition of that island." He even tried to include an "elaborate appeal to the party in which it was an influential organ"—the Republicans—although the editor, William C. Bryant, "would not insert it."[45] Under the editorship of Kentucky's George Sanders, the *Democratic Review* argued that Cuban annexation would put a stop to the importation of enslaved laborers. One article in 1858 claimed that "so long as Spain suffers Cuba to be used for the furtherance of the African slave trade," the United States would be "desirous to prevent importation . . . into its own territory, and to take away the inducements and temptations which the trade of that island presents to American citizens and others."[46] In 1859 the *Review* said, "The inhumanity and cruelty of the system in Cuba is of a character to excite the commiseration of the most thoughtless," while the American system promoted a mutually beneficial relationship between the races.[47] The Americans would also shut down the coolie trade, a system of bound labor more cruel than slavery since it affected Asian races, who "feel slavery more acutely" than Blacks. It was shocking to the periodical that the Republicans, claiming "exclusive friendship for the oppressed races," can "take ground against a measure calculated in a greater degree than any other, to promote the cause of humanity and the principles of liberty."[48]

Having abolished the slave trade in 1808, the United States was by "providence" the only power capable of outlawing the importation of Black labor in Cuba, or so argued Young America. When Governor-General Pezuela attempted his reforms in 1854, the Pennsylvania paper the *Democrat and Sentinel* reiterated the fact that the United States was the only nation prepared to eradicate the slave trade for good: the Union has "vigorously arrested and annihilated the

African slave trade with her people since 1808; and England, who professes to be so anxious to put an end to it between Cuba and Brazil, refuses to consent to the acquisition of the former by this country, although fully aware that such an acquisition is the only way effectually and forever to annihilate that traffic." The paper quoted statistics that apparently showed the Spanish continuing to import slaves during this period, concluding that "the negroes clandestinely carried into Cuba from Africa, from 1841 to the present day, amount to the number of *about 15 thousand every year!*"[49] As Maturin Ballou noted in his *History of Cuba*, the Spanish were bound by "treaty stipulations" to "make war" on the slave trade, but "she tacitly connives at its continuance"; furthermore, "Everyone knows that slaves are monthly, almost weekly, landed in Cuba." Spain's real aim was, in fact, to import slaves with a view to creating a "war of the races" on the island.[50]

This desire to suppress the slave trade fitted within Young America's broader program. Ohio Democrat George E. Pugh argued the abolition of the slave trade in Cuba was a corollary to the Democrats' professed anti-imperialism and faith in free trade. In 1859 many of Pugh's fellow senators complained that the Union's liberal trade policy with the island rewarded Cuban planters for continuing to exchange slaves on the global market.[51] By importing slave labor from abroad, creoles could produce sugar more cheaply than American planters in Louisiana. Without trade barriers to compensate, the United States was allowing the Cubans to undercut American prices on the open market by virtue of their immoral and illegal modes of production. Instead of raising tariffs as a retaliatory measure, Pugh argued that America should simply take control of the island, suppress the trade in slaves, and implement free trade. At the same time, the Union could lower Cuban duties on American products.

These sentiments echoed across the Atlantic within the circles of British liberalism. During his consulship in London, George Dallas made the antislavery case for Cuban annexation to Lord Henry Brougham, the British campaigner against the international slave trade. Brougham apparently believed the current method of policing the trade—through visitation and search—was "utterly inconsistent with fundamental or universal principles of international law." "Why not put an end to the trade by passing Cuba over to the United States?" Dallas suggested, to which Brougham replied that "it might come to that." In relation to domestic slavery, Brougham also approved of the Democrats' moderate policy of allowing the "institution" to expire in its own time. "As to domestic servitude," Dallas reported, "your lordship is aware that its cessation in the United States must be the slow effect of time," for America "cannot get rid of it without consequences more dreadful than the thing itself."[52] In 1857 Dallas reported that the Liberal Party he admired so much in England was "reconciling itself" to an

American Cuba. He said there may be an "abatement in the crusading spirit" against Cuban annexation because the Liberals "despair of stopping the trade from Africa" and "may see reason to prefer the institution as it exists with us to the one on the island."[53] In a letter to Lewis Cass in 1858, Dallas optimistically alluded to "an opinion which, though adverse to slavery in general, deems it to be less reprehensible under the laws and morals of the United States than elsewhere, and would feel rather philanthropically employed than otherwise in being accessory to its transfer from Spain to us."[54]

In 1858 a friend and ally of Richard Cobden, Henry Ashworth, wrote to Henry Gilpin, lending his support to the United States' annexation of Cuba. Ashworth did not see the policy as one that extended slavery, since that institution already existed under Spanish rule. Instead, he claimed that "the slavery of Cuba is much worse in every way and under Spanish rule there is no hope of any amelioration of the atrocious system now pursued." Ashworth also revealed a distaste for philanthropy and imperial intervention consistent with the anti-abolitionism of his Democratic friend. He wrote, "Were it not for the busy-body meddling spirit which such men as Palmerston have been but too ready to adopt at the insistence of the philanthropists we should withdraw from the prosecution of this expensive marine police upon the coasts of Cuba." Instead, the British government should "remove our coast guard from these distant places" and "no longer be the receivers of the vile plunder" of cotton and sugar imported into Liverpool every day. Like his Democratic brethren, Ashworth revealed an abstract opposition to slavery combined with a reluctance to take immediate action. However "abhorrent the system may be," he insisted, "it is not quite in readiness to be removed by a mere stroke of the pen."[55] This anti-abolitionism espoused by British free traders and American Democrats alike must be taken seriously as an aspect of a liberal worldview that reached beyond the borders of the United States. Men like Gilpin, Dallas, and Ashworth could be in favor of Cuban annexation, suspicious of centralized power, and tolerant of slave labor as a response to the wider problem of racial inferiority, while also being abstractly opposed to slavery and even willing to stand against its extension into territory where it did not already exist.[56] This worldview certainly aided the Slave Power in an instrumental way, but it was also a distinct aspect of transatlantic liberalism in the mid-nineteenth century.

Young Americans also diverged from some Southerners in their view that Cuban annexation could be a means of eradicating slavery—and Black labor itself—from the American mainland. Indeed, there were Southerners opposed to expansion for exactly this reason. As late as 1857 the Northern *Democratic and Sentinel* worried that "the scruples and misgivings of the South" about maintaining a grip on slavery where it already existed would "have to be over-come." The paper implored the South not to fight the dynamics of the "safety-valve" theory, since it was an inevitable process. Slaveholders should be prepared to "withdraw their capital and labor from present employments" and "leave these lands worthless," since it was a "natural" process, already underway.[57] The future was not "backing up" slavery in Texas but taking slaves to Cuba, where they could labor more productively, without degrading or undercutting white workers in the border states. By fighting to preserve the balance of power, Southerners were clinging to an outdated version of statecraft that had blighted Europe for years. Instead, Young America urged them to reject federal inter-vention and embrace the natural laws driving national development.

Some Young Americans went further, arguing slavery in Cuba would come to an end under American rule. California's Edward C. Marshall railed against North Carolina's Abraham Venable for opposing Cuban annexation on the grounds the island would become a series of free states. He complained that Venable's opposition was motivated by "jealousy of the North." In Marshall's view, Southerners should not concern themselves with using the federal govern-ment to maintain the balance of power between the states. In the absence of federal intervention, the institution would stand or fall on its own terms. By withdrawing the support slavery received from the federal government, Marshall believed he was depriving it of life. Nothing as fundamentally unjust, social regressive, or economically efficient as slavery could exist for long in indepen-dent, democratic communities, even in the tropics. In Marshall's words: "It is a conviction, now nearly universal, that the progress of slavery in American terri-tory is arrested. That in all future acquisitions, from the operation of many ac-tive causes, the institution of slavery will not exist." The North's "greater energy and aptitude for emigration" meant that any territory "seeking admission to the Union" would be free without recourse to federal intervention. As long as it was protected by the "Constitution and the laws," it did not matter that the natural laws of political development would bring slavery to an end. Since the "conditions of human society and the progress of free states militate against it," there was no point attempting to prolong slavery's downfall. "In its own nature," slavery was "temporary and evanescent, and about to disappear before the demo-cratic energies and the laws of political economy."[58] In a powerful articulation of "free labor" ideology, Marshall explained that emigrants settling in Cuba from the northern and western states would protect the "aristocracy of labor" in the absence of federal intervention.

However, these pronouncements still rang a little hollow. Marshall never ex-plained, for example, what would happen to the existing enslaved people already living in Cuba. If the prospect of a free Black population was such a menace, would they be colonized to Africa, as many Young Americans proposed elsewhere? Moreover, many of his compatriots did not go as far as Edward Marshall and merely argued that America could better control the international slave trade than Spain. But this concession was tepid at best: Many proslavery Southerners would not have disagreed. The question of whether these bound laborers would one day be emancipated, and how this would be done, went unanswered. Finally, paradoxes remained. Enslaved labor might be particularly appropriate to the tropics, where the climate supposedly made Black workers more efficient than white. But this did not stop slavery being a blight on the free Cuban population, who were imagined as white, as well as on the planters themselves. Given these tensions within their worldview, it is perhaps surprising that Young Americans advocated the annexation of Cuba with quite so much relish. Yet a wide cross section of figures still made a case that fitted within Young America's larger program and was at least compatible with moderate antislavery beliefs.

Like most other issues, territorial expansion was one aspect of the Jacksonian program that transcended party affiliation during the 1850s. As the Democrats hemorrhaged voters to the antislavery Republican Party, Jacksonian figures took their enthusiasm for expansion into the Republican fold. In the midst of this process, Young America remained a coherent faction within the Democracy. As he campaigned for Stephen Douglas in the presidential election of 1860, George Sanders promoted national expansion to voters in the free and slave states as a means of preventing secession. Drawing on common assumptions about the cruelty of Spanish slavery, Sanders pleaded with the Republicans: "If the ultra sections of your party are actuated only by humanitarian motives, why not bravely begin the war on Cuba, where neither constitutional pledges, nor hallowed memories of patriot ancestors forbid, and where the condition of the Ethiopian is so much below the 'persons held to service' in our country?"[59] But, as these appeals also suggest, expansionism did not exclusively appeal to supporters of the Democratic Party. Many former Democrats who had previously contributed to the *Review* took their ideas into the Republican fold. With Jacksonian voters up for grabs in the free states, even Whiggish figures recognized the need to incorporate Democratic principles and policies into the Republican platform. The coeditor of the *New York Tribune,* Joseph Medill, feared the Democrats would bring forward the issue of Cuban annexation "conspicuously and constantly next campaign," arguing the Republicans could not afford to oppose, or ignore, the policy.[60]

Thus, the migration of Jacksonian figures into the ranks of the antislavery movement combined with the need to peel off Northern Democratic voters made expansionism an appealing issue in Republican circles. Some figures made the case for expansion into free territory. John P. Hale proposed, in 1853, that Lewis Cass's resolution to reaffirm the Monroe Doctrine in Cuba should, in fact, be applied to Canada, while German immigrant Carl Schurz argued that Pierce's expansionist program should continue once the United States had abolished slavery.[61] But others made a case for expansion in the tropics that sounded remarkably similar to Young America's; they even tolerated the annexation of territories with slavery intact. Northerners knew that confining slavery to the South was not the only means of eradicating the institution. In fact, Young America's vision of an expansionist white republic appealed beyond the ranks of the Democracy.

Like their Democratic counterparts, the antislavery figures who supported the annexation of Cuba saw Young America's nationalist program as fully compatible with free labor ideology. One of these was the radical abolitionist Gerrit Smith, who ran for president in 1848 as the candidate for the abolitionist Liberty Party. In the 1850s Smith argued that antislavery feeling in the United States had already put the institution on the path to extinction, unlike in monarchical Spain, where concentrations of power and wealth facilitated its spread. The American system was also less cruel than the Spanish one. As Smith told abolitionist Wendell Phillips, "The type of slavery in Cuba is, in some respects, more terrible than in any other part of the world." He pointed to the absence of the "family relation," low life expectancy, and high fertility rates, while in America, "slavery encounters, and is modified by, a higher civilization than that, which pervades the dominions of Spain, and rejoices in bull-fights."[62] Furthermore, Smith argued that America was the only power prepared to abolish the international slave trade. Despite acknowledging rumors that the South planned to reopen international traffic, he believed that, in actuality, both the interests of the South and its people's moral feeling would forbid it: "They have outgrown the barbarism of the African slave trade. May they speedily outgrow other barbarisms, which fall but little short of it."[63] Other Free-Soilers affiliated with the Republican Party accepted the view that free labor would naturally outcompete slave labor in the tropics and would do so without explicit federal intervention. Eli Thayer, for example, argued that Central America will "prove abundantly sufficient to carry emigration southward, even across many parallels of latitude"; a process that would ultimately "cut off . . . the umbilical cord of an embryo Southern Empire." Indeed, he speculated to much laughter, it was "cut off already," since "everybody knows the psychological consequences" of this act.[64]

More significantly still, Gerrit Smith modified the "freedom national" argument popular in antislavery circles and applied it to Cuba. He suggested the annexation of the island would cordon off enslaved labor—under American control—within a circle of freedom. Like a scorpion that appears to sting itself to death when surrounded by fire, these enslaved territories would soon become free through a combination of moral pressure, economic exhaustion, and fugitivity. By tempering "the cruelties of Cuban slavery" and eventually "lead[ing] to its abolition," annexation, Smith believed, would "contribute, mightily, to the overthrow of the whole system of American slavery."[65] Contained within America, the "institution" would be isolated from the rest of the world and subject it to international condemnation. In his final letter to his constituents, he wrote: "Let all the other nations of the earth shake themselves of slavery—even though it be into the lap of America. For were the whole of the foul thing gathered there, no sympathy with it could be found elsewhere; and, hence, its years would be few."[66] This international pressure would combine with the beneficial effect of American culture and institutions in bringing slavery to an end. Despite rejecting the more forceful assertions of American exceptionalism, Smith nevertheless believed "bad, as we now are, even in that case, few of our neighbors would become worse, and most of them would become better, by becoming like us."[67]

In practical terms, Smith would not pay any sum for the island. He claimed that although he would not pay $250 million for Cuba, nor $200, or even $100 million, he would "have her come" when "she wishes to come" and that he "would not have her wait, always, for the consent of the Spanish government." Rejecting the frequent accusations that this put him in league with petulant expansionists in the grip of Slave Power, Smith cried, to great laughter in Congress, "Now, if this is *filibusterism,* then all I have to say is 'make the most of it!'"[68] Although Gerrit Smith was too much an abolitionist to constitute a supporter of the Young America movement, prominent Young America Democrats did express their admiration for his Jacksonian principles. New York's John A. Dix, for example, wrote, "He makes strong antislavery, and reform and free trade speeches."[69] Although historian Yonatan Eyal attributes this admiration to Dix's antislavery credentials, it could also reflect his support for Smith's Jacksonian ideology, which not only included free trade but also territorial expansion. Like John O'Sullivan, Samuel Tilden, Thomas Kane, and many other Young Americans, Dix's antislavery beliefs were most significant insofar as they related to a broader Jacksonian vision—one that took all these men back into the Democratic fold after the Free-Soil revolt.

Similarly, Parke Godwin's publication *Putnam's Monthly Magazine* disagreed with "those who think that the possession of Cuba by the United States, would strengthen the hands of the supporters of the slave system in America itself."[70]

Instead, one writer stated that it was his "conviction" that "it would just leave the slave question where it is; while, at the same time, it would effectually put an end to the traffic in slaves, at least in as far as Cuba is concerned."[71] Furthermore, although keen to discredit the South's corrupt and outdated foreign policy, Godwin himself was somewhat sympathetic to the spirit that lay behind filibustering expeditions. In an article in *Putnam's Review,* he proclaimed, "We cannot . . . regard the disposition of the people, even those of more wild and turbulent spirits, who yield too unreservedly to the intoxication of a pervading influence as a mere marauding and piratical rage."[72] Apparently, "beneath the superficial propensity" to exert influence over other countries lay a "deep feeling of inspiration." Godwin maintained that only "the system of constitutional federal union" could "assure to each [state] a complete republican independence."[73]

Godwin was, in some respects, a strange ideological bedfellow for the Young Americans. He was an associationist, committed to the ideas of the French philosopher Charles Fourier. Drawing on Fourier's work, Godwin promoted a form of communal living within a "phalanx," or commune. Few Jacksonians moved in these circles. Proponents of Fourierism more often found a home in the pages of Horace Greeley's Whig paper the *New York Tribune,* with America's most prominent adherent, Albert Brisbane, writing a regular column. These radicals from the Whig tradition were growing in number during the 1850s and broke with many of the party's orthodox positions.[74] Some certainly embraced expansionism and were drawn into the orbit of Young America, which, for its part, saw itself at the vanguard of the Democratic Party.[75] But the associationists' emphasis on social interdependence and the subversion of traditional gender roles sat uneasily with the Democrats' stress on the political and social independence of the white male sovereign. For the most part, Godwin remained alienated from his fellow travelers. Before the Mexican War he wrote a famous letter to the Fourierist magazine the *Harbinger* chastising the American Union of Associationists for passing an official condemnation of the conflict. Echoing the Young Americans, Godwin admitted that he wished the extension of democracy could be done "without 'war' and without 'slavery'—but if those two subjects are accidently involved in it [he] would rather overlook the incidental evil than fail of the greater good."[76] In another letter justifying his stance, Godwin argued that the associationists' "universal scheme of social regeneration" should not be confused with the "narrow" and "unpatriotic sentiments of a one-sided and bigoted moralism."[77]

Like Godwin, the poet Walt Whitman was a former contributor to the *Democratic Review* who carried his support for territorial expansion into the Free-Soil movement. During the presidential contest of 1856, he published a pamphlet entitled *The Eighteenth Presidency* that betrayed the same expansionist fervor with which he had supported the Mexican War a decade earlier. He wrote, for example, that the United States had started to colonize "the shores of the Pacific" and the "Asiatic Indias." This expansion of American principles would usher in a new era in the history of human progress: "On all sides tyrants tremble, crowns are unsteady, the human race restive, on the watch for some better era, some divine war." Conflating technological and moral progress, he wrote that America's expanding influence, aided by the telegraph and printing press, would do nothing short of "re-making" the nature of "man."[78] Like Smith and Godwin, Whitman wanted "no reforms, no institutions, no parties" to govern this new age, but simply "a living principle as nature has, under which nothing can go wrong."[79] Specially addressing Cuba in 1851, Whitman wrote that "it is impossible to say what the future will bring forth, but 'Manifest Destiny' certainly points to the speedy annexation of Cuba by the United States."[80] In *Democratic Vistas,* which was mostly written during the 1850s, he predicted, "There will be forty to fifty great states, among them Canada and Cuba."[81] These pronouncements suggest Whitman still adhered to the same expansionist ethos that made him an enthusiastic supporter of the Mexican American War, when he wanted Texas "to come under the wings of our eagle" as part of a political system that could "extend to any extent."[82]

There is some evidence to suggest that, despite his Free-Soil politics, Whitman retained a residual loyalty to the Democratic Party throughout the 1850s— even supporting Douglas before he finally voted for Lincoln in 1860. Although his newspaper, the *Brooklyn Eagle,* backed the Republican candidate John C. Frémont in 1856, Whitman's editorials argued for a Democratic candidate who would represent a middle way between Frémont's antislavery position and Buchanan's tacit support for the Slave Power—possibly someone like Stephen Douglas, whose enthusiasm for territorial expansion seems to have chimed with Whitman's. In 1858 the poet wrote in the *Brooklyn Eagle* that he wanted "a great middle conservative party, neither proscribing slavery, like Seward, nor fostering it, like Buchanan."[83] Since he was comfortable with expansion farther southward and deemed slavery's "doom" already "sealed," it is perhaps fair to class Whitman alongside pro-Douglas Democrats like William Richardson and Edward Marshall, who believed a renewed commitment to Jacksonian nationalism was perfectly compatible with the eventual extinction of slavery. Like many of this group, Whitman imagined that the future for Blacks was in Africa, since "nature" had set her "seal" against racial amalgamation.[84]

Just as Young Americans believed America's intellectual and political life were intertwined, Whitman's support for territorial growth went hand-in-hand with his status as a poet. The *Brooklyn Daily Times* argued that Whitman's literary talents made him comprehensible to humanity as a whole. He was an example "for the present and future of American letters and American young men, for the south the same as the north, and for the Pacific and Mississippi country and Wisconsin and Texas and *Canada and Havana* just as much as New York and Boston." Similarly, Whitman was confident that American expansion was "in the interest of mankind," precisely because in the Romantic culture of the mid-nineteenth century, poets were perfectly placed to interpret human nature.[85] For Young Americans, natural law constituted the voice of the masses, independent of congressional enactments or customary practices. As a Democrat embedded in these Romantic sensibilities, Whitman therefore believed he could express a popular voice that "can be neither captured by representation nor finally embodied by political institutions."[86] As this voice had inherent moral authority, popular support for the Mexican War was sufficient justification for America's "claim to those lands . . . by a law superior to parchment and dry diplomatic rules."[87] Similarly, in the preface to the 1855 edition of *Leaves of Grass,* he wrote that the poet "imaginatively" "incarnates" the nation's geography, including the "Texan and Mexican and Floridian and Cuban seas" and those "off California and Oregon."[88] The political role of the literary figure in Whitman's writings echoed that of Shelley, who deemed poets "the unacknowledged legislators of the world."[89] As nature became a source of political authority, the Romantic poet was perfectly placed to interpret its laws, even foreseeing how the nation would grow in the future. Similar ideas about the political purpose of literature had long been found in the pages of the *Democratic Review.* Southerner William Gilmore Simms chose to title a poem on the Oregon crisis, *Progress in America; Or, a Speech in Sonnets, on Great Britain and the United States; not delivered either in Parliament or Congress.*[90] Proudly declaring that this speech was "not delivered in . . . Congress," Simms drew attention to its political status as a speech while emphasizing that the proper context for such a political document was outside the formal legislature. Reporting on the nation's progress was clearly the preserve of the poet, not the politician.

The political space in which Free-Soil expansionism flourished certainly narrowed during the 1850s. In the early republic, Jeffersonians could talk confidently about extending free labor over the territory purchased from Napoleon in 1803 as part of the Louisiana Purchase. But bound labor proved to be highly profitable in Mississippi and Alabama, and then in parts of Missouri when it was admitted as a state in 1820. Later, in the 1840s, the annexation of Texas strengthened the South even further, while the growth of explicitly proslavery nationalism made it difficult to ignore the chorus of Southern voices calling for tropical acquisitions.

In this context, support for the expansion of free labor seemed to ignore the reality of imperial politics in the nineteenth century. In their confident assertions otherwise, Young Americans appeared to be politicking or providing a fig leaf for the expansion of slavery. Stephen Douglas, for his part, was often ambiguous about the future of slavery in the tropics, allowing both Northern and Southern Democrats to lay claim to the region. To unite the party and placate slaveholders ahead of the 1860 election, Douglas promoted the annexation of Cuba as a slave state in front of an audience in Alabama. In this speech, he made the seemingly bizarre claim that abolitionists would come to accept slavery if they migrated to a tropical climate.[91] Understandably, Republicans accused Douglas of collaborating with Southerners to strengthen their peculiar institution. Greeley's *New York Tribune* was adamant that the movement for Cuban annexation was a betrayal of the liberal cause. The paper threw its support behind the "the revolutions in Europe" that advocated the "Enfranchisement and the Elevation of the Laboring Class," while the "'revolution in Cuba'" sought "to leave the cultivators of *her* soil in the position of beasts or chattels."[92] Undoubtedly, Douglas was making cynical political calculations throughout the decade and courting proslavery Democrats for whom the protection of their labor system was more important than popular sovereignty for white men.[93]

While antislavery politicians slandered Douglas as a Southern puppet, not all proslavery Democrats saw things that way. Although Douglas made an explicitly proslavery case for annexation in Alabama, more often he was silent on the issue, implying that slavery would be left up to a popular vote. This was totally inadequate for most proslavery figures. Indeed, the first day he arrived in Alabama, Douglas was pelted with a stream of eggs.[94] Many Southerners, in line with their Northern counterparts, simply rejected the idea that popular sovereignty would facilitate slave labor in Latin America. Fire-Eaters refused, for example, to support Douglas's annexationist plank in the 1860 election without an explicit federal guarantee for slavery. And, in the end, Douglas's expansionist program probably attracted far more support north of the Mason-Dixon line than it did in the South.[95] We cannot, therefore, discount the idea that Douglas believed he was using the South, rather than the other way around.

Moreover, on their own terms, Douglas's ideological commitments were compatible with the acquisition of Cuba as a slave state. His desire for a lily-white republic, free from Black labor of any kind, might have led him to oppose slavery in the most abstract sense as a threat to the white population: Young Americans freely admitted that slavery would continue to degrade white masters in the tropics. But out of all the options facing the United States in the 1850s, a proslavery Cuba was most compatible with the political rights of white men—as Douglas envisioned them. Enslaved laborers would be transported from white communities on the US mainland to an area with a relatively small white population where slavery already existed and nonwhite laborers were supposed to work efficiently. All this could be achieved without infringing on the democratic rights of white slave owners or giving political influence to what historian Joshua Lynn calls "the antislavery power."[96] The slave trade would, then, be abolished and the harsher elements of Spanish slavery meliorated under democratic rule. The trade-off for Douglas's free-labor ideology was that enslaved workers would continue to degrade Cuba's white population by association. However, out of all the options on offer, admitting the island with slavery intact could still be attractive to Democrats who otherwise supported free labor. Simply put, the economic and political gains to white male sovereigns could trump their tepid opposition to slavery, but this did not mean the latter stance was an utter sham or complete fabrication. Overall, among Northern and Southern supporters of Young America, and even among Northerners themselves, there were clearly differences of opinion on whether slavery would be a desirable or practical outcome of popular sovereignty in Cuba. John O'Sullivan came close to admitting that the economic gains from forcing Black workers to labor in the tropics, where they were relatively efficient, outweighed the degrading effects on their owners and the nation at large.[97] But in the end Young Americans' first commitment to the political rights of white men led many to tolerate either slavery or free labor, confident the most just and efficient system would arise without external intervention.

This hierarchy of priorities, with white male democracy at the top, explains why such a large proportion of the Northern population, who subscribed to what Stephen Maizlish rightly calls an "antislavery consensus," could support the annexation of Cuba as a slave state. In contrast, Graham Peck and James Oakes conclude that proslavery sentiment was actually more prevalent in the North than historians previously suspected.[98] Perhaps we will never know Douglas's personal views, or intentions, with any precision—if, indeed, he knew himself. What is more important was that he was able to draw on a discourse of antislavery expansion that was popular among his circle of Young America Democrats and beyond. Even by the end of the 1850s, these assumptions had considerable influence in the northern and western states, as Douglas's impressive popular vote in the election of 1860 shows.[99] To understand Young America as essentially antislavery is not to apologize for their complicity in the extension of the institution but to recognize that abstract opposition is sometimes not enough.[100] Moreover, it brings into view a form of Unionism not built around anti- or proslavery beliefs but around a vicious racial taxonomy and a naïve faith in the inherent morality of white communities. This mainstream American nationalism was opposed to Black labor of any kind, and it was deeply implicated in the perpetuation of slavery until, as we shall see, the world shifted from under Young America's feet.

6

A State of Nature

SLAVERY AND THE CRISIS OF DEMOCRACY, 1854–1857

After the Whigs lost the argument over the Mexican War in 1846, their conception of the Union came under increasing strain. Texan annexation in the West joined events in Europe to further embolden the Young America movement. American expansionism remained incredibly popular in the antebellum North during the early 1850s, while the Revolutions of 1848 popularized ideas about natural rights that the *Democratic Review* had promoted since its inception in 1837. Convinced that democracy was not just a political system but a natural means of ordering society, George Bancroft and Stephen Douglas saw no bounds to the expansion of the American republic.[1] Just as European nations were reordering themselves according to natural laws, America too could start again in the West. Vast areas of imagined wilderness provided a receptacle for the natural laws of political science and economics that the *Review* had promoted for so long. As one congressman explained, Americans were now "engaged" in laying the "foundations of society" as if they were still in the "state of nature."[2]

It is certainly true that in the aftermath of the Mexican War a burgeoning Free-Soil movement emerged, which divided the Democratic Party and allowed the Whigs to defeat the Democrats in the presidential election of 1848. A Democratic congressman from Pennsylvania, David Wilmot, issued a proviso in 1846 that proposed the exclusion of slavery from any new territories acquired during the Mexican War. Two years later, in 1848, former president Martin Van Buren left the Democrats to lead the Free-Soil Party into an election where they won 10 percent of the vote. Partly owing to these high-profile defections, Mexican War veteran Zachary Taylor beat Democratic nominee Lewis Cass in the election of 1848. The coeditor of the *Democratic Review,* Thomas D. Reilly, compared this setback to the counterrevolution in Europe after 1848. Just as France was "deceived into an outrage upon her existence," the United States was "similarly duped into the worship of a name merely victorious on the battlefield." Due to these problems at home, the nations' foreign policies suffered accordingly: "France did not defend Republican principle or existence in Berlin, Vienna or Budapest, neither did we, there, nor anywhere else, neither in Cuba, the Isthmus or Mexico."[3]

However, Democrats went on to win the election of 1852, heavily influenced by Young Americans' bellicose nationalism, and with this victory came a renewed hope about the revolutions in Europe. By midcentury the slavery question had been legislated to a draw due to the efforts of Whig statesman Henry Clay together with Douglas himself. In 1850 the Little Giant had helped pass a series of compromise bills, originally drafted by Clay, that decided the status of slavery in the vast areas of land acquired during the Mexican War. After Clay failed to pass the bills as a package, Douglas managed to squeeze them through Congress as individual pieces of legislation. In its totality, the so-called Compromise of 1850 guaranteed slavery in Texas but made California a free state. It also carved two new territories, New Mexico and Utah, out of land that Texas claimed on its southwestern border. Slavery in these areas would be left to a popular vote. In an effort to appease the South, the compromise included a much stricter Fugitive Slave Law, which made the federal government responsible for the capture and return of runaway slaves. For a time, this delicate balancing act was successful in bringing the Union together. President Millard Fillmore declared that it was a "final settlement" on a problem that had plagued the nation since before the founding. Democrats and Whigs both lined up behind the compromise, curbing the possibility of another Free-Soil revolt ahead of the presidential election in 1852.

The Compromise of 1850 was a curious blend of measures proposed by Democratic and Whig politicians—of a kind the Union would not see again. The hand of the "Great Compromiser" and old-line Whig Henry Clay was apparent in the careful balance between free and slave states. Moreover, the stronger Fugitive Slave Law, which suspended habeas corpus for self-emancipated people and compelled Northerners to assist slave catchers, was clearly a boon to the slave states. Indeed, many Northern Democrats with strong antislavery inclinations were horrified not only because this strengthened the South's hand but also because it infringed on states' rights north of the Mason-Dixon line.[4] Scholars such as Richard Blackett point out the new Fugitive Slave Law remained highly controversial. "For many in the North, especially those opposed to the extension of slave territory," Blackett argues, "the law became the one element of the Compromise that was totally unacceptable."[5]

But this did not stop politicians in both parties from lining up behind the Compromise of 1850 and justifying the Fugitive Slave Law in their own terms. The *Democratic Review*, as well as Young Americans like Stephen Douglas and

George Dallas, argued the law was compatible with Democratic principles. The *Review*, for example, claimed to be upholding the states' rights of the South. "Slavery is no national charge because we have no national slavery," one writer claimed, pointing out the institution had been abolished in the free states during the early nineteenth century.[6] Instead, the *Review* took aim at the idea that an appeal to individual conscience could trump the collective will of the community as manifested in the passage of the Fugitive Slave Law through congress.[7] One writer pounced on the notion that "individuals, and collections and associations of individuals, are justified in deciding that any law thus duly passed is wicked, unjust or inexpedient, in the light of individual conscience." Similarly, George M. Dallas complained that individual critics of the act aimed to trample on the rights of the "whole people."[8] For the *Democratic Review*, the will of white majorities trumped both the rights of Black people and the individual consciences of white Americans who could not command the support of the majority.[9] This argument appears to have been subtly different from Whiggish defenders of the Fugitive Slave Law, such as George T. Curtis.[10] Unlike the Young Americans, Curtis conceded that slaves did have natural rights. But he argued the "self-preservation" of the North meant the free states did not constitute the "soil" on which to secure them. This was a typically Burkean argument that the needs of a specific community should trump the immediate implementation of abstract justice.[11] That said, in spite of these arguments, Richard Blackett has correctly noted that the Fugitive Slave Law could not, in reality, command the respect of even the white majority in the free states.[12] For all their faith in majoritarianism, it would not be the first time the Young Americans' political program did not match up with the will of white communities.

Other elements of the Compromise of 1850 lent themselves more easily to the nationalist aspirations of Young America. The idea of popular sovereignty, which would decide the status of slavery in Utah, California, and New Mexico, had distinctly Democratic origins. Certainly, Douglas showed flexibility in the course of the debates over the future of slavery in the Mexican Cession. Before settling on popular sovereignty, he entertained two other proposals, one of which was President Polk's original idea to extend the Missouri Compromise all the way to the Pacific.[13] But popular sovereignty was first proposed by Democrats who wanted a Jacksonian route to ending slavery in the territories. Indeed, New York's Daniel Dickinson first coined the principle as a way to avoid the extension of the Missouri Compromise line in the dispute over Oregon statehood in 1847. Whatever happened, few denied Oregon would become free. But Dickinson feared that extending the 36° 30' line would sanction the expansion of slavery south of that latitude—almost indefinitely given the possibilities in

Latin America. By contrast, popular sovereignty was a means for communities of white male sovereigns to consecrate free labor in Oregon via a majority vote, without losing vast swathes of territory to the South. The principle thus originated in free labor—as well as Democratic—ideology.

Likewise, in the dispute over the Compromise of 1850, popular sovereignty was championed by proponents of free labor and was quickly couched in the language of Young America. Two congressmen from the western states with close ties to Stephen Douglas, Ohio's James Shields and Illinois's William A. Richardson, defended its immediate application in California, a territory that would almost certainly become free given the makeup of its population. They argued that slave owners' fears about congressional representation, just like that of Whiggish compromisers, mirrored Metternich's calls for a balance of power following the Napoleonic Wars. Shields told Congress, "The idea of equilibrium is the dream of a visionary." Moreover, "You cannot balance political power, you cannot weigh it in scales." After the fall of Napoleon, "the Holy Alliance" had apparently "tried a similar experiment," only to see it fail. The slave states were losing influence "every day," losses engendered "not by the action of Government, but by the action of irresistible laws—laws that control the moral, social and political condition of man."[14] William Richardson saw sectional tensions between the North and South as a mere sideshow rooted in outdated notions of realpolitik. Much more important were the inexorable laws affecting a gradual transfer of power from the eastern to the western states. Richardson asked the House, "If the slaveholding States are to have a balance of power, why should not the Atlantic States demand a balance of power also?" During the early republic, "the Atlantic States planned and won the Revolution"; they erected the "structure" of the Union. But while they once had "all the political power, [e]mpire and political power will soon pass from them to return no more."[15] Outdated notions of the balance of power could not prevent the operation of these natural laws.

Despite what Young Americans claimed, however, popular sovereignty was just one aspect of the Compromise of 1850, which sat alongside federal directives that denied settlers control over their own affairs.[16] Although Douglas's supporters argued it was rooted in principle, in fact the compromise rested on the same notions of the balance of power that Shields and Richardson so despised. New states, so desired by Douglas and his supporters, posed an existential threat to the fragile equilibrium on which the balance rested. To maintain the steady expansion of the Union, the Young America movement needed a principle that was applicable in all places and at all times. Indeed, these Democrats longed to see the organization of more territories to keep pace with what they called the "spirit of the age." With the quietening of sectional animosities, and with the

Democratic Party in power, the Young America movement looked to further their cause: the expansion of the Union and the extension of Democratic principles for white men. To do so, they were eager to facilitate the construction of a huge transcontinental railroad. From the very first issue of the *Democratic Review*, these gigantic infrastructure projects had been lauded as a means of binding the Union together and extending the Democratic principles of self-government and free trade. But since the new railroad would wind its way through the territories of Kansas and Nebraska on route to the Pacific, these areas required organization as states, either slave or free.

Faced with this dilemma, Douglas and his followers enshrined the principle of popular sovereignty within the Kansas-Nebraska Act of 1854. At its heart was a simple idea: white settlers in Kansas and Nebraska could adjudicate the status of slavery for themselves. Just like in the previous decade, Young Americans believed that democracy for white men was an inherently just means of deciding fraught moral issues. The collision of ideas and opinions among an enlightened race would generate a solution that was practical, economically efficient, and morally right. The only problem was that the Kansas-Nebraska Act repealed the sacred Missouri Compromise of 1820 that prohibited slavery north of the 36° 30' parallel. Among the free states this precedent was sacrosanct, and its overthrow signified the dangerous encroachments of an expansionist Slave Power. Furthermore, even among those Democrats who remained loyal to the party, the Kansas-Nebraska Act was controversial. Specifically, the legislation did not make clear when settlers could vote to outlaw slavery. Antislavery Democrats argued that a territorial legislature should be permitted to exclude slavery long before admission to the Union. This would assist migrants from the free states, who moved into newly opened territories much faster than slave owners slowed down by their human capital. By contrast, Southerners argued that the issue of slavery should be decided when the new state's constitution was ready for ratification. During the territorial phase, Southerners insisted that slavery should be protected by law. In the meantime, slave owners could move into the territory, intimidate free settlers, and make their presence felt at the polls.

The backlash against the Kanas-Nebraska Act took a massive chunk out of the Democrats' northern vote in 1856. The new Republican Party, whose public face was the explorer John C. Frémont, attracted a majority of former Whigs and several disaffected Northern Democrats. Although the Democracy won the election of 1856, the Republicans beat them in the north with 45.2 to 41.5 percent of the vote share and picked up vital states such as New York.[17] Conscious of his dip in popularity, Stephen Douglas declared that he could have made his way from Boston to Chicago by the light of his own burning effigies. By the middle of the 1850s, sectionalism came to dominate US politics, as an increasing number of Americans described themselves either in anti- or proslavery terms.

The renewed agitation over sectional issues during the 1850s presents a central problem for historians interested in Stephen Douglas and the Young America movement. As historian David Potter puts it, "Why would an administration triumphantly elected on the 'finality' platform . . . sponsor a measure so certain, as Douglas recognized, to raise 'a hell of a storm'?"[18] There were, of course, local concerns. The quicker Douglas could organize the territories, the faster his home state of Illinois would have access to the Pacific. If the eastern terminus of the proposed transcontinental railroad was located within its borders, the state would also benefit from the economic activity and population flows that would result. Douglas stood to gain personally too. He had profited substantially from investments in real estate outside Chicago, which boomed when a new railroad was constructed from there to Mobile, Alabama. Just in case the terminal was stationed elsewhere, Douglas hedged his bets. With the help of the successful financier William Walker Corcoran, he invested in a northern route with an eastern terminal at Superior City, Wisconsin. Fellow Young America Democrat Robert J. Walker was so enthusiastic about Douglas's decision that he declared his intention to bid on the route himself—which also proved popular with proslavery Democrats.[19] As head of the Committee on the Territories, Douglas presented Congress with a variety of options for the new railroad, but he made sure that he stood to gain from each one.

Furthermore, proslavery Southerners molded the Kansas-Nebraska Act to comply with their interests and ambitions. Douglas's original draft preserved the Missouri Compromise line in the territories, meaning that only free settlers could decide whether to include slavery at the constitutional stage. A proslavery Senate faction named after their shared living quarters—the F Street Mess—was instrumental in forcing Douglas to change course.[20] Missouri Democrat David Atchison, as president pro tempore of the Senate, threated to strip Douglas of his position as chairman of the Committee on the Territories if he did not explicitly repeal the compromise line. Douglas made alterations in a second version of the bill that still failed to satisfy the South. At this point, Kentucky Whig Archibald Dixon made a crucial intervention. Dixon invited Douglas for a carriage ride—a sure sign of shady activity during this period—where he convinced the Little Giant to make an explicit repeal. With Douglas on board, the F Street Mess swung into action. The senators used their connections to force a meeting with President Franklin Pierce on the Sabbath. Although he was reluctant to approve the changes, Pierce signed, knowing these influential Southerners could make or break two other pieces of legislation he wanted to get through

Congress: an acquisition of territory from Mexico known as the Gadsden Purchase and the free trade Canadian Reciprocity Treaty—both of which conformed to the Young America program. Without telling moderate Northern Democrats William Marcy or Lewis Cass, Pierce signed off on the repeal. Finally, Douglas rushed the bill through the Committee on the Territories denying the other members time for any meaningful scrutiny. This is, perhaps, the behavior of an archetypal political insider. Pressure from the Slave Power, old-fashioned politicking, and material self-interest all pushed a much-revised Kansas-Nebraska Act through Congress.

But the act had not been changed beyond recognition. None of these political or financial concerns were incompatible with the Young America program.[21] A desire for material prosperity and personal advancement, as well as an interest in a unified Democracy, had always complemented, rather than contradicted, the principles of the movement. Moreover, Young Americans had pushed free-labor policies past supporters of Calhoun before. In the previous decade the Northern Democrats had used the issue of popular sovereignty to make Oregon a free state without setting a precedent for the expansion of slavery below the Missouri Compromise line. Perhaps Democrats in the free states still believed they were calling the shots. More importantly, political ties to the South and economic interests do not fully explain the path to statehood that Douglas tried to pursue. The language of the Kansas-Nebraska Act was of a very particular sort, and Douglas's decision to press on in the face of widespread unpopularity, congressional stalemate, and political division is simply inexplicable purely in the context of the senator's practical and material considerations.

In fact, Douglas's support for the nationalism of Young America helps explain his behavior in this decade. Knowing the Kansas-Nebraska Act would be controversial, especially after the proslavery revisions, Douglas's ideological commitments made him proceed regardless. Despite the inevitable backlash, Douglas and his supporters constantly claimed that the people would come to embrace his principles due to the inherent justice of white majoritarianism.[22] Douglas's view of social progress as inseparable from territorial expansion and material prosperity also made the organization of the territories a matter of upmost urgency. The enlargement of the national domain not only took precedence over slavery but also presented its own solution to this moral problem. Meanwhile, Douglas woefully underestimated the potential for sectional conflict—he simply did not see the nation's ideological battleground in these terms. While historians will always struggle to gauge the sincerity of an individual's ideological commitments, the Young America movement essentially provided Douglas with a—very particular—solution to sectional strife, one that rested on a whole set of assumptions long detailed in the *Democratic Review*. As we shall see, the principled language Douglas settled on also constrained the scope of his political action further down the line. Although he certainly entertained other options, it was difficult for Douglas to abandon popular sovereignty when he had framed it in such idealistic terms. At crucial moments, both his supporters and opponents warned him of hypocrisy, which prevented him from wavering. Drawing on his Democratic roots, Douglas decided to "persevere and abide the consequences" in the hope of a final triumph.[23] It was, therefore, not the unbridgeable cleavage between Northern and Southern ideologies that paved the way for the sectional crisis, but the very political program that was supposed to bring peace and prosperity to the nation. Indiana's John G. Davis could not possibly have appreciated the irony when he declared in the House of Representatives that the railroad would remove "deep seated prejudices of a sectional character" that were caused by "want of correct knowledge of the habits, feelings and institutions of each other."[24]

Ideological polarization would not have emerged in 1854 had it not been for the misplaced confidence of Young America's Enlightenment project. Stephen Douglas drew on the young Democracy's expansive vision of the Union to silence those critics who accused him of reopening the sectional controversy for the sake of a reckless nationalist agenda. Douglas hit back, saying, "You cannot fix bounds to the onward march of this great and growing country. You cannot fetter the limbs of the young giant."[25] Similarly, John G. Davis praised his country for catching up with the spirit of Young America: "The idea of constructing a railway across this continent was, but a few years since, regarded by the masses as a wild, visionary and Utopian scheme." Davis chastised the "class of men who fold their arms and quietly sit down in the belief that human skill, science and improvement have reached the utmost limit of perfection" and who always "hang as an incubus on the skirts of progress and advancement." Fortunately, the "North American mind" had not "been idle or inactive." Having "read, thought and investigated," the American people had become convinced of the need for technological progress.[26] Cyrus L. Dunham, another Democrat from Indiana, shouted down a Whig colleague for "taking alarm at the 'progressive spirit of Young America'": "Fears of the progress of Young America! Sir, the hoarse murmurs of the Pacific unite with the resounding roar of the profound Atlantic to hush them into silence."[27] Outside Congress, Springfield postmaster Isaac Diller framed the act in generational terms. He told Douglas that from Washington it was impossible to "judge of the strength and depth of feeling in your favor" in their home state of Illinois. Diller informed his ally that "old men who have grown gray in the ranks of Whiggery threw up their hats and huzaad for you when I announced to them at the post office window that the Nebraska Bill had passed."[28]

For these Democrats, the principle of popular sovereignty was inextricably connected to intellectual independence from the Old World. Popular sovereignty was a new law for the territories that would replace "the plan of our territorial governments" that was "copied from the colonial system of Europe."[29] Like Young Americans before him, Cyrus Dunham believed the Democrats were fighting a much broader struggle to reform the international order in accordance with the "law of nations." Unless explicitly regulated by the Constitution, Dunham argued, natural and international law should control the relations between the sovereign states of the Union, just as they should the nations of Europe. Dunham's desire was to make "Kentucky and Indiana, Ohio and Virginia, stand in the same relation in which England stands to France, or France to Germany" under "a regulation controlled by international law only."[30] In this liberal international order, each state and nation would stand independent of each other within a vast political union, free from both federal and imperial interference.

Other western Democrats and Douglas supporters argued the natural right to popular sovereignty, even for territorial legislatures, was an American idea; replacing the vestiges of European despotism. David T. Disney agreed that "popular sovereignty" was an affront to "all forms of colonial government" that "assume . . . the people have no natural rights"—this position was "as old as the law of force, and has been applied in every age wherever it has ruled."[31] Similarly, in a pamphlet endorsing James Buchanan for president in 1856, the Democratic writer and phrenologist Nahum Capen described the universalism of Young America as such: "Democracy is based on eternal principles, and is limited to no season, age or nation. It is the conservator of humanity . . . a living system, based upon natural laws, responding to, and providing for, the unnumbered and unceasing wants of mankind, in all their multiplied relations." Capen considered that popular sovereignty was not a "wandering move" of "expediency" but constituted "the great laws of progress." Rejecting a geographically determined view of the nation, Capen wrote, "The great truths of Democracy are not of a *territorial* nature, but moral. Territory is an *interest* incident to progress, and its boundaries are marked for the conveniences of sovereignty." Dismissing territorial boundaries as arbitrary divisions of power, Capen's worldview totally subsumed the very notion of "interest" within an overarching commitment to democracy. In a world governed by "natural laws," there would be no need for competing or conflicting factions—the entire notion of the "balance of power" would be a moot point. Like territorial boundaries, the Democrat also "look[ed] upon slavery as an evil, yet to be removed by improvement in condition, and not as a power."[32] Certainly, not all Young Americans supported the Kansas-Nebraska Act. As we shall see, figures such as the Pennsylvanian Galusha Grow abandoned the Democratic Party, turning the language of Young America against Douglas and his allies. Others like Thomas L. Kane also rallied against the Kansas-Nebraska Act but remained within the Democratic Party. (Kane even claimed to be a "Douglasite" in 1858.)[33] Still, a core group did remain loyal to Douglas and rooted their support for popular sovereignty in the ideology of the Young America movement.

Democratic newspapers also understood "popular sovereignty" as a universal principle rooted in natural law that transcended the divisions between individual nations. The Democratic organ in Washington, DC, the *Daily Union*, stated that under the Kansas-Nebraska Act the North and South had agreed that "the natural law of peaceful and spontaneous immigration" should decide whether slavery would expand. It made the case that the Democrats were battling for the application of the same natural law in Kansas as the supporters of self-government in Europe: "The advocates of the 'divine right of kings' resorted to every shift, whether by argument or force, to crush out the idea of popular self-government—just as the Republicans are now laboring to defeat the application of the same idea in Kansas."[34] A strident advocate of the Kansas-Nebraska Act, the *Democratic Review* also spoke of popular sovereignty as a "natural right" to which both native-born Americans and immigrants were entitled by virtue of being white men. In 1856 one writer explained, "Those whose natural right it is to share the patrimony of freedom, are not, like plants, which neither think nor act, the product of a particular soil, but men manumitted and enfranchised from the slavery of despotic principles, by the force of intellect and virtue."[35]

The Democrats often saw the struggle in Kansas as a microcosm of a larger battle for the consecration of popular sovereignty as a natural right around the world. The future secretary of the Navy, Isaac Toucey, claimed that the "principle of popular sovereignty" had "penetrated far and wide into the Old Word" and had "already wrought a mighty change in the condition of oppressed and suffering humanity"—it was "destined to prevail wherever earth has an inhabitant."[36] Toucey was struck that the principle's applicability to "a hundred thousand Americans" needed to be "gravely debated" when—in reality—it should form the bedrock of a new international order. Without popular sovereignty Congress would become "the despotism practiced by the worst Governments over the most abject and down-trodden people of Europe, Asia and Africa."[37] At the vanguard of a global struggle, the Young Americans aimed their pamphlets at immigrants within the United States. In 1856 Robert J. Walker had issued his *Pittsburgh Letter* to galvanize support for popular sovereignty before the presidential election. This document was a powerful appeal for national unification according to Jacksonian principles; it was translated into French, Italian, and German to maximize its circulation among European immigrants. Walker pictured the crowned heads reveling in their "exulted shouts" while sowing discord in the United States. "Upon their gloomy banners" they would inscribe "as they believe never to be effaced, their motto, 'man is incapable of self-government.'"[38] Likewise, in his inaugural address as governor of Kansas, Walker tied the political struggles in Kansas to events in Europe. He told his audience that "our country and the world are regarding with profound interest the struggle now impending in Kansas: whether we are competent for self-government: whether we can decide this controversy peacefully. . . . Upon the plains of Kansas may now be fought the last great and decisive battle involving . . . the liberties of the world."[39] Ultimately, Walker saw the conflict in Kansas as one part of a broader struggle against centralized power, whether against the federal government on the American continent or the monarchical powers of Europe.

This faith in principle, rather than the balance of power, explains how Douglas managed to mobilize support, despite the initial unpopularity of the measure. The idea that popular sovereignty was inherently just imbued Douglas's supporters with false confidence. In free and open discussion, the principle would surely earn the recognition it deserved. One Democrat wrote to the Little Giant: "Your measure is gaining strength day by day. The people are just beginning to get hold of the doctrine upon which it is based. Popular sovereignty will win if it is thoroughly and properly discussed and understood." The same letter denounced older members of the party for not fully backing Douglas, accusing Lewis Cass of being "frightened at the resurrection of his own offspring."[40] Similarly, John O'Sullivan told Douglas that by arguing for the "non-intervention Principle," he had "performed a duty of no small importance . . . to the cause of truth and right; and I am satisfied that time will prove it, in spite of any present imaginary apprehensions in regard to the sentiment of the North."[41] Finally, Ohio's Samuel Cox praised Douglas for "keeping our democracy in line on the bill with a very big opposition against it," reassuring him that "opposition is growing less by degrees as men understand the question." Acknowledging the ideological similarity between himself and Douglas, Cox wrote that, despite only being introduced briefly, "I feel that I know you," so he would therefore speak "frankly." In any case, Cox declared, "You ought to know me" due to services he had lent the Little Giant's cause. If only the "alien clause was replaced," Cox predicted, "we can today whip the Whigs and abolitionists clean out." The only danger was men who had made up their minds about Douglas "a priori," "without regard to the principles of your bill," and were therefore immune from free debate.[42] This was reminiscent of protestors at pro-Nebraska rallies whose shouts drowned out Douglas's speeches in an attempt to force him off the stump. The fundamental division at work was as follows: those Democrats who held that the will of white men, expressed through free and open discussion, was itself a natural right and therefore the ultimate arbiter of national life arrayed against those who believed that certain rights were so sacred as to transcend racial divisions and be exempt from political debate.

Despite this liberal discourse, antislavery politicians in the free states accused the Democrats of acting to further the interests of Slave Power. Ohio's Salmon P. Chase asked Douglas to postpone Senate debate over the Kansas-Nebraska Act only to hastily publish a fierce denunciation of the bill titled the *Appeal of the Independent Democrats*. The *Appeal* argued that just as the Free-Soil movement had condemned the annexation of Cuba as a plot to extend slavery, an oligarchy of slaveholders intended to turn the territories into a "dreary despotism" that would be "inhabited by masters and slaves."[43] According to the *Appeal*, the slaveholding class conspired to make slaves of white Americans and European migrants by robbing them of their right to free labor. What was significant about this document is that it staked out a Northern ideology based around opposition to the Slave Power that transcended partisan divides. Indeed, the Independent Democrats were not Democrats at all. Signatories included conscience Whigs such as Charles Sumner and Joshua Giddings; former Democrat Alexander DeWitt; and Free-Soil stalwarts like Gerrit Smith, Salmon Chase, and Edward Wade. Both the fundamentalist and revisionist schools, which have dominated writing on the Civil War for over a century, argue the Independent Democrats unified the free states in defense of what Michael Holt calls a "republican" ideology under threat from an aristocratic slaveholding class.[44] Similarly, Eric Foner points out that "historians have tended to agree that the *Appeal* was one of the most effective pieces of political propaganda in our history."[45] The idea that a unified Northern ideology emerged in antagonism with its proslavery counterpart dramatizes the coming of the Civil War and creates a coherent narrative around competing worldviews.

But recent scholars have successfully questioned the significance of the *Appeal*. Mark Neely points out that anti-Nebraska papers neither mentioned the document itself nor drew on the defense of republicanism that informed its authors. In fact, Neely argues that opposition to Douglas's bill was self-consciously "conservative."[46] Papers tended to eschew attacks on aristocracy in favor of the charge that Stephen Douglas and his supporters had no respect for political compacts.[47] Rather than focus on the Slave Power, anti-Nebraska forces blasted

Douglas for his recklessness in abandoning the Missouri Compromise. William Penn certainly saw Douglas as a "transgressor," primarily for "trampling upon solemn compacts" and "exciting discord among brethren."[48] Others mourned the death of an older tradition of compromise associated with the conservative statesmen of a previous generation. Pennsylvania representative I. E. Hiester proclaimed, "It would have required even more than the nerve and enterprise of Young America to encounter the flashing eye and indignant sneer" with which the late Henry Clay would have greeted "this stammering effort to amend the last and noblest of his works," the Compromise of 1850.[49]

In this context, Young America's claim to the mantle of revolutionary nationalism makes more sense. Indeed, these Democrats believed themselves to be replacing outdated political compacts with principles. Explaining his support for Douglas's measure, Democrat John Cochrane told Secretary of State William Marcy, "I have no regard for compromises. They are made to be broken; and a repeal is their just fate. Substitute a principle; and the country will fair repose."[50] Young Americans thus continued to see their political role in terms reminiscent of the second party system rather than as brokering power between sectional extremes. For them, popular sovereignty was a practical and moral means of establishing free labor in the territories. The fact that the burgeoning Free-Soil movement disagreed did not reflect just their suspicion of the Slave Power but supposedly their hostility to the Democracy: Free-Soil supporters did not trust the decisions of white male settlers.

Still fighting the same battles as a decade earlier, the Young Americans believed both the Free-Soil movement and the proslavery Democrats advocated Whig principles in new forms. Since the Democratic program would lead to free labor, the Republicans' push for federal intervention seemed unnecessary and disingenuous. Similarly, the proslavery zealots would sacrifice the principles of the Democracy to expand their own labor system. Although racism was baked in from the start, Young Americans saw no place for slavery in their natural order. Wiley Harris from Mississippi compared Nebraska to "an island, fresh risen from the sea," where the Constitution could not tell wherever "black or a white person" should be enslaved.[51] Drawing on a fictitious state of nature, Democrat Cyrus Dunham argued, "If . . . a black man and a white man should rise up out of the ocean upon some naked island, over which human legislation had never extended, it would be very hard to decide by any show of natural law, which should be the slave." If free labor represented the triumph of natural law, then slavery was the result of positive government enactment. "At the outset," Dunham went on, the territories will be "without law, and without law as I have shown there can be no slavery," while only the "introduction of slavery" could be facilitated through "positive law."[52] Similarly, one newspaper claimed that slavery could only exist by "positive enactment" and therefore could not take root in an area untouched by human legislation.[53] Likewise, Robert J. Walker's Mississippi Report explained, "The right of the master exists, not by force of the law of nature or of nations, but by virtue only of the positive law."[54] Since slavery was condemned by "reason and the law of nature," it would be struck down by a majority vote, unprotected—as it was—by the same constitutional provisions as other forms of "property." Moreover, as slavery was a product of "positive law," it mattered little that slave owners wanted to prohibit legislatures from explicitly outlawing their "property" during the territorial phase—before settlers had formed a convention and were ready to draw up a state constitution. In an argument that echoed Stephen Douglas's Freeport Doctrine (articulated in his debates with Lincoln in 1858), Young Americans argued that territorial legislatures would not need to rule against slavery, since it required the passage of positive law to survive. If the territorial governments simply withheld this legislation, slavery would be denied the protections, like local police powers, on which its existence depended. White communities would, in turn, fall back on their natural rights: namely, to practice democratic rule unencumbered by the interference of slaveholders.

For Young America, Republicans not only hindered the cause of free labor by promoting unjust and unnecessary interventions but also by ignoring the effectiveness of popular sovereignty. Dunham specified that slavery was contrary to "natural right" but argued that settlers would only obey laws they had made themselves. "In a country like ours where the people have been accustomed to yield obedience only to laws self-imposed," he said, "they will but little respect those which may be imposed upon them, against their wish, by a legislature they have not selected."[55] Young America Democrats saw slavery itself as a result of federal overreach. *Democratic Review* editor George Sanders and historian George Bancroft both argued that the British had established it in the American colonies in the first place—a legacy propped up by the federal government ever since. Sanders implored the "republican statesmen of Europe" to believe that "the existence of slavery in the United States is an inheritance from the British government."[56]

Since the unconstrained exercise of territorial sovereignty was an inherent moral good, Young Americans believed that free labor would inevitably triumph over slavery. The Democratic program, featuring both racism and hostility to government intervention, was a more powerful motor toward a free-labor society than federal intervention. True friends of free labor, Young Americans maintained, would not lament the repeal of the Missouri Compromise. Rather, the Republican Party should rejoice that the territories had become what California's

David Broderick called a "common battle-field in which the conflicting rights of free and slave labor might struggle for supremacy." Echoing the free-labor argument that Eli Thayer and Edward C. Marshall had made for the annexation of Cuba, Broderick said that "Northern opinions, Northern ideas, and Northern institutions" would monopolize the new territories. Even a "dissolution of the Union" would not prevent the flow of free labor southward, according to Broderick: it could not "lessen the amount of immigration, or the number of free white men seeking for homes and a market for their labor." It was simply inevitable that the "compulsory labor of slaves" will give way before the "intelligent labor of free men."[57] Likewise, Dunham argued that Northerners "have nothing to fear from a free and fair competition with the people of the south."[58] "Scores of her hardy laborers" will "press forward into the western wilds with greater facility than a single slaveholder with his negroes and the paraphernalia of his plantation."[59]

Other Democrats believed the Kansas-Nebraska Act would bring about a "natural order" without slavery. Although initially opposed to the repeal of the Missouri Compromise, in 1856, Martin Van Buren held no doubt that popular sovereignty—properly enforced—would prevent the South's expansion. He told Samuel Tilden's brother Moses, "If Mr Pierce had from the beginning . . . interfered against all foreign interference" as soon as he "noticed the movements" of the Missourians, "Kansas would have been a Territory so decidedly free as to put an end to attempts to make it a slave State." Just like national independence movements in Europe, all Pierce had to do to ensure the success of popular sovereignty was to prevent the intervention of foreign powers—be they the federal government or the Border Ruffians of Missouri. Only then would the principle of nonintervention be vindicated in the "estimation of the world."[60] Successful in their application to any problem—including slavery—Democratic principles would finally assume their just influence on the international stage.

As well as taking the law of nature to mean universal political principles, the Democrats also drew on the physical geography of the United States to reinforce their argument that slavery was contrary to the natural order. In the Senate in 1854, Douglas maintained that the "law of physical geography" trumped the authority of the Missouri Compromise and undermined its status as a "solemn compact."[61] While the compromise reached in 1820 was based on "Congressional interference," the Kansas-Nebraska Act, like the Compromise of 1850, rested on "the laws of God" manifested in the "physical geography" of the United States. Similarly, in his inaugural address as governor of the Kansas Territory, Robert J. Walker told his audience, "There is a law more powerful than the legislation of man, more potent than passion or prejudice, that must ultimately determine the location of slavery in this country; it is the isothermal line, it is the law of the thermometer, of latitude, or altitude, regulating climate, labor and productions and, as a consequence, profit and loss."[62] Although former Whigs also referenced this environmental pseudoscience, the Young Americans used it—much like their theory of natural rights—to justify a long-running opposition to federal intervention. These environmental laws worked in tandem with God's will on earth, offering an alternative to the federal policy that Jacksonians had long distrusted. Putting his environmental determinism in a wider context, Walker declared that the isothermal line "can no more be controlled by the legislation of man than any other moral or physical law of the almighty"—of which the Democrats' doctrine of natural rights was one.[63]

Of course, the idea that the inherent dynamism of free laborers, combined with the laws of physical geography, shaped the development of the West was an illusion. In fact, enslaved labor, the power of the state, and the manipulation of the natural world had always been key factors driving the settlement and economic exploitation of the American continent. The Bank of the United States, which was hated by Democrats of all kinds, had played an important role in this story. By 1832 lending by the bank in the lower Mississippi valley was sixteen times the level it had been in 1824.[64] Federal intervention in the economy thus provided a vital source of credit, allowing speculators to purchase large swathes of land. Rather than facilitating the emigration of free labor, the majority of these loans went to powerful slave-trading partnerships. Enslaved labor proved especially useful in building levees to prevent flooding in the fertile land around the Mississippi River.[65] To be sure, the Bank of the United States was a distant memory by the 1850s, while slavery likely would not have proved as central to the development of Kansas as it had further south. But Young Americans still ignored the historical role of federal intervention and bound labor in the settlement of the West.

Furthermore, in the mid-nineteenth century, the federal government continued to fund the infrastructure that brought western produce to an international market and to raise troops to forcibly remove indigenous populations. Indeed, their mania for national expansion and economic development at times led even Young Americans to embrace a larger role for intervention in the economy—polices that violated their professed faith in the natural law and their opposition to international improvements.[66] John O'Sullivan, for example, advocated federal aid for the construction of a canal across the Isthmus of Darien (the Isthmus of Panama), while Stephen Douglas defended appropriations for harbor improvements on the Illinois River.[67] Yet Douglas dodged the traditional Jacksonian argument that federal intervention in the economy favored some states at the expense of others. In Douglas's estimation, the fact that the waterway connected the Atlantic to the Gulf of Mexico meant improvements could be justified in the interests of national commerce. Moreover, these inconsistencies should not lead us to dismiss Young Americans' ideological concerns in their entirety but rather acknowledge how these mythologies rubbed up against the realities of western expansion. Overall, the huge amounts of private capital flowing into the United States by the 1850s made federal intervention in the economy less of a divisive issue than it had been. Foreign investment in the antebellum era peaked in 1853, diminishing the government's role in economic development.[68] Exploiting this situation, Young Americans, more often than not, argued these private revenues should fund much-needed infrastructure in the West.[69]

The Dissolution of the Whig Party and the New Radicalism

As a distinctly Northern opposition to the Kansas-Nebraska Act took shape after 1854, formative ideologies rooted in the old second party system still mattered. Despite taking many different political trajectories, ex-Whigs in the Northern states remained uncomfortable with the idea that popular sovereignty was a natural right for white men.[70] Even when this diverse group agreed on little else, many former Whigs simply could not accept the idea that natural and divine law arose from a mere majority vote. Some could not countenance the imposition of natural law at all. Just like the Democratic Party, the Whig Party of the 1850s had always been a loose coalition containing progressive and conservative factions. On the one hand, there were patrician conservatives, such as Rufus Choate, who were hostile to immigration and believed in cultural deference to Britain. On the other, there were progressives like Charles Sumner, who welcomed new arrivals from Europe, talked confidently about the Revolutions of 1848, and supported the United States' intellectual and cultural independence from her former imperial master. Both factions urged compromise over slavery and faith in positive law during the 1840s. But in the 1850s the two groups diverged. The progressives took a principled opposition to the expansion of slavery, rooted in the idea of positive moral government and the federal guarantee of natural rights—not to democracy but to the fruits of one's labor. This stance earned them the name "Wooly Whigs," based on their alleged sympathy for "wooly haired" slaves. Conversely, the conservative faction, known as the "Silver Grays," advocated the preservation of the Union at any cost. Some believed in the existence of natural rights to the fruits of one's labor but argued these should be subsumed to preserve the nation as a geographical, cultural, and political community. Others rejected the idea of natural rights altogether, claiming that whatever rights Americans enjoyed emanated from the stability and prosperity engendered by the Union.

As historians like David Potter have demonstrated, it was these tensions over both immigration and slavery that divided the Northern wing of the Whig Party during the 1850s and ultimately brought about its demise in 1854.[71] After the Whig Party imploded, the more progressive wing took their antislavery convictions into the Republican fold. By contrast, the Silver Greys joined the Know-Nothings, due to their hostility to immigration, and later the Constitutional Unionists, to preserve the nation as it threated to split in two. Some even joined the Democratic Party, although more out of a desire to preserve the last bisectional force in politics than respect for its ideology. But regardless of their new political homes, all these former Whigs were united in one fundamental way. Just like in the previous decade, politicians from the Whig tradition opposed the idea that popular sovereignty constituted a natural right for white men. The more conservative Whigs dismissed all talk of natural rights as mere "glittering abstractions," while the progressive faction argued that slavery violated natural law and was therefore exempt from the democratic process.

Looking at his political writings from the early antebellum period through the Civil War, there is little doubt that man of letters Sidney George Fischer was in the conservative camp. Fischer noticed that the Young Americans were proposing the same principles with the Kansas-Nebraska Act that had been so controversial in the 1840s. In one political tract he wrote, "The principle announced by the President is precisely that on which Dorr, of Rhode Island, assisted by a rabble rout of followers . . . undertook to overturn the government of a populous and flourishing state." He criticized the metaphysical pretensions of Democratic Unionism, claiming "ideas, principles, are sharp tools to play with, and he who uses them has need of a mind that can see far into the future and calculate remote consequences."[72] During the political tumult of the 1850s, this arch-conservative sided with the Constitutional Union Party. Nevertheless, Fischer found something to admire in Lincoln's political outlook, applauding him for sharing the same attitude toward the Union as Henry Clay. Undoubtedly, Fischer admired some Republicans for their hostility to Douglas's newfound doctrine of popular sovereignty and for their fidelity to older ideas.

The conservative periodical the *North American Review,* which had rallied against the Dorrites ten years earlier, shared Fischer's opposition to Douglas's supporters within the Democratic Party. One article warned that the question of slavery was too sacred to be left to the whims of majority rule. In contrast to the mob, the "enlightened, patriotic, and humane people, are shocked by the monstrous dogmatism that denies to them the power to forbid forever the establishment of slavery, or polygamy, or castes, or sutteeism, or cannibalism, or any other wrong . . . within the limits of their common territories."[73] Popular sovereignty was a political right based on membership in the national community rather than simply the white race. The *Review* referenced the situation in Georgia after the American Revolution, arguing that "wise and good men" struggled to consecrate the state for free labor, only to have their voices drowned out by popular rule.[74] Indeed, the state's founder, James Oglethorpe, had modelled Georgia on the Enlightenment principles of the eighteenth century. Oglethorpe had wanted to create a home for British ex-convicts and paupers where slavery and alcohol would be outlawed. But, in pursuit of profit, planters from the nearby Carolinas migrated and quickly changed the law. The colony, which had been conceived with such high ideals, ended up one of the first states to secede from the Union before the Civil War.

The *North American Review* was adamant that popular sovereignty was not a natural right for white men. Those "inevitable deductions from the mere fact of [man's] creation"—contained within the Declaration of Independence—entitled people to "life, liberty and the pursuit of happiness," but not the right to vote.[75] For the *Review*'s readers, democracy involved competing freedoms and interests. There was no voice of the people that conformed to the voice of God, nor was there an economic order that could function without trade-offs or compromise. One person's decision to pursue a particular policy enhanced his individual liberty only at the expense of another. For all their talk of "organic" nationalism, conservative Whigs acknowledged the reality of class interests. Unlike the Democrats, however, Whigs sought to balance these competing claims within an overarching whole rather than overcome them entirely through struggle. It was "modern Democrats" who claimed power over others as a "personal prerogative"—"for each inhabitant of a free state in virtue simply of his age and sex."[76] Democrats were misguided to talk about popular sovereignty in terms of "eternal justice" or "eternal truth" without "acknowledging that there are any limits to its operation or that it is open to any more question . . . than a man's right to his life, or to the fruits of his industry." It was dangerous for "every ignorant peasant" to hear that voting is a "right to which his age and sex entitle him . . . not simply by the laws of the land, but by the laws of nature." In a direct shot at Young America, the publication complained that the "modern" Democracy "generally manage to cover everybody who directly assails them . . . with odium . . . and drive him into private life as . . . an 'old fogy.'"[77]

The Protestant clergyman Caleb S. Henry shared the *Review*'s distinction between the natural right to personal autonomy and the political right to popular sovereignty. Henry made the case that "logical deductions from metaphysical principles of absolute right, when carried recklessly out in practical application to great social questions, are often very absurd and mischievous." Instead, he argued that it was "quite enough" to fall back on the ancient principles of personal autonomy laid down in the Declaration of Independence, but not to argue that the Union was grounded in "natural justice" or in "any general theory of human rights."[78] Henry believed the fallacy of Douglas's nationalism was that it confused the idea of universal right with the concept of democracy. In fact, the Declaration of Independence did not refer to "political rights[,] for these are not *natural* but prescriptive rights" entrusted by virtue of belonging to the nation and not common to all humanity.[79]

After the implosion of their party, then, former Whigs continued to oppose Young America. In particular, all pushed back on the idea of an unqualified right to majority rule that was rooted in nature—even for white men. But during the 1850s their political priorities did begin to change. While the Whig Party had advocated an organic conception of the Union on which the right of self-government depended, many former Whigs now stressed their own—alternative—conception of natural rights. Situating ethical foundations in a new state of nature, these figures could not rely on their historicist view of the Union. After all, the territories had no coherent American history or culture to bind them to the existing states. In this new political context, these ex-Whigs found themselves on more radical ground, wrestling with the essential dilemma of liberal nationalism: How should the universalist idea of natural rights be reconciled with the particularist demands of national existence?

Certainly, some ex-Whigs proposed some very conservative answers. They argued the territories should be carved up by a geographical line to retain equilibrium between free and slave states. But many others made an explicit defense of their understanding of the liberal tradition and clarified its relationship to the nation. Threatened by Young America's Democratic foundations for national existence, these Whiggish figures proposed an alternative version of natural rights: that the rights to life and to the fruits of one's labor were the only pre-political principles, and incorporated races that almost all Americans excluded from the political community. They thought that the nation had an obligation to resist the spread of slavery—which would actively infringe on natural rights—to areas where it had not previously existed. Similarly, Young America's faith in popular sovereignty could not be allowed to become the highest moral value within the Union. If these two battles were lost, the nation would be robbed of its moral force in the world, becoming another state mired in European realpolitik or actively furthering the cause of despotism. Previously wrestling with a more cautious and conservative Whig Party, Young Americans were thus forced to contend with this principled stance, as articulated by the Republican Party. In some respects, the movement had become a prisoner of its own success. It had not only forced the question of territorial organization onto the national agenda but also pushed a radically Democratic version of natural rights into the mainstream. To resist, previously conservative figures staked out more radical positions and joined the ranks of the antislavery movement.

We see this transition most clearly in the thinking of former Whig Abraham Lincoln. Before 1854 Lincoln did not mention the Declaration of Independence in his political writings or speeches. As he declared in his debates with Stephen Douglas in 1858, the Whig Henry Clay was his "beau ideal of a statesman."[80] Following Clay's conservative course, Lincoln urged fidelity to the Constitution, including the protections afforded to slavery where it already existed. That is not to say the Whigs were amoral or lacking a conception of natural or divine justice. Outside the political realm, they channeled these impulses into evangelical reform. If the Union remained secure, then moral reformation, along the lines of evangelical Protestantism, would facilitate the extension of natural and divine law. Thus, Lincoln could implement legislation he profoundly disagreed with, such as the return of fugitive slaves, in order to preserve national stability. To keep the nation together, many Whigs argued that observing existing laws was in itself a religious duty. At the same time, Lincoln could rest assured that natural law would finally triumph. If the majority of the nation was still committed to God's "higher law," progress was possible, and slavery would be eradicated eventually.

After the passage of the Kansas-Nebraska Act, Lincoln took more decisive action. Faced with Young America's new conception of natural rights in the territories and an expansionist Slave Power, he could no longer be sure the nation was heading in the right direction. There was no guarantee that local white communities would make intrinsically just decisions, since self-government was a political procedure rather than a natural right. Pushed to respond, he joined the antislavery movement alongside many of his former Whig colleagues. The idea that popular sovereignty was a practical route to free labor held little appeal for him. The abolition of slavery was not sought because it happened to win favor among white communities but because it was inherently just. At the core of his ideology, Lincoln distinguished between the right to the fruits of one's labor— rooted in natural law—and the political privileges that came with membership of the national community. In a speech in 1858, for example, Lincoln claimed that "necessity" forbade "political and social equality" between the races.[81] Moreover, in a Springfield speech in June 1857, he told his audience that the Black slave woman "in some respects . . . certainly is not . . . my equal; but in her natural right to eat the bread she earns with her own hands without asking leave of any one else, she is my equal, and the equal of all others."[82] Historian Dorothy Ross highlights this distinction between the natural right to labor and the political right of suffrage. She argues, "Lincoln and the free soil movement forced a wedge into the right of self-government to avoid equal citizenship for blacks." Lincoln distinguished between "membership in humanity"—which entitled people to freedom from slavery—and "membership in the nation."[83] The way Lincoln "made the nation into a moral source of universalist liberal principle and a living center of spiritual force," then, certainly echoed the Young America historian George Bancroft.[84] But Lincoln redefined the universal principles underlying nationality to mean freedom from slavery rather than recommending O'Sullivan's "Democratic principle," which encompassed much more: popular sovereignty, free trade, and territorial expansion, as well as a more tepid commitment to the extinction of slavery in the fullness of time.

Many Democrats, including several from the Young America faction, joined these former Whigs in the Republican Party. Unhappy with Douglas's interpretation of popular sovereignty, they were less concerned with the rights of the enslaved than those of white communities. These figures believed that slavery, by its very nature, relied on federal intervention. The mere presence of slave owners among the democratic communities of the western territories prevented white men from exercising their political rights, especially if slavery could not be excluded until the formation of the state constitution. This argument sometimes came from figures who had been directly involved in the Young America movement and was couched in the same language of natural rights and generational difference. Galusha Grow, for example, was a Democrat from Pennsylvania who had called for intervention in the Revolutions of 1848 and reform of the American navy in the aftermath of the Koszta Affair of 1853—all in the name of Young America. After the passage of the Kansas-Nebraska Act, he turned on Stephen Douglas and rallied against his former party for betraying their principles. Grow passionately supported the Topeka Constitution, an antislavery document drawn up by settlers in Kansas without federal approval, viewing it as the legitimate result of the true principle of popular sovereignty. During the debates in Congress over its approval, many figures in the House of Representatives wondered whether there was a precedent for such an action. In language typical of the Young Americans, Grow bellowed, "What is the odds whether there is a precedent or not? . . . The existence of the Republic itself and its whole history are in violation of all precedent. . . . Truth, justice, and humanity need no precedent—they make them."[85]

As historian Matthew Karp has made clear, this sort of populist, anti-institutional ideology formed a vital component of the antislavery movement. Karp points out that the authority of "natural rights and popular democracy" was used to justify the extralegal action of the Topeka Constitution. In this context, the language of "Young America" was sometimes explicitly associated with the Republican Party. One editor in Ohio declared, "One of the strongest proofs that a mighty and wholesome revolution is involved in the present tremendous popular movement for Frémont may be found in that most of the old party hacks and political fogies of the country shrink from it. It threatens to abolish all the old party machinery, the corrupt cliques, the little regencies of old wire-pullers here and there."[86] As an explorer and western pioneer, the Republican presidential candidate in 1856, John C. Frémont, was also clearly calculated to appeal to the supporters of Young America. As historian Jon Grinspan writes, Frémont and his wife, Jessie (daughter of Democratic senator Thomas Hart Benton of Missouri), "promised youth, vigor, Democratic connections, and romantic adventure."[87] In the election of 1856, Frémont, then forty-three, and thirty-year-old Jessie contrasted with the stuffy old bachelor James Buchanan. The *New York Times* called Frémont "the embodiment of the spirit of Young America."[88]

Whig-Republicans found unlikely compatriots, then, in the form of Young Americans who bolted from their old party. Moreover, just as Burkeans began to adopt a more principled stance, new progressive groups took liberal ideas to greater lengths.[89] A growing abolitionist movement advocated the immediate application of natural rights, while socialist groups and labor movements made the case for the communal ownership of property. Thus, the Republican Party became a broad church, encompassing everyone from ex-Whigs who worshipped Henry Clay to truly revolutionary figures, with several Jacksonian Democrats in between. A decade earlier, progressive Democrats only had to protest against a crumbling status quo in the form of the Whig Party. Young America now had to defend an inherently unstable republic of its own making—one that had given rise to new forms of radicalism.

Young America's Conservative Transformation

Just like Young America, the "young" liberal movements in Europe faced new radical groups after 1848 who were determined to resist them. Although the revolutions of that year had certainly posed a powerful challenge to monarchists and conservatives across the continent, gains proved temporary and incredibly fragile. France succumbed to a dictatorship more violent than the old monarchical regime; the Crimean War plunged Eastern Europe into a conflict over the balance of power; and the British tightened their hold on India and Ireland after failed uprisings. But new "isms," in the form of socialism and communism, also threatened the liberal order with intervention, this time from below rather than above. Now, liberal and democratic ideas that had been deemed radical a decade earlier could be put to work defending the status quo—particularly in the protection of property rights. Alexis de Tocqueville, for example, advocated universal suffrage as a means of enfranchising the rural population in France because it was predominantly conservative. Tocqueville reasoned that voters in the countryside would oppose the radicals in Paris, thus protecting individual rights against the incursions of socialists in the capital. As J. A. S. Grenville has written, "The surest way to maintain the social order was to ask for its sanction by the majority through the electoral process."[90] For all the radical connotations previously attached to the term, democracy's conservative potential would continue to resonate from the mid-nineteenth century onwards. As historian Russel Kirk points out, British prime minister Benjamin Disraeli passed the Second Great Reform Act in 1867 upon the realization that "the great body of the English peoples are conservative."[91] Although not exclusively the property of conservativism, parts of the classical liberal agenda—including direct democracy—took on a conservative style and function after 1848, a trend that persisted in the conservative movements of the twentieth century.[92]

Meanwhile, in the United States, under Democratic watch, the territories seemed to be giving way to the same disorder that plagued European nations in the nineteenth century: the right of Kansas to govern itself was becoming as contested as it was in Hungary or France. Despite the Young Americans' great predictions, a cosmopolitan community was certainly not emerging from the shadows of national self-determination. Reluctant to change course or reevaluate their political outlook, how could Young Americans draw on conservative forces to stabilize the nation? And who could they turn to for blame?

The apparently reckless egalitarianism of the new Republican Party proved to be a convenient scapegoat—what Democrats termed "Black Republicanism." This new target appealed to an electorate terrified by political upheaval from below rather than oppression from patrician elites. It also made political sense for the Young Americans to single out the Republicans for blame: these predominantly Northern Democrats still had to abide by the proslavery extremists within their own party. That said, in private correspondence Douglas supporters did criticize Southern Fire-Eaters, like the Republicans, for their interventionist instincts. And, as we shall see, they did so more publicly as tensions in the Democratic Party worsened, culminating in the divided convention of 1860. Overall, radicals within both sections now threatened to wield the power of the federal government in service of what Young Americans considered dangerous ends.

An increasing number of more moderate Democrats blamed the Young America movement itself for this state of affairs. Many became critical of the term, believing that social progress had to be coupled with a renewal in the nation's spirit of moderation. At the Pennsylvania Democratic State Convention held in Harrisburg in 1856, William Montgomery of Washington County told the delegates, "We are emphatically a 'fast people'" who "begin to feel that we have been progressing too rapidly, and the masses with one accord demand of 'Young America' to halt in her headlong career."[93] Whereas in 1852 Pierre Soulé had pushed for a departure from Washington's Farewell Address on the question of foreign intervention, Montgomery argued that "we must go back to the true and tried statesmen of the past." Similarly, James Porter of Northampton said that "all we can ask" of Young America is to "take a little advice . . . from the experience of age."[94] Montgomery and Porter were typical of their party in supporting James Buchanan because of his conservative qualities. Despite his role in writing the Ostend Manifesto, Buchanan retained a reputation for conservative statesmanship at a time when the Democratic Party was moving away from the adventurism of Young America.

Sensing the changing winds of political opinion, Young Americans shifted their language accordingly. With independence movements in retreat across the world and state sovereignty threatened within the Union, Democrats like Stephen Douglas couched their program in more conservative terms. Their fundamental principles and polices remained unchanged. But, as in Europe, parts of the classical liberal agenda could now be put to conservative ends. The principles of direct democracy and individual liberty were turned against abolitionists and socialists, who threatened private property and social stability, and against proslavery Southerners, who compromised the rights of ordinary white Americans with their dangerous interventionism.

The Young Americans began to call themselves "conservative" as the radical connotations attached to their movement fell out of favor. In the 1840s and the early 50s, the Little Giant and his followers were almost synonymous with adventurism and the extension of the Declaration of Independence to embrace new, untried principles. However, Young Americans now claimed to be a force for moderation and conciliation. None other than Pierre Soulé, the author of the Ostend Manifesto, who had been exiled from France for revolutionary activities, declared that the "conservatism of the north" will "group around Stephen Douglas."[95] It is important to note, however, that neither Douglas, Soulé, or any of the

Young Americans had changed their commitment to the essential components of Jacksonian nationalism, nor did they eschew the idea of natural laws, which would have been so repugnant to an older generation of conservatives.[96] Rather, the world had changed around them. The advent of socialism, abolitionism, and more interventionist forms of liberalism, together with the death of patrician conservatism, had made popular resistance to interventionism a conservative, rather than a radical, force.

In Democratic discourse the idea of progress was more frequently welded to the term "conservative," while natural law was accompanied by a new strand of anti-intellectualism aimed at perceived elites. The moderate Democrat from Michigan, Lewis Cass, encapsulated the new combination of conservative and progressive values. For him, popular sovereignty was a universal principle encoded in the laws of nature. But it was also one that had been tested by experience rather than the theorizing common to abolitionism and socialism. In a speech in 1854, Cass drew on the language of Young America as he justified popular sovereignty according to those rights "written in the great volume of nature." He claimed that there were "certain inalienable rights which the bountiful creator has given to man as it emphatically announced in our Declaration of Independence." Nevertheless, Cass denounced those who sought to reorganize the American nation according to their political theories. The "questions of human rights" could not be "solved with the precision of a mathematical problem, substituting Euclid for Jefferson." Applying "the square and compass to human rights" was a "subject beyond our reach." To imagine "angels in the shape of Congressmen" governing the territories was to "make slaves of white communities." If congressmen attempted to impose their own ideas on the settlers, "political metaphysics" in America would play the same role "the sword" played in Europe. Cass trusted the Democrats Bright, Dickinson, and Dodge to be "on the side of human rights," owing to their patriotism and intellectual power, while, at the same time, he warned against the "philanthropists" who used political metaphysics to undermine the established principles underlying national existence.[97]

This opposition to "metaphysics," which was more often dubbed a priori reasoning, was a common one among Young Americans. Although he drew on the language of "divine law," Stephen Douglas argued that universal values were properly expressed through the will of the majority, not by an elite class of philosophers or clergymen. Douglas pushed back, in particular, against the outpouring of hostility towards the Kansas-Nebraska Act among the Protestant clergymen in the free states. Religious figures organized meetings to denounce Democratic policy and sent petitions to Congress to protest against the extension of slavery into the territories. As William Seward famously argued in the debates over the admission of California in 1850, these clergymen asserted that a "higher law" prohibited slavery in the territories, irrespective of the wishes of white majorities or the words of the Constitution. Douglas was careful to point out that he recognized the right to protest against government policy, but he resisted attempts by church leaders to dictate Congressional decisions over and above the wishes of the majority.[98] In response to the Republicans' assertion of God's higher law, the Little Giant exclaimed, "If we recognize three thousand clergymen as having a higher right to interpret the will of God than we have, we destroy the right of self-action, of self-government, of self-thought." True democracy would be undermined as Americans would simply "refer" political questions "to this body of clergymen" to inquire into whether they are "in conformity with the law of God . . . or not."[99] Douglas believed that the only moral response was to leave politics to "the people"—communities led by white men. He pointed out that "when God created man, he placed before him Good and Evil and endowed him with the capacity to decide for himself and held him responsible for the consequences of the choices he might make."[100] Similarly, George Sanders took aim at the idea of a higher law interpreted and sanctioned by religious authorities. But he also went after proslavery zealots, such as Virginia's Robert M. T. Hunter, who used this argument to defend the South. Although Sanders pointed out that "a man may, with the highest patriotism, become a revolutionist to overthrow an oppressive government," he could not do so in a democracy simply because "his religious sentiments" might "impel him." If a person insisted on following a higher law in conflict with the will of the white majority, he was obliged to renounce or leave the republican government under which he lived, becoming an exile or martyr.[101]

Democratic intellectuals like historian George Bancroft also believed that the voice of the people was an expression of God's will. Bancroft urged the people not to defer their judgement to a "superior" class of thinkers. In an 1854 lecture before the New York Historical Society, he declared, "The many are wiser than the few; the multitude than the philosopher; the race than the individual and each successive generation than its predecessor." He argued that "common sense" took priority over the wisdom of the philosopher, teaching that "each individual is to contribute some share toward the general intelligence."[102] On another occasion he claimed, "The husbandman or mechanic of a Christian congregation solves questions regarding God and man and man's destiny, which perplexed the most gifted philosophers of ancient Greece."[103]

Other Democrats shared Douglas's and Bancroft's skepticism toward intellectual elites, preferring to trust the conservative instincts of the common people. Thomas L. Kane, the Young America Democrat from Philadelphia, drew on the French social scientist August Comte to ground his liberalism in a positivist worldview that he defined in opposition to a priori reasoning.[104] Between 1830 and 1842 Comte published the four volumes that constitute his *Course of Positive Philosophy.* The Frenchman outlined three distinct stages of thought: the theological, the metaphysical, and the positivist. The theological stage dominated early phases of human history before giving way to metaphysical authorities that emphasized abstract rights. The final, positivist, stage was supposed to have arrived with the advent of social science in the mid-nineteenth century, which was meant to use logical deductions based on empirical evidence. Kane drew on these ideas to dismiss his Republican opponents as a priori thinkers. Conversely, he equated both popular rule and racial hierarchy with empiricism. As a former member of the Free-Soil movement, Kane explained that he became disillusioned when it failed to win widespread support among the American people. He argued that it was useless to win over such intellectual luminaries as "Emerson, the *Tribune* and Uncle Tom's Cabin" when antislavery could not convince "the champions of . . . fair play" who "profess the Gospel of the Declaration of Independence." "The true philosophy of our country," Kane insisted, was to study public opinion "with a view of understanding it," which would then allow the "law of our own social conditions" to be "deduced." Mirroring the language of Douglas and Bancroft, he argued that the "voice of the people" amounted to "divine common sense," and it was "to the world" "the voice of God."[105]

In another lecture, "Old England or New England—Who Will Govern the United States?," Kane rallied against the idea that philosophers and theologians rather than democratic majorities were the rightful guardians of the natural law. "As a Democrat and non-interventionist," Kane claimed, he "detested . . . a priori reasoning." Citing the empiricist philosopher Aristotle as the "greatest thinker the earth" has ever known, Kane complained that too many New Englanders tried to make the nation conform to their own ideals and prejudices. Having established "principles" with "rules of conducts based thereupon," they exerted power to "exact a complete conformity with them." They would establish a "theocratic dictatorship," disrespecting the "laws" of "elected men" by interrogating them "in terms of right or wrong." Turning his ire on the disrespect for majority rule among northeastern reformers, Kane recalled in horror how "a single line of father, son and grandfather in Massachusetts, can boast of having concocted and coddled the alien and sedition and Main Liquor laws, the anti-Masonry and anti-Texas movements around one and the same old family mahogany." In New England, Kane saw nothing less than "champions of Old England's imperial system." He hoped that one day Americans would discuss

Kansas's "right to enter the Union" and not "our privilege of compelling her to come in."[106]

In these speeches Kane conflated both popular opinion and racial hierarchy with empirical reasoning. Contrasting himself with the abolitionists, Kane believed that social laws could only be deduced through observing how people lived and thought. Democracy was inherently empirical because it allowed politicians to test whether policies worked without resorting to harmful federal interventions. This "scientific" perspective also lent itself to racism. If the lived experiences of the masses constituted an empirical reality, racial inequalities, or conflict between the races, became an observable fact. By the 1850s, then, the social sciences allowed figures like Kane to justify inequalities according to the principles of the Enlightenment. Thus, while modern historians sometimes associate the Enlightenment with abolitionist ideas about the brotherhood of man, this did not seem quite so clear to Americans in the nineteenth century. In fact, Kane correctly identified abolitionist ideas as secular outgrowths of religious thought that had been handed down through generations. Nevertheless, Kane was not, of course, as empirical as he liked to think. Convinced that his own work lay on the cutting edge, he failed to recognize the absurdity of what passed for social science in this period. Although he did not start from beliefs about the essential equality of human beings, he nonetheless assumed that scrutinizing evidence would facilitate the discovery of social laws—a supposition that was, in itself, more deterministic than evidence based.

Despite these inconsistencies, Kane fused liberal ideas with new conservative sensibilities and did so in a way typical of Young America in the middle of the decade. On the one hand, he believed his ideas were based on the most developed modes of social thought, while New England abolitionists, crowded around their "old mahogany," relied on outdated metaphysical reasoning. On the other, he showed a new distaste for literary culture and emphasized practical and empirical reasoning that typified conservatism. At heart, though, his shift toward more conservative discourse was a rhetorical, rather than a substantive, move. Kane still uncritically applied the "truths" contained in the Declaration of Independence to white men, while his empirical reasoning continued to betray the same universalist assumptions that Young Americans had long embraced. Indeed, many Whig-Republican politicians had a hard time accepting Young America's conservative credentials. From their perspective, the antislavery movement sought to defend ancient rights against the newfangled ideas propagated by "Modern Democrats." In a climate where political realities had been altered beyond recognition, former conservatives were forced to take uncompromising stands, while the radicals who had helped shaped the crisis tried desperately to conserve their imagined future.[107]

As what it meant to be a conservative became unsettled, the patrician elites of New England took a second look at the Democracy. In the 1830s and 40s, democracy was a radical proposition that still held negative connotations for many in the New England elite. Some preferred the term "republic," refusing to countenance the idea that the nation was "democratic" at all.[108] But in the 1850s people began to see democracy, even in its most direct incarnations, as a conservative feature of American institutions. Simultaneously, some of the New England elite flocked to the party of that name. These men were now convinced the Union could only be safeguarded through the same robust populism they had rallied against a decade earlier. In a decision that would have been unimaginable a few years before, patrician Whig Rufus Choate voted Democratic in the presidential election of 1856. In a pamphlet justifying his decision, this old Burkean went on the defensive. Choate had not "join[ed] the Democratic Party," he insisted, nor did he "retract" his "opinion on the details of its policy," nor "acquit it of its share of blame in brining on the agitations of the hour." But these trying times required an organization that would "fight fire with fire—to encounter by a sharper, more energetic, and more pronounced antagonism the precise type of evil which assails the State." Even the Democratic Party under Buchanan still "burned ever with that great master passion that this hour demands," Choate wrote. It was "a youthful vehement exultant and progressive nationality" that displayed "gay and festive defiance of foreign dictation." Although this spirit had led the party into "some perils" and would no doubt continue to do so, Choate believed that it was nonetheless required to save the Union from interminable division. After fulfilling this function, Choate could once again pass into that "minority of conservatism" that seeks to "temper" the influence of the Democracy.[109]

Even conservatives like Rufus Choate, who ended up voting Democrat, made their role as fellow travelers perfectly clear. Like former Whigs who had gravitated toward the Know-Nothing or Republican Parties, Choate still kept his distance from the ideology of Young America. Support for direct democracy was merely a strategy designed to fend off sectionalism, which had become an inescapable fact of American life. Choate retained an older vision of nationalism that valued the geographical integrity of the Union above all else. Even in the midst of the sectional crisis, the ideologies of the second party system continued to resonate.

But if some Whigs became fellow travelers out of a desire to preserve the Union for its own sake, Young Americans were still anxious to conserve what were perceived to be Democratic principles. In one letter, former president

Martin Van Buren told Moses Tilden that Americans should resist "flying to unknown evils," because the "conservative character of the Democratic Party" had a distinct purpose: to "preserve the sovereignty of states." By contrast, under the leadership of Frémont, the Republicans would preside over the "long lost ascendency" of "ancient federalism."[110] Although the party hoovered up what one historian has called the "conservative diaspora" during this decade, the Democracy did not merely become a vehicle for keeping the nation together.[111] In fact, even while courting former Whigs, the Young America movement, however misguided, never lost sight of the universal principles that were at stake in the decade before the Civil War. Samuel Tilden agreed with Van Buren that what the Republicans were proposing amounted to a dangerous infringement on state sovereignty, akin to European imperial power. He argued that the Founding Fathers formed the Union when the states "existed as independent sovereignties." They "might have constructed a system . . . imperial in character" that subjected "all the internal affairs of the states to the dominion of a centralized government," but instead chose to grant independence to individual states—a principle "binding" not only "by compact" but "by its intrinsic wisdom and righteousness." So great was this principle of nonintervention that Tilden could not imagine slavery coming to an end in any other way. "So wonderful are the laws of mutual action" resulting from state and territorial sovereignty, that they would "work for the welfare of all better than foreign government, and better than the propagandism of any system by foreign force."[112] Events in Kansas nonetheless confounded Tilden's naivety. The fight for popular sovereignty for white men became more desperate as the decade wore on, especially as the Buchanan administration came to sacrifice states' rights to the Slave Power.

1

Popular Sovereignty and the Struggle against Slavery, 1857–1861

Conflict had been a constant feature of life on the frontier since the Kansas-Nebraska Act passed in 1854, particularly in the territory of Kansas, where the climate was conducive to establishing slavery in some form. Border Ruffians sympathetic to slavery streamed in from Missouri, while Eli Thayer's Emigrant Aid Company struck back by organizing the emigration of free laborers. Fighting for its foundational principles, Kansas fell victim to the same violence and instability that characterized Europe and Latin America during the midcentury Age of Revolutions.[1] From the outset, antislavery forces were losing the battle to establish a free state. In December 1855 they made a doomed lunge for freedom by passing the antislavery Topeka Constitution. When the constitution was put to the settlers for approval in January the following year, most proslavery men boycotted the vote. Lacking the approval of the entire territory, President Franklin Pierce condemned the document. Although passed by the House of Representatives, it was ultimately held in committee by the Senate.

The proslavery settlers answered the Topeka Constitution with one of their own, drawn up at Lecompton in September 1857. Free-Soil settlers did not participate in the election for its approval—a process that was marred by corruption, with six thousand fraudulent votes cast in favor of the constitution. Nevertheless, Lecompton fared better in Washington, DC. Sympathetic to slavery and eager to preserve political order, it won the endorsement of President James Buchanan. With the official backing of the Democratic administration, it looked like slavery would prevail. Dissent, however, came from an unlikely source: Young America Democrats within Buchanan's party turned on their own leader. Having supported Buchanan in the election of 1856, Congressman Stephen Douglas did everything in his power to prevent the decisions made at Lecompton from becoming a reality. Aided by the work of Free-Soil lawyer Thomas Ewing Jr., who directed an investigation into fraudulent ballots, Douglas claimed the document debased the true principle of popular sovereignty and argued vehemently against its passage in Congress. Three senators from the western states, David Broderick, Charles Stuart, and George Pugh, allied themselves with Douglas in Congress, while outside Washington many others rallied to his cause. Free-labor advocate George Bancroft provided Douglas with historical precedents from the colonial era to delegitimize the Lecompton Constitution. Moreover, Robert Walker resigned from his position as governor of Kansas rather than oversee its implementation, despite being appointed by Buchanan just a year earlier. Finally, Philadelphia Democrat and prominent newspaper editor John Forney attacked Buchanan for crumbling before the will of Southern slave owners. Ostensibly abiding by the Kansas-Nebraska Act, Buchanan was being attacked by the same "progressive" Democrats who had introduced the legislation in the first place. In the words of Stephen Douglas, "By God, sir, I made James Buchanan, and by God sir, I can unmake him."[2]

Young America's hostility to Buchanan created new alliances between their faction and the antislavery movement that would have been unimaginable a few years prior. As William C. Bryant observed in 1858, politics had become "like some of the games I used to play at when a boy in this respect, that the principal players form new associations—take new postures and discard old ones."[3] In the county of Westchester, New York, antislavery activists (with many former Whigs among them) supported ex-Democrat John B. Haskin in his run as an independent in the elections of 1858. Haskin had backed the Baltimore Convention of 1852 and Douglas's Kansas-Nebraska Act in 1854. Although he had worked alongside the South for so long, Haskin was outraged at Buchanan's endorsement of the Lecompton Constitution. Like Douglas and his allies, he argued that the Democracy was undermining the principle of popular sovereignty and truckling to the Slave Power. Haskin declared he would "sooner co-operate with that (Republican) Party than with those who have . . . endeavored to force a slave state into the Union."[4] And that is exactly what he did. In an appeal to Democratic voters, the Republican Party ran Haskin's name at the top of their ticket.

But this alliance in Westchester County was temporary and fragile; it was a marriage of political convenience rather than ideological affinity. Just a year earlier, in the election of 1857, Republicans had courted nativist Know-Nothing voters, attacking the Democrats' stance on immigration and temperance. It was only when this strategy failed that Republicans threw their support behind anti-Lecompton Democrats, letting former Know-Nothings flock to Buchanan's National Democracy out of fear of "Black Republicanism." The Republican *Yonkers Examiner* conceded the new alliance was a concession to political realities: the "election of a Republican was an impossibility," meaning the choice was between Haskin or a "full blown Lecompton Democrat."[5] Moreover, skilled political operatives like Horace Greeley sought alliances with Jacksonians to exaggerate divisions in the Democratic Party over the Lecompton Constitution ahead of the presidential election of 1860. When that election arrived, the *Examiner* rejected Douglas's popular sovereignty platform as a "threat to law and order."[6]

By the late 1850s, then, the antislavery movement subsumed all other political considerations within a larger goal of halting the extension of slavery, an outcome that appealed to a broad spectrum of Northern voters. For their part, Young Americans were being drawn into the orbit of sectional politics. Douglas's defiance of the Slave Power, for example, proved popular with voters in the free states. One Republican noted that "the enthusiasm with which Douglas' championship of the cause of Kansas has been received all over the northwest shows that the heart of the northern people is with those who resist the entrance of slavery into the territories."[7] As one would expect, Democrats loyal to the administration viewed this sectionalism with alarm. The official organ of the Buchanan administration, the *Washington Union*, stressed that there were now "three factions" working to bring down the Democratic Party through Haskin's election: Stephen Douglas's anti-Lecompton Democrats; Henry Winter Davis of the "Dark Order," who constituted the Know-Nothings; and Horace Greeley of the Black Republicans.[8]

However, the anti-Lecompton Democrats did not see themselves as sectionalists. Consistent with their earlier program, they had altered their allegiances only as the Slave Power became the most immediate threat to their principles. Earlier in the decade, these Democrats had reached out to Calhounites to pass the Kansas-Nebraska Act, while they now required the Republican vote to oppose Lecompton. But throughout the decade Young Americans continued with efforts to expand the Union and to solve the problem of slavery in accordance with Democratic principles. Only the circumstances the movement itself had helped to create were changed. If before they had naively courted the Slave Power in the service of national expansion, Young Americans now aggressively opposed the proslavery Democracy they had brought into being.

Indeed, although John B. Haskin ran for Congress as an independent in 1858, appealing to Northerners across the political spectrum, his offer to the electorate was still essentially Jacksonian. A meeting was organized at Tarrytown to rally support for Haskin that was designed to appeal to antislavery figures. It was, for example, advertised "without regard to party," revealing an effort to transcend partisan differences. Similarly, Democrat Charles Goepp (who had written the homage to Young America, *The United States of the World,* in 1853) predicted "a great coming together" of the two Northern parties.[9] But the principles on which this unity would rest were eminently Democratic. John Forney, the prominent Philadelphia Democrat and Douglas supporter, cried that the people were "coming to popular sovereignty," imploring Republicans to "let us take that as a single principle. Everything else that is right will follow."[10] For these Democrats, the establishment of popular sovereignty remained an obtainable goal during the late 1850s: it was the only hope for settling the fate of slavery in a just and enduring manner, compatible with the true principles of American nationality. Forney framed his opposition to the Buchanan administration in terms of Young America's older commitment to an international order free from centralized power. He claimed that in Haskin's election, "the principle which has made every liberal government in the world is at stake." Forney compared the current struggle with the enthusiasm for Kossuth and the Hungarian Revolution that had swept the nation earlier in the decade; the same enthusiasm that had provoked the Pennsylvanian to go on a speaking tour in favor of the European revolutions in 1851. Apparently, "Kossuth came to this country, and by the power of his eloquence, extracted from a money loving . . . people hundreds of thousands of dollars . . . because the people of Hungary had been debarred these privileges of self-government by Austria." Forney recalled how his blood had been made to "boil at the butcheries of Haynau [the ruthless Austrian general] in Hungary," just as his "blood has been made to boil by the butcheries of Buchanan in Illinois." Accordingly, "Every American who has not come up to the test on Lecompton has been beheaded."[11] The same democratic principles that Forney and Goepp hoped to see flourish in Europe and Latin America during the 1840s would—they thought—provide the only satisfactory solution to the crisis over slavery.

Once he was successfully elected to Congress, John Haskin defied Buchanan and tried to rally Democrats *and* Republicans around Douglas's commitment to popular sovereignty. On the floor of Congress, he attacked Buchanan for being beholden to Southern interests: "The fundamental principle of popular sovereignty which underlies . . . our national government is sought to be overthrown and destroyed by the south." Carving out a political niche above partisan squabbling, he glorified the anti-Lecompton Democrats for prioritizing principle over party. Placing himself in a tradition of great philosophers and statesmen, Haskin singled out the "Necker of the administration of James Polk—Governor Walker" and "the Gibbon of American history—George Bancroft." A western nationalist to the core, he also praised the "father of the new states of the West, the heroic, the honest, the able, the fearless, the determined Douglas."[12] This combination of western nationalism, radical cosmopolitanism, and concern for intellectual culture revealed Haskin's continued debt to Young America. Even as the crisis over slavery became interminable, Democrats advanced a Jacksonian solution to the sectional crisis that had changed little from the previous decade. Whether allying with Southerners or Republicans, they sought, in the words of Democrat William Montgomery, to "defend the right of the *white man* to govern himself" (author's emphasis).[13]

Outside Congress, editor John Forney continued his assault on the Buchanan administration for pandering to despotic Southerners. In the face of widespread criticism from the pro-Buchanan press, the newspaperman parodied the administration's position. In his own paper aimed at Independent Democrats, the *Philadelphia Press,* Forney made fun of the idea of Buchanan asking "Walker and Douglas" to "unite in support of my Kansas policy" and back the territorial election at Lecompton, even though it was "held under circumstances of fraud and infamy."[14] Buchanan was portrayed as begging Douglas and Walker: "I know you have the strong side of the question. I know that you can carry off the people but I appeal to you to stand with me otherwise Georgia, Mississippi and Alabama will secede from the Union."[15] The administration's *Democrat and Sentinel* might have believed that Forney "does not utter one broad national sentiment."[16] But Forney painted James Buchanan as a "Northern Democrat with southern principles." It was Douglas, Haskin, and Walker who were defending Young America's cosmopolitan vision, albeit this time with Republicans rather than Southerners.

Stephen Douglas made similar comparisons in a speech on the Lecompton Constitution in March 1858, likening Buchanan's use of executive power to "continental despots."[17] While in the heyday of Young America Douglas had rallied against British-backed abolitionists, he now attacked the Democratic administration for being beholden to the Slave Power. Of course, Douglas had to placate voters in Illinois as he was up for reelection to the Senate in 1858. The electorate certainly did not want to see slavery extended to Kansas where many believed it would crowd out free labor. But observers like John Bigelow confessed, "Douglas, I am satisfied, is in earnest." Furthermore, "He does not disguise his conviction that he can never be forgiven by the south if he were ever so much disposed to ask forgiveness."[18] Similarly, Douglas's behavior reveals a politician with genuine ideological commitments. When his spokesperson in the House, John McClernand, wrote a public letter denouncing Lecompton, the Little Giant "read [it] with pleasure and admiration."[19] In turn, McClernand implored his mentor to "agitate! Rouse the people!"[20] Unwilling to further bend popular sovereignty to the will of southerners, Douglas told McClernand, "We must stand on this principle and go wherever its logical consequences may carry us."[21]

More significantly, the behavior of Douglas and his allies was not at odds with their professed principles, even as their allegiances shifted dramatically. In his comparisons with Europe, Douglas suggested that the current crisis presented a profound challenge to America's exceptionalist mission. Without the cornerstone of popular sovereignty, he implied that American democracy would fade and die. The Illinois senator pointed out that at least "in Old England, whose oppressions we thought intolerable, an administration is hurled from power in an hour when voted down by the representatives of the people upon a government measure."[22] Although he conceded that Louis Napoleon's France was the greatest despotism of them all, the famously Anglophobic Stephen Douglas admitted that Buchanan's behavior in Kansas constituted a usurpation of executive power hitherto unknown in Britain. He said: "In that monarchical country, where they have a queen by divine right . . . and where Republicanism is said to have but a slight foothold, the representatives of the people can check the throne, restrain the government, check the ministry and give a new direction of the policy of the government, without being accountable to the king or to the queen."[23] Of course, in the eyes of administration Democrats, Douglas had finally succumbed to sectional prejudices. One paper wrote, "The warm hearted, impulsive southerner, the cool calculating northern man and the progressive pioneer of the west" all once extended their support to Douglas, but, after Lecompton, his appeals were made "exclusively to the North."[24] But others criticized this narrative. One pamphlet claimed, "Tories prated about the Divine right of kings . . . and talked about 'rebel Americans' just as King James I (Buchanan) and his tools now talk about 'rebel Douglas' and his 'popular sovereignty.'"[25]

Rallying against the Buchanan administration, Young Americans drew on the intellectual and political networks they had created during the previous decade. Stephen Douglas maintained an active correspondence with historian George Bancroft as the sectional crisis worsened. Not content with mere partisan maneuvering, both men drew on intellectual culture to argue that their principles for national unification were rooted in the universal authority of history and political science. For example, in 1857 Douglas asked Bancroft to furnish him with precedents for the policy of popular sovereignty from the colonial era. Bancroft responded that "the principle of democracy requires popular sovereignty" and that "all precedents are that way." Bancroft cited Congress's willingness to let the original thirteen colonies decide on the status of slavery within their new states—a policy that led to emancipation in the Northern states. According to the historian, "the principle and prevailing practice in Virginia" during the eighteenth century "utterly repudiate[s] the proceedings of the Lecompton Constitution." These historical precedents amounted to a larger philosophical truth: that the case for popular sovereignty should be self-evident among "anyone who studies the history of human nature."[26]

As well as supplying Douglas with colonial precedents, George Bancroft actively campaigned for Douglas's version of popular sovereignty against the Lecompton Constitution. After returning from a diplomatic post in London in 1849, the historian retired from the frontline of political life. In the 1850s he focused instead on writing his magnum opus—the ten-volume *History of the United States of America from the Discovery of the American Continent*. Apart from an oration before the New York Historical Society in 1854, Bancroft was largely absent from politics, and, in particular, he abstained from providing his services to the Democratic Party.[27] But in 1858 he burst back onto the scene, chairing an anti-Lecompton meeting in New York City alongside a host of Young Americans. These Jacksonians were outraged at Buchanan's usurpation of popular sovereignty. Bancroft told the meeting that the Kansas constitution amounted to a "concentration of power" in the hands of a convention, which was not an "American idea." As ever, Bancroft linked the struggle for popular sovereignty against federal encroachment to the fate of nationalist movements in Europe, connected, as they were, by the universal principle of nonintervention and democracy for white men. Thus, Buchanan's usurpation of the peoples' rights was "borrowed from those republics of Europe"—those that were "not capable of existing for the very reason that power was so concentrated."[28]

Although Bancroft acknowledged that the conflict in Kansas related to slavery, he primarily perceived it through the Jacksonian lens of resistance to the consolidation of centralized power. If the federal government had the ability to legislate for slavery, it would create dangerous precedents for intervention in other areas of social life. Emboldened by the growth in federal capacity, the administration would soon enough "limit the right of suffrage" and do so "by force." Bancroft reached out to European immigrants, particularly the Irish, since they were aware of the "bitter fruits" that resulted from "complicity between a shameless minority and central power."[29] Far from a mere measure of compromise, this was an attempt on Bancroft's behalf to protect a universal principle, or natural law, in the form of resistance to federal power. Like his friend and ally Stephen Douglas, Bancroft attacked the Buchanan administration for its "neglect of principle for terrorizing expediency."[30]

Within this broader commitment to Democratic universalism, Bancroft was a staunch critic of slavery and believed that popular sovereignty would lead to the triumph of free labor. The historian told Stephen Douglas that he approved of the antislavery Topeka Constitution in Kansas, saying that "it is probably the voice of the people," despite lacking "form."[31] In another letter, Bancroft denounced the Dred Scott decision, saying Blacks should have the right to testify in court and pointing out that they had political rights in some colonial legislatures.[32] Turning against the Fire-Eaters within his own party, Bancroft began to oppose the Slave Power in a manner reminiscent of leading Republicans. But what set him apart from several of the Republicans—and made him suspicious of their motives—was a continued commitment to the Jacksonian vision of state sovereignty. Although he opposed slavery and hailed from the free states, it was Bancroft who declared he was "of the old states' rights school."[33] After the Civil War, Bancroft reminded fellow Young American Samuel Cox that they had "stood together" with Stephen Douglas to prevent the "outrageous attempt to force slavery upon Texas." Bancroft evidently saw the Young America Democrats as proposing a Jacksonian solution to the problem of slavery by making decentralized, local democracy the route to a free-labor society. Advancing a Jacksonian vision of free-labor ideology, the historian told Cox that without slavery, free labor would "rush towards the south with surprising swiftness."[34] Without the blight of chattel slavery, "Texas will be our Italy."[35]

Despite this emancipatory rhetoric, Bancroft did show a new concern for conservatism, which was characteristic of Democrats in this period. The historian said, for example, that although he wished to "keep bright" the "eternal principles of justice," he did not want to do so by "warring against all existing institutions."[36] With the emergence of socialism, abolitionism, and more interventionist forms of liberalism after the Revolutions of 1848, threats to the libertarian order now came from below as well as above. Thus, Bancroft might have compared the Buchanan administration to a despotic tyranny, but he also believed it was emblematic of the "worst periods of revolutionary France," which "usurped power over a nation by terror and reckless daring."[37] This suspicion of the French Revolution was a far cry from the Democrat Edmund Burke, who had defended the Jacobins against monarchical France a decade earlier.[38] Unlike longstanding conservatives like Rufus Choate, Bancroft did not abandon universalist principles. However, in common with many Young America Democrats, he increasingly defended them in the language of conservatism.

Like George Bancroft, the expansionist Young Americans Charles Goepp and Samuel Cox pushed for popular sovereignty as a principled route to free labor from within the Democratic Party. But like the great American historian, who eventually defected to the Republicans, Goepp saw popular sovereignty as a Jacksonian principle that transcended party affiliation. In a letter to Stephen Douglas, Goepp expressed his belief that the Republican Party should adopt as its own the Democrats' principle of nonintervention in the territories. Goepp envisioned popular sovereignty not as a mere compromise measure but as a principle of "self evident justice." Far from being a boon to the Slave Power, it was also "not in any manner antagonistic to the position of the Republican

Party heretofore." Goepp held out for a unification of the two Northern parties on the basis of Jacksonian principles. Once the Republican platform embraced nonintervention and popular sovereignty, the position of the Republicans and anti-Lecompton Democrats would be "identical." Finally, the great obstacle to the "formation of a unitary opposition party" would be removed.[39]

Fellow Young American Samuel S. Cox agreed that popular sovereignty was a principled route to a free-labor society. Far from just a pragmatic solution to the sectional crisis, Cox believed popular sovereignty was a transcendent principle across time and space. Echoing his efforts to reform the economic and political order of Europe, Cox told Congress, "that principle," which was "above all precedents, settlements, or compromises" has "a history . . . at least since the repeal of the Corn Laws in 1846, or the French Revolution of 1848." Cox believed popular sovereignty, inherently just, would bring peace and stability to the territory of Kansas. But, ultimately, he was at pains to emphasize that "whether there be peace or not," he "would not sacrifice the principle involved." For this Young American, "expediency" was a dangerous doctrine "when in collision with principles."[40] Like Bancroft, Goepp and Cox both saw popular sovereignty as a universal axiom. Their political aims in Kansas were just one part of Young America's larger project of transforming the international order, which they had begun a decade earlier.

Tensions between the Northern and Southern wing of the Democracy were further inflamed by Douglas's allies in the Senate. A triumvirate composed of Ohio's George E. Pugh, Michigan's Charles E. Stuart, and California's David Broderick defended Douglas after the fallout from the Lecompton Constitution. All three believed themselves to be spokesmen for western Democracy. Pugh took Republican Salmon P. Chase's seat in 1855, a fate that would be reversed when Chase won it back in 1861. Although he initially spoke out in favor of the Lecompton Constitution, Pugh voted against it in accordance with the wishes of the electorate in Ohio. And, in time, he became incensed by Southerners who denounced Douglas for failing to explicitly guarantee slavery in the territories prior to the formation of a state constitution. The demand for this guarantee effectively repudiated what would become known as Douglas's Freeport Doctrine: that settlers could outlaw slavery in the territories by refusing to pass local legislation (positive law) in support of it. Long before Douglas made the point in his debates with Lincoln, this was the reason many of Douglas's supporters did not think slave owners would exert significant influence on the territorial legislatures, despite their right to enter the territories under the Kansas-Nebraska Act. Despairing of the South's complaints, Pugh lamented that the Northern Democracy had always stood up for their Southern brethren, to the detriment of their own support in the free states. The Democracy was a "vast mountain of democratic strength" in March 1854—before the Kansas-Nebraska Act—when it held every single northwestern state. Although he would stand by the national principle of popular sovereignty, Pugh refused to bend to Southern demands, furious at their inability to recognize the North's truly national stance. The problem was that Southerners misunderstood the purpose of popular sovereignty. Just like the defunct Whig Party, Southern partisans merely sought to resurrect "the ancient idea of an equal partition of territories, as between the north and south." In fact, Pugh believed popular sovereignty was about principle, not power. The South should not mind if the application of Democratic ideas brought a succession of free states into the Union. Indeed, California was to be "the example in future cases; declaring that what her people had done, even without the assent of Congress, should be ratified and forever established."[41]

While some Northern Democrats crafted proposals for further compromise with the South, Douglas's allies held firm. One such proposal was a bill put forward by Indiana Democrat William English in 1858. English had opposed the Lecompton Constitution when it was first put to Congress on the grounds that it forced slavery into the territory. But he quickly became impatient of congressional deadlock. In 1858 English worked with Georgia's Alexander Stephens to create a bill that offered the settlers a land grant as part of the Lecompton Constitution. English hoped the free settlers might go for Lecompton under these conditions, furnishing the constitution with some democratic legitimacy. Eager as ever to break congressional stalemate, Stephen Douglas considered voting for English's bill. But his ally from California, David Broderick, stood firm. Broderick told the Little Giant that if he abandoned his opposition to Lecompton, he might as well "go into the street and blow his brains out."[42]

It turned out that David Broderick more accurately described the fate that lay in store for him in his home state of California. The following year, in 1859, a proslavery Democrat named David Terry took revenge on Broderick and his Free-Soil supporters when Terry failed to win reelection as chief justice to the California State Supreme Court. Outraged at what he perceived to be Broderick's antislavery politics, Terry compared the Northern Democrats to supporters of the Black abolitionist Frederick Douglass. He is reported to have said of the Young Americans, "Perhaps they do sail under the flag of Douglas, but it is the banner of the Black Douglass, whose name is Frederick, not Stephen."[43] Broderick denounced Terry as corrupt, grouping him with President Buchanan and the proslavery Californian William Gwin. Furious, Terry challenged Broderick to a duel, which he accepted. After Broderick's pistol discharged before the final count, Terry was left with a free shot, which he fired straight into the senator's chest. The caning of the antislavery Charles Sumner might be the most famous example of violence at the hands of the Slave Power. But at the time of his death, Broderick was honored as an antislavery hero who was martyred for the cause of popular sovereignty and free labor in the West. On his deathbed, the Californian was even reported to have said, "I die because I was opposed to a corrupt administration and the extension of slavery."[44] The principle of popular sovereignty advocated by Young Americans like Douglas, Broderick, and Pugh was considered, at the time, a Jacksonian route to a free-labor society.

This was not an isolated instance of violence between the Young Americans and the Slave Power. Rumors circulated in 1859 that there was a plot to assassinate Stephen Douglas. Many Southerners and their Democratic allies wanted to strip the Illinois senator of his role as chair of the Committee on the Territories for his opposition to the Lecompton Constitution. In this context, *Harper's Weekly* circulated a story that there was a conspiracy to kill him. The plan was to exploit Douglas's fiery temper. Louisiana's John Slidell would insult the Little Giant on the Senate floor, provoking Douglas to challenge him to a duel. Slidell was an expert marksman and would have easily dealt with his hot-tempered opponent. According to historian Michael E. Woods, "There were compelling reasons to believe this story."[45] Notably, Slidell had helped to orchestrate the campaign to elect pro-Lecompton Democrat Sidney Breese in the Illinois senate race of 1858. During the campaign Slidell spread rumors that Douglas mistreated the slaves on the Mississippi plantation that he managed on behalf of his sons after the death in 1853 of their mother—herself the daughter of a prominent North Carolina planter. Douglas denied the allegations, and a flurry of speculation and personal accusations ensued in the press.

We will never know whether Slidell really conspired to murder Douglas. But people had certainly dueled over far smaller disputes in the nineteenth century. Indeed, Young Americans were particularly given to this method of resolving arguments. New York's August Belmont was wounded in a duel in 1841, while Louisiana's Pierre Soulé instigated multiple clashes in Spain. The anti-institutional nature of the practice, combined with its emotional charge and connotations of manhood, appealed to the political culture of Young America. In the middle of the decade, the *New York Herald* noted "a mania among our fast young men for dueling."[46]

As sectional tensions transformed the Democracy, Young Americans like Douglas became increasingly alienated within their own party. Proslavery Democrats put the expansion of slavery before any other issue, while Cotton Whigs flocked to the Democracy to defend Unionism against the Republican threat. In the late 1850s both groups went after Douglas.[47] Firstly, Southern

Democrats argued that slavery was, under the Constitution, entitled to federal protection in the territories, regardless of the decisions of the territorial legislatures. The Supreme Court appeared to uphold this position in the Dred Scott decision of 1857, alongside the ruling that African Americans could not be citizens under the Constitution. This seemingly threatened Douglas's position that slavery should be left to white communities to decide for themselves. In effect, it suggested that slavery could not be outlawed in the territories at all. Nevertheless, in the course of the famous Lincoln-Douglas debates, Douglas articulated his Freeport Doctrine, which posited that slavery did not need to be explicitly banned, since local communities could simply refuse to pass positive laws in its support. Without these local protections, slavery would have no future in territories governed by natural law—an intolerable proposition for many Southern Democrats. Cotton Whigs, for their part, were uncomfortable with the idea that popular sovereignty was an inherent right, even for white men. Unpopular within his own party, Douglas was stripped of his position as chair of the Committee on the Territories, which he had held for the last eleven years. The Little Giant knew that he would need to mount a robust of defense of his principles if he was ever to bridge the divisions within the Democracy and earn his party's nomination for the presidency in 1860.

In this context, Douglas published a remarkably theoretical article in the popular literary magazine *Harper's Weekly*.[48] This was an unprecedented move for a potential presidential candidate and suggests that Douglas considered himself as much a political theorist as a congressional power broker. In the article he drew on a long-established discourse that originated in the debates, which took place in 1844, over the Dorr Rebellion of 1841. Conflating natural and political rights, he wrote that "the right of local self-government" was "inalienable" and backed that claim up with colonial precedents that he had taken from Bancroft earlier in the decade.[49] Similarly, in a speech given in 1860, Douglas claimed, "The doctrine of the revolutionary war was, that the right of local government was inherent in the people." He complained, "We are now told that this inherent right of self-government only pertains to States."[50] Douglas admitted that Congress granted political authority to the territories but argued that congressional power stopped there.[51] Instead, territorial settlers made decisions, subject only to the US Constitution, according to their natural right to self-government. Crucially, this inherent right to majoritarianism applied not just when constitutions were made but throughout the territorial phase. It was this right, Douglas contended, that the American colonies had defended in the revolution against the British Empire. In 1860 Douglas and his supporters sought to do the same against sectional extremists and conservative Whigs.

George T. Curtis, among the latter category, profoundly disagreed with Douglas's assertions. In the pamphlet war that Douglas's remarks provoked, Curtis emerged as one of his most powerful critics. As a Cotton Whig, Curtis's critique was steeped in a patrician conservatism that had its origins in the pages of the *Whig Review*. In contrast to Douglas, he argued, "The sovereignty of the 'states' [is] founded in something more than an *abstract* right of self-government." Instead, Curtis subscribed to a historicist view of the Union in which democracy emerged over time. Certainly, Douglas's view of the Union was also grounded in history, but only insofar as the nation came to free itself from constraints to the exercise of self-government. New technologies were, of course, a spur to progress, but only because of their power to obliterate old cultures and customs. Conversely, Curtis was a historicist in the sense that the qualities of history, culture, and custom were preconditions for democracy to thrive. There were natural rights to the fruits of one's labor that preceded the contingent facts of national existence.[52] But Curtis viewed these as pre-political in the proper sense of the term. Democracy could not exist, even for white men, independent of a social, political, and legal order rooted in positive law. Popular sovereignty could not take root in the territories, for example, where people "come from communities of differing political ideas; where some have had no civil training at all, where others are entirely lawless, while a few are perhaps skilled in the arts of political management; where no homogenous popular character has been formed; and where there are as yet none of the institutions which brace together, and none of the settled habits of order which precedents supply."[53] This theoretical debate that raged before the presidential election of 1860 was remarkably similar to the ones that had taken place over the Dorr Rebellion, the Mexican War, and the Revolutions of 1848.

As well as former Whigs, Douglas was forced to confront Fire-Eaters and their doughface allies, who argued that neither congressional nor territorial legislatures could interfere with slavery in the territories, as it was protected by the Constitution. Since the debates over the Dorr Rebellion, proslavery Southerners—like conservative Whigs—had been suspicious of unqualified majoritarianism.[54] But tensions became particularly acute as the Douglasites demonstrated their willingness to break from the party over Lecompton. If Young Americans were prepared to put principle over party, the proslavery Democrats would need to confront their ideas head-on. Buchanan's attorney general, Jeremiah Black, attacked the Little Giant's conception of natural rights, arguing that settlers could not vote to outlaw slavery during the territorial stage. In a pamphlet responding to Douglas's *Harper's* article, he wrote, "The territories are either sovereign powers by natural and inherent right, or else they are political corporations, owing all the authority they possess to the acts of Congress which create them."[55] Black argued that slavery could only be outlawed when settlers were ready to form a political convention that would decide on a state constitution. In this precise moment, settlers would go from being a band of migrants, existing in a natural relation, to a political society that was necessary to constitute self-government. To make this distinction between man as a natural being and man as a political entity, Virginia's Henry Wise used the metaphor of the settlers growing to maturity—in a stark contrast to Young America's unqualified celebration of youth. Wise wrote that when the settlers form a political community, they "put on the attributes of sovereignty. . . . They are to put away childish things, and become more than men—an American, self-governed, sovereign people."[56] Before this moment when territories became sovereign, the South's human property was protected under the Constitution. The states' combined authority over the territories meant that no section of the Union could be excluded from their enjoyment. Thus, Black and Wise repudiated the idea that the American colonies and the British Empire stood in the same relation as the territories and the federal government. This eighteenth-century relation was only comparable to that which existed between the federal government and the *states*, since only the latter were sovereign entities.

While Douglas did battle with proslavery Democrats and conservative Whigs within his own party, he was also forced to reckon with Jacksonians who had left to join the antislavery movement. Former Democrats in the Republican Party shared many of Young America's Jacksonian commitments, but they differed from Douglas in their interpretation and application. Jacksonians within the Republican fold still defined themselves as the true guardians of popular sovereignty and nonintervention. But, for them, it was Douglas and his allies who had betrayed the Democracy. Salmon P. Chase, in a widely republished letter of January 1854, wrote that slavery extension was essentially incompatible with a genuine Democratic government. He claimed not to object, in theory, to the clause in the Democratic Party's Baltimore convention of 1852 that condemned "all interference by Congress with the question of slavery." Chase argued that this "fundamental proposition . . . as an original one was sound," saying that "every intelligent man knows that slavery, outside of state limits, could not exist under our Constitution and system of government without the interference of Congress." Chase, though, believed the federal government had so ingrained slavery into American society through years of congressional legislation that Congress itself would have to "repeal acts, heretofore passed without constitutional authority on the subject." By maintaining "neutrality" on the question of slavery, Democrats like Douglas were facilitating previous congressional injustices:

the existence of slavery in the District of Columbia; "the sale of men, women and children under federal process"; and the Fugitive Slave Law. By contrast, Chase wanted to see the federal government actively uncouple itself from slavery: "The Independent Democracy demand the divorce of the national government from slavery as sternly and uncompromisingly as Jackson demanded it from the banks." In theory at least, Chase claimed that it was still "the Democracy which attracts my devotion"—one that constitutes "the law of Nature pervading the law of the land." But compromise with slaveholders was impossible because, by their very nature, they used the federal government to achieve their ends. Chase's letter was influential among Jacksonians in the Democratic as well as Republican Parties and can be found in the papers of Ohio Democrat William Allen.[57]

Other antislavery Democrats who became prominent members of the Republican Party reached out to Douglas and his supporters, acknowledging their shared ideals. The *New-York Evening Post* maintained a respect for Samuel Tilden's Jacksonian nationalism throughout the 1850s, despite his association with the proslavery wing of the Democratic Party. For example, the *Post* asked Tilden for a copy of a speech he had given at the Cooper Union Institute in 1860 so they could republish it in the paper. According to Tilden, the editors told him that he had "friends among their readers" who "would be glad to know" how he had "reasoned [himself] into the associations" with which he stood on the "Presidential question." Tilden responded warmly to the *Post*'s request, eager for the opportunity to enlighten the "mass" of its readers, "among which are many cultivated intellects and some friends of my earlier years" who "are widely and dangerously wrong in their present political action." Tilden promised to send his former allies an explanation of his political loyalties in the coming days. He acknowledged "the sacred duty of showing" *Post* readers "a decent way out" of their trajectory towards Republicanism. Commenting on this letter in his memoir of Tilden, *Evening Post* editor and former contributor to the *Democratic Review* John Bigelow claimed to understand Tilden's position better than his own followers. Bigelow believed that Tilden's audience was "unaccounted for debris of the old Whig Party," who "did not care to listen long to so prominent a political partisan of Jackson and Van Buren." Indeed, Tilden had been a "most formidable critic of all Whig measures during all their successive administrations." The *Post* observed that his current supporters were "conspicuously impatient of anything savoring of old-fashioned Democracy." Suggesting that Tilden would receive a fairer hearing in the pages of the *Post,* it offered to publish his speech "cheerfully." That way, it would "reach a great many more of Tilden's friends . . . , and they will be glad to know by what process so clever a man has reasoned himself into such bad company."[58]

Elsewhere, the *Evening Post* maintained its scorn for Samuel Tilden's fellow travelers. It attacked his pamphlet *The Union! Its Dangers!!!*, written on the eve of the 1860 election, on the grounds that it was addressed to William Kent, an old Whig. The *Post* argued: "An uninterrupted political antagonism . . . existed since the days when their fathers were active opponents, but who now, like Pilot and Herod, are brought together and united by the bond of common outrage upon what we regard as the cause of truth and justice."[59] Addressing Tilden's pamphlet, writers at the *Post* also claimed the mantle of Jacksonian nationalism for themselves. Tilden had argued that the election of Lincoln placed the federal government in the same relation to the South as a foreign government. He believed Lincoln's was an unrepresentative administration eager to use the powers of central government in dangerous ways. The *Post* shot back that "the character and objects" of the Republican Party had never been "fairly discussed in the southern states," meaning that "the policy and purposes of the Republican Party are not much better understood in the south today . . . as they are in Mongolia."[60] Nor, would they be, argued the Free-Soil paper, until the federal government was free from the grip of "oligarchy." Here, the *Post* reversed Tilden's powerful image of Lincoln's federal government tyrannizing over the South by depicting Southern elites using the central government to subdue the North. In both images the struggle was depicted as one for state sovereignty in the face of a federal reach that was un-American in its power and influence.

These Republican attacks hit home. Democrat John Forney worried that his party had become a shell of its former self. It was no wonder the Republicans had assumed the mantle of the Democracy. "The opposition have seized our armor and our weapons and almost our standard," he wrote in 1858, while "using our own arguments to destroy us."[61] Despite his estrangement from the Democratic Party, Forney declared that he was "standing in my independent attitude, yet as ever profoundly Democratic in all my feelings." With the political climate shifting underneath his feet, Forney despaired: "I daily ask myself where all this is to end!" In a new world of sectional allegiances, where were Democrats to stand? On the one hand, Forney railed against the South for betraying the principles of the Democratic Party, but, on the other, he remained suspicious of the Republicans. Their rhetorical commitment to democracy was overshadowed by the tariff, which they tried to "weave . . . into our popular sovereignty creed."[62]

As the second party system collapsed, its attendant ideologies did not simply disappear. Rather, these identities came untethered to official affiliations. While the parties became outlets for sectional outlooks, many Young Americans stood in the same "independent attitude" as John Forney. They fought for Jacksonian principles within the Democracy itself while also reaching out to former

Democrats within the Republican fold. Old animosities between Young Americans and former Whigs (now in both the Democratic and Republican ranks) were still apparent, while disputes with the Southern Democrats came to the fore. At the same time, Young Americans acknowledged their old Democratic colleagues who had migrated to the Republican ranks. Partisan battles were not over, but they no longer corresponded with party affiliations, just as sectional disputes had once raged below the surface of the second party system.

Douglas and his supporters tried to stand aloof from the sectional alliances that emerged in the 1850s. A core group of Young Americans were sufficiently alienated by *both* the Republicans and Democrats to back Douglas as the Northern Democratic candidate in the election of 1860.[63] On the one hand, Douglas was estranged from the Fire-Eaters and Cotton Whigs who now dominated his former party. On the other, he refused to join the Democrats who defected to the Republican ranks, suspicious of the party's attitude toward race, social progress, and the federal government. Up until secession, Douglas and his supporters pleaded with Americans to sustain their vision of Unionism on both sides of the Mason-Dixon line. Thus Jacksonian nationalism still provided the lens through which Young Americans understood the period before the Civil War. Moreover, it offered a common language that made sense to their former colleagues in the Republican Party. Of course, popular sovereignty was, in the end, a procedure rather than an inherent value. Even former contributors to the *Democratic Review* disagreed about how it should work. However, by tracing the continued salience of the second party system, the unwillingness of Northerners to pursue Reconstruction to a radical conclusion begins to make painful sense. If many Northerners fought for Democratic principles rather than against slavery per se, the emphasis on national unity, federal withdrawal, and racism that came to overwhelm the Reconstruction project can be traced back to this formative period.[64]

Indeed, after the Civil War, Northern Democrats reached out to Republicans, particularly those with Jacksonian sympathies, who were growing impatient with their radical colleagues. Historian Erik B. Alexander suggests that as early as 1868, Northern Democrats courted more moderate Republicans, paving the way for the Liberal Republican revolt in 1872 and the eventual withdrawal of federal troops from the South. This began during the presidential election of 1868, when leading Democrats appealed to none other than Republican Salmon P. Chase to run as the party's nominee. Many of these figures had been supporters of the Young America program before the Civil War, including August Belmont, Robert J. Walker, and Samuel Tilden. In their efforts to persuade Chase, they explicitly played on his Jacksonian inclinations. August Belmont, for example, appealed to Chase's "sympathies with the broad principles of the

Democratic party on the questions of free trade, finance and states rights." True to what he said before the war, Chase replied that for "more than a quarter of a century, I have been in my political views and sentiments, a Democrat; and I still think that . . . the old democratic principles afford the best guidance."[65] To be sure, the Ohioan also drew attention to his more pronounced feelings on the subject of slavery. But he quickly walked back on these sentiments, running for the Democratic nomination on a platform that buried a vague commitment to Black suffrage under the stipulation that individual states would determine voting rights. The Democrats' faith in white majoritarianism, then, remained salient even after partisan realignment and civil war. This ultimately weakened the Republican Party as a coherent organization as Black rights gave way to other priorities. The legacy of the second party system remained relevant long after its demise, and, with more research, we can see how it contributed to the downfall of Reconstruction during the 1870s.

Race and Slavery in Young America Nationalism

The Young America movement fell apart because its supporters were, in the end, unable to bridge the sectional divides that their politics had brought into sharp relief. Democrats never provided a compelling answer to the fundamental question of what to do with the four million enslaved people already living within the southern United States. It was all very well to support popular sovereignty for white men, but they still had to confront the question of what to do with America's existing slave population. Young Americans proposed that territorial expansion and colonization would naturally draw slaves and free Blacks away from the mainland United States toward tropical regions and advocated colonization to Latin America and Africa. At a purely abstract level, these policies were antislavery, promoting a racially homogenous democracy free from Black labor of any kind. Even a Kentuckian like George Sanders had "long ago [probably dating back to the 1840s] pondered over a plan for the settlement of the free negro population," while his wife predicted "as the black empire rises in Africa, the American negroes will see their own advantage in going."[66]

The new western territory of Oregon provided a model for this opposition to Black labor of any kind. In 1844 the territory passed a Black Exclusion Law that outlawed Black people from its boundaries either as slaves or free people. If slaves were found in Oregon, their master would be given notice of three years before they were forcibly freed. Free Blacks in the territory would be imprisoned, beaten, and forced to leave. In an editorial in 1858, Walt Whitman wrote that "this sort of total prohibition of colored persons should become quite a common thing in the new Western, Northwestern and even Southwestern states." The poet predicted that "the whole matter of slavery agitation will assume another phase" with "the totality of White Labor, on the one side, and on the other, the interference and competition of Black Labor, or of bringing in colored persons on any terms." Even as slavery divided the nation in two, many Young America Democrats saw the conflict in these terms. Although slavery was rooted in positive law (and was therefore "artificial"), the poet also insisted that "nature has set an impassible seal" against the integration of races "on any terms."[67] Oregon was admitted as a state in 1859 with a "whites only" clause in its original constitution.

Nevertheless, this outlook could not escape the realities of the sectional conflict. On the one hand, it chimed with free-labor ideology by clearing ground for white Americans in the West. But in the Caribbean it could certainly function as a proslavery policy. For people like Whitman, the annexation of Cuba as a slave state was a price worth paying to avoid racial amalgamation in the West, while not technically contributing to the expansion of slavery. Thus, the Young America movement is best characterized as a form of white nationalism that could count itself for and against slavery at different times and in different places. Its significance lay in forcing the country to confront problems that had previously been settled through caution and compromise. The solutions the Young Americans proposed were impractical in the context of the 1850s and forced Americans of all diverse political persuasions to take a stand on the issue of slavery. As such, they inadvertently fueled the growth and ambition of the Slave Power and forced the Republicans to stake out radical ground.

Written on the eve of secession in 1860, Samuel Tilden's *The Union! Its Dangers!!!* contained an entire section entitled "Natural and Material Laws" to explain how he viewed the future of slavery in the United States. He argued that slavery was being slowly eradicated from the mainland as it moved toward warmer climates nearer the equator. Tilden made the case that slave owners were selling their property southward as they found it increasingly difficult to compete with free labor. The tide of immigration into the Northern states kept wages down, ensuring that it was always cheaper to hire diligent and industrious free laborers to do jobs instead of buying and supporting slaves. Thus, "A man who today employs slaves in raising wheat or corn on the southern bank of the Ohio, uses labor at least twice as costly as it was ten years ago." At present, Tilden claimed, the chivalry of the South prevented masters from selling their slaves southward at the rate that nature demanded: "Family and social habits, an honorable sentiment against selling dependents . . . resists." However, eventually "the social laws at last prevail as the unceasing current of a stream outlasts the strokes of the swimmer."[68] Tilden thus saw slavery as a barrier to fulfilling Blacks "natural" destiny in the tropics.

The fact that the tropics were such an attractive destination for slave labor made the proposition to annex Cuba more appealing to Northerners eager to keep slavery out of western territories like Kansas and Nebraska. As chapter 5 outlines, an antislavery case for Cuban annexation was closely entwined with the case for popular sovereignty. Even some abolitionist newspapers recognized the beneficial effect of Cuban annexation for draining Blacks away from the mainland United States. Once Cuba had come into the Union, the Liberty Party paper the *National Era* wrote, "The domestic trade will either drain off the domestic population of the more northern slave states, or convert them into merely slave-breeding establishments for their southern customers." For this reason, the paper said it would "give up much of our hostility towards the acquisition of Cuba," if there was a guarantee that families would not be disrupted. Although the paper insisted, "We shall always oppose the extension of the area of slavery," it also claimed, "We should not regret the concentration of the Slave population in the extreme south."[69] Nevertheless, it was still not apparent how enslaved people in Cuba would eventually be emancipated. Democrats made it clear that a free Black population was not an option. Yet the continuation of slavery would cause the white population on the island, including the creoles, to be degraded by association.

While the annexation of Cuba was mired in contradictions, colonization in Africa presented a clearer yet more fanciful solution. The editor of the *Democratic Review*, George Sanders, was an enthusiastic proponent of this policy. In an "Address to the People of France" in 1854, he set his sights on the vast coast of Africa as a viable destination. While enslaved laborers who were moved to Cuba would still be forced to work, those colonized to Africa would become free. Sanders was optimistic about their prospects. He claimed the "beginning of a great republican empire" would emerge from the "modest American settlement" in Liberia. In turn, this would "extend the germ of American civilization" into the "bosom of Ethiopia." Sanders took pride in the American system of colonization and compared it favorably with monarchical empires. He implored "Frenchmen of all parties, in justice to republican principles, to compare the action of American colonization in Liberia with monarchies anywhere else the world over." The genius of American colonization, according to Sanders, was that Blacks would carry with them America's enterprising spirit and knowledge of democratic institutions. In Sanders's view, colonization formed a kind of Black Manifest Destiny, whereby the United States would "redeem" Africa just as it had done for Europe. While Sanders watched the exodus of Frenchmen coming to America with "exultation," he "turn[ed] with no less pride to a thriving colony on the western coast of Africa" that exhibited a "new species of immigration."[70] Having laid out his vision for the region, he chastised the French for using Africa merely as a site to send dissident "Republican authors and men of science," who had been exiled for their political beliefs. Nevertheless, this projection of Manifest Destiny into Africa was different than the one envisioned for the American West. Nowhere did Sanders argue that Black laborers would establish democratic communities through the same natural right to self-government that white men exercised in the territories.[71] In fact, he implied that, unlike white men, Black laborers could only exercise democratic rights after a period of tutelage in America.[72] It seemed that as a dependent and permanently inferior population, Black people derived their political rights not from nature but from the "master race."

Like Sanders, Philadelphia Democrat Thomas L. Kane rejected Republican proposals to limit the acquisition of new slave territories, arguing that colonization was the only way to banish enslaved labor from the mainland United States once and for all. In a lecture from 1856, he explained his decision to support the Buchanan administration despite his prior enthusiasm for the Free-Soil movement. Part of the reason was bound up in what Kane saw as the changing preferences of white society. Although he professed pride in bolting from the Democratic Party in 1848, he explained that his antislavery sentiments waned as time went by. Despite the Republican Party's surge in popularity, Kane claimed the American people were not receptive to the antislavery message. Only after accepting the wisdom of the common people did he begin to declare, in the mid-1850s: "All men are created free and equal but not negroes." Like Whitman, Kane retained his belief that Blacks should not take up space in the western territories, whether as free laborers or slaves. Although he was not in danger of "entangling alliances" with "social inferiors," Kane argued that the "poor man" was, by seeing Blacks "at his side every day, in the field, factory or workshop." He may even have to "live every day in the same confined room with him."[73]

Unlike Republicans, Kane decided that enclosing slavery within the Southern states was not the best way to prevent its spread to Kansas. Such a policy of "shutting all the doors and windows on [slavery] as we do a fire" would only unduly punish the South. In a neat summary of what has become known as the "freedom national" argument against slavery, Kane remembered how in 1848 he proposed that "all the avenues for emigration" for the Black population should be "fixed" while the whites moved west and settled.[74] As demand for cotton grew, Southern planters would breed more slaves until eventually the soil would become "exhausted" and the economy unprofitable. As a result, the "relation" between "employer" and "employee" would adjust itself "naturally." By 1856 Kane was disenchanted with a solution that would "starve the master into emancipation." Professing sympathy for the enslaved, he painted a horrific picture of a "starved" slave "dragging" himself to work with "skin as fleshless as his hoe hands."[75] According to Kane, it was this picture of the individual that abolitionists neglected in their grand theories of human amelioration. By taking their cue from a priori ideas, antislavery Republicans, Kane spuriously contended, forgot the wellbeing of the individual in their plan to make freedom national.

Although he could tolerate admitting Cuba to the Union—presumably as a slave state—Kane saw no future for the peculiar institution within the mainland United States. He was both unwilling to confine enslaved laborers to the South and adamant that popular sovereignty would keep them out of new territories like Kansas. The only "humane" future he imagined would come via the deportation of the Black population to their "natural" home in Africa. In a lecture entitled *Transportation, Extermination, Fusion,* he dwelt on what would become of America's Black population. Rejecting a program of total extermination and dismissing fusion with the white race as undesirable, Kane proposed a program of colonization. Like Sanders, he was positive about Blacks' prospects. Kane claimed that "on the banks of the river Niger . . . or the Amazon," Blacks "compete with the descendants of Celts and Saxons with excessive odds in their favor." Moreover, emancipation in the tropics meant Africa was not the only compelling destination. Although not long before the West Indies had been a "fortress of slavery" and all America "south of the Gulf of Mexico" was a "sealed book" for colonization, Kane now argued these islands of free Blacks were suitable destinations for ex-slaves. Furthermore, technological innovations in the form of railways and steamships facilitated the transportation of human beings to warmer climes: "We are now days from St. Domingo, from Guama, and the mouth of the Amazon and from . . . Trinidad," Kane claimed.[76]

The editor of the *Democratic Review,* John O'Sullivan, viewed the expansion of slavery into the tropics as a means of drawing Blacks out of the United States. Like Thomas Kane, Samuel Tilden, and Martin Van Buren, O'Sullivan supported the Free-Soil ticket in 1848 before returning to the Democratic fold in 1852. O'Sullivan's decision to abandon antislavery politics was partly due to his changing attitude toward race. In the 1840s he believed "without question" in the "old doctrine of the unity of the Human Race." O'Sullivan explained that this carried with it "the consequence that the negro was merely a Black White man degraded by a long course of external influences to a present merely temporary and accidental inferiority." Thus, "Slavery involved an idea, to me, of wrongful oppression in conflict with the essential American idea." The former editor of the *Democratic Review* explained that he changed his view in the early 1850s after reading the work of Harvard zoologist Louis Agassiz, who pioneered the theory of polygenesis, or separate creation myths for the Black and white race. From that day forward, O'Sullivan deemed "slavery to the inferior race . . . a better as well as a more natural relation than freedom side by side, especially in a democratic country."[77]

O'Sullivan's view of the beneficial effects of slavery for African Americans seems to have mirrored a larger transition in the Northern Democratic Party. The *Democratic Review,* for example, was sympathetic to the idea of the unity of the races during the mid-1840s. By the early 1850s, however, articles about race were more complimentary of the pseudoscience and accepted the underlying thesis that different races did not share the same origins.[78] John Campbell, the British ex-chartist who eventually became a follower of Stephen Douglas after emigrating to the United States, also tried to promote polygenesis in the North prior to the Civil War. Like Kane and O'Sullivan, Campbell initially joined the Free-Soil Party in 1848. But by the 1850s he chastised "negro philanthropy" for distracting from the uplift of the white race.[79] Concerns over Black rights should not interfere with the natural right of white men to rule by popular sovereignty.[80]

That is not to say, however, that Democrats wanted to see slavery expanded into territories that would otherwise be reserved for free whites, and, as such, they still maintained an allegiance to the ideology of free labor. Like Kane, O'Sullivan made clear, in a private letter, that "there is no chance of either Kansas or Nebraska becoming a slave state," and he maintained that the presence of slavery there would degrade free white labor. Despite coming to believe that slavery benefited African Americans, O'Sullivan continued to oppose the institution in the abstract due to what he saw as its adverse effect on the white population—whether they were yeomen or enslavers.[81] Accustomed to total control over another human being, the planter elite failed to comprehend the "Democratic principle," behaving with arrogance in Congress and taking a dim view of labor itself. Similarly, John Campbell's racial science never led him to unequivocally endorse slavery in America. He always maintained Douglas's position that the western territories would be filled with free labor and that slavery's future, if it had one, was south of the Gulf of Mexico.

Overall, the Young Americans' virulent racism was compatible with their vision of Jacksonian nationalism and abstract antislavery politics. Sanders, Kane, Dallas, Walker, and Tilden all advocated territorial expansion and colonization as solutions, however impractical, to the crisis over slavery. The most contentious issue was Cuba, where some believed the suitability of enslaved laborers to the tropical climate outweighed the degrading effects on the white population.[82] In these areas, annexation with slavery intact was the best of a range of undesirable options that would ameliorate the worst aspects of the institution under Spanish rule. Young Americans were, therefore, advocates of free-labor ideology only in the abstract, while their schemes for territorial growth instrumentally worked to protect slavery.

Progress: The Republican Alternative

While Young Americans confidently predicted that popular sovereignty and territorial expansion would create a homogenous white republic, former Whigs within the Republican Party were more skeptical. For some of these figures, it was not just that a confident and powerful Slave Power could mold the Young American program to meet its own needs. They also believed that democracy alone was not sufficient to drive moral progress. An alternative conception of nationhood was required, rooted in correct ideas about natural rights. These men argued that Young Americans' fundamental ideas about the future were misplaced. Social and moral progress did not inevitably accompany material development, while human intervention was necessary to make society conform to divine law. In short, the "people" were liable to corruption, and democracy was a contingent force. Universal rights applied to all humanity, as God created it, not to different racial groups based on "scientific" authorities. The Republicans who made these arguments took on the spokesmen of Young America explicitly, rejecting their version of Enlightenment thought.

On February 11, 1859, the ex-Whig Abraham Lincoln gave his "Second Lecture on Discoveries and Inventions" that offered up a powerful critique of the Young America movement and its figurehead, Stephen Douglas. The soon-to-be president of the United States declared, "We have all heard of Young America. He is the most current youth of the age. . . . He has a great passion—a perfect rage—for the 'new.'"[83] Addressing the political program of Douglas, Bancroft, and Forney directly, he joked that their "desire for land is not selfish, but merely an impulse to extend the area of freedom."[84] But Lincoln did more than point out the hypocrisy of these men. He also took aim at the arrogance and naivety of their worldview. He criticized, in particular, the idea that the past was a relic of barbarism and that the future would belong to these independent and intellectually emancipated Americans. By contrast, Lincoln sought to remind Young America that cooperation and collaboration, in the form of discussion and writing, were indispensable drivers of technological progress. Lincoln's speech was a homage to inherited wisdom and the accumulation of knowledge—qualities he did not think were sufficiently credited in Young America's future-orientated view of the Union. It was only by combining "powers of observation and reflection" that people could create useful "discoveries and inventions." By exchanging ideas with one another, a "result is . . . reached" between two collaborators, "which neither alone would have arrived." Adam and Eve were the first to exploit this dynamic, when Eve sewed Adam a fig leaf to preserve his modesty in the Garden of Eden—the "first and most perfect 'world's fair.'"[85] This gentle mocking of international exhibitions calls to mind two of Young America's most ardent enthusiasts, Charles Goepp and Samuel Cox. As we saw in chapter 4, both became besotted with the Great Exhibition when they travelled Europe in the early 1850s.

By using the Genesis story as its basis, Lincoln's lecture took as a touchstone a pre-Enlightenment fable that warned of the dangers of eating from the Tree of Knowledge. Of course, Lincoln humorously inverted the original meaning of the Genesis myth by turning Adam into the first "inventor"—a man who had to "invent the art of invention." Despite this, the original meaning of the story was not lost. Just as Genesis teaches us that we cannot truly overcome original sin, Lincoln criticized Young America's unqualified faith in moral progress. He told his audience that human character had not changed since Adam's day—the first man and father of humankind was "quite as much of a man as his very self-complacent descendent" (the Young American). In fact, Adam had an advantage over Young America in that he "had dominion over all the earth," while Young America seeks only to "re-annex it."[86] By championing the past in this way, Lincoln was abiding by a long tradition of Whig thinkers who valued the intellectual and political ancestry of the American Union. Furthermore, he articulated a skepticism about the inevitability of moral progress that was a characteristic of many Whiggish criticisms of Young America. In this conservative political tradition, cooperation and accumulated wisdom were highly valued, at the expense of Douglas's blind fixation on decentralization and intellectual emancipation.

Like Lincoln, the Protestant Episcopal clergyman Caleb S. Henry wrote extensive critiques of the progressive doctrines of Young America during the 1850s. By the time he joined the Republican Party, Henry offered an alternative vision of Unionism that bore a strong resemblance to Lincoln's. As a professor of history and philosophy at New York University, Henry was in a unique position to do this, addressing Democratic intellectuals like George Bancroft head-on. In 1854, for example, he wrote the lecture "Young America—The True Idea of Progress" to undermine the Democrats' beliefs about the universal laws underlying national existence. Like Lincoln, he noted that "the phrase 'Young

America' has become one of frequent utterance among us." He implored his audience to take the label seriously, writing, "The wise will not regard it merely as a phrase—merely as designating a certain number of ardent young men." Rather, "It involves ideas, thoughts, sentiments, instincts and practical tendencies of the gravest significance in the political and social sphere."[87]

Like other Whig critics of Young America, such as Edward Everett, Henry did not dismiss the movement in its entirety. If it was not taken to its extremes, the historian believed that Young America's vision of the Union could stimulate the imagination and inspire Americans to strive patiently for national greatness: "So far as Young America is the feeling of this idea, the stirring of this impulse, it is a noble and sacred thing."[88] Nevertheless, Henry warned of dangers that mirrored Lincoln's critique: namely, the tendency to disavow and disrespect the past, to push abstract ideas too far into practice, and to ignore the indispensable role of religion in bringing about social progress and political cohesion. While Young America Democrats were turning toward more conservative language in 1854, Henry nonetheless chastised them for pushing "an abstract idea out with reckless absoluteness." They apparently forgot that politics was a "practical science" and were therefore too keen to "uproot what works well merely to replace it with something more theoretically perfect."[89] Added to this dangerous tendency, Young America applied principles to areas of political life that were best governed by practical considerations. To be sure, Henry recognized that "eternal principles of justice" governed human behavior, such as the right to the fruit of one's own labor.[90] Nevertheless, "Questions of economical policy are not questions of political principle."[91] Confronted with George Bancroft's and Robert Walker's faith in the democratizing power of free trade, Henry wrote, "It has no more to do with the question of political freedom, than the question of gas or oil in street-lighting; and to argue it (because of the word 'free') as if it had, is absurd and mischievous."[92] Henry made clear that he did not think free trade was necessarily wrong or inefficient but that it was profoundly misguided to think of it as a natural right, synonymous with enlightened thought and political liberation.

In another lecture aimed at Young America, entitled "Remarks on George Bancroft's Oration on Human Progress," Henry attacked the "chief intellectual spokesperson" of the Democratic Party for paying insufficient attention to religion in his view of national progress.[93] He criticized Bancroft for arguing that democratic government, rather than religious salvation, should provide the foundations for social advancement. Furthermore, he took aim at popular sovereignty and territorial expansion. Firstly, Henry described Bancroft's assertion that the "last political state of the world . . . is ever more exulted than the old" as "pernicious rigmarole." It was "a poor thing, in our judgement, to tell mankind at this age, that they are going gloriously onward in a perpetual movement towards something better."[94] The problem for Henry lay in the fact that Bancroft saw the twin forces of technological development and democratic government driving human advancement, leaving no room for religion or individual conscience. The theologian wrote that even if "all the nations of the earth" were "in enjoyment of free governments," they would not "contain the guarantees for the continual progress of humanity."[95] Similarly, technological and cultural sophistication could not do the work of religious faith: "Progress in civilization, in science and knowledge, in the subjugation of the tremendous forces of nature to man's earthly uses, has not been a proportional progress of humanity in true rational, moral and spiritual development."[96] This critique of the natural and political sciences as the true drivers of social progress aimed squarely at Bancroft's internationalist political outlook. Without Protestant piety, the enlightened society Bancroft hoped to create through technology, free trade, and territorial expansion was only "the increase and expansion of what we are now."[97] Social progress without the directing force of Protestantism was aimless and destructive.

Caleb Henry equally rejected the idea that the will of the majority, as given expression in American democracy, would always be just and righteous. He devoted a lengthy passage to undermining Bancroft's claim that "the multitude is wiser than the philosopher." Henry found this phrase absurd, as it argued that "the voice of the people is the voice of God." This was not, as Bancroft would make out, a "universal truth," but one that applied only when "the voice of the people is the echo of God's voice in man." Just as he dismissed the inherent value of territorial growth, Henry condemned majority rule if it was not tempered by the wisdom of divine judgment. To think otherwise, it may "be rightfully pleaded as a divine sanction for all the crimes that have ever been committed under the impulse of popular frenzy." In fact, for Henry, it was God who had "appointed the few to be the guides of the many." Without their beneficial influence, "individuals, nations, the race, can go the road downward, as well as the road upward."[98] Although he did not mention slavery in this reply to Bancroft's oration, this statement had undeniable implications for Henry's attitude toward popular sovereignty. Unlike Douglas or Bancroft, Henry knew the public mind was liable to corruption. The majority might well vote for slavery in the territories and declare it just. Instead, Henry preached the right to the fruit of one's own labor, rooted in God's transcendent laws, over the fickle demands of American democracy.

Ultimately, the two historians disagreed on the final authority in national life: Bancroft deferred to the will of the people, which was tantamount to the voice of God. By contrast, Caleb Henry thought that Protestant ethics were the ultimate arbiter in human affairs, assuming an importance above even majoritarian rule. Placing the United States at the heart of historical development, Bancroft taught that humankind could flourish only through the influence of American democracy. By contrast, Henry recognized that religious salvation had been achieved in other eras and under different political systems. For him, it was the crucial ingredient of Protestant faith that brought about true progress, rather than Bancroft's eulogy to technological advance and democratic government. While Bancroft believed that America's political system would transform humanity, Henry recognized that "every age has had its side of true and right"— just like the present one. He declared, "Young America . . . must not be ignorant of the past, nor despise it, much less hate it," for this risked God's time-honored laws in favor of a novel, but misguided, form of democratic morality.[99]

As rival visions of progress did battle, Democratic nationalism remained a powerful means of making sense of the world even at the very height of the sectional crisis. The ideology of the Democratic Party did not merely fade away after the collapse of the second party system in 1854. Historian Michael Holt might argue that "the Jacksonian Democratic Party that had helped constitute the Second American Party System died just as the Whig party did."[100] But sectional ideologies, on their own, are not sufficient for understanding the politics of the 1850s. The Democracy was not a mere a pawn of the Slave Power, nor the Republican Party purely a vehicle for the extinction of slavery.[101] Once we look beyond the fragile sectional and partisan coalitions that emerged in the 1850s, we begin to see that Jacksonian nationalism continued to shape Northern politics within both the Democratic and Republican folds. As civil war loomed on the horizon, a great many politicians maintained a commitment not to Northern or Southern sections but to a Jacksonian vision of free labor and popular sovereignty for white men within a decentralized republic, propped up by the colonization or extermination of Black laborers.

Liberal Nationalism in an Age of Civil Wars

Many Americans in the late 1850s thought the Union was breaking apart, with several discrete nationalities jostling for dominance where there should have been one. But these different nationalities did not always divide along sectional lines, based around the geographical entities of North and South. Rather, as one congressman noted in 1857: "Intellectual anarchy reigns throughout the land. There is no social doctrine, no scientific maxim of government, assured of general assent or free from incessant discussion. The entire population of the country appears to be slowly dividing into distinct nationalities, as perverse in their prejudices, as opposite in their peculiarities of thought and feeling, as if they were severed by the breadth of angry seas, or the height of icy mountains." This particular American believed that nationality had nothing to do with geographical markers or even cultural homogeneity. Instead, "unity in fundamental opinions" constituted "the spiritual essence, the very soul of nationality." Furthermore, in describing the ideas that divided the nation, he did not turn exclusively to Northern, or Southern sectionalism. Rather, the "general antagonism of primary opinions" included those Northern politicians who "proclaim[ed] a frightful despotism in Congress to rule the people of the Territories as the mere serfs of government."[1] For many other antebellum Americans, a shared intellectual culture, rather than geographical or cultural homogeneity, provided the foundations of national existence. And the ideas that defined the nation did not just hinge on the question of slavery.

Observing the Revolutions of 1848 in Europe, the French political thinker Alexis de Tocqueville noted that people had not always seen nationality in this way. Before the French Revolution at the end of the eighteenth century, people defined themselves in terms of a shared history and a common territory. Only afterward did the revolution create "beyond separate nationalities, an intellectual homeland, where men of all nations could become citizens." Tocqueville argued that this was a new phenomenon in political life. "No similar feature can be discovered," he said, "in any other political revolution recorded in history." Tocqueville understood that the universalist ideology behind these political upheavals more accurately resembled religious, rather than political, conflicts. The French aristocrat summarized: "Religions commonly affect mankind in the abstract without allowance for additions or changes effected by laws, customs or national traditions." They dealt with "the reciprocal duties of men, independent of social institutions. . . . Based on principles essential to human nature, they are applicable and suited to all races of men."[2] If religious questions referred to anything involving principle rather than specific theological doctrines, then the religious disposition was equally relevant for a secular age. What Tocqueville was getting at were the religious roots of secular liberalism—how political conflicts during the mid-nineteenth century began to assume a religious character.

Tocqueville observed that it was precisely this new form of political mobilization that was responsible for the violent revolutions presiding over the mid-nineteenth century. Since 1789 revolutions had addressed themselves to "*natural principles of social order and government*" and were therefore capable of "simultaneous imitation in a hundred different places." This did not simply increase the scale of the violence over a larger geographical area but made the upheavals themselves particularly intense. "By seeming to tend to the regeneration of the human race than to the form of France alone," Tocqueville wrote, the revolution "roused passions such as the most violent political revolutions had been incapable of awakening." The French Revolution had transformed a discrete political conflict into a millenarian struggle; it was an intellectual revolution that refused to die on the guillotine with Robespierre. These doctrines went on "uniting or dividing men"—not according to territorial boundaries but in spite of them. They "turned fellow citizens into enemies, strangers into brothers . . . despite their laws, traditions, personality of language."[3] In effect, the cosmopolitanism of the French Revolution had created a global civil war. By making universal ideas the basis of political loyalty, people came to see groups divided by mountains and oceans as allies and friends. At the same time, common territory, shared history, and tradition lost their role as markers of political belonging.

Several of the thinkers admired by Young America Democrats were less cynical than Tocqueville about the prospects of internationalism. In 1758 the Swiss theorist of international law Emer de Vattel looked forward to a time when "nations would communicate to each other their products and their knowledge; a profound peace would prevail all over the earth, and enrich it with its invaluable fruits."[4] Others, however, seemed to tacitly acknowledge the connection between cosmopolitanism and civil conflict. As historian David Armitage notes, the French author Victor Hugo, who contributed to the *Democratic*

Review during the 1850s, dwelt on this relationship in his most famous novel, *Les Misérables.*[5] One of his characters, Marius Pontmercy, heads to the barricades in 1832 to do battle with the Bourbon monarchy. He asks: "Civil war, what does this mean? Is there any foreign war? Is not every war between men, war between brothers? War is modified only by its aim. There is neither foreign war, nor civil war. There is only unjust war, and just war. . . . War becomes shame, the sword becomes a dagger, only when it assassinates right, progress, reason, civilization, truth. Then civil war is a foreign war."[6] Here, Hugo perfectly describes the same intellectual transformation as Tocqueville. With the rise of cosmopolitanism, territories and borders became increasingly unimportant. As such, war between different countries began to assume the cast of conflicts between brothers. At the same time, new sites of political loyalty—perhaps new nations—emerged in place of geographical lines on the map. The question of being foreign came to relate to principle—the "sword only becomes a dagger" when set against "right, progress, reason," and "truth." As a result, neighbors within the same territory were no longer necessarily allies and friends. If set against right and progress, they became part of a different nation altogether. Twenty years before America's own great civil conflict, John O'Sullivan touched on the same relationship between cosmopolitanism and civil war in the *Democratic Review.* In an 1840 article entitled "Democracy," O'Sullivan predicted that the different states of the Union would soon go to war. He wrote, "A long warfare will infringe on the civilities of life" that would divide families in two.[7] But from the vantage point of 1840, the conflict O'Sullivan expected to see was not the one that divided the nation in 1861. Rather than a fight over slavery, he thought the two antagonistic principles were democracy and centralized government, encapsulated by America's proto-Federalists—the Whig Party.

John O'Sullivan's call to arms was a unique product of his universalist view of the American nation. Rejecting the historicist vision of the Whig Party, Young America Democrats situated the Union in a much wider context. Rather than looking to precedent and positive law, writers at O'Sullivan's periodical turned to the intellectual authorities of political science, political economy, and international law. They argued these disciplines could interpret nature and uncover the fundamental principles of national existence. Although they rejected the Enlightenment's static view of a "state of nature," these Young Americans still believed the nation should conform to the natural laws that emerged in democratic society. Examining O'Sullivan's *Democratic Review* and its congressional allies, my book has traced one of the ways in which cosmopolitanism came to shape American political discourse during the antebellum era. To use Benedict Anderson's phrasing, O'Sullivan and his allies created an "imagined community" at the international level, one that actually made national existence more precarious.[8] Drawing on the "Democratic principle" to define national loyalty, O'Sullivan turned on his fellow Whigs as enemies of the nation. It is much harder to imagine Whigs pushing for this kind of conflict within the Union. Their vision of the nation's political system was very different. It might be called historicist: prioritizing the territory of the United States and the traditions associated with it over reforming the international order in line with a Democratic idea of justice.

As historian Daniel Howe has convincingly shown, the Whigs presented a view of the nation at odds with the radical cosmopolitanism of Young America. Rather than the tradition of natural law, their conception of the nation was rooted in a divine obligation to respect positive, or local, legislation, as contained in the British tradition of common law. More wedded to their British ancestry, Whigs saw the institutions and traditions they had inherited from their Anglo-American forbearers as bulwarks of national stability. Whigs embraced their specific Protestant heritage drawn from colonial New England to drive individual and national uplift. This was not defined as liberation from the central government but individual moral development based on restraint and self-control. These components amount to a view of the nation that Howe, and many of the Whigs he writes of, called "an organic community."[9] Place, precedent, and a specific religious culture mattered much more than universalist values, amounting to a more conservative view of the nation.

Of course, the Declaration of Independence still played a significant role in the Whig political tradition. But, as we have seen, it was defined in a more qualified way: democracy itself was not a natural right but a system of government designed to safeguard the more fundamental freedoms of "life, liberty and the pursuit of happiness."[10] Furthermore, when Whigs did promote natural rights, they did so through extrapolitical evangelical reform rather than wielding legislative influence. Historian Stewart Winger refers to the Whigs' "Augustinian" distinction between the higher law emanating from God and the national law that bound political life.[11] Because the Whigs' vision of the nation was conservative and territorial, they were far less likely to imagine ideological conflict within the Union. For them, the primary markers of national identity were a shared sense of place and cultural tradition. In this context, nations might fight each other, particularly over their spheres of interest, but they would not turn on their fellow citizens. Living under the same set of positive laws engendered loyalty; natural law was less relevant.

The Whigs saw the nation as a means of harmonizing competing interests rather than setting different groups against each other. They recognized that citizens might have different ideas about good government and different priorities and expectations within society. But people could still be brought together under a shared legal system and common cultural traditions. With careful statesmanship, political leaders could hold inevitable social conflicts in check. Whigs talked about being "national" or "above party" just as much as Democrats, but they meant a very different thing by it. Young America Democrats meant abiding by natural law applicable in all times and places. Whigs meant weighing up competing interests. Both looked to an authority higher than mere politics. But where Democrats turned to political science, Whigs more often looked to a sense of patriotism or disinterested concern for the common good.

O'Sullivan's efforts to divide the nation into two ideological factions, and his prediction of a global civil war, are absent in Whig political writing. In this sense, we can see how Young America's tradition of universalist nationalism acted as a catalyst for the Civil War. Almost all scholars view Stephen Douglas and his political allies as pragmatic politicians, committed to keeping the Democratic Party and the Union together at a time of deepening sectional conflict.[12] The recent historian of Young America, Yonatan Eyal suggests that Douglas's movement postponed the Civil War through its successful attempts at compromise.[13] However, Young America Democrats came to the language of accommodation late in the game. Faced with a conciliatory Whig opposition, they opened fissures in the Union by seeding nationalism in natural law. Long before Lincoln started using the discourse of natural rights in 1854, Douglas, Bancroft, and O'Sullivan advanced a universalist conception of the nation to replace the territorially binding vision of the antebellum Whigs.

The imagined global community of Young America turned all foreign wars into civil wars. As Democratic politicians envisaged their place in an international order, territorial markers lost their significance. They justified intervention in faraway conflicts on the grounds they were fighting for the same values within a shared global community. At the same time, since territory was no longer the primary marker of national identity, the bonds between people living in geographic proximity lost their intrinsic strength. The Young America movement, therefore, illuminates the relationship between cosmopolitanism and conflict historian David Armitage has highlighted. Drawing on European examples at the turn of the eighteenth century, he reminds "contemporary political theorists" that cosmopolitanism is not necessarily "a philosophy of peace."[14] The prevailing wisdom assumes that "cosmopolitanism's imagined community would be tolerant, egalitarian and universalist." "Only recently," Armitage points out, "have scholars acknowledged that cosmopolitanism might have something to say about war or that war might shed light on the limits and possibilities of cosmopolitanism."[15] He remarks later, "Just as the Enlightenment itself had its shadows, so there is a dark side to enlightened cosmopolitanism."[16] My book reinforces Armitage's central argument: that these "least likely of all conceptual companions"—cosmopolitanism and civil war—are in fact mutually reinforcing.[17]

Although a civil war did break out in 1861, it was not, as O'Sullivan predicted, a conflict between different visions of democracy. However, this book has demonstrated that the Young America movement played a role in shifting the debate over nationalism onto the grounds of natural law in the first place. Ascendant in the years from 1846 to 1854, Young America became a touchstone for a broad range of politicians and writers in- and outside Congress. Edward Everett, John Bell, George W. Curtis, and Abraham Lincoln all defined new visions of nationalism with reference to Douglas's and Bancroft's Young America. Although these ex-Whigs rejected the equation of political and natural rights, they nevertheless drew on the natural law tradition and framed their political position in terms of the international, as well as the national, order. The Whig-Republicans who formed the backbone of the fight against slavery came to champion a form of nationalism very different from their old party. Rejecting the classical republicanism that dominated Colton's *Whig Review*, the Republicans advanced a conception of positive moral government rooted in the natural law tradition—one that owed much to the millenarianism of O'Sullivan, Bancroft, and Douglas.

Furthermore, during the sectional crisis, Young Americans believed they were primarily fighting against the encroachments of the federal government. Stephen Douglas and his allies—George Bancroft, John McClernand, and Samuel Cox—resisted calls by both the North and South for federal legislation on the subject of slavery in the territories. These Jacksonian nationalists believed that both abolitionists and the Slave Power threatened the Democratic principles of popular sovereignty and nonintervention. Once implemented, these universal laws would bring stability and social progress in equal measure. In this sense, then, Democratic Unionists *were* fighting O'Sullivan's conflict, even if Whig-Republicans like Lincoln were not. When viewed in this context, O'Sullivan's prediction is eerily prescient.

More broadly, the Young America movement can help us reevaluate our own accounts of social progress and think again about the place of the Civil War in our larger histories of the American nation. While historians of the South have long recognized that the slave owners' hierarchical and racist worldview was also outward-looking and distinctly modern, historians of the antebellum North have been slower to appreciate the ambivalent sides to progress in the mid-nineteenth century. As historians Edward Ayers and Dorothy Ross have observed, we still see the coming of the Civil War as a melioristic narrative. The dominant accounts argue that abolitionists forced the universalist values of human rights onto the political agenda. In this scenario, the emancipation of the slaves becomes the culmination of a half-century-long struggle on behalf of the values of liberal individualism. As Dorothy Ross describes: "Since the 1960s emancipation has been influentially portrayed as a result of the gradual, halting, but growing triumph of universalist liberal and Christian principles, a key moment in a progressive national narrative of growing freedom."[18] Or, as Edward Ayers suggests, this story "reassures Americans by reconciling the great anomaly of slavery with an overarching story of a people devoted to liberty."[19] By bringing Young America's vision of progress into focus, we can challenge our more teleological assumptions about mid-nineteenth-century America. Many Americans might have looked to natural rights to secure the promises of the Declaration of Independence. But there was a darker side to the liberal tradition that did not see the future this way. Young America was the group perhaps most closely associated with the notion of progress during the mid-nineteenth century. Yet the future they envisioned was not primarily defined in terms of opposition to slavery. Rather, it constituted the rollback of the federal government, free trade, and popular sovereignty. The natural laws they championed worked on behalf of white majorities, not individuals, and championed a racial pseudoscience that instrumentally assisted Southern slave owners. It was not inevitable for the liberal tradition to culminate in the election of Lincoln and the emancipation of the slaves. There were other powerful currents of universalist thought that pointed in very different directions—visions of progress that, thankfully, never came to pass.

By rejecting Young America's arguments for territorial expansion and popular sovereignty, Republican opposition to slavery involved as much a conservative as a progressive impulse. Some Republicans had to do battle with the idea that unbridled democracy would bring about an inherently just social order. Others remained closer to Young America's worldview even as they moved in explicitly antislavery circles. But from the vantage point of the antebellum years, Young Americans seem, in important respects, more liberal and forward-looking than some of their Republican counterparts, and as having a greater claim to the values of the Enlightenment. The effort to root politics in natural, not positive, law led many Democrats toward the racial pseudoscience of phrenology. For them, African American inferiority was inherent in the psychological makeup of the race. The possibility that slaves could thrive outside Africa and the tropics or integrate into American society was anathema: "extermination" and colonization were seriously entertained as alternatives. These Young Americans saw themselves on the cutting edge of Enlightenment thought, abandoning the metaphysical speculations that made the antislavery movement an outdated political force. The idea of a universal right to labor, which cut across racial and gender divisions, flew in the face of phrenological developments. It also privileged religious values over science, economic efficiency, free-market capitalism, and unqualified majoritarianism.[20] In opposing Young America, many Republicans, including Abraham Lincoln, criticized their reckless progressivism as much as the inhumanity of their position on the slavery question. The idea that the free exchange of ideas would always produce moral outcomes and that material development went hand-in-hand with moral progress were criticized as hallmarks of Young America's political thought.

By contrast, several members of the Republican Party, sometimes quite explicitly, recognized the limitations of the Enlightenment project. There was no progress without religious guidance, the multitude was often corrupt, and Providence was frequently inscrutable. The physical and material laws that governed the human world were distinct from the divine. Figures like Caleb Henry noted that a priori ideas about fundamental equality were necessary to guard against the direction in which public opinion might be tending. Less sure of social progress than George Bancroft, Henry knew the nation was as likely to degenerate as improve if democracy alone was the highest standard of morality. Theological certainties were necessary for just and enduring government, together with a healthy skepticism about new scientific developments. The capacity for "negative capability" some historians have attributed to Lincoln meant making peace with the things that could not be known.[21]

The Democrats' use of the natural law, then, did not lead them to the egalitarianism of the Declaration of Independence; in fact, quite the opposite. Blurring the boundary between natural and political rights, Democrats criticized fixed ideas about equality as belonging to an anterior age. Instead, Young Americans wanted to investigate society as it was—to find the workings of nature in the political and social order rather than in metaphysical abstractions. Texts such as Elisha Hurlbut's book on natural rights made the case that the white race's instincts made them uniquely suited to democratic society.[22] Similarly, the races with no grounding in Europe's intellectual or political traditions were deemed inherently inferior and were excluded not only from the political order but from humanity itself. Finally, these Democrats displayed a reverence for public opinion, believing the prejudices of white society revealed general laws.[23] It was the Young Americans, not the Republican Party, who most often claimed to represent the "spirit of the age." As much as anyone in antebellum political culture, these "progressive" Democrats advocated new principles to deal with unprecedented problems in domestic and foreign policy. Thankfully, a majority of Northerners rejected their vision, arguing the ancient values contained in the Declaration of Independence were worth preserving. Conscious that moral issues were not settled through the operation of providential laws, these men and women took action. Only then did Americans ensure that slavery had no place in the future of the United States.

Notes

Abbreviations

GNSFP   George Nicholas Sanders Family Papers, Library of Congress
HSP   Historical Society of Pennsylvania, Philadelphia
LC   Library of Congress, Washington, DC
MHS   Massachusetts Historical Society, Boston
NYPL   Manuscripts and Archives Division, New York Public Library
TLKP   Thomas L. Kane Papers, Brigham Young University, Provo, Utah

Introduction

1. As explored in chapter 7, a number of key Young Americans supported Stephen Douglas in the election of 1860 from both sides of the Mason-Dixon line, including Kentucky's George Sanders, Mississippi's Robert J. Walker, Louisiana's Pierre Soulé, Illinois's William Richardson, Ohio's Samuel S. Cox, as well as New York's George Bancroft, Samuel Tilden, August Belmont, Martin Van Buren, and John O'Sullivan. Former contributors to and allies of the *Democratic Review* who defected to the Republican Party include John Bigelow, William C. Bryant, Galusha Grow, and John Forney, albeit very late in the day.

2. For the only book-length study of the politics of Young America, see Eyal, *Young America Movement*. Eyal primarily examines how the Young America movement transformed the internal politics of the Democratic Party. Building on this contribution, my book focuses on the role of Young America within the broader political culture, with a particular focus on its critics and the extent of its influence beyond the Democratic ranks. Moreover, Eyal's sources are almost entirely political, while my book examines how and why political figures drew on intellectual and literary culture so extensively during this period. Finally, he does not aim to fully examine Young America ideology during the sectional crisis; in particular, he does not show how the wider program related to slavery and race as well as the specific policy of popular sovereignty. Indeed, Eyal characterizes the movement's progressive agenda as "antislavery" and downplays Democrats' racism. Conversely, I argue that neither anti- nor proslavery categories can adequately describe an ideology that was ultimately Jacksonian throughout the entire decade before the Civil War. Furthermore, Young America's self-consciously "progressive" agenda was entirely compatible with their racist worldview. Eyal does provide a compelling account

of Young America's relationship with the Kansas-Nebraska Act: see Eyal, "With His Eyes Open." For more on the politics of the Young America movement, also see Curti, "Young America"; and Danborn, "Young America Movement." For the literary culture of the Young America movement, see Miller, *Raven and the Whale.* For both the politics and culture of the Young America movement, which are nevertheless treated as distinct entities, see Widmer, *Young America: Flowering of Democracy.* Like Eyal, Widmer does not fully extend his analysis of the politics of Young America into the 1850s.

3. G. Dallas, *Great Speech of Hon. George M. Dallas,* 14.

4. Shields, *Letter of the Hon. James Shields,* 3.

5. Trevelyan is quoted in Kinealy, *Repeal and Revolution,* 1.

6. Rudolph Vecoli observes that the 1840s saw the beginning of the "first wave" of European immigration to the United States, which lasted from 1841 to 1890; during this time a total of almost fifteen million new arrivals were recorded. "Significance of Immigration," 11.

7. The first issue that lists Thomas P. Kettell as editor is *Democratic Review* 21 (July 1847), and the last is *Democratic Review* 29 (July 1851). In his *Memoir of Thomas Devin Reilly,* Irish revolutionary John Savage wrote that in 1852, Reilly "finally found his true place as editor of the *Democratic Review* in connection with his friend George Sanders" (27). In 1853 he began editing the official Democratic organ the *Union* in Washington, DC, before dying from a stroke the following year.

8. See, for example, "Chicago Convention. Speech of David Dudley Field," *Democratic Review* 21 (September 1847); and T. F. Meagher, "Ireland and the Holy Alliance," *Democratic Review* 31 (July 1852).

9. *New York Evening Post,* January 22, 1838, quoted in Widmer, *Young America: Flowering of Democracy,* 42.

10. For these figures, see Widmer, *Young America: Flowering of Democracy,* 228.

11. *Boston Post* quoted in ibid., 47.

12. "Introduction," *Democratic Review* 1 (October 1837), 14.

13. "The Great Nation of Futurity," *Democratic Review* 6 (November 1839), 427.

14. Foletta, *Coming to Terms with Democracy.*

15. "Great Nation of Futurity," *Democratic Review* 6 (November 1839), 428, 427.

16. "Popular Sovereignty and States' Rights," *Democratic Review* 25 (July 1849), 5.

17. "Political Portraits with Pen and Pencil: Hon. Edmund Burke," *Democratic Review* 20 (January 1847), 75.

18. "Political Portraits: George Dallas," *Democratic Review* 10 (February 1842), 166.

19. "Political Portraits: John. C Calhoun," *Democratic Review* 12 (January 1843), 93; "Political Portraits: James Buchanan," *Democratic Review* 11 (July 1842), 650.

20. *Cong. Globe,* 32nd Cong., 2nd Sess. (1853), 243.

21. As Illinois's William Richardson had done before him, Marshall attacked Breckenridge for "denouncing the editor of the *Review* and the whole character of the publication, without measure or moderation." *Cong. Globe,* 32nd Cong., 1st Sess. (1852), 723.

22. Journal of Anna J. R. Sanders, March 9, 1852, GNSFP, LC.

23. *New York Herald,* May 16, 1853.

24. By invoking the term "Young America" and tracing its actual usage in the political culture, I hope to convey how this movement was in the process of constant construction and reconstruction as people identified with the ideology to different degrees over time. I hope this addresses David Potter's warning that where the historian's "theory tells him that nationalism is a relative thing existing in partial form, his practice may impel him to treat it as an absolute thing, existing in full or not at all." "Historian's Use of Nationalism," 927.

25. Although formerly a supporter of the Whig Party, Caleb Cushing switched to the Democrats during the 1840s and became associated with the Young America program. The *New York Herald* said of him "with respect to his political proclivities, we apprehend he is identified with the progressive school of 'Young America.' . . . He is not afraid of Cuba. . . . The atmosphere of the Democratic Party has expanded his views on the tariff question into the conviction that the policy of Robert J. Walker and the policy of Sir Robert Peel have done more for our commerce and that of the world than all the high protective tariffs of the last quarter of a century." *New York Herald,* February 19, 1853.

26. For a classic biography see Johannsen, *Stephen A. Douglas.* Martin Quitt draws on a huge range of sources, as well as insights from psychology, in *Stephen A. Douglas and Antebellum Democracy.* Rather than studying Douglas's place within the Democratic Party, scholars usually study him in relation to his rival Abraham Lincoln. See Jaffa, *Crisis of the House Divided;* and Burt, *Lincoln's Tragic Pragmatism.* A recent and highly illuminating exception is Woods, *Arguing until Doomsday.*

27. Butler, "Anti-slavery, Liberalism and Empire Building."

28. Winger, "Lincoln's Economics and the American Dream."

29. Southern suspicion of the Revolutions of 1848 is outlined in Roberts, *Distant Revolutions.*

30. The Southern transition toward seeing the imperial powers of Europe as allies who recognized the necessity of bound labor is explored in Karp, *This Vast Southern Empire.*

31. "Eighteen Fifty-Two, and the 'Coming Man,'" *Democratic Review* 30 (January 1852).

32. John Geiss to Stephen Douglas, August 12, 1856, SADP. George Sanders voted for Buchanan over Douglas at the Democratic Convention owing to a dispute detailed in chapter 4, but he later came to regret this choice, and in 1860 championed Douglas's swift attempt to restore sectional harmony in the face of secession, as outlined in chapter 7.

33. For the politics of Young America, see Eyal, *Young America Movement;* Curti, "Young America"; Danborn, "Young America Movement." Like Eyal, Curti does not trace the way Young America Democrats in the political arena drew on intellectual and literary culture, nor does he examine Young America ideology during the sectional crisis or how it relates in particular to the policy of popular sovereignty.

34. To be sure, Duyckinck was a Democrat and political ally of O'Sullivan, who edited the literary section of the *Democratic Review* from 1844 to 1846. He supported the reform of capital punishment, among other causes of the periodical. But by the 1850s he had turned away from both Democratic politics and strident literary nationalism. For

the literary culture of the Young America movement, see Miller, *Raven and the Whale;* Widmer, *Young America: Flowering of Democracy.* A more recent study of the influence of a postcolonial mentality on the art, culture, and intellectual life of the United States is Haynes, *Unfinished Revolution.* There was also a paper dedicated to land reform entitled *Young America* that was distinct from the group of expansionist Democrats. See Lause, *Young America.*

35. There is a tendency in the current literature to separate the intellectual and political ambitions of Young America. Edward Widmer acknowledges the importance of studying the literary and political elements of Young America together. But, ultimately, he separates the movement into "Young America I" and "Young America II," which William Kerrigan has termed an "unconvincing distinction." In this interpretation, "Young America I" denotes the literary movement associated with Cornelius Matthews and Evert Duyckinck, while "Young America II" refers to the political movement pushing for territorial expansion, which is presented as a fig leaf for Southern interests. This argument falls prey to two weaknesses common to the broader swathes of Jacksonian historiography. First, it separates the militaristic and racist aspects of the Young America program from their intellectual and ideological roots as well as from Jacksonian ideology as a whole. Second, by presenting Young America as a mere fig leaf for Southern interests, Widmer obscures the continued importance of Democratic principles throughout the 1850s—which found a home in both the two major Northern parties. See Widmer, *Young America: Flowering of Democracy;* Kerrigan, "Review: E. Widmer, 'Young America: Flowering of Democracy.'"

36. As Michael Zuckert points out, "Although the Declaration declares government an artifice made by human beings, that is not at all the case with rights for they are said to derive from the Creator. Rights thus precede government and result from no human making." Zuckert, *Natural Rights,* 3.

37. Dorothy Ross does not tie this development explicitly to Young America. Nevertheless, the *Democratic Review* and its congressional allies were at the vanguard of the antebellum Democracy, especially interested in theoretical questions and the propagation of Democracy as a universal principle to be extended around the world. See D. Ross, "Lincoln and the Ethics of Emancipation." James Oakes identifies three categories of rights in antebellum America: natural rights, citizenship rights, and states' rights, including laws regulating voting, marriage, and jury duty. Oakes carefully outlines how Lincoln was an egalitarian on natural rights, believing these transcended racial divisions, and was "cautiously egalitarian" on citizenship rights. In both cases Lincoln "resisted" the idea that these rights were "subject to majority rule." By contrast, qualifications for voting fell into a category of rights decided by individual states to be determined by "state legislatures elected by the people at large." On this question, Lincoln deferred to the prejudices of the people as constituted in the political communities of the states. Although Lincoln undoubtedly shared many of these prejudices, Oakes astutely concludes, "Lincoln's prejudicial views had as much to do with democracy as racism." Oakes, "Natural Rights, Citizenship Rights," 110–11. For a view of the American nation as legitimized by nature,

see Miller, *Nature's Nation.* Nonetheless, Miller does not explore how Americans parsed these different authorities and sites of political belonging.

38. Young Americans were clearly not the most precise or sophisticated political thinkers—John O'Sullivan was no John Locke. They were also directly engaged in the political process—or were trying to influence those who were. Many times, ideas had to give way to political prerogatives, and language was imprecise. Indeed, the tendency to blur the boundaries between political relations and natural laws often stemmed from an overzealous imprecision rather than any attempt to reevaluate the relationship between nation and natural law. Nevertheless, the elision of these different categories of rights was still the consequence of Young America's thought and was picked up on explicitly by their rivals within the Whig and Republican Parties, as well as by their own opponents within the Democracy.

Young Americans used different terms interchangeably to describe their idea of white men as independent and inherently political beings. The idea of the "sovereign" often took the place of "natural rights" precisely because these figures did not distinguish between nature and politics or make natural rights a distinct category. Moreover, this mode of thought often led to confusion about exactly when a political community was formed. Young Americans implied that this was as soon as possible and that riots and mobs constituted authentic forms of political expression. But because Young Americans collapsed the boundaries between the people as an undifferentiated mass and the people as a political community, it became difficult to identify exactly when—and through what means—the change occurred. Surely, one or two men wandering through an unexplored territory did not constitute a political community, in the absence of positive laws or a common history? As we shall see, thinkers in the Whig tradition mercilessly exploited these contradictions long after the party itself collapsed. The difficulty of establishing the bounds of a political community is a central theme in the work of historian Edmund Morgan. He makes clear that as far back as the seventeenth century, the concept of popular sovereignty and the very idea of a political community were necessary fictions. He explains that "the sovereignty of the people, like the divine right of kings, and like representation itself, is a fiction that cannot survive too close examination or too literal application. It requires that we believe not only in the existence of something we call the people but also in the capacity of that something to make decisions and to act apart from the elected representatives of particular localities." Even John Locke was not "clear about just how the people, already embodied in a society (however that may have been achieved), could go about forming a government." *Inventing the People,* 256.

39. Zuckert points out that the revolutionary generation conceived of government "as a thing made for the sake of securing rights." *Natural Rights,* 3. It is important to note that the Founders also *compromised* fundamental rights for the sake of securing government. But these compromises were deemed necessary to safeguard those liberties that could be protected and allow for the realization of further freedoms over time.

40. This focus on the relationship between liberalism and nationalism will answer calls for a theory of nationalism to be developed in the American context, rather than

to merely shade in the content of the imagined memories that make up the nation or to evaluate their strength. As Michael Bernath argues, "We all know that we are supposed to cite Benedict Anderson when talking about nationalism (and we almost always do in our introductions) . . . but relatively few Civil War–era historians have undertaken the task of engaging and challenging these theories. This is a missed opportunity not simply to bring parity to the American side of the story but to advance the overall discussion about the workings of nationalism in the nineteenth century generally." "Nationalism," 6. Or as Mark Neely wondered in 2009: "Lincoln was America's most important nationalist, but what does his career mean when measured" against the ideas of Ernest Geller, Benedict Anderson, and Eric Hobsbawm? "Lincoln, Slavery," 456–58. For the idea that Manifest Destiny represented a future-orientated and distinctly American nationalism, see Merk, *Manifest Destiny.* Also see Parish, "Exception to Most of the Rules."

41. John Locke has had a tremendous influence on American political thought, most particularly through his conception of natural rights. But many other European figures popularized these ideas, which were, in turn reinterpreted by American thinkers. In the nineteenth century natural rights and natural law were so integral to the American lexicon that writers and politicians would draw on these ideas without any reference to Locke. Historian of political thought John Dunn concludes, "The historical question of just how much American political perception or sentiment [was] at any point clearly attributable to the more or less attentive reading of passages from Locke's writings is extremely complicated and very hard to answer at all convincingly." "Measuring Locke's Shadow," 264. Merle Curti concludes that Locke remained "America's philosopher" right up until the outbreak of the Civil War in areas of education, religion, and reform, as well as politics. Curti concludes, "Divergent interests appealed to contradictory doctrines and implications in Locke's political thought." "The Great Mr. Locke," 136. A defense of natural right as the right to autonomy and the fruits of one's labor also appeared in the early eighteenth-century text *Cato's Letters,* by John Trenchard and Thomas Gordon. Indeed, Clinton Rossiter argued that this text was more influential than Locke's work for the American founders. *Seedtime of the Republic,* 140. My book is less concerned with the intellectual antecedents of the ideas of natural rights and natural law as it is the way this discourse played out in the political culture of mid-nineteenth-century America.

42. Pocock, *Machiavellian Moment;* Bailyn, *Ideological Origins of the Revolution.*

43. Historian Herman Belz writes that "when Abraham Lincoln said in 1858 that the real issue in the slavery controversy was the eternal struggle between right and wrong throughout the world, he spoke the language of natural law," since "the natural law tradition posits the existence of an objective and universal moral order external to subjective human intellect." "Abraham Lincoln and Natural Law," 1. For an examination of antislavery politics and the natural law tradition, see Dyer, *Natural Law;* and Jaffa, *Crisis of the House Divided.* Jaffa contrasts Lincoln's faith in the natural law tradition with Douglas's supposedly pragmatic and materialist concerns. Similarly, Stewart Winger argues that "it was Douglas, not Lincoln, who wanted Americans to put economic development (and political compromise) above morality." "Lincoln's Economics," 58. For Douglas

as being "Burkean" in his pragmatism, see Baker, *Affairs of Party*. Steven Smith usefully draws attention to the Kantian dimensions of Lincoln's thought, viewing politics as "not only protectionist but progressive," which "bespeak[s] a moral perfectionism—even a utopianism—that goes well beyond the Whiggish and contracturalist language of natural law prudentialism." But, again, Smith contrasts this perspective with Stephen Douglas's "historicist view," which held that the Declaration "served merely to restore to the American colonies the rights of British subjects." "Lincoln's Kantian Republic," 218–19, 224. Like Lincoln, Douglas was steeped in the Enlightenment tradition of natural law as well as the German idealism of Immanuel Kant and his successors, via the influence of the American Transcendentalists, who traced certain "innate ideas" across time and space.

44. For the development of nationalism at the beginning of the early republic period, see Murrin, "Roof Without Walls"; Kramer, *Nationalism in Europe and America*.

45. According to one scholar, "Herder referred to happiness as an individual good which was everywhere climactic and organic, the offspring of practice, tradition and custom." Schmidt, "Cultural Nationalism in Herder," 408. Kloppenberg writes, "Attachment to the Union is easier to understand when placed alongside the nationalism of . . . John Gottfried Herder in Germany and Giuseppe Mazzini in Italy, as well as that of historians George Bancroft and Francis Parkman in the US," but he does not attend to differences between these forms of nationalism or their interaction with the liberal tradition. *Toward Democracy*, 664.

46. "The Democratic View of Democracy" *North American Review* 101 (July 1865), 107.

47. Howe writes that conservative Whigs tried to create "artificial constraints—prescriptive, legal, historical, cultural—for America." *Political Culture*, 235. Of Whig Rufus Choate, Howe notes, "The source of the pollution he found in the doctrine of Rousseau and Locke, and our own revolutionary age . . . [was] that the state is nothing but a contract." Nevertheless, "For all his talk of 'organic forms,' he admitted that American nationality and American institutions were manufactured. Our national consciousness 'is, to an extraordinary degree, not a growth, but a production.'" Ibid., 230.

48. Dorothy Ross points out the unsettling implications of Romantic nationalism for many nineteenth-century liberals: "As the construction of human action, history was subject to the frailty and contingency upon which events turned. As a process of continuous qualitative change, it also presented the constant challenge of novelty. What stable basis for understanding and praxis could be found in a historical world?" Ross points above all to the idea of historical progress that replicated aspects of Enlightenment universalism and provided a comforting teleology. In the American case, it was particularly important to mitigate against "the unsettling implications of historicism." Ross writes, "Historicist tendencies in American culture were not absent, as we shall see, but they had to contend against this larger prehistoricist framework. As 'nature's nation,' and as God's, America could more easily be seen as the domain of eighteenth-century natural law: The course of American history followed the prescriptive forms of nature." *Origins of American Social Science*, 15–16, 26.

49. O'Sullivan wrote in 1839, for example, "So far as regards the entire development of the natural rights of man, in moral, political and national life we may confidently assume that our nation is to be *the great nation* of futurity." "The Great Nation of Futurity," *Democratic Review* 6 (November 1839), 426. He also wrote, "Man surrenders none of his rights on entrance into society," so long as the state does not "intervene unduly with his affairs." "Democracy," ibid., 7 (March 1840), 223.

50. Christian Fritz argues in *American Sovereigns* that in the Revolutionary era, some Americans did argue "a majority of the people possessed the inherent right to make constitutional changes, even independent of government" (5). This view had a conservative counterpart in the argument that a constitutional revision would need to abide by an existing constitution's amendment provisions and that a constitutional convention would need the sanction of an existing state legislature. This doctrine found a home in the antebellum Whigs Party. Young Americans went further than both by arguing that the people possessed a natural right not only to revise constitutions but to preside over every aspect of government and the political community.

51. For Jacksonians' view of the market as an embodiment of nature, see Zakaras, "Nature, Religion and the Market."

52. "Democracy," *Democratic Review* 7 (March 1840), 223, 224.

53. As Barbara Fields wrote of the founding, "When self-evident laws of nature guarantee freedom, only equally self-evident laws of equally self-evident nature can account for its denial." "Slavery Race and Ideology," 107. Fields's statement describes the founding era but resonates even more in the antebellum period when natural rights were increasingly elided with political rights, making the personal truly political. Laura Clarke Shire is particularly effective in upturning the idea that "antebellum Americans kept politics out of the home, and domestic concerns out of their politics" in her analysis of Andrew Jackson's enslavement of Lyncoya. "Sentimental Racism," 119. In contrast to Shire, I downplay the importance of "separate spheres" in sustaining racial and gender hierarchies. In distinctly Jacksonian fashion, a political order based purely on natural rights blended the public and private spheres, making the maintenance of a racial and gendered hierarchy at home indistinguishable from the task of upholding an exclusionary political order.

54. *Speech of Mr Soulé of Louisiana*, 14.

55. Stephen Sawyer writes about the importance of Bancroft's idea of himself as a poet. Sawyer argues, "The poet animated history by bringing the past into the present." While German figures like Goethe were preoccupied with the specifics of the past as well as the decay of an older order, Bancroft was interested in bringing a political ideal into being, in "pulling out the essential lessons" from the past as "both poet and historian." "Between Authorship and Agency," 53–54. Dorothy Ross points out that for all their emphasis on empirical research, mid-nineteenth-century historians in Europe and the United States attempted to trace universal laws working themselves out in history. She writes that they combined a "'romantic' or 'mystical' insight with sifting through sources

to define the progressive course of development hidden in the empirical substance of history." *Origins of American Social Science,* 20.

56. At first glance, it appeared that Young Americans, Whigs, and more moderate Democrats disagreed only on the speed at which expansion should take place. Nevertheless, beneath the surface of this distinction was a set of assumptions about the nature of popular sovereignty. The extent to which democracy was considered a natural right for white men or a product of history largely determined attitudes to the speed of territorial expansion and revolution in Europe, as well as perspectives on the future and the past. Regarding the former, nations would emerge spontaneously in the absence of external interference, while in the latter case, time was necessary precisely to develop the customs and institutions necessary for democratic governments.

57. The sociologist Karl Mannheim proposes that generational consciousness depends on the rate of technological change. As a relatively youthful group of political figures, Young Americans were more accustomed to the technological changes that had occurred in the United States during the market revolution of the first half of the nineteenth century, particularly the growth of the penny press, the telegraph, steamships, canals, and railroads. The Young Americans often observed that time was moving faster in the 1840s. Obviously this was not literally true, but it captured the extent to which technological and social change had created a generational identity in opposition to an elder group of statesmen. Mannheim argues that generational consciousness is not inevitable. In times of slower technological development, other distinctions, like class, might come to the fore. In a sense Young America's generational discourse did mask class divisions in the United States by curbing resistance to the Slave Power: see *Problem of Generations.* The Young America movement's embrace of the market revolution, in contrast to an older generation of Democrats, is explored in Eyal, *Young America Movement.* Although this part of the thesis is compelling, I think Young America's support for federally funded internal improvements was a concession to practical realities rather than a core part of their ideology. For the market revolution in the United States, see Sellers, *Market Revolution.*

58. "The Position of the Parties," *Whig Review* 1 (January 1845), 6, 9 (italics in the original).

59. "Human Rights," *Whig Review* 2 (November 1845), 445.

60. Ibid., 445.

61. A. Smith, *Stormy Present.*

62. For Hawthorne's most famous attack on the reformist elements in Whig thought, see *The Blithedale Romance.*

63. Although scholars are fond of pointing out that Burke was a liberal, it is crucial to remember that his liberal principles were based on a particularist, or preliberal, foundation. This distinguishes Burke from a less conservative tradition of liberal thought found in the writings of British and American theorists such as Thomas Paine and, in a more extreme form, the Young America movement. For Burke's understanding of the

nation, see *Reflections*. For a work wonderfully alive to these distinctions within liberal thought, see Gray, *Liberalism*.

64. For histories of Jacksonian Democracy that end before the 1850s, see Schlesinger, *Age of Jackson;* Wilentz, *Chants Democratic;* Feller, *Jacksonian Promise;* Myers, *Jacksonian Persuasion*.

65. Despite the differences between these two schools, both foreground Northern and Southern worldviews in their accounts of ideological conflict before the Civil War. The classic fundamentalist interpretation of the coming of the war is Eric Foner's *Free Soil, Free Labor, Free Men*. Foner locates the rise of a mass antislavery movement in the birth of free-labor ideology in the Northern states that channeled resistance to the Southern masterclass. But this approach fails to fully appreciate the role of the Northern Democrats, who shared the same faith in free labor as their Republican counterparts but remained, in large part, a distinctive political force. In contrast, revisionists downplay the power of ideology as a causal factor in creating sectional tensions in the first place. This provides a useful sense of contingency to our explanations of the conflict, which was certainly not an inevitable consequence of irreconcilable ideologies. But when the revisionists do look at ideology, it is, eventually, to focus on sectional polarization. In the classic revisionist account, Michael Holt argues that the dissolution of lively partisan competition in the early 1850s created a political vacuum in which Americans channeled their fears about republicanism into opposition to the Slave Power. Holt might distinguish effectively between the breakdown of the second party system and the ensuing sectional crisis as two discrete events with different causes. But his account still foregrounds a distinctly Northern worldview at the expense of nationalism within the Democratic Party. Indeed, Holt argues, "The Jacksonian Democratic party that had helped constitute the Second American Party System died just as the Whig party did." *Political Crisis of the 1850s*, 104.

66. Literature on the nationalisms of the 1850s is also divided between North and South. Grant, Oakes, Peck, and Parish have explored a strand of antislavery nationalism in the antebellum North without fully exploring alternative conceptions of the nation that were popular in the Northern states—of Jacksonian or Constitutional Unionist varieties: Oakes, *Freedom National;* Grant, *North over South;* Peck, *Making an Antislavery Nation;* Parish, *North and the Nation*. On the other side, Quigley, Brettle, Bernath, and Tucker have traced varieties of Southern nationalism: Quigley, *Shifting Grounds;* Brettle, *Colossal Ambitions;* Tucker, *Newest Born of Nations;* Bernath, *Confederate Minds*. For recent scholarship on the center position of Civil War politics, or at least those who sought to reconcile North and South in some way, see Conlin, "Dangerous *Isms*"; Mason, *Apostle of Union;* A. Smith, *Stormy Present;* Furniss, "Devolved Democracy." However, at times these scholars elide the different forms of bisectional and nationalist worldviews into one homogenous group. This is unhelpful, since Americans held different theories of national development even while they were loyal to the same Union. Furthermore, terms like "centrist" and "conservative" can be misleading in the rapidly changing political climate of the 1850s. As was the case with Young America, an unmistakably radical movement could become conservative in a matter of a few years, while

the center of politics constantly shifted. What was once mainstream could be an irrelevance five years later. Moreover, the tacit equation between centrism, on the one hand, and conservative and moderate politics on the other, is perhaps hasty. In any period, centrist politicians can smuggle in fairly radical views, often forcing conservatives to take radical stands. Indeed, I argue that the truly conservative Whig position was largely destroyed in the 1850s, leading to national breakdown. Paradoxically, politicians insisted on their conservatism precisely because voters craved stability in a climate where the mainstream parties assumed radical, universalist positions. For a book refreshingly alive to these distinctions, see Lynn, *Preserving the White Man's Republic.*

67. The prevailing view that Douglas Democrats became ideologically insignificant originated in Roy Nichols's *Agents of Manifest Destiny.* Nichols argues, "Two new masses were prominent on the political landscape, the Republican party and the Solid South. Douglas had disappeared" (212). For works that sectionalize Democratic ideology by turning it into a vehicle for the Slave Power, see Landis, *Northern Men with Southern Loyalties;* and Widmer, *Young America: Flowering of Democracy.* For an opposite interpretation that nonetheless sectionalizes the party, see the Democracy as an antislavery force in Eyal, *Young America Movement.* For work that sees the Democracy as a force for compromise and reconciliation, see Baker, *Affairs of Party.* Baker views Democrats, particularly Stephen Douglas, as pragmatic, and Burkean, in their commitment to local communities. She writes, "Like many Democrats, Douglas wished to replace moral judgements on good and evil with what he considered an effective policy" (192). I argue instead that Douglas and the Young America movement were universalist in outlook, committed to direct democracy, and explicitly disdainful of Edmund Burke's brand of conservatism. For a very recent book that takes Jacksonian Democracy seriously during the sectional crisis, see Lynn, *Preserving the White Man's Republic.*

Scholars of individual components of the Jacksonian program, such as territorial expansion and popular sovereignty, also tend to tell their stories from a Southern perspective. Territorial expansion is almost always narrated from a Southern vantage point by the 1850s: see Karp, *This Vast Southern Empire;* and Johnson, *River of Dark Dreams.* Moreover, histories of popular sovereignty miss an opportunity to explore the considerable appeal of the principle for members of the antislavery Republican Party: see Childers, *Failure of Popular Sovereignty.* A notable exception to this broad trend on economic ideology is Marc-William Palen, who recognizes a Jacksonian commitment to free trade persisting underneath the sectional tensions of the 1850s: see Palen, *"Conspiracy" of Free Trade.* Palen argues, "The newly formed Republican party's rally around antislavery . . . temporarily overshadowed the Republican coalition's conflicting free trade and protectionist ideologies" (31).

68. Although vitally filling a lacuna in the historiography, Eyal does not spend much time on the sectional crisis and argues that Young America had a "healthy and unifying" effect on the Democratic Party that delayed the onset of war (*Young America Movement,* 219–20). By contrast, he convincingly portrays Douglas as a force for instability in "With His Eyes Open."

69. For the Democrats' favorable interpretation of the French Revolution, see Burke, *Rhode Island*, 50.

70. The *Democratic Review* termed "patriotism" a "false bond," preferring the recognition of "expanded philanthropy." "The East and West," *Democratic Review* 22 (May 1848), 401.

71. For an insightful study of the Democratic Party rebranding itself as conservative during the middle of the nineteenth century, see Lynn, *Preserving the White Man's Republic*.

72. See Quigley, "Interchange." Quigley writes that while it is "tempting" to contrast Lincoln's vision of the Union with Alexander Stephens's "cornerstone" speech, in fact "both men drew on a nation-wide antebellum faith that America's historic mission was to model self-government for the rest of the world" (468). Stewart Winger notes that Lincoln appropriated a variant of Bancroft's millenarian nationalism: see *Lincoln, Religion*. Some Southern expansionists in Nicaragua aped the generational politics of Young America, calling themselves the "Young South": see Moore, "Pierre Soulé: Southern Expansionist," 211.

73. Requesting that the Republican *Evening Post* publish one of the speeches he delivered at the Cooper Institute in 1860, Democrat Samuel Tilden told the editors that he would be glad to address himself to the "many cultivated intellects and some friends of my earlier years." Samuel J. Tilden to the Editors of the *Evening Post*, October 3, 1860, in Tilden, *Letters and Literary Memorials*, 1:132. Before publishing this speech, the *Evening Post* ran an editorial that said: "The readers of the *Evening Post* know . . . that Mr Tilden never writes or speaks without having something to say worth hearing, though they have not lately been unfortunate enough to agree with him on Federal politics" (ibid.).

74. Writing to Tilden in 1861, John O'Sullivan blamed the triumph of the Republican Party on the "cooperation of the deluded Democracy that has enabled the Republican administration to undertake this war," urging the Democracy to put a stop to the conflict and allow the Southern states to secede if necessary. But while O'Sullivan stood by the South and labored on behalf of their war effort, Tilden sided with the North, albeit campaigning actively for Peace Democrats, who wanted to negotiate a settlement with the South. O'Sullivan to Tilden, June 5, 1861, Samuel J. Tilden Papers, NYPL.

75. Bancroft's view that Spanish imperialists were responsible for spreading slavery to the United States can be found in Bancroft, *History of the United States of America*, 1:159–64. Bancroft's view of the relationship between slavery and European imperialism led him to believe that chattel slavery was incompatible with a truly democratic society. He believed the fact that slavery still existed in the United States only proved the extent to which the Union had not escaped its European past. Even while rallying against abolitionism as a British plot, Bancroft saw the steady expulsion of slavery as a way of cleansing America of the lingering influence of European monarchism. In the historian's words, "Slavery was an anomaly in a Democratic society." See Bancroft to Dean Milman, August 15, 1861, in Bancroft, *Life and Letters*, 2:133.

76. One might argue that this mirrored the Southern argument that slavery was a necessary evil. Indeed, several historians see Northern Democrats as spokespeople for the Slave Power in the free states, as I discuss in chapters 1, 5, and 7. In the end, it is more useful to think of the Young Americans navigating a hierarchy of priorities rather than contending with a clear binary. Historian David Potter urges historians not to ask "Did the people of the North really oppose slavery?" but "What was the rank of antislavery in the hierarchy of northern values?" *Impending Crisis.* Certainly, Young Americans could be proslavery at times, but they could also count against slavery. Even the idea of Southern expansion was not inherently proslavery; it attracted a number of unlikely bedfellows in the antislavery movement, as I discuss in chapter 7. For a nuanced discussion of the Northern Democrats' attitude to slavery that nonetheless concludes they came down in favor of it, see Peck, "Was Stephen Douglas Antislavery?"

77. For a discussion of Black manifest destiny and the supposed efficiency of Black labor in tropical climates, see chapter 7, especially Thomas L. Kane's "Transportation, Extermination, Fusion," XI, TLKP.

78. For a discussion of the extinction of the Black race, see chapter 1, particularly the discussion of "Slaves and Slavery," *Democratic Review* 19 (October 1846), 254. For extinction through racial mixing, see Goepp and Poesche, *The New Rome.* Goepp anticipated a "'white washing' process" whereby white males would procreate with black females, and "eventually . . . efface all traces of the black race not capable of adventurous admixture with the white," 55.

79. For the connections between British liberalism, empire, and racism, see Mehta, *Liberalism and Empire.* For the relationship between Democratic thought and British liberalism, see R. Kelley, *Transatlantic Persuasion.*

1. The Intellectual Culture of the Young America Movement, 1844–1854

1. Towers, *Looking Past the Lower North,* 1.

2. Although political theorists during the early republic, such as Thomas Paine, did advocate universal rights, these did not refer to direct democracy at the local level. As historian Robert Lamb writes, "Paine's commitment to democracy, though explicit, is not to its pure, direct Athenian form. In the late eighteenth century, the idea of democracy suffered a poor reputation: it was regarded even by many radical thinkers as an essentially dangerous idea, one to be associated with mob rule and the 'swinish multitude' of which Burke is fearful. This worry is visible even in the new world that Paine lauded." See Lamb, *Paine and the Idea of Human Rights,* 77. In response, Paine shied away from the idea that popular sovereignty was a natural right, advocating instead for the mediating effects of representative government. The Whigs certainly saw Young America's transcendent democracy as a novel phenomenon, associated with a new generation. (See

the introduction to this work.) For popular cosmopolitanism in the early republic, see Cotlar, *Tom Paine's America*.

3. As one historian points out, "Whatever differences exist between the views of the Founders and Van Buren . . . they both accepted the premise that the electoral process should be considered as an institution that controlled candidate behavior." Caeser, "Political Parties and Presidential Ambition," 9.

4. For antipartisanship in mid-nineteenth-century America, see A. Smith, *No Party Now*. For nationalism in the early republic, see Parke, *American Nationalisms*. The view that the nation should be an organic community with culture and values specific to a particular place was popularized by the Irish statesman Edmund Burke. See Burke, *Reflections on the Revolution in France*. The historian Benedict Anderson draws attention to nationalism as a cultural construction during the nineteenth century. But he nonetheless believes the "imagined community" that constitutes a nation is rooted in a particular place rather than in competing theories about a nation's development: see Anderson, *Imagined Communities*. For the talismanic role of the Union in American political culture, see Varon, *Disunion!*

5. Fritz argues that "one view [of sovereignty] saw the people dependent on government and procedure while another view did not," although "both views shared the general consensus of American revolutionaries that a majority of the people were the sovereign." *American Sovereigns*, 3.

6. Conservative Whig Millard Fillmore argued, "Our own free institutions were not the offspring of our Revolution. They existed before. They were planted in the free charters of self-government under which the English colonies grew up, and our Revolution only freed us from the dominion of a foreign Power, whose government was at variance with those institutions." *Cong. Globe*, 32nd Cong., 2nd Sess. (1852), 11

7. According to Fritz, "Americans had a natural right of revolution, as did every other people, but as the collective sovereign Americans also possessed the inherent right to revise their constitutions." *American Sovereigns*, 28.

8. There is too much emphasis in the historiographical literature on the pragmatism of Stephen Douglas and his supporters. See *Crisis of the House Divided*. Jaffa contrasts Lincoln's faith in the natural law tradition with Douglas's supposedly pragmatic and materialistic concerns. Similarly, Jean Baker sees the Democrats, especially Stephen Douglas, as Burkean pragmatists. She cites "the casual intermixing of means and ends, the priority given to the past (other things being equal), the acceptance of the people's right to decide local politics and the reliance on the Constitution." *Affairs of Party*, 191.

9. O'Sullivan complained of "a theory which places the social and natural state in a certain mutual contradiction and equipoise." He wrote, "In defining the rights of man, we must consider his whole constitution—all the laws and relations of his being. Every science respecting human nature, save political, resorts immediately to that nature itself." "Democracy," *Democratic Review* 7 (March 1840), 220, 221.

10. D. Ross, *Origins of American Social Science*. Historian Stewart Winger writes that Ross misses an opportunity to examine Democratic social scientists as well as Whigs.

He argues that Whigs such as Henry Carey certainly made the case that "governmental activity was not necessarily at odds with the working of the natural order." However, he also notes, "Contrary to Dorothy Ross' analysis . . . , the economic tenets of the Democratic party were exceptionalist in the extreme, and . . . in general it was the Whigs who questioned American exceptionalism." "Lincoln's Economics," 72.

11. O'Sullivan, "Democracy," *Democratic Review* 7 (March 1840), 222, 221.

12. "Compromises," *Democratic Review* 34 (July 1854), 15.

13. O'Sullivan, "Democracy," *Democratic Review* 7 (March 1840), 226.

14. "Poetry for the People," *Democratic Review* 13 (September 1843), 267.

15. "Democracy," *Democratic Review* 7 (March 1840), 228, 226.

16. For Glipin's involvement in the early life of the *Democratic Review,* see Widmer, *Young America: Flowering of Democracy,* 37.

17. Gilpin, *Address Delivered at the University of Pennsylvania,* 13, 11.

18. Goepp and Poesche, *The New Rome,* 70.

19. For the classic accounts of the literary culture of Young America, see Miller, *Raven and the Whale;* and Widmer, *Young America: Flowering of Democracy.*

20. Edmund Burke wrote an entire article in the *Democratic Review* praising Capen for his "labors as an investigator and writer in the fields of science, politics and literature." "Nahum Capen," *Democratic Review* 41 (May 1858), 399, 402.

21. Capen, *Republic of the United States of America,* 4–5.

22. Ibid., 7.

23. Capen, *History of Democracy,* xvii.

24. Ibid. Also see "Introductory Statement," *Democratic Review* 1 (October 1837), 7.

25. Carey, *Principles of Social Science,* 105.

26. See Widmer, *Young America: Flowering of Democracy;* and Eyal, *Young America Movement.* Neither book makes a sustained analysis of the *Democratic Review* in relation to its conservative counterparts, with which it was in constant dialogue.

27. W. A. Jones, "Criticism in America," *Democratic Review* 15 (September 1844), 244.

28. F. Bowen, "French Ideas of Democracy and a Community of Goods," *North American Review* 69 (October 1849), 299, 300.

29. Ibid., 309.

30. Ibid., 312.

31. Ibid., 325.

32. F. Bowen, "The Recent Contest in Rhode Island," *North American Review* 58 (April 1844), 421.

33. Ibid., 373, 375.

34. "The Science of Politics," *North American Review* 80 (April 1855), 367.

35. Ibid., 373, 368, 367.

36. Scholnick, "Whigs and Democrats," 72.

37. "The Presidential Veto," *Whig Review* 10 (August 1849), 113.

38. Ibid.

39. "The Future Policy of the Whigs," *Whig Review* 7 (April 1848), 330.

40. "Human Rights," *Whig Review* 2 (November 1845), 443.

41. Ibid., 450.

42. Ibid., 447.

43. Hurlbut, *On Human Rights,* 25, 33, 52.

44. Ibid., 36.

45. "Hurlbut's Essays on Government," *Democratic Review* 17 (September 1845), 190.

46. Ibid.

47. Ibid., 194.

48. Throughout this book I argue that Young Americans' defense of racial hierarchy was drawn from the same "scientific" sources as their conception of democracy as a natural right. Rather than standing in tension with one another, these were two conceptions of a universalist and progressive worldview.

49. "Human Rights According to Modern Philosophy," *Whig Review* 2 (October 1845), 332.

50. Ibid., 334.

51. Ibid., 340.

52. "Democracy and Literature," *Democratic Review* 11 (August 1842), 199.

53. Ibid. The article pointed out: "Hardly with one exception, our writers of the first class have not only spoken out freely their belief in the stability and integrity of the Republic but have also expressed themselves plainly in the terms of the democratic creed."

54. Ibid.

55. "Federalism and Democracy," *Boston Post,* October 11, 1838, 1–2, cited in Scholnick, "Ultraism of the Day," 174.

56. "The Culture, the Support and the Objects of Art in a Republic, A Lecture by George Bancroft," *New York Times,* December 10, 1852.

57. Ibid.

58. Bancroft's place in the network of Young American Democrats is apparent in the course of this book, but particularly in chapters 2, 4, and 7.

59. "Nationality of Literature," *Democratic Review* 20 (April 1847), 317.

60. "Mr. Forrest's Second Reception in England," *Democratic Review* 16 (April 1845), 385. The belief that literary figures understood and expressed democratic principles better than most is one of the reasons so many authors and artists were promoted to diplomatic positions during the two administrations most influenced by Young America—those of James Polk and Franklin Pierce. The two most notable examples were George Bancroft (United Kingdom under Polk) and Nathaniel Hawthorne (United Kingdom under Pierce), but *Democratic Review* editors John O'Sullivan and George Sanders also served under Franklin Pierce (Portugal and the United Kingdom). This is discussed in more detail in chapter 4.

61. Lueger, *Henry Wikoff and the Development of Theatrical Publicity in America,* 86.

62. "American Actors in England," *Democratic Review* (September 1846).

63. "Mr Forrest's Ovation," *Democratic Review* 3 (September 1833), 56. The turn away from philanthropy toward more conservative language is explored in chapter 6.

64. A. Smith, *Stormy Present,* 104.

65. "Hawthorne's New Spirit of the Age," *Democratic Review* 15 (July 1844), 61.

66. "Nathaniel Hawthorne," *Democratic Review* 16 (April 1845), 376.

67. Hawthorne, *The Scarlet Letter,* 5.

68. "Hawthorne's Life of Pierce—Perspective," *Democratic Review* 31 (September 1852), 276, 277.

69. Ibid., 278.

70. Ibid., 279, 280.

71. Ibid., 283.

72. The *Whig Review* quoted in Casper, "Two Lives of Franklin Pierce," 213.

73. "Nathaniel Hawthorne," *Whig Review* 4 (September 1846), 304, 308.

74. Hawthorne, "Earth's Holocaust," In *Works of Nathaniel Hawthorne,* 10:396.

75. "Earth's Holocaust" quoted in *Whig Review* 4 (September 1846), 308.

76. "Nathaniel Hawthorne," *Whig Review* 4 (September 1846), 308.

77. "Nathaniel Hawthorne," *North American Review* 76 (January 1853), 231.

78. The argument that the Young America movement was essentially liberal but for blind spots on race can be found in Eyal, *Young America Movement;* and Sampson, *John O'Sullivan.* Both authors are right to stress the free-labor credentials of Young Americans and their emancipatory rhetoric, but they do not focus on its relationship with white supremacy. Indeed, without focusing on the faction's racial politics, Eyal's characterization of Young Americans as straightforwardly antislavery is misleading, since it makes them out to be more racially egalitarian than they were.

79. For the interpretation that Young America became a vehicle for the Slave Power, see Widmer, *Young America: Flowering of Democracy,* on the role of "Young America II." Also see Landis, *Northern Men with Southern Sympathies.* For the view that racism was the driver behind Jacksonian ideology, while liberal rhetoric provided a mere smokescreen, see Horsman, *Race and Manifest Destiny.* Part of the problem is one of framing—historians such as Horsman focus exclusively on race, while Eyal and Sampson examine the movement's liberal politics. My study aims to explore how racial hierarchy might function within a broader liberal (and Jacksonian) worldview.

80. Studies that integrate race within the broader ideology of Jacksonian Democracy include Ashworth, *"Agrarians" and "Aristocrats,"* 221; Ford, "Making the 'White Man's Country,'" 71; Shire, "Sentimental Racism," 119.

81. "Annexation," *Democratic Review* 17 (July–August 1845), 8.

82. Kettell, *Southern Wealth and Northern Profits,* 101.

83. This is one example of how—in the words of the historian Rogers Smith—"The Jacksonians' consenualist posture served racially exclusionary purposes." *Civic Ideals,* 230.

84. Van Evrie, *Negroes and Negro "Slavery,"* 289.

85. "Slaves and Slavery," *Democratic Review* 19 (October 1846), 247.

86. "The Indian Lover," *Democratic Review* 19 (October 1846), 272, quoted in Scholnick, "Extermination and Democracy," 128.

87. "Thayendanegea," *Democratic Review* 3 (October 1838), 115.

88. Chambers, *Vestige of the Natural History of Creation.*

89. "Vestiges of the Natural History of Creation," *Whig Review* 1 (May 1845), 525, 539.

90. "The Past and Present of the Indian Tribes," *Whig Review* 1 (May 1845), 509.

91. Ibid., 508, 507.

92. "Do the Various Races of Man Constitute a Single Species?," *Democratic Review* 11 (August 1842), 113–39.

93. The *Review* maintained that "all the evidences of our senses" pointed to the fact that the black and white races were separate and distinct. "Notices of New Books: 'The Unity of the Human Races Proved to be the Doctrine of Scripture, Reason and Science, with a Review of the Present Position and Theory of Professor Agassiz,' by Rev. Thomas Smyth, D.D.," *Democratic Review* 26 (June 1850), 570.

94. Ibid.

95. "European Views of American Democracy," *Democratic Review* 2 (July 1838), 352–53.

96. "Slaves and Slavery," *Democratic Review* 19 (October 1846), 254.

97. Anderson, *Imagined Communities.*

2. The Dorr Rebellion

1. *Providence Journal,* quoted in Wiecek, "A Peculiar Conservatism," 247. Wiecek also effectively traces how anti-Dorrites self-identified as conservatives during the crisis in Rhode Island.

2. Conley, "No Landless Irish Need Apply," 82.

3. Wilentz, *Chants Democratic,* 330.

4. Chaput, "Rhode Island Question," 66.

5. Ibid., 53.

6. A. Smith, *Reimagining Democracy,* 31.

7. Chaput, "Proslavery and Antislavery Politics," 693.

8. Edmund Burke to Bancroft, July 19, 1844, George Bancroft Papers, MHS.

9. "Political Portraits with Pen and Pencil: Hon. Edmund Burke," *Democratic Review* 20 (January 1847), 75.

10. Edmund Burke and the Select Committee, *Rhode Island,* 27.

11. This interpretation of Jacksonian thought is dominant in the scholarship. The most extreme example of Jacksonian Democracy as folkloric is in Mead, "Jacksonian Tradition and Foreign Policy." For the Democrats as backward-looking, anti-intellectual, and pragmatic, see Baker, *Affairs of Party.*

12. Burke, *Rhode Island,* 33.

13. Ibid., 33, 41.

14. Ibid., 50.

15. For an eloquent example of the Whigs' critique of majoritarianism, see Lincoln, *Perpetuation of Our Political Institutions,* January 27, 1838, *Collected Works,* vol. 1.

16. Winger, *Lincoln, Religion.*

17. Burke, *Rhode Island,* 50. This idea that people could restrain themselves, free of federal interference, mirrored an argument put forward in the *Democratic Review.* In the very first issue, John O'Sullivan wrote, "Government is best which governs least, because its people discipline themselves." *Democratic Review* 1 (1837), 6.

18. *Democratic Review* 1 (1837), 50.

19. Ibid., 164, 165.

20. *Cong. Globe,* 28th Cong., 1st Sess. (1844), 328.

21. Ibid., 328, 330.

22. Ibid., 330.

23. Ibid., 378.

24. *Cong. Globe,* 28th Cong., 2nd Sess. (1845), 278.

25. Ibid., 279.

26. Ibid.

27. *Cong. Globe,* 28th Cong., 1st Sess. (1844), 384–85.

28. Ibid.

29. Ibid.

30. "The Protestant Puritan's Legacy" quoted in Chaput, "Rhode Island Question," 64.

31. *Cong. Globe,* 28th Cong., 1st Sess. (1844), 378.

32. Thomas W. Dorr quoted in Chaput, "Rhode Island Question," 55.

33. Bancroft quoted in Curtis, *Merits of Dorr and Bancroft,* 26.

34. Ibid., 34.

35. Ibid.

36. "Political Portraits: Thomas Wilson Dorr No. XXXII," *Democratic Review* 11 (August 1842), 205.

37. "Compromises," *Democratic Review* 34 (July 1854), 15.

38. F. Bowen, "The Recent Contest in Rhode Island," *North American Review* 58 (April 1844).

39. Ibid., 386.

40. Ibid., 405.

41. See Curti, "Impact of the Revolutions of 1848," 213.

42. Barnard, *Man and the State,* 44, 14, 15.

43. Ibid., 38.

44. One writer complained about Chambers's brutal view of human evolution, writing, "Individual men and individual nations and even races have suffered and perished in those backward cycles which the scheme admits to be necessary to the

general progress." See "Vestiges of the Natural History of Creation," *Whig Review* 1 (May 1845), 525.

45. O. Brownson, "Origin and Ground of Government," *Democratic Review* 13 (October 1843), 139.

46. Colton, *Junius Tracts*, 88, 89.

3. Global Transformations

1. Edward Widmer characterizes Young America's expansionist program as a fig leaf for Southern interests and separates it from their cultural and intellectual ambitions: see *Young America: Flowering of Democracy*. Several historians acknowledge that Southern expansionism coexisted with Southern Unionism and that the sectional goal of territorial acquisition was pursued through nationalist channels. Nonetheless, the current scholarship overwhelmingly focuses on expansionism from a Southern perspective and portrays slave owners manipulating the federal government for explicitly sectional ends. While this is part of the story, Young America's expansionism was based on a truly national vision. For Southern expansionism, see Karp, *This Vast Southern Empire;* May, *Southern Dream of a Caribbean Empire;* Johnson, *River of Dark Dreams*. These interpretations inform a larger view of the Democratic Party of the 1850s as a mere shell of its former self, a view that is explored in the introduction. For Southern expansionism as an impetus for secession as well as a mission throughout the Civil War and beyond, see Brettle, *Colossal Ambitions*. With regards to expansionism, two recent works explore the cultural and political factors driving support for expansionism in the free states: Amy Greenberg draws attention to concepts of masculinity in *Manifest Manhood;* and Michael Gobat focuses on an explicitly antislavery, sometimes abolitionist, case for expansion in Nicaragua in *Empire by Invitation*.

2. For a masterful account of how the United States justified the war with Mexico because of the nation-state's perceived inability to defend against Comanche raids, see Delay, "Independent Indians."

3. *Letter of Mr. Walker, of Mississippi, Relative to the Annexation of Texas*.

4. Freehling points out that "no one called Walker's (analysis) 'untrue.'" *Road to Disunion*, 1:422.

5. *Letter of Mr. Walker, of Mississippi, Relative to the Annexation of Texas*, 8, 17.

6. John O'Sullivan to Henry Gilpin, March 30, 1844, Henry Gilpin Collection, HSP.

7. "The Texas Question," *Democratic Review* 14 (April 1844), 425.

8. Ibid.

9. Ibid., 429.

10. According to Everett, slaves could not be in "two places at the same time." "Territorial Aggrandizement," *Democratic Review* 17 (October 1845), 269, 258.

11. *Cong. Globe*, 28th Cong., 2nd Sess. (1845), 141, 111.

12. Herschel Johnson argued this was partly due to the fact that a thousand "Anglo-Americans" could be fed on the same amount of land that sustained the hunting practices of one Native American. *Probable Destiny of Our Country,* 7.

13. John O'Sullivan to George Bancroft, May 23, 1845, Bancroft Papers, MSH.

14. Sampson, *John L. O'Sullivan,* 201. O'Sullivan's pacifism might seem odd in light of his reputation as one of the most bellicose proponents of the Mexican War. But it was not a mere smokescreen and shows the extent to which some nineteenth-century Americans distinguished between a war of liberation and a war of conquest. Sampson draws attention to O'Sullivan's outspoken pacifism during his time in the New York State Assembly.

15. George Bancroft to President Polk, London, January 28, 1848, in Bancroft, *Life and Letters,* 2:29.

16. George Bancroft to his Wife, December 31, 1847, ibid., 2:76.

17. George Bancroft to James Polk, June 3, 1847, Bancroft Papers, MHS.

18. Philip Foner argues that Bancroft deliberately mischaracterized Humboldt as an expansionist after his death in 1859: see "Alexander Von Humboldt on Slavery in America," 334.

19. Humboldt's stance against territorial expansion and the extension of slavery, as well as his dispute with J. S. Thrasher, is detailed in P. Foner, "Alexander Von Humboldt on Slavery in America."

20. Johnson, *Probable Destiny of Our Country,* 37.

21. For the relationship between custom and natural law in Vattel's political thought, see Iurlaro, "Vattel's Doctrine of the Customary Law of Nations."

22. "Intervention," *Democratic Review* 30 (January 1852), 52.

23. Armitage, "Cosmopolitanism and Civil War." 19.

24. Ibid.

25. Ibid.

26. *Cong. Globe,* 32nd Cong., 1st Sess. (1852), 161.

27. "'The Texas Question,' A letter from Alexander Everett," *Democratic Review* 15 (September 1844), 251.

28. *Cong. Globe,* 28th Cong., 2nd Sess. (1845), 112.

29. *Cong. Globe,* 30th Cong., 1st Sess. (1848), 175.

30. D. D. Field, "*The Edinburgh* and *Foreign Quarterly* on Oregon," *Democratic Review* 17 (November 1845), 327, 330.

31. "Lopez and His Companions," *Democratic Review* 29 (October 1851), 296.

32. "Laws of Nations," *Democratic Review* 21 (July 1847), 27.

33. *Cong. Globe,* 28th Cong., 2nd Sess. (1845), 112.

34. Robert J. Walker, June 29, 1844, R. J. Walker Letter Book, University of Pittsburgh, 47.

35. Although some—but by no means all—of the cultural and intellectual figures associated with Young America were opposed to expansionism, the politicians within the movement still used these ideas to bolster their foreign policy. The connection was

certainly not inevitable, but the liberal intellectualism of Young America was perfectly compatible with a violent and acquisitive form of nationalism. Furthermore, the connections between the intellectual and political sides to the Young America movement suggest that Edward Widmer's division between Young America I and Young America II might not tell the whole story. See *Young America: Flowering of Democracy.*

4. Nature and the Political Order

1. George Bancroft to James Buchanan, March 24, 1848, in Bancroft, *Life and Letters,* 2:33.

2. "The East and West," *Democratic Review* 22 (May 1848), 401.

3. In this context, the term "exceptional" is employed in a similar manner to Timothy Roberts in *Distant Revolutions.* However, American exceptionalism can also refer to the idea that the Union is similar to the rest of the world (rather than unique), but more advanced and therefore destined to take a leading role in international affairs.

4. For a masterful account of American responses to the Revolutions of 1848, see Roberts, *Distant Revolutions.* Roberts argues that the failure of the revolutions reinforced the United States' exceptionalist self-image as Americans became convinced that only the United States possessed the required conditions for a stable, democratic society. Mischa Honeck also identifies a turn away from international affairs after the initial burst of enthusiasm for 1848: see "Freemen of All Nations." While these arguments are certainly true of the Whigs and many Democrats, the ideology of Young America made the group uniquely optimistic about the prospects of self-government in Europe. For the argument that European revolutionary movements also remained influential on the Continent and won many achievements during the 1850s, see Clarke, "After 1848."

5. In one article Democratic writer and diplomat Henry Wikoff wrote that secret societies in France were "fermenting like an unseen volcano": see "Prince Napoleon Louis Bonaparte in Prison," *Democratic Review* 23 (December 1848), 501.

6. This provides a parallel to the Republican Party, which believed federal intervention was necessary to promote the natural right to the fruits of one's labor. Democrats, by contrast, believed this right could only be achieved within sovereign—and racially homogenous—political communities, which they too were prepared to protect through federal intervention.

7. Hendrickson, *Union, Nation or Empire,* 1.

8. For an account of the political activities of the Irish in the United States and their influence on American foreign policy, see Sim, *A Union Forever.* Sim traces the circulation of bonds issued by the Fenian Brotherhood in "Following the Money."

9. For a more extensive account of the activities of European migrants in the United States, see Eichhorn, *Liberty and Slavery.* For the influence of European revolutions on different forms of Confederate identity, see Tucker, *Newest Born of Nations.*

10. Daniel Howe also identifies "deliberate modernizers" within the Whig Party, such as William Seward and Horace Greeley. Howe, *Political Culture of the American Whigs*, 184.

11. *Cong. Globe*, 32nd Cong., 1st Sess. (1852), 105.

12. *Cong. Globe*, 32nd Cong., 1st Sess. (1851), 173; "Speech of Mr. Douglas of Illinois at the Congressional Banquet to Kossuth," 8.

13. *Cong. Globe*, 32nd Cong., 1st Sess. (1852), 351.

14. Cox, *The Scholar*, 19.

15. *Cong. Globe*, 32nd Cong., 1st Sess. (1852), 161.

16. "The Contrast: The Whig and Democratic Candidates for the Presidency," 1852, William Allen Papers, LC.

17. *Cong. Globe*, 32nd Cong., 1st Sess. (1852), 243.

18. Ibid., 442. The editor of the *North American Review*, Francis Bowen, also argued against the idea that the Revolutions of 1848 proved the universal nature of democratic government. See "The War of Races in Hungary," *North American Review* 70 (January 1850).

19. *Cong. Globe*, 32nd Cong., 1st Sess. (1852), 442.

20. Ibid.

21. Thomas Richardson to Stephen Douglas, September 16, 1851, SADP.

22. Goepp, *E Pluribus Unum*, 25.

23. *Cong. Globe*, 32nd Cong., 1st Sess. (1852), 302.

24. Ibid.

25. For a discussion of this correspondence, see Curti, "Young America," 44.

26. William Grandin to Stephen Douglas, February 7, 1852, SADP.

27. George Sanders to Stephen Douglas, April 12, 1854, SADP.

28. "Correspondence between Consul Sanders and M. Kossuth," *New York Times*, June 24, 1854.

29. Joseph Barker, in *Liberator*, November 24, 1854.

30. The Whig Party Platform, June 17, 1852, American Presidency Project, accessed September 6, 2021, https://www.presidency.ucsb.edu/documents/whig-party-platform-1852.

31. *Cong. Globe*, 32nd Cong., 1st Sess. (1852), 791.

32. Ibid.

33. Savage was quoting an article in the *Democratic Review*: see *Our Living Representative Men*, 69.

34. Stephen Douglas to Franklin Pierce, March 1853, in Douglas, *Letters*, 260.

35. Reilly, "Eighteen-Fifty-Two and the Presidency," *Democratic Review* 30 (January 1852), 2.

36. Thomas L. Kane to William Wood, January 10–11, 1852, TLKP.

37. Roberts, *Distant Revolutions*.

38. Congressman Edmund Burke quoted in Curti, "Young America," 45.

39. *True American*, August 8, 1855.

40. Of course, this optimism was naïve and misguided and, ultimately, destabilized the nation Pierce tried to bring into being.

41. G. M. Dallas to Francis Markoe, March 15, 1855, Francis Markoe Papers, LC.

42. *Cooper's Clarksburg Register,* December 7, 1853.

43. *Baltimore Sun,* December 8, 1851.

44. Jane Cazneau to George Bancroft, June 20, 1848, Bancroft Papers, MSH.

45. The idea that antislavery Democrats were opposed to internationalism was a particularly egregious misrepresentation. In fact, many Barnburners wanted to aid the Revolutions of 1848 and expand the bounds of the American union—as long as it did not involve the acquisition of more slave territory. Nevertheless, a private letter of this sort suggests that Cazneau did portray the Barnburners as a conservative force that was either using antislavery as a cover to hide their opposition to territorial expansion or focusing on the incidental issue of slavery at the expense of national growth. For Cazneau, slavery was incidental, since expansion would lead to its demise in the fullness of time.

46. Goepp and Poersche, *The New Rome.*

47. Isaac R. Diller to Stephen Douglas, December 22, 1853, SADP.

48. *Spirit of the Times,* April 5, 1853.

49. August Belmont to Stephen Douglas, November 15, 1853, SADP.

50. Kelley referenced in "Our Mission—Diplomacy and Navy," *Democratic Review* 31 (July 1852), 39.

51. For a discussion of the dress circular, see David, "Diplomatic Plumage," 175–79.

52. August Belmont to Stephen Douglas, November 15, 1853, SADP.

53. Ibid.

54. Ibid.

55. Sanders's letter to the Swiss appeared in the *London Times,* August 21, 1854; "Correspondence between Consul Sanders and M. Kossuth," *New York Times,* June 24, 1854.

56. "Americans in Europe: Another Letter from George N. Sanders: Address to the People of France," *New York Times,* October 27, 1854. Yonatan Eyal points out Ledru-Rollin and Giuseppe Mazzini joined Kossuth in denouncing Sanders's recall. Eyal, "Romantic Realist," 111.

57. William Marcy to James Buchanan, December 15, 1854, William Marcy Papers, LC.

58. August Belmont to George Sanders, September 19, 1854, GNSP, LC.

59. This letter from the *New York Times* was recorded by George Sanders's wife Anna. Journal of Anna J. R. Sanders, September 26, 1855, GNSFP LC.

60. Ibid.

61. John Mason wrote, "I have no doubt that the French government sincerely believe that Mr. Soulé's presence in France is dangerous," although Mason did not believe Soulé had given them proper reason to justify this belief. John Mason to William Marcy, December 21, 1854, William Marcy Papers, LC. Soulé's relationships with prominent revolutionary leaders in Europe would have been known to the French authorities. See Blumenthal, *Reappraisal of Franco-American Relations,* 82.

62. Marcy wrote to Buchanan that one of Sanders's letters, stamped with the seal of Buchanan's legation, had been "placed into the hands of Jerome Bonaparte." Jerome had shown the letter to the emperor, and it entered onto a list of France's "pretended grievances." William Marcy to James Buchanan, December 4, 1854, William Marcy Papers, LC. The *Daily Pennsylvanian* pointed out that Sanders's letter was a mere pretense because Sanders had already been dismissed by the time the letter was made public. *Daily Pennsylvanian,* November 14, 1854.

63. This account derives from Blumenthal, *Reappraisal of Franco-American Relations,* 80–84.

64. William Marcy to John Mason, December 12, 1854, William Marcy Papers, LC.

65. *Daily Pennsylvanian,* November 14, 1854.

66. George Dallas to Francis Markoe, November 14, 1854, Francis Markoe Papers, LC.

67. P. Foner, *History of Cuba,* 97.

68. Green and Kirkwood, "Reframing the Antebellum Democratic Mainstream."

69. Soulé's attempts to purchase Cuba while he was serving as a diplomat in Europe mirrored the piratical style of the filibustering expeditions and helped to turn public opinion against Young America diplomats. Indeed, the authors of the Ostend Manifesto, discussed in chapter 5, were themselves compared to the filibusters. See "The Ostend Manifesto: The Three Filibusters—Buchanan, Mason and Soulé," *New York Herald* August 6 ,1856. Ultimately, the outrage around the Kanas-Nebraska Act (explored in chapter 6) and these unorthodox attempts at territorial expansion worked together to turn the Northern public against the Democratic Party. These two aspects of the Young America agenda were unwelcome reminders of the instability that plagued the nation. They forced many Northerners to take a radical stand against the idea that popular sovereignty was the highest authority in national life and to resist the encroachments of the Slave Power.

70. Soulé's exploits in foreign policy during the late 1850s are traced in Preston Moore, "Pierre Soule," 204–23. After returning from Spain, Soulé actively supported William Walker's campaign to take power in Nicaragua and annex the country to the United States. From 1856 Soulé raised money for Walker in his home state of Louisiana, partly by selling bonds that could be recuperated after Walker took power.

71. For an analysis of Young Americans' response to the Koszta Affair, see Power Smith, "Young America Movement."

72. *Cong. Globe,* 33rd Cong., 1st Sess. (1854), 131.

73. Caleb Lyon quoted in Schroeder, *Shaping a Maritime Empire,* 121.

74. Kossuth expressed these sentiments while he was working as a foreign correspondent for the *New York Times.* See "Democratic Letters on European Matters and Foreign Policy," No. 7, Tuesday, July 12, 1853, *New York Times,* August 2, 1853.

75. Reilly, "The Policy of the Administration in Regard to American Citizens Abroad," in Savage, *Memoir of Thomas Devin Reilly,* 46.

76. Millard Fillmore to Joseph P. Kennedy, October 14, 1853, Joseph P. Kennedy Papers, Enoch Pratt Free Library, Baltimore.

77. Some Republicans undoubtedly were motivated by a concern for universal rights that transcended racial divides. But others believed that curbing the influence of the Slave Power would serve white communities in Europe and the United States, irrespective of the rights of nonwhite groups.

78. A Republican like Galusha Grow had embraced Young America in 1853 when he argued the American navy should dispense with "old fogey commanders" in favor of men like Captain Ingraham. *Cong. Globe*, 33rd Cong., 1st Sess. (1853), 808.

79. One speaker at the meeting hoped the administration's response would be "worthy of the sentiment of Young America, an echo of the convictions of the American republic, and an interpretation of the charter of human rights." *New York Times*, September 23, 1853.

80. For Robert J. Walker's comments at the Ingraham Testimonial Meeting, see ibid. Anna Sanders recorded in her diary a gathering with George Sanders and Robert J. Walker in which "Col. [Charles] Henningsen was the toast of the whole company. They talked to him when he was present, and about him when he went out and read his book *The White Slave* when they went to their rooms." Journal of Anna J. R. Sanders, July 1852, GNSFP, LC. *The White Slave* was typical of Henningsen's work, and the Young America outlook more broadly, in emphasizing the injustice of Russian serfdom because the slaves were white. See Henningsen, *The White Slave*.

81. Anna Sanders cheered on Charles Henningsen's and William Walker's exploits in Nicaragua. Journal of Anna J. R. Sanders, January 26, 1857, GNSFP, LC.

82. Originally, William C. Brant (who had defected to the Free-Soil movement in 1848 and would do so again) asked George Bancroft to preside over the Testimonial Committee in 1853. Between the election of 1852 and the passage of the Kansas-Nebraska Act in 1854, these former contributors to the *Democratic Review* were, once again, united over free trade as well as a broader hope that the Democracy would inspire Europe's revolutionary movements. Bancroft did not accept the offer, but he undoubtedly would have had fewer clashes with George Sanders than the explicitly antislavery president Hugh Forbes.

83. George Sanders remarks to Hugh Forbes are recorded in his wife's journal. Journal of Anna J. R. Sanders, September 12, 1855, GNSFP, LC.

84. This was George Sanders's response to Gollovin in the *Tribune*, as recorded by his wife. Sanders also pointed out that the French Democrat Ledru-Rollin would have rather seen the death penalty for the accomplices in Louis Napoleon's coup than for the common criminal. Nevertheless, this obviously did not amount to an endorsement in either case. Journal of Anna J. R. Sanders, September 22, 1855, GNSFP, LC. This was a surprising position when we consider that many Young Americans, including John O'Sullivan and the *Democratic Review*, had taken a staunch position against capital punishment during the 1840s. See Widmer, *Young America: Flowering of Democracy*.

85. More work will have to be done on attitudes to violence among Young Americans and the Democratic Party more broadly. But from the Mexican War to the Astor Place

Riot, it would appear that Young Americans were more tolerant of violent means to justify revolutionary ends than their progressive counterparts in the Whig Party.

86. Everett, *Stability and Progress. Remarks,* 5, 6, 10.

87. "Mr Curtis' Lecture before the Young Men's Association, 'Young America,'" *Chicago Tribune,* December 14, 1853.

88. "Practical Annexation of England," *Democratic Review* 19 (July 1846).

89. H. Wikoff, "Is It the Policy of England to Fight or Trade with the US?," *Democratic Review* 18 (June 1846), 423.

90. Goepp and Poesche, *The New Rome,* 151.

91. Cox, *A Buckeye Abroad,* 30.

92. George Dallas to Mr. Cass, London, October 26, 1858, in Dallas, *Series of Letters from London,* 60.

93. Dallas to Henry Gilpin, October 31, 1858, in ibid., 60.

94. Dallas to L. Cass, December 17, 1868, in ibid., 73.

95. Dallas to William Marcy, April 20, 1856, in Dallas, *Series of Letters from London,* 24.

96. Ibid.

97. Dallas to Judge Joel Jones, May 9, 1856, in ibid., 34.

98. Cox, *"Territorial Expansion,"* 15; Walker, *Speech at Banquet.* Walker's letter proposing union between the United States and Great Britain is quoted in Horsman, *Race and Manifest Destiny,* 296. Walker also admired Bright and Cobden: see Letter of R. J. Walker to Mr Deacon, the Town Clerk of Southampton, reprinted in the *London Daily News,* October 15, 1851.

99. Thomas L. Kane to William Wood, November 15, 1851, TLKP.

100. Goepp and Poesche, *The New Rome,* 88.

101. Dallas to Mr. J. P. H., May 16, 1856, in Dallas, *Series of Letters from London,* 40.

102. Dallas to Mr. Miles, London, November 25, 1856, ibid., 109.

103. Ibid. For Dorothy Ross's discussion of the nation as an "ethical factor," see "Lincoln and the Ethics of Emancipation," 379.

104. The turn toward conservatism among Young America Democrats will be discussed in more detail in chapter 6. After the Revolutions of 1848, these "progressive" Democrats increasingly saw the threat to their liberal democracy emanating from below as well as above. By the mid-nineteenth century, abolitionists and socialists presented a threat to self-government as well as to despotic monarchical regimes.

105. Dallas to Judge Joel Jones, May 9, 1856, in Dallas, *Series of Letters from London,* 33.

106. Dallas to John O'Sullivan, January 12, 1857, in ibid., 129.

107. Ibid.

108. A. Belmont to G. Sanders, August 1854, quoted in Curti, "Young America," 54.

109. *Cong. Globe,* 33rd Cong., 1st Sess. (1853), 808.

110. A. Belmont to G. Sanders, no date, referenced in Curti, "Young America," 44.

111. Cox, *Scholar, as the True Progressive,* 25.

112. Cox, *"Territorial Expansion,"* 15.

113. Walker, *Speech at Banquet*, 8.

114. Ibid.

115. Existing literature tends to argue that "Anglophobia" became less pronounced during the 1850s. For this reason, Samuel Haynes concludes his masterful study in the late 1840s. See *Unfinished Revolution*. Sexton argues that one of the reasons the Civil War broke out was that Americans were no longer united around their fear of Great Britain as an external enemy. See *Monroe Doctrine*.

5. Cuban Annexation and the Problem of Slavery

1. Southern attempts to acquire new territory in the tropics are well documented in the historical literature. See May, *Manifest Destiny's Underworld;* Karp, *This Vast Southern Empire*.

2. John O'Sullivan was one example of a politician who advocated both strategies. Polk, who was certainly influenced by Young America's ideas even if he was not a strict supporter of the movement, believed that López's expedition would scuttle the administration's attempts to purchase the island through legal means. See Chaffin, "Sons of Washington," 79.

3. Parker H. French to Stephen Douglas, February 14, 1856, SADP.

4. James D. Welphy to Stephen Douglas, February 14, 1856, SADP.

5. George Dallas to Francis Markoe, May 9, 1854, Francis Markoe Papers, LC.

6. Robert J. Walker to Stephen Douglas, May 4, 1850, SADP.

7. *Cong. Globe*, 32nd Cong., 1st Sess. (1852), 1083.

8. William Marcy quoted in Nester, *Age of Lincoln*, 63.

9. The Democratic platform of 1856, in D. Johnson and Porter, *National Party Platforms*, 26.

10. For the relationship between Sanders and Marshall, see the introduction to this book.

11. Marshall, *American Progress*, 4, 7.

12. Marshall, *Speech on the Conduct of the Administration in Cuba*, 2.

13. Eyal, *Young America Movement*, 109.

14. Cox, *"Territorial Expansion,"* 2.

15. "Continental Policy of the United States—The Acquisition of Cuba," *Democratic Review* 43 (April 1859), 24.

16. Cox, *"Territorial Expansion,"* 13.

17. Pugh, *Speech on the Acquisition of Cuba*, 1, 9, 15.

18. Ibid., 15.

19. Thomas L. Kane referenced in M. Grow, *Liberty to the Downtrodden*, 105.

20. Ibid.

21. "Eighteen Fifty-Two and the Presidency," *Democratic Review* 30 (January 1852), 3.

22. Ibid., 5.
23. Ibid., 6.
24. *Star of the North,* May 28, 1856.
25. Ballou, *History of Cuba,* 197.
26. Ibid., 217.
27. Ibid., 220.
28. *Democratic Sentinel and Harrison County Farmer,* December 1, 1852.
29. *Weekly Indiana State Sentinel,* April 19, 1855.
30. Cushing, "Mexico," *Democratic Review* 18 (June 1846), 440. Although formerly a supporter of the Whig Party, Caleb Cushing switched to the Democrats during the 1840s and became a strong supporter of the Young America program. The *New York Herald* said of him: "With respect to his political proclivities, we apprehend he is identified with the progressive school of 'Young America.' . . . He is not afraid of Cuba. . . . The atmosphere of the Democratic Party has expanded his views on the tariff question into the conviction that the policy of Robert J. Walker and the policy of Sir Robert Peel have done more for our commerce and that of the world than all the high protective tariffs of the last quarter of a century." *New York Herald,* February 19, 1853.
31. Dix, *"The War with Mexico": Speech of Hon. J. A. Dix,* 7.
32. See the *New York Herald,* March 31, 1854. The *Herald* relayed a report from the Democratic organ based in Washington, DC, the *Union,* which predicted "an alliance more formidable to our enemies than any ever contracted among the crowned heads." The *Herald* reported that "the most important feature in this grand program is not George Law's muskets but Kossuth's policy of intervention, which is threatened by our government organ. The interference of France and England in our quarrel with Spain about Cuba will be the signal for armed cooperation, therefore, with the third party in the European war—the revolutionary elements—who are yet to rise up and make the contest a grand triangular fight."
33. Curti, "Young America," 49.
34. George Dallas to Francis Markoe, August 28, 1854, Francis Markoe Papers, LC.
35. *Cong. Globe,* 35th Cong., Special Sess. (1857).
36. Cox, *"Territorial Expansion,"* 15.
37. Ibid.
38. Karp, *This Vast Southern Empire.*
39. Ibid., 190.
40. George Dallas to Francis Markoe, May 9, 1854, Francis Markoe Papers, LC.
41. James to Buchanan to William Marcy, May 11, 1854, William Marcy Papers, LC.
42. The Ostend Manifesto, quoted in May, *Slavery, Race and Conquest,* 116.
43. John O'Sullivan to Stephen A. Douglas, February 10, 1854, SADP.
44. John O'Sullivan to James Buchanan, March 19, 1848, James Buchanan Papers, HSP.
45. John O'Sullivan to Stephen A. Douglas, February 10, 1854, SAPD.

46. "Non-intervention of Nations," *Democratic Review* 42 (August 1858), 100.

47. "Continental Policy of the United States—The Acquisition of Cuba," *Democratic Review* 43 (April 1859), 28.

48. Ibid., 37.

49. "Cuba," *Democrat and Sentinel,* June 2, 1854.

50. Ballou, *History of Cuba,* 189, 190.

51. Pugh, *Speech on the Acquisition of Cuba,* 189.

52. Dallas, *Diary,* 292.

53. Dallas to Lewis Cass, July 28, 1857, in Dallas, *Series of Letters from London,* 183.

54. Dallas to Lewis Cass, January 21, 1858, ibid., 249.

55. Henry Ashworth to Henry Gilpin, June 10, 1858, Henry Gilpin Papers, HSP.

56. At first glance, this combination of support for territorial expansion and abstract opposition to slavery suggests the "freedom national" doctrine was not the only strategy for bringing about emancipation during the mid-nineteenth century. But in another sense, this Democratic outlook was a variation of the same idea, aiming to cordon off areas of slave labor under American control. Cuban annexation could certainly appeal to Americans who did not want to see slavery expanded into areas where it did not already exist—a view almost unanimous in the Northern states, according to some historians and observers at the time. For the "freedom national" approach to ending slavery, see Oakes, *Freedom National.*

57. *Democrat and Sentinel,* June 3, 1857.

58. Marshall, *Speech on the Conduct of the Administration in Cuba,* 2.

59. Saunders, *George N. Sanders on the Sequence of Southern Secession.*

60. Joseph Medill to "Friend Gurley," August 15, 1859, Joseph Medill Papers, Chicago Historical Society.

61. In January 1853 Lewis Cass reaffirmed the Monroe Doctrine in Cuba, hinting that European intervention in the Caribbean would be met with a swift rebuttal. In response Hale issued an amendment that would repeat word-for-word the section on Cuba, only substituting "Canada" and "Great Britain" for "Cuba" and "Spain." See Murphy, *Hemispheric Imaginings,* 63. For expansionism as an element of Republican policy after the war, see Guyatt, "America's Conservatory." Despite Smith's support for Cuban annexation in the antebellum period, explored below, Guyatt points out that Smith opposed the annexation of Santo Domingo in 1870. Ibid., 980.

62. G. Smith, "Final Letter to his Constituents," in *Speeches of Gerrit Smith,* 390.

63. Ibid., 391.

64. Thayer, "The Suicide of Slavery," 7.

65. G. Smith, "Final Letter to his Constituents," 390: G. Smith, "Letter to Wendell Phillips," 397, both in *Speeches of Gerrit Smith.*

66. G. Smith, "Final Letter to his Constituents," in ibid., 393.

67. G. Smith, "Speech on the Mexican Treaty and 'Monroe Doctrine,' June 27, 1854," in ibid., 299.

68. Ibid., 299–300.

69. Eyal, *Young America Movement,* 187.

70. "Cuba," *Putnam's Monthly Magazine* 1 (January 1853), 15.

71. Ibid.

72. "A Letter to John Bull," *Putnam's Monthly Magazine* 1 (February 1853), 229.

73. Ibid., 120.

74. Adam Tuchinsky explores the radical figures emanating from the Whig Party in *Horace Greely's* New York Tribune. The radicals who congregated around the *Tribune* broke with more conservative Whigs through their involvement in land reform. This placed many of them in the orbit of Young Americans, who also supported the cause of land and labor, with Stephen Douglas being the first senator to introduce the Homestead Act in 1849. Furthermore, like the Young Americans, many figures associated with the *Tribune* were outspoken advocates of the Revolutions of 1848. Nonetheless, Whiggish figures were more likely than Democrats to support the communal ownership of property. This stance was, ironically, derived from an emphasis on social interdependence, which was shared with more conservative members of the party. Radical Whigs were also concerned more with the question of labor than popular sovereignty, eschewing the conflation of political and natural rights characteristic of Young America. This willingness to look past the white male as an independent sovereign whose political rights were a product of nature allowed radical Whigs to bring disenfranchised nonwhites into their movement for natural rights.

75. For a study that incorporates Whiggish figures in the world of nineteenth-century expansionism, see Gobat, *Empire by Invitation.* Although the Whigs' historicist view of the American nation often turned them against the rapid expansion of the Union, some radical figures from this tradition nonetheless believed that new nations liberated from monarchical rule would spontaneously produce natural laws, albeit more cooperative and interdependent ones than Jacksonian Democrats had in mind.

76. Parke Godwin to the editors of the *Harbinger,* postmarked June 5, 1846, Bryant-Godwin Papers, NYPL.

77. Parke Godwin to Charles H. Dana, May 1846, ibid.

78. Whitman, *The Eighteenth Presidency!,* 43, 44.

79. An extract from one of Walt Whitman's notebooks, found in Reynolds, *Walt Whitman's America,* 327.

80. Ibid., 136.

81. Whitman, *Democratic Vistas.*

82. *Brooklyn Eagle,* June 6, 1846.

83. *Brooklyn Eagle,* November 5, 1858.

84. Whitman, *I Sit and Look Out,* 87–88, 89–90.

85. "Walt Whitman: A Brooklyn Boy," *Brooklyn Times,* September 29, 1855.

86. Frank, "Aesthetic Democracy," 404.

87. Whitman quoted in Scholnick, "Whigs and Democrats," 83.

88. Whitman, *Preface to Leaves of Grass* (1855 ed.), 618.

89. Shelley, "In Defence of Poetry," 508.

90. Simms, "Progress in America: Or, a Speech in Sonnets, on Great Britain and the United States; Not Delivered Either in Parliament or Congress," *Democratic Review* 18 (February 1846).

91. May, *Slavery, Race, and Conquest,* 197.

92. *New York Tribune,* April 28, 1851.

93. In the senate race of 1858, Douglas claimed the outcome of popular sovereignty in Cuba would be "obvious," since the inhabitants "will never turn loose a million free negroes to desolate that beautiful island." Moreover, Young America certainly garnered some support south of the Mason-Dixon line. Alabama's John W. Womack told John McClernand that his home state revered Douglas as a spokesperson for Young America. May, *Slavery, Race and Conquest,* 189, 160.

94. Ibid., 197.

95. May argues that "it is more likely . . . that Douglas's expansionist record did him more good with northern Democrats than southern Democrats, since expansionists like George N. Sanders and National Democratic Chairman August Belmont were still laboring for his campaign and only 163,568 of his total 979,425 popular votes came from the slave states." Ibid., 201.

96. Lynn, "From the Money Power to the Antislavery Power."

97. John O'Sullivan came close to advocating for slavery in the tropics as a positive good. Writing to Stephen Douglas in 1854, O'Sullivan said that slavery was "not beneficial to the country in which it exists, or to the superior race," but added the caveat, "except perhaps for the necessities of tropical labor." O'Sullivan to Douglas, February 10, 1854, SADP.

98. The historiographical verdict on Stephen Douglas's personal view of slavery is mixed. Both his acclaimed biographer Robert Johannsen and the historian of the Lincoln-Douglas debates, Harry Jaffa, argue that Douglas was opposed to slavery on moral grounds. But Graham A. Peck reverts to the original interpretation put forward by historian Allen Nevins that, based on the available evidence, he can be called proslavery. Peck points out that the historiographical tide is turning in his favor, pointing to works by Leonard Richards and Jonathan Glickstein. Where historians come down in this debate depends on whether they accept the argument, most recently advanced by Stephen E. Maizlish and Adam I. P. Smith, that there was a broadly antislavery consensus in the antebellum North; or whether they believe that the battle between pro- and antislavery forces was also being waged within the free states themselves, as James Oakes and Michael Landis suggest. It also depends on whether support for free labor can be readily taken as moral aversion to slavery. Historian David Potter provides a way of thinking past the anti- and proslavery binary, urging historians not to ask, "Did the people of the North really oppose slavery?" but rather, "What was the rank of anti-slavery in the hierarchy of northern values?" Johannsen, *Stephen Douglas;* Jaffa, *Crisis of the House Divided;* Peck, "Was Stephen A. Douglas Antislavery?," 1–2; Richards, *Slave Power;* Glickstein, *American Exceptionalism,* 253; Nevins, *Ordeal of the Union;* Maizlish, *Strife of Tongues;* A. Smith, *Stormy Present;* Oakes, "Taming the Antislavery Revolution"; Landis, *Northern Men with Southern Loyalties;* Potter, *Impending Crisis,* 44.

99. Although I disagree with his argument that Stephen Douglas was essentially pro-slavery, Graham Peck is right to highlight Douglas's appeal to the Northern electorate. He points out that Douglas was "the leading spokesperson for well over one million northern Democratic voters, receiving approximately forty percent of the northern popular vote in the 1860 presidential election." See "Was Stephen Douglas Anti-Slavery?," 20.

100. David Brion Davis argues in *Slavery and Human Progress* that gradualist anti-slavery figures could often be the most significant obstacle to abolition in the nineteenth century. Unlike proslavery figures who could galvanize the opposition, moderates bred complacency about what was required for emancipation and took the idea of progress for granted.

6. A State of Nature

1. Jaffa, *New Birth of Freedom*. In a discussion of the parallels between ancient Rome and the American Union, Jaffa argues that the "universalization of Roman citizenship" meant that Rome "was not a political regime because a political regime, properly so called, is always one of many." Ibid., 137.

2. *Cong. Globe*, 33rd Cong., 1st Sess. (1854), 789.

3. "Eighteen Fifty-Two and the Presidency," 2, 3.

4. For an exploration of the Fugitive Slave Law as an infringement of the states' rights of the North and a source of controversy among Northern Democrats (and later Republicans), see Woods, "Tell Us Something about State Rights."

5. Blackett, *Captive's Quest for Freedom*, 8.

6. "The Fugitive Slave Law: Shall it be Enforced?," *Democratic Review* 28 (April 1851), 359.

7. These arguments bore a striking resemblance to Stephen Douglas's opposition to religious critics of the Kansas-Nebraska Act.

8. "The Fugitive Slave Law; Shall it be Enforced?," *Democratic Review* 28 (April 1851), 353. The quotation from George Dallas is in Blackett, *Captive's Quest for Freedom*, 31.

9. The idea that Black people were inferior according to the law of nature was clearly expressed in "The Fugitive Slave Law: Shall It Be Enforced?," *Democratic Review* 28 (April 1851).

10. Matthew Mason deftly draws attention to the way older partisan identities informed competing conceptions of Unionism during the 1850s; see "In an Evil Hour."

11. Quotation from George Curtis is in Blackett, *Captive's Quest for Freedom*, 45. In the same section, Curtis argued that the free states had the right to exclude slaves for the sake of security in the same way that states had the right to exclude Irish immigrants degraded by English oppression.

12. Blackett notes, "If it is true that laws only gain their legitimacy by being assented to by all they wish to bind, then the 1850 Fugitive Slave Law was doomed to failure from its very inception." *Captive's Quest for Freedom*, 8.

13. Polk's other idea was to admit the entire Mexican Cession as a single state under the principle of popular sovereignty.

14. *Cong. Globe,* 31st Cong., 1st Sess. (1850), 649.

15. Richardson, *"The Admission of California,"* 5.

16. The Compromise of 1850 was also designed to sit alongside, rather than overturn, the Missouri Compromise, despite what Douglas claimed in 1854.

17. "The American Presidency Project," Presidency.ucsb.edu, accessed February 9, 2019, https://www.presidency.ucsb.edu/statistics/data/voter-turnout-in-presidential-elections.

18. Potter, *Impending Crisis,* 167.

19. Malavasic, *F Street Mess,* 82.

20. This account of how Southerners shaped the Kansas-Nebraska Act draws on ibid., 86–112.

21. Historians generally argue that the reworking of the Kansas-Nebraska Act sectionalized American politics. Alice Malavasic writes, "What had been a partisan issue for more than a decade became a sectional issue overnight"; while Michael Holt argues that partisan disagreement over the Kansas-Nebraska Act gave way to a debate between free and slave states. Malavasic, *F Street Mess,* 112; Holt, *Political Crisis of the 1850s,* 112. While I agree that national politics started to revolve around sectional issues, this was not true for all Americans in the period. For Young America Democrats, older loyalties associated with the second party system continued to shape their political choices.

22. A very effective article that aims to situate Douglas's Kansas-Nebraska Act within the context of the Young America movement is Eyal's "With His Eyes Open."

23. Johannsen, *Letters of Stephen Douglas,* 322.

24. Ibid., 296.

25. *Cong. Globe,* 33rd Cong., 1st Sess. (1854), 337.

26. Ibid., 961.

27. Ibid., 1134.

28. Isaac R. Diller to Stephen Douglas, May 31, 1854, SADP.

29. *Cong. Globe,* 33rd Cong., 1st Sess. (1854), 1132.

30. Ibid.

31. Ibid.

32. Capen, *Plain Facts and Considerations,* 26, 28, 27.

33. Grow, *"Liberty to the Downtrodden",* 111.

34. "The Struggle Between Truth and Falsehood," *Daily Union,* August 19, 1856.

35. "Know-Nothingism," *Democratic Review* 37 (June 1855), 490.

36. *Cong. Globe,* 33rd Cong., 1st Sess. (1854), 319.

37. Ibid., 318.

38. Walker, *Appeal for the Union,* 11.

39. Walker, *Inaugural Address.*

40. S. D. Johnston to Stephen Douglas, March 24, 1854, SADP.

41. O'Sullivan to Douglas, February 10, 1854, SADP.

42. Samuel Cox to Stephen Douglas, March 24, 1854, SADP.

43. "Appeal of the Independent Democrats in Congress to the People of the United States," *Cong. Globe,* 33rd Cong., 1st Sess. (1854), 281–82.

44. Holt, *Political Crisis of the 1850s,* 152. The fundamentalist Civil War historians emphasize the role of Chase's *Appeal* in forging a Northern ideology committed to Free Soil. This fits into a larger narrative about the crystallization of sectional worldviews before the Civil War. The classic account of this thesis is Eric Foner's *Free Soil, Free Labor, Free Men.* But the revisionists also foreground the *Appeal* and the sectional ideologies it helped to forge.

45. E. Foner, *Free Soil, Free Labor, Free Men,* 94–95.

46. Mark Neely argues persuasively that "people at the time recognized this position as conservative, and in general historians have underestimated the importance of the conservative protest against the Kansas-Nebraska Act." See "Kansas-Nebraska Act," 38. My exploration of how ex-Whigs drew on their formative ideology in opposition to the Kansas-Nebraska Act aims to address this gap in the scholarship.

47. Ibid., 40.

48. William Penn to Stephen Douglas, March 25, 1854, SADP.

49. Paulus, "America's Long Eulogy for Compromise," 36.

50. John Cochrane to William Marcy, February 9, 1854, William Marcy Papers, LC.

51. "Slavery: A Creature of Municipal Law," *Grand River Times,* September 13, 1854.

52. *Cong. Globe,* 33rd Cong., 1st Sess. (1854), 1134.

53. "Slavery: A Creature of Municipal Law," *Grand River Times,* September 13, 1854.

54. Ibid.

55. *Cong. Globe,* 33rd Cong., 1st Sess. (1854), 1133.

56. "Kossuth against the Slavery Agitation—Mazzini's Letter Explained," *New York Times* June 24, 1854. For Bancroft's view on slavery as an inheritance from the British, see the introduction to this work.

57. Broderick, *Against the Admission of Kansas,* 3, 10, 11.

58. Cong. Globe, 33rd Cong., 1st Sess. (1854), 1133.

59. Ibid.

60. Letter from Martin Van Buren to Moses Tilden, September 1, 1856, in Tilden, *Letters and Literary Memorials,* 1:119, 120.

61. *Cong. Globe,* 33rd Cong., 1st Sess. (1854), 333.

62. Walker, *Inaugural Address.*

63. Ibid.

64. Baptist, *Half Has Never Been Told,* 239.

65. Woods, *Arguing until Doomsday,* 19.

66. Douglas continued to oppose federal appropriations for internal improvements in 1854 and even argued they repelled private investors who expected the government to carry out the same tasks. See Douglas, *River and Harbor Improvements,* 3.

67. Widmer, *Young America: Flowering of Democracy,* 29; Woods, *Arguing until Doomsday,* 61.

68. Holt, *Political Crisis of the 1850s,* 110.

238 NOTES TO PAGES 149–156

69. See Douglas, *River and Harbor Improvements*, 3.

70. For the classic account of Northern opposition to the Kansas-Nebraska Act, see E. Foner, *Fee Soil, Free Labor, Free Men.*

71. Potter, *Impending Crisis.*

72. Fischer, *Law of the Territories*, 106, 122.

73. "Kanzas [*sic*] and Nebraska," *North American Review* 80 (January 1855), 104.

74. Ibid., 98.

75. "The Democratic View of Democracy," *North American Review* 101 (July 1865), 109.

76. Ibid., 110.

77. Ibid., 111, 114, 125.

78. Henry, *Great Republican Movement*, 13–14.

79. Henry, *Patriotism and the Slaveowners Rebellion*, 20.

80. "Mr. Lincoln's Reply in the Ottawa Joint Debate," Lincoln, *Collected Works*, 3:255.

81. Lincoln, "Fourth Lincoln-Douglas Debate," in *Speeches and Writings*, 636.

82. Lincoln, "Speech at Springfield," in *Collected Works*, 2:329–30.

83. D. Ross, "Lincoln and the Ethics of Emancipation."

84. Ibid.

85. Grow quoted in Karp, "People's Revolution," 536–37.

86. Karp, "People's Revolution," 536; Ohio editor quote, ibid., 531.

87. Grinspan, *Virgin Vote*, 70.

88. Ibid., 70.

89. Although more universalist, Republicans like Lincoln still defended this principled stance as essentially conservative by referring to "ancient rights," in contrast to the Young Americans' departure from the Founders.

90. Grenville, *Europe Reshaped*, 38.

91. Kirk, *Conservative Mind*, 275.

92. Joshua Lynn argues the Democratic Party rebranded majoritarian democracy and liberal individualism as a conservative program during the 1840s and 1850s. According to Lynn, this connection has persisted in the American conservative movement of the late twentieth century: see *Preserving the White Man's Republic.* Lynn is absolutely right to argue that the Democratic Party rebranded itself as conservative in the middle of the nineteenth century. I would add that this was part of a broader transformation in the relationship between liberalism and conservatism that resonated across the Atlantic world. As liberals in Europe and the United States took power after 1848, they were forced to think about how to conserve their social order, especially from the threat of new radical movements. Since many of the most outspoken American liberals found a home in the Republican Party, the Democracy underwent a corresponding reinvention as a conservative force. But Democrats were not the only ones to characterize themselves as "conservative" during the nineteenth century. In fact, the Whig Party had long used the term, and former Whigs did not stop doing so during the 1850s. However, this group moved in the opposite direction to the Democrats described in Lynn's book. Just as the dissolution of organic nationalism shifted

Democrats into a more conservative position, Burkeans came to embrace a principled stance. Abraham Lincoln, for example, was forced to grapple with the natural law tradition amid the revolutionary upheavals of the mid-nineteenth century, while even Rufus Choate came to vote for a party he praised for their youthful vim and "progressive nationality." In the political vacuum left after the demise of organic nationalism, Americans of all stripes came to realize that some conception of natural rights had to be tied explicitly to national existence, even if they had very different ideas about how this might be done.

93. *Proceedings of the Pennsylvania Democratic State Convention,* 50.

94. Ibid., 57.

95. Soulé's speech quoted in *New York Times,* July 28, 1860. For another Douglas supporter couching their politics in conservative terms, see Richardson, *Speech Delivered in Burlington, New Jersey,* 4. In 1860 Richardson declared, "Between the position of Mr Breckenridge and Mr Lincoln, the great body of conservative men in this country can have no choice. . . . It is their right, it ought to be their privilege." However, Richardson continued to see politics in millenarian terms, as an eternal battle between opposing principles, of which he had always been on the right side. "The difference between the Republican Party and the party to which Breckenridge belongs is this: they are both in favor of intervention"; while Douglas and Richardson favored popular sovereignty and what they described as nonintervention.

96. It is also important to note that both Soulé and George Sanders chose to support Stephen Douglas in 1860, rather than the Southern candidate John Breckenridge. This suggests that Young Americans cannot purely be understood in terms of sectional ideologies, even by the end of the decade; they continued to rally around Jacksonian nationalism. In 1856 Soulé supported Douglas for the presidential nomination and Sanders supported Buchanan. Nevertheless, this was due to the personal animosities discussed in chapter 4 more than ideological differences. By 1860 Sanders regretted his choice and attacked Buchanan as being "too old" for the presidency. For discussions between Soulé and Sanders about their choices for president before the nominating convention, see Journal of Anna J. R. Sanders, May 30, 1856, GNSFP, LC. For Sanders's attacks on Buchanan in 1860, see George Sanders to President Buchanan, July 30, 1860, ibid. Sanders wrote, "Had I then known your real age . . . I should have avoided my share in the error of your elevation."

97. *Cong. Globe,* 33rd Cong., 1st Sess. (1854), 277, 279.

98. Douglas, *Letter of Stephen Douglas Vindicating His Character,* 6.

99. Ibid., 621.

100. Douglas, *Speech at Independence Square Philadelphia, July 4, 1854,* 5.

101. George Sanders, reprinted in *New York Times,* May 21, 1855.

102. Bancroft *Necessity, Reality, and Promise,* 10.

103. Bancroft, *Literary and Historical Miscellanies,* 512–13, quoted in Winger, *Romantic Cultural Politics,* 132.

104. Scholars of the antebellum South have noted the tendency to utilize scientific discourse in opposition to the idea of natural rights. Drew Gilpin Faust argues that the desire to infer natural laws from empirical rather than a priori ideas was how "the Revolutionary

concepts of natural law were thus transmuted into the tenets of social organicism; the prestige of modern science served to legitimate tradition and conservatism." Faust, "Southern Stewardship," 78. To nineteenth-century observers in the North, however, it would not be quite so clear that science was being used to legitimate conservativism. This would largely depend on how they viewed the trajectory of historical progress.

105. "The English System, III," TLKP.

106. "Old England or New England—Will Either Govern the United States?," TLKP. It is important to note that although Kane rallied against authors and philosophers from New England as well as abstract a priori reasoning, he presented himself as more intellectually advanced than these thinkers. Inspired by August Comte's explanation of the three stages of reasoning, Kane evidently considered himself an empirical thinker, more attuned to social progress than the metaphysical antislavery zealots. Indeed, Kane maintained an active correspondence with Comte.

107. Historian Adam I. P. Smith also tries to decenter sectional ideologies in narratives of the 1850s. With regards to Whig-Republicans such as Abraham Lincoln, I aim to explain the paradox that Smith presents of "essentially conservative people being drawn to act in fundamentally revolutionary ways." *Stormy Present*, 15.

108. For the conservatives of New England, see Howe, *Political Culture of the American Whigs*. Whig Calvin Colton warned about the dangers of democracy as late as 1839 in *Voice from America to England*.

109. "Glittering and Sounding Generalities—Speech of Hon. Rufus Choate," *New York Times*, October 30, 1856.

110. Letter from Martin Van Buren to Moses Tilden, September 1, 1856, in Tilden, *Letters and Literary Memorials*, 121.

111. Lynn, *Preserving the White Man's Republic*.

112. Tilden, *The Union! Its Dangers!!!*, 7, 8.

7. Popular Sovereignty and the Struggle against Slavery, 1857–1861

1. Historians characterize the period from 1850–70 as marked by violence driven by the ideology of liberal nationalism. As Patrick Kelley explains, the "period between 1840–1880" was one of "extraordinary violence," driven by "economic development, national unification, and democratic government, a nineteenth-century ideology Enrique Dal Lago has termed 'progressive nationalism'"; it was a time that connected "concurrent rebellions occurring in China, Europe, and South America." See "European Revolutions of 1848," 432.

2. Stephen Douglas, quoted in Walters, *Lincoln, the Rise of the Republicans*, 117.

3. William C. Bryant to John Bigelow, January 22, 1858, Bryant-Godwin Papers, NYPL.

4. John B. Haskin, quoted in Baum, "Loose Party Times," 58–59.

5. Ibid., 57.

6. Ibid., 57, 61.

7. William C. Bryant to John Bigelow, January 22, 1858, Godwin-Bryant Papers, NYPL.

8. *Washington Union,* September 9, 1858.

9. Charles Goepp to Stephen A. Douglas, June 3, 1858, SADP.

10. Forney, *Speech at Tarrytown,* John Forney Papers, HSP.

11. "The Anti-Lecompton Meeting at Tarrytown," *New York Tribune,* September 3, 1858.

12. *Cong. Globe,* 35th Cong., 1st Sess. (1858), 1052.

13. Ibid., 1197.

14. "Forney and Popular Sovereignty, Including a Reprint of Forney's Justification of Popular Sovereignty in the 'Philadelphia Press,'" *New York Tribune,* October 1, 1858.

15. Ibid.

16. "Does Senator Douglas endorse John W. Forney?," *Democrat and Sentinel,* January 12, 1859.

17. Douglas, "Speech in the Senate on the Lecompton Constitution, Delivered March 22, 1858," in Douglas, *Life, Public Services,* 234.

18. John Bigelow to William C. Bryant, December 28, 1857, John Bigelow Papers, NYPL.

19. Douglas to John McClernand, February 21, 1858, in Douglas, *Letters,* 417.

20. John McClernand to Douglas, February 17, 1858, SADP.

21. Douglas to John McClernand, November 23, 1857, in Douglas, *Letters,* 403.

22. Douglas, "Speech in the Senate on the Lecompton Constitution, Delivered March 22, 1858," in Douglas, *Life, Public Services,* 234.

23. Ibid.

24. Ibid.

25. *Campaign Plain Dealer and Popular Sovereignty Advocate,* October 13, 1860, 27.

26. Bancroft to Douglas, December 2, 1857, in Bancroft, *Life and Letters,* 2:130, 131.

27. Bancroft *Necessity, Reality and Promise.*

28. *Democratic Anti-Lecompton Meeting,* 9, 6. In another speech Bancroft connected the struggle for popular sovereignty in Kansas to "our fellow citizens of foreign birth to whom we hold out the hand of brotherhood, remember that liberty in Europe has been trodden underfoot by a complicity between the central government and a miserable minority in the several states." Ibid., 7.

29. Ibid., 6.

30. Ibid. Also see Douglas to W. A. Richardson, June 3, 1856, in Douglas, *Letters,* 361. Douglas told Richardson that he would withdraw his name from the nomination for the presidency at the Democratic Convention in 1856 if it meant the principle of popular sovereignty was accepted. He wrote, "I have a thousand fold more anxiety for the triumph of our principles than for my own personal elevation." Ibid.

31. Bancroft to Stephen Douglas, December 2, 1857, in Bancroft, *Life and Letters*, 2:152.

32. Bancroft to James Mason, July 24, 1857, ibid., 2:126–28.

33. Ibid., 2:127.

34. George Bancroft to S. S. Cox, January 28, 1865, ibid., 2:156.

35. Ibid.

36. Bancroft to Reverdy Johnson, January 2, 1868, ibid., 2:185.

37. *Democratic Anti-Lecompton Meeting*, 6.

38. For the Democrats' favorable interpretation of the French Revolution, see Burke, *Rhode Island*, 50.

39. Charles Goepp to Douglas, June 3, 1858, SADP.

40. Cox, *Speech on the President's Message*, 2–3. Under administration pressure Cox did eventually vote for Lecompton.

41. Pugh, *"Vindication of the Northern Democracy,"* 4, 9.

42. Broderick, quoted in Burt, *Lincoln's Tragic Pragmatism*, 46. Conversely, Walker voted for the bill.

43. O'Meara, *Brief History of Early Politics in California*, 266.

44. These final words became something of a rallying cry in the western states for Jacksonian supporters of free labor. Ibid., 256.

45. This idea was first raised in Woods, "Was There a Plot to Kill Stephen Douglas?," blog entry, January 30, 2018, Muster (*Journal of the Civil War Era*), https://www.journalofthecivilwarera.org/muster/.

46. *New York Herald*, June 12, 1855, in Neely, "Kansas-Nebraska Act," 20.

47. These were the two groups that presented the greatest threat to Young America's control over the Democratic Party in the late 1850s. As we shall see, both were uncomfortable with the idea that popular sovereignty was a natural right. Proslavery Democrats subscribed to "joint sovereignty," while Cotton Whigs clung to the social organicism of the *Whig Review*. Although conservative Whigs went in various directions after the collapse of their party, Cotton Whigs were members of the New England elite who were attracted to the Democrats because of the party's emphasis on national unity and their economic ties to the South. Many Cotton Whigs were owners of textile factories that relied on the slave South for cotton production.

48. The background to Douglas's article in *Harper's* is explored in Johannsen, "Douglas, 'Harper's Magazine,' and Popular Sovereignty." Joshua Lynn also explores Douglas's article and the pamphlet war it inspired in Lynn, *Preserving the White Man's Republic*.

49. Douglas wrote that "it was the birth-right of all freemen—inalienable when formed into political communities—to exercise exclusive legislation in respect to all matters pertaining to their internal policy—slavery not accepted." Douglas, *Dividing Line*, 11. Douglas is vague as to precisely what makes a collection of people constitute a "political community," ultimately undermining the crux of his argument. On the one hand, if there were political communities wherever people gathered together, there was no need for Douglas's caveat. On the other, if the formation of a political community

was based on contingent factors, then popular sovereignty could hardly constitute a natural right. This contradiction was exploited by former Whigs and proslavery Democrats who argued that Douglas had given insufficient attention to the factors that created political communities in the first place.

50. Douglas, "Let the People Rule," 3.

51. Douglas's opponents argued that Congress could not confer powers on the territories that it did not itself possess. According to Douglas, the opposite was true. Those powers that the Constitution *had* invested in Congress, such as the regulation of commerce, were the ones that could not be delegated to the territories. In fact, Douglas argued that Congress often created institutions, or political bodies, that wielded powers that it could not exercise itself. Douglas referred to Congress's power to create courts that had the absolute authority to decide judicial questions. Douglas, *Dividing Line*, 7.

52. Curtis, *Just Supremacy of Congress over the Territories*, 21. It was common for Cotton Whigs to acknowledge the natural right to the fruit of one's labor, like their Republican counterparts. Nevertheless, this remained a theoretical ideal, even in the territories, that should be sacrificed for national unity. The problem for Curtis was that Douglas had also misunderstood the theory of natural rights.

53. Ibid., 22.

54. Erik Chaput points out that "after conferring with Democrats from around the country in Washington, New Hampshire Congressman Edmund Burke informed Thomas Dorr in February 1844 that Democrats in the South, concerned about a threat to Southern slavery, 'do not hold so absolutely to the doctrine of popular sovereignty as we do in the North.'" Chaput, "Rhode Island Question," 55.

55. Black, *Observations on Senator Douglas' Views of Popular Sovereignty,* 21.

56. Wise, *Territorial Government and the Admission of New States,* 92.

57. *Politics in Ohio: Senator Chase's Letter to Hon. A. P. Edgerton,* January 1, 1854, William Allen Papers, LC.

58. Samuel J. Tilden to the editors of the *Evening Post,* October 3, 1860, in Tilden, *Letters and Literary Memorials,* 1:132, 135.

59. Bigelow, *Life of Samuel J. Tilden,* 1:155.

60. Ibid.

61. John Forney to Henry Wise, May 26, 1858, John Forney Papers, LC. A Virginia Democrat, Henry Wise nonetheless opposed the Lecompton Constitution, viewing the establishment of free labor in Kansas as a logical outcome of popular sovereignty. Indeed, Wise's views on slavery were remarkably similar to Young America's, as he argued the Mexican War would cause slavery to drain into Latin America. Nevertheless, these views made Wise incredibly unpopular in his home state of Virginia and jeopardized his chances of running for the presidency. In 1859 he swung around to Calhoun's joint sovereignty idea in a pamphlet discussed earlier in this chapter. See Wise, *Territorial Government and the Admission of New States.* For the way Wise's pragmatism informed his political career, see Ambrose, *A Good Southerner.*

62. Forney to Wise, May 26, 1858, John Forney Papers, LC.

63. These Democrats included Samuel Tilden, Martin Van Buren, Samuel S. Cox, George Sanders, John O'Sullivan, Robert J. Walker, and August Belmont. John Forney voted for the Republican candidate, Abraham Lincoln, while Young America Democrat Thomas L. Kane voted for John Breckenridge. However, Douglas showed flexibility after the election, proposing, once again, that the Missouri Compromise line be extended across the continent to avoid secession and proposing a free-trade agreement with the Latin American states instead of annexation. May, *Slavery, Race, and Conquest*, 228.

64. Historian Fitzhugh Brundage argues: "There are ample grounds to expand the discussion of Reconstruction to the antebellum era." Brundage points out that "we await a comprehensive history of the ideas of social transformation that circulated in the mid-nineteenth century United States and informed ideas about reforming the South." He calls on historians to examine the "conceptual rehearsals" that paved the way for this period. See "Reconstruction in the South." I would add that framing Reconstruction in terms of the Democratic ideologies prevalent in the 1850s helps us to understand the failures of the period.

65. Alexander, "Fate of Northern Democrats," 195–96.

66. Anna Sanders mentioned these plans in the context of praising George Sanders's support for the annexation of Texas, making the 1840s a likely decade. Anna Sanders to George Sanders, n.d., GNSFP, LC.

67. "Prohibition of Colored Persons," *Brooklyn Daily Eagle*, May 6, 1858. For a similar outlook from Whitman, see "Black Labor Versus White Labor," *Brooklyn Daily Eagle*, May 25, 1857.

68. Tilden, *The Union! Its Dangers!!!*, 9.

69. *National Era*, September 7, 1854.

70. "Address to the People of France," *New York Times*, October 27, 1854.

71. The relationship between racial segregation and liberal benevolence has a long history in the United States. For an earlier period, see Guyatt, *Bind Us Apart*. Unlike Guyatt's protagonists, Young Americans generally saw nonwhites as separate and inherently inferior races. By contrast, Americans in the early republic believed racial differences were less stark. Nonwhites were common descendants of the same ancestors whose differences were shaped by environmental influences.

72. The idea that natural rights applied to men but that the rights of dependent populations like women were contingent on circumstance can be found in Zagarri, "Rights of Man and Woman."

73. *The English System III*, TLKP.

74. *What a fine thing is a theorist? XII*, TLKP; Oakes, *Freedom National*.

75. *What a fine thing is a theorist? XII*, TLKP.

76. *Transportation, Extermination, Fusion XI*, TLKP.

77. O'Sullivan to Douglas, February 10, 1854, SADP.

78. For an exploration of the attitudes to race in the *Democratic Review*, see chapter 1.

79. For John Campbell's view of race, see Campbell, *Negro-Mania*, 4.

80. For an account of Campbell's political positions during the 1840s and 50s, see Heath, "Producers on the one side."

81. O'Sullivan to Douglas, February 10, 1854, SADP.

82. Stephen Douglas asserted that Black slavery was particularly suited to tropical regions. See May, *Slavery, Race,* 197.

83. Lincoln, "Second Lecture on Discoveries and Inventions," February 11, 1859, in *Collected Works,* 3:356.

84. Ibid., 357.

85. Ibid., 358, 360.

86. Ibid., 358.

87. Henry, "Young America—True Idea of Progress," in *Considerations on Some of the Elements and Conditions,* 198, 199.

88. Ibid., 200.

89. Ibid., 204, 205.

90. Henry, "California: Historical Significance of Its Acquisition," in ibid., 175.

91. Henry, "Young America—True Idea of Progress," in ibid., 205.

92. Ibid.

93. Winger, "To the Latest Generations," 29.

94. Henry, "Remarks on Mr G Bancroft's Oration on Human Progress," in *Considerations on Some of the Elements and Conditions,* 289.

95. Henry, "The Destination of the Human Race," in ibid., 229–30.

96. Henry, "Remarks on Mr G Bancroft's Oration on Human Progress," in ibid., 270–71.

97. Ibid.

98. Ibid., 278, 281, 284.

99. Henry, "Young America—True Idea of Progress," in ibid., 203, 201.

100. Holt, *Political Crisis of the 1850s,* 104.

101. Landis, *Northern Men with Southern Loyalties;* Oakes, *Freedom National.*

Conclusion

1. *Cong. Globe,* 34th Cong., 3rd Sess. (1857), 229.

2. Tocqueville, *Ancien Régime and the Revolution,* 25.

3. Ibid.

4. Vattel, *Law of Nations,* 268.

5. Armitage, "Cosmopolitanism and Civil War," 14.

6. Hugo, *Les Misérables,* quoted in ibid., 164–65.

7. John O'Sullivan, "Democracy," *Democratic Review* 7 (March 1840), 228.

8. Anderson, *Imagined Communities.*

9. Howe, *Political Culture of the American Whigs.*

10. For a discussion of popular sovereignty and natural rights in relation to the Dorr Rebellion, see chapter 2; for the sectional crisis, see chapter 6.

11. Winger, *Lincoln, Religion*, 205.

12. See Jaffa, *New Birth of Freedom*. Jaffa contrast Douglas's pragmatism and material self-interest against Lincoln's use of the natural law tradition. He writes, "Neither Thrasymachus or Machiavelli espoused more completely than Douglas the doctrine that 'justice is in the interest of the stronger'" 311.

13. Eyal, *Young America Movement*, 223.

14. Ibid., 1.

15. Armitage, "Cosmopolitanism and Civil War," 1, 3.

16. Ibid., 26.

17. Ibid., 3.

18. D. Ross, "Lincoln and the Ethics of Emancipation," 1.

19. Ayers, "Worrying about the Civil War," 156.

20. This argument fits with the most recent literature on the history of capitalism, which reframes the slave South as a foundation of the globalized economy in the mid-nineteenth century rather than a backwater out of step with modernity. This being the case, I would add that conservative figures within the antislavery movement were actually at odds with some of the more virulent supporters of secular, free-market capitalism in both the North and South. Furthermore, support for slavery as an engine in the global economy resonated beyond the slave states, as some Northerners became attracted to the economic efficiency of slavery in tropical regions. As such, the 1850s constitute an important moment when the association between antislavery morality and economic and moral progress, traced masterfully by historian David Brion Davis in *Slavery and Human Progress*, was in flux. In this context, a wide variety of critics of capitalism found a home in the antislavery movement: not only radicals, but conservatives seeking to preserve older religious ideas against the economic and political forces of modernity. For the relationship between slavery and capitalism, see Baptist, *Half Has Never Been Told*.

21. Burt, *Lincoln's Tragic Pragmatism*, 11.

22. For a discussion of Elisha P. Hurlbut's book on natural rights, see chapter 1.

23. For Young America's privileging of popular attitudes to race, see the discussion of Thomas L. Kane in chapter 7.

Bibliography

Primary Sources

Printed Sources

Appeal of the Independent Democrats in Congress to the People of the United States: Shall Slavery be Permitted in Nebraska? Washington, DC: Tower's Printers, 1854.

Ballou, Maturin. *History of Cuba, or Notes of a Traveller in the Tropics.* Boston: Phillips, Sampson and Co., 1854.

Bancroft, George. *History of the United States of America: From the Discovering of the Continent.* 10 vols. New York: D. Appleton, 1888.

Barnard, Daniel. *The Life and Letters of George Bancroft.* Edited by M. A. De Wolfe Howe. 2 vols. New York: Scribner's, 1908.

———. *Man and the State, Social and Political: An Address Before the Phi Betta Kappa Society of Yale College, August 19, 1846.* New Haven, CT: B. L. Hamlin, 1846.

———. *The Necessity, the Reality and the Promise of Progress of the Human Race: Oration Delivered before the New York Historical Society, November 20, 1854.* New York: Printed for the Society, 1854.

Black, Jerimiah. *Observations on Senator Douglas' Views of Popular Sovereignty as Expressed in Harpers' Magazine for September 1859.* Washington, DC: Thomas McGill, 1859.

Broderick, David C. *Against the Admission of Kansas under the Lecompton Constitution, Delivered in the Senate of the United States, March 22, 1856.* Washington, DC: Lamuel Towers, 1858.

Burke, Edmund. *A Philosophical Enquiry into the Origin of Our Ideas of the Sublime and Beautiful and Other Pre-Revolutionary Writings.* Edited by David Womersley. London: Penguin, 1998.

———. *Reflections on the Revolution in France.* London: Penguin, 1968.

Bushnell, Horace. *A Discourse Delivered on the Sunday after the Disaster of Bull Run in the North Church, Hartford.* Hartford, CT: L. E. Hunt, 1861.

Campbell, John. *Negro-Mania, Being an Examination of the Falsely Assumed Authority of the Various Races of Men.* New York: Campbell and Power, 1851.

Capen, Nahum. *The History of Democracy, or, Political Progress, Historically Illustrated from the Earliest to the Latest Periods.* Hartford, CT: American Publishing Co., 1875.

———. *Plain Facts and Considerations Addressed to the People of the United States without Distinction of Party in Favor of James Buchanan for President and John Breckenridge of Kentucky for Vice-President.* Boston: Brown, Bazin and Co., 1856.

————. *The Republic of the United States of America: Its Duties to Itself and Its Responsible Relations to Other Countries.* New York: D. Appleton, 1848.

Carey, Henry. *Principles of Social Science.* Philadelphia: J. P. Lippincott, 1858.

Chambers, Robert. *Vestige of the Natural History of Creation.* London: John Churchill, 1844.

Colton, Calvin. *Junius Tracts.* New York: Greeley & McElrath, 1844.

————. *A Voice from America to England.* London: Henry Colburn, 1839.

Cox, Samuel S. *A Buckeye Abroad; Or, Wanderings in Europe and in the Orient.* G. P. Putnam, 1852.

————. *The Scholar, as the True Progressive and Conservative, Illustrated in the Life of Hugo Grotius and by the Law of Nations, an Address Delivered before the Athenian Literary Society of the Ohio University.* Columbus, OH: Scott and Bascom, 1852.

————. *Speech of Samuel S. Cox of Ohio on the President's Message, December 16, 1857.* Washington, DC: Lemuel Towers, 1857.

————. *"Territorial Expansion": Speech Delivered in the House of Representatives, January 18, 1859.* Washington, DC: Lemuel Towers, 1859.

Curtis, George T. *The Just Supremacy of Congress over the Territories: Intended as an Answer to the Hon. Stephen A. Douglas on Popular Sovereignty.* Boston: A. Williams and Co., 1859.

————. *The Merits of Thomas W. Dorr and George Bancroft as they are Politically Connected.* Boston: John H. Eastburn, 1844.

Curtis, George W. *The Duty of the American Scholar to Politics and the Times: An Oration, Delivered on Tuesday, August 5, 1856, before the Literary Societies of Wesleyan University, Middleton., Conn.* New York: Dix, Edwards & Co., 1856.

Dallas, George. *Diary of George M. Dallas while United States Minister to Russia, 1837 to 1839, and to England, 1856 to 1861.* Edited by S. Dallas. Philadelphia: Lippincott, 1892.

————. *Great Speech of Hon. George M. Dallas upon the Leading Topics of the Day, Delivered at Pittsburgh, Pennsylvania, September 18, 1847.* Philadelphia: Time and Keystone Job Office, 1847.

————. *A Series of Letters from London Written during the years 1856, '57, '58, '59, and '60.* Edited by J. Dallas. Philadelphia: Lippincott, 1869.

Democratic Anti-Lecompton Meeting, Held Wednesday 17, 1858. New York: John T. Trow, 1858.

Dix, John A. *"The War with Mexico": Speech of Hon. J. A. Dix of New York in the Senate of the United States, January 26, 1848.* Washington, DC: Congressional Globe Office, 1848.

Douglas, Stephen. *The Dividing Line between Federal and Local Authority.* New York: Harper and Brothers, 1859.

————. *Letter of Senator Douglas, Vindicating His Character and His Position on the Nebraska Bill Against the Assaults Contained in the Proceedings of a Public Meeting*

Composed of Twenty-Five Clergymen of Chicago. Washington, DC: The Sentinel Office, 1854.

———. *The Letters of Stephen Arnold Douglas.* Edited by R. W. Johannsen. Urbana: University of Illinois Press, 1961.

———. *"Let the People Rule": Speech of Hon. Stephen A. Douglas, at Concord, New Hampshire, July 31, 1860.* n.p.

———. *River and Harbor Improvements: Letter of Stephen Douglas to Governor Matteson, of Illinois.* [Washington, DC]: n.p., 1854.

———. *Speeches of Mr. Douglas, of Illinois, at the Democratic Festival at Jackson Hall, January 8, 1852. And at the Congressional Banquet to Kossuth, January 7, 1852.* Washington, DC: Lemuel Towers, [1852].

———. *Speech of Senator Douglas at the Democratic Celebration of the Anniversary of American Freedom, in Independence Square Philadelphia, July 4, 1854.* [Philadelphia]: n.p., [1854].

———. *Stephen Douglas: His Life, Public Services, Patriotism and Speeches.* Edited by Clark E. Carr. Chicago: A. C. McClurg, 1909.

Everett, Edward. *Stability and Progress. Remarks Made on the 4th of July 1853.* Boston: Eastburn's Press, 1853.

Fischer, Sidney George. *The Law of the Territories.* Philadelphia: Sherman & Son, 1859.

Gilpin, Henry. *Address Delivered at the University of Pennsylvania before the Society of Alumni, on the Occasion of Their Annual Celebration, November 13, 1851.* Philadelphia: King and Baird, 1851.

Goepp, Charles. *E Pluribus Unum: A Political Tract on Kossuth and America.* F. W. Thomas, 1852.

———, and Theodore Poesche. *The New Rome; or, the United States of the World.* G. P. Putnam, 1853.

Hawthorne, Nathaniel. *The Blithedale Romance.* New York: Penguin, 2014.

———. "Earth's Holocaust." In *The Works of Nathaniel Hawthorne,* vol. 10: *Mosses from an Old Manse.* Edited by George Parsons Lathrop. Boston: Houghton Mifflin, 1891.

———. *The Scarlet Letter.* London: Penguin Classics, 2002.

Henningsen, Charles. *The White Slave, or, the Russian Peasant Girl.* 3 vols. London: Henry Colburn, 1845.

Henry, Caleb. *Considerations on Some of the Elements and Conditions of Social Welfare and Human Progress.* New York: D. Appleton, 1860.

———. *The Great Republican Movement: What We Want, Why We Want It, and What Will Come If We Fail; Remarks Made at a Public Meeting in Geneva, NY, July 19, 1856.* New York: Dix, Edwards & Co., 1856.

———. *Patriotism and the Slaveowners Rebellion—An Oration.* New York: D. Appleton, 1861.

Hugo, Victor. *Les Misérables . . . A Novel.* Translated by Charles Edward Wilbour. 5 vols. New York, 1862.

Hurlbut, *On Human Rights and their Political Guarantees*. New York: Greeley and McElrath, 1845.

Johnson, Herschel. *The Probable Destiny of Our Country, the Requisites to Fulfil that Destiny; and the Duty of Georgia in the Premises; an Address before the Phi Delta and Ciceronian Societies of Mercer University; Delivered on the 14th of July, AD 1847*. Penfield, GA: Temperance Banner Office, 1847.

Kettell, Thomas P. *Southern Wealth and Northern Profits, as Exhibited in Statistical Facts and Official Figures Showing the Necessity of Union to the Future Prosperity and Welfare of the Republic*. New York: George W. and John A. Wood, 1860.

Lincoln, Abraham. *Abraham Lincoln: Speeches and Writings*. 2 vols. New York: Library of America, 1989.

———. *Collected Works of Abraham Lincoln*. Edited by Roy P. Basler. 3 vols. Ann Arbor, MI: University of Michigan Digital Library Production Services, 2001.

Marshall, Edward C. *"American Progress—Judge Douglas—the Presidency": Speech of Mr Marshall of California in the House of Representatives, March 11, 1852*. Washington, DC: [Globe Office], 1852.

———. *Speech of Mr. E. C. Marshall of California on the Conduct of the Administration in Cuba Delivered in the House of Representatives, January 6, 1853*. Washington, DC: Globe Office, 1853.

McClernand, John A. *Address of John A. McClernand to His Constituents*. Washington, DC: Globe Office, 1848.

O'Meara, James. *A Brief History of Early Politics in California*. San Francisco: Bacon and Company, 1861.

Proceedings of the Pennsylvania Democratic State Convention Held at Harrisburg, March 4th, 1856. Philadelphia: W. M. Rice, Pennsylvanian Office Printer, 1856.

Pugh, George E. *Speech of Hon. G. E. Pugh of Ohio on the Acquisition of Cuba Delivered in the Senate of the United States, February 10, 1859*. Washington, DC: Lemuel Towers, 1859.

———. *"Vindication of the Northern Democracy," Speech of Hon. George E. Pugh of Ohio Delivered in the Senate of the United States, December 19, 1859*. Washington, DC: Lemuel Towers, 1859.

Richardson, William. *"The Admission of California," Delivered in the House of Representatives, April 3, 1850*. Washington, DC: Globe Office, 1850.

———. *Speech of Hon. W. A. Richardson, of Illinois, Delivered in Burlington, New Jersey, Tuesday Evening, July 17, 1860*. [Philadelphia: Ringwalt & Brown], 1886.

Sanders, George. *George N. Sanders on the Sequence of Southern Secession, New York, 30th October 1860. To the Republicans of New York Who Are for the Republic*. New York: n.p., 1860.

———. *George N. Sanders to President Buchanan*. [New York: 1860].

Savage, John. *Memoir of Thomas Devin Reilly: A Lecture Delivered by John Mitchel, in the Tabernacle, New York*. New York: P. M. Haverty, 1857.

———. *Our Living Representative Men: From Official and Original Sources.* Philadelphia: Charles and Peterson, 1860.

Shelley, Percy Bysshe. "A Defense of Poetry." In *Shelley's Poetry and Prose.* Edited by D. H. Reiman and S. H. Powers, 478–511. New York: Norton, 1977.

Shields, James. *Letter of the Hon. James Shields Addressed to a Committee of His Fellow Citizens, Delivered at Galena, Illinois, August 5, 1852.* Washington, DC: Robert Armstrong, 1852.

Smith, Gerrit. *Speeches of Gerrit Smith in Congress.* New York: Mason Brothers, 1856.

Soulé, Pierre. *Speech of Mr Soulé of Louisiana on Colonization in North America and the Political Condition of Cuba Delivered in the Senate of the United States, January 25, 1853.* [Washington, DC: n.p., 1853.]

Stockton, Robert. *Remarks of the Hon. R. F. Stockton of New Jersey upon Non-intervention, Delivered in the Senate, February 2, 1852.* Washington, DC: J. N. O. Towers, 1852.

Thayer, Eli. *"The Central America Question": A Speech of Eli Thayer Delivered in the House of Representatives, January 7th, 1858.* Washington DC: Buell & Blanchard, printers, 1858.

———. *The Suicide of Slavery: Speech of Hon. Eli Thayer, of Mass. Delivered in the House of Representatives, March 25, 1858.* Washington DC: Buell & Blanchard, printers, 1858.

Tilden, Samuel J. *Letters and Literary Memorials of Samuel J. Tilden.* Edited by John Bigelow. 2 vols. New York: Harper and Brothers, 1908.

———. *The Life of Samuel J. Tilden.* Edited by John Bigelow. 2 vols. New York: Harper and Brothers, 1895.

———. *The Union! Its Dangers!!! And How They Can Be Averted—Letter from Samuel Tilden to Honorable William Kent, October 26, 1860.* New York: n.p., [1860].

US House of Representatives. *Interference of the Executive in the Affairs of Rhode Island,* 29th Cong., 1st sess., 1844, report no. 546.

Van Evrie. *Negroes and Negro "Slavery": The First an Inferior Race: The Latter Its Normal Condition.* New York: Van Evrie, Horton & Co., 1861.

Vattel, Emer de. *The Law of Nations* [1758]. Edited by Bela Kapossy and Richard Whatmore. Indianapolis, IN: Liberty Fund, 2008.

Walker, Robert J. *An Appeal for the Union, Letter from the Hon. Robert J. Walker, September 30, 1856.* New York: J. F. Trow, [1856].

———. *Inaugural Address of R. J. Walker, Governor of Kansas Territory, Delivered in Lecompton, K.T., May 27, 1857.* Lecompton, KS: Union Office, 1857.

———. *Letter of Mr. Walker, of Mississippi, Relative to the Annexation of Texas, in Reply to the People of Carroll County, Kentucky, to Communicate His Views on the Subject, January 8, 1844.* Washington: Globe Office, 1844.

———. *Speech at Banquet Given by the Mayor & Municipal Authorities of Southampton, to Lewis Kossuth, Late Governor of Hungary, 1851.* London: Waterlow and Sons, 1851.

Wayland, Francis. *The Affairs of Rhode Island: A Discourse Delivered in the Meeting-house of the First Baptist Church, Providence, May 22, 1842.* [Providence, RI]: B. Cranston & Co. and H. H. Brown, 1842.

Whitman, Walt. *Democratic Vistas and Other Papers.* New York: Fredonia Books, 2002.

———. *The Eighteenth Presidency: A Critical Text.* Edited by Edward F. Grier. Lawrence: University of Kansas Press, 1956.

———. *I Sit and Look Out: Editorials from the "Brooklyn Daily Times."* Edited by E. Holloway and V. Schwartz. New York: AMS Press, 1996.

———. *Leaves of Grass: The First Edition* [1855]. London: Penguin Classics, 1961.

Wise, Henry A. *Territorial Government and the Admission of New States into the Union: A Historical and Constitutional Treatise.* [Richmond, VA: n.p.], 1859.

Manuscript Collections

Baltimore, MD: Enoch Pratt Free Library
Joseph P. Kennedy Papers

Boston: Massachusetts Historical Society (MHS)
George Bancroft Papers

Chicago Historical Society
Joseph Medill Papers

New York City: New York Public Library (NYPL). Manuscripts and Archives Division. Astor, Lenox, and Tilden Foundations.
Bryant-Godwin Papers
George Bancroft Papers
Samuel J. Tilden Papers

Philadelphia: Historical Society of Pennsylvania (HSP)
George M. Dallas Papers
Henry Gilpin Collection
James Buchanan Papers

Pittsburgh, PA: University of Pittsburgh
Robert J. Walker Papers

Provo, UT: Harold B. Lee Library, Brigham Young University
Thomas L. Kane Papers (TLKP)

Special Collections Research Centre, University of Chicago
Stephen A. Douglas Papers (SADP)

Washington, DC: Manuscript Division, Library of Congress (LC)
  Francis Markoe Papers
  George N. Sanders Family Papers (GNSFP)
  John W. Forney Papers
  Martin Van Buren Papers
  William Allen Papers
  William L. Marcy Papers

Newspapers and Periodicals

Illinois
Chicago Democrat
Chicago Tribune
Ottawa Free Trader

Indiana
Weekly State Indiana Sentinel

London
London Daily News
Reynolds's Weekly Newspaper

Maryland
Baltimore Sun

Massachusetts
Boston Post
North American Review

Michigan
Grand River Times

New York
American Whig Review [a.k.a. the *Whig Review*]
Brooklyn Daily Eagle
Harper's Weekly
New-York Evening Post
New York Herald
New York Times
United States Democratic Review [a.k.a. the *Democratic Review*]

Ohio
Champaign Plain Dealer and Popular Sovereignty Advocate
Democratic Sentinel and Harrison County Farmer
Spirit of the Times

Pennsylvania
Democrat and Sentinel
Jeffersonian Republican
Star of the North

Virginia
Cooper's Clarksburg Register

Washington, DC
Daily Union
Washington National Intelligencer

Secondary Sources

Alexander, Erik. "The Fate of Northern Democrats after the Civil War: Another Look at the Presidential Election of 1868." In *A Political Nation: New Directions in Mid-Nineteenth-Century Political History,* edited by R. A. Sheldon and G. W. Gallagher, 188–213. Charlottesville: University of Virginia Press, 2012.

Ambrose, Douglas. *A Good Southerner: The Life of Henry A. Wise of Virginia.* Chapel Hill: University of North Carolina Press, 1985.

Anderson, Benedict. *Imagined Communities: Reflections on the Origin and Spread of Nationalism.* New York: Verso, 1991.

———. *Reflections on the Origin and Spread of Nationalism.* Rev. ed. London: Verso, 2006.

Armitage, David. "Cosmopolitanism and Civil War." In *Cosmopolitanism and the Enlightenment,* edited by Joan Pau Rubies and Neil Safier. Cambridge, UK: Cambridge University Press, forthcoming. Accessed November 1, 2021. https://scholar.harvard.edu/files/Armitage/files/cosmopolitanism_and_civil_war.pdf.

Ashworth, J. *"Agrarians" and "Aristocrats": Party Political Ideology in the United States, 1837–1846.* Cambridge, UK: Cambridge University Press, 1983.

Ayers, Edward. "Worrying about the Civil War." In *Moral Problems in American Life,* edited by Karen Halttunen and Lewis Perry, 145–65. Ithaca: Cornell University Press, 1998.

Bailyn, Bernard. *The Ideological Origins of the American Revolution.* Cambridge, MA: Harvard University Press, 1967.

Baker, Jean. *Affairs of Party: The Political Culture of Northern Democrats in the Mid-Nineteenth Century.* New York: Fordham University Press, 1983.

Baptist, Edward. *The Half Has Never Been Told: Slavery and the Making of American Capitalism.* New York: Basic Books, 2016.

Baum, Zachary. "Loose Party Times: The Political Crisis of the 1850s in Westchester County, New York." *Gettysburg County Journal of the Civil War Era* 2 (2011): 27–65.

Belz, Herman. "Abraham Lincoln and the Natural Law Tradition." In *Natural Law, Natural Right and American Constitutionalism.* Witherspoon Institute, 2011. Accessed November 1, 2021. https://www.nlnrac.org/american/lincoln.

Bensel, Richard. *Yankee Leviathan: The Origins of Central State Authority, 1859–1877.* Cambridge, UK: Cambridge University Press, 1991.

Bernath, Michael. *Confederate Minds: The Struggle for Intellectual Independence in the Civil War South.* Chapel Hill: University of North Carolina Press, 2010.

———. "Nationalism: The Future of Civil War Studies." *Journal of the Civil War Era* 2.1 (March 2012): 4.

Blackett, Richard J. M. *The Captive's Quest for Freedom: Fugitive Slaves, the 1850 Fugitive Slave Law, and the Politics of Slavery.* Cambridge, UK: Cambridge University Press, 2018.

Blumenthal, Henry. *Reappraisal of Franco-American Relations, 1830–1871.* Chapel Hill: University of North Carolina Press, 1959.

Brettle, Adrian. *Colossal Ambitions: Confederate Planning for a Post-Civil War World.* Charlottesville: University of Virginia Press, 2020.

Brundage, Fitzhugh. "Reconstruction in the South." Muster: Blog of the Journal of the Civil War Era. Accessed September 7, 2021. https://www.journalofthecivilwarera.org /forum-the-future-of-reconstruction-studies/reconstruction-in-the-south/.

Burt, John. *Lincoln's Tragic Pragmatism: Lincoln, Douglas, and Moral Conflict.* Cambridge, MA: Harvard University Press, 2013.

Butler, Leslie. "Anti-slavery, Liberalism, and Empire Building in Transatlantic Perspective." Paper presented at the Organization of American History Annual Meeting, New Orleans, January 3–6, 2013.

Caeser, James W. "Political Parties and Presidential Ambition." *Journal of Politics* 40.3 (August 1978): 708–39.

Casper, Scott. "The Two Lives of Franklin Pierce: Hawthorne, Political Culture, and the Literary Market." *American Literary History* 5.2 (Summer 1993): 203–30.

Chaffin, Tom. *Fatal Glory: Narciso Lopez and the First Clandestine War against Cuba.* Charlottesville: University of Virginia Press, 1996.

———. "'Sons of Washingon': Narciso López, Filibustering, and U.S. Nationalism, 1848–1851." *Journal of the Early Republic* 15.1 (Spring 1995): 79–108.

Chaput, Erik. "Proslavery and Antislavery Politics in Rhode Island's 1842 Dorr Rebellion." *New England Quarterly* 85.4 (December 2012): 658–94.

———. "'The Rhode Island Question': The Career of a Debate." *Rhode Island History* 68.2 (Summer/Fall 2010): 47–76.

Cheatem, Mark. *Andrew Jackson: Southerner.* Baton Rouge: Louisiana State University Press, 2013.

Childers, Christopher. *The Failure of Popular Sovereignty: Slavery, Manifest Destiny, and the Radicalization of Southern Politics.* Lawrence: University of Kansas, 2012.

Clarke, Christopher. "After 1848: The European Revolution in Government." *Transactions of the Royal Historical Society,* Sixth Series, 22 (2012): 171–97.

Conley, Patrick T. "No Landless Irish Need Apply: Rhode Island's Role in the Framing and Fate of the Fifteenth Amendment." *Rhode Island History* 68.2 (Summer/Fall 2010): 46–77.

Conlin, Michael. "The Dangerous *Isms* and Fanatical *Ists:* Antebellum Conservatives in the South and the North Confront the Modernity Conspiracy." *Journal of the Civil War Era* 4.2 (June 2014): 205–13.

Cotlar, Seth. *Tom Paine's America: The Rise and Fall of Transatlantic Radicalism in the Early Republic.* Charlottesville: University of Virginia Press, 2011.

Curti, Merle. "The Great Mr. Locke: America's Philosopher, 1783–1861." *Huntington Library Bulletin* 11 (April 1937): 107–51.

———. "The Impact of the Revolutions of 1848 on American Thought." *Proceedings of the American Philosophical Society* 93.3 (June 1949): 209–15.

———. "Young America." *American Historical Review* 32.1 (October 1926): 34–55.

Danborn, Daniel. "The Young America Movement." *Journal of the Illinois State Historical Society* 67.3 (June 1974): 294–306.

David, Ralph. "Diplomatic Plumage: American Court Dress in the Early National Period." *American Quarterly* 20.2, pt. 1 (Summer 1968): 164–79.

Davis, David Brion. *Slavery and Human Progress.* Oxford: Oxford University Press, 1984.

Delay, Brian. "Independent Indians and the U.S.-Mexican War." *American Historical Review* 112.1 (February 2007): 35–68.

Doyle, Don. *The Cause of All Nations: An International History of the American Civil War.* New York: Basic Books, 2013.

Dunn, John. "Measuring Locke's Shadow." In John Locke, *Two Treatises of Government and a Letter Concerning Toleration,* 257–85. New Haven, CT: Yale University Press, 2003.

Dyer, Justin. *Natural Law and the Antislavery Constitutional Tradition.* Cambridge, UK: Cambridge University Press, 2012.

Eichhorn, Niels. *Liberty and Slavery: European Separatists, Southern Secession, and the American Civil War.* Baton Rouge: Louisiana State University Press, 2019.

Eustace, Nicole. *Passion Is the Gale: Emotion, Power, and the Coming of the American Revolution.* Chapel Hill: University of North Carolina Press, 2012.

Eyal, Yonatan. "A Romantic Realist: George Nicholas Sanders and the Dilemmas of Southern International Engagement." *Journal of Southern History* 78.1 (February 2012): 107–30.

———. "With His Eyes Open: Stephen A. Douglas and the Kansas-Nebraska Disaster of 1854." *Journal of the Illinois State Historical Society* 91.4 (Winter 1998): 175–217.

———. *The Young America Movement and the Transformation of the Democratic Party, 1828–1861.* Cambridge, UK: Cambridge University Press, 2007.

Faust, Drew Gilpin. "A Southern Stewardship: The Intellectual and the Proslavery Argument." *American Quarterly* 31.1 (Spring 1979): 63–80.

Feller, Daniel. *The Jacksonian Promise: America, 1815 to 1840.* Baltimore: Johns Hopkins University Press, 1995.

Field, Corinne. *The Struggle for Equal Adulthood: Gender, Race, Age and the Fight for Citizenship in Antebellum America.* Chapel Hill: University of North Carolina Press, 2014.

Fields, Barbara. "Slavery, Race and Ideology in the United States of America." *New Left Review* 181 (May/June 1990): 95–118.

Finkelman, Paul, and Daniel Kenon, eds. *Congress and the Crisis of the 1850s.* Athens: Ohio University Press, 2011.

Fleche, Andre. *The Revolution of 1861: The American Civil War in the Age of Nationalist Conflict.* Chapel Hill: University of North Carolina Press, 2012.

Foletta, Marshall. *Coming to Terms with Democracy: Federalist Intellectuals and the Shaping of American Culture, 1800–1828.* Charlottesville: University of Virginia Press, 2001.

Foner, Eric. *Free Soil, Free Labor, and Free Men: The Ideology of the Republican Party before the Civil War.* Oxford: Oxford University Press, 1995.

Foner, Philip S. "Alexander Von Humboldt on Slavery in America." *Science and Society* 47.3 (Fall 1983): 330–42.

———. *A History of Cuba and Its Relations with the United States. Vol. 2: 1845–1895: From the Era of Annexationists to the Outbreak of the Second War for Independence.* New York: International Publishers Co., 1963.

Ford, Lacey K., Jr. "Making the 'White Man's Country' White: Race, Slavery, and State Building in the Jacksonian South." *Journal of the Early Republic* 19.4 (Winter 1999): 713–37.

Frank, Jason. "Aesthetic Democracy: Walt Whitman and the Poetry of the People." *Review of Politics* 69.3 (Summer 2007): 402–30.

Franklin, John H. *The Militant South, 1800–1861.* Cambridge, MA: Harvard University Press, 1956.

Freehling, William. *Prelude to Civil War: The Nullification Controversy in South Carolina, 1816–1836.* New York: Harper and Row, 1996.

———. *The Road to Disunion. Vol. 1, Secessionists at Bay, 1776–1854.* Oxford: Oxford University Press, 1991.

Fritz, Christian. *American Sovereigns: The People and America's Constitutional Tradition before the Civil War.* Cambridge, UK: Cambridge University Press, 2008.

Furniss, Jack. "Devolved Democracy: Federalism and the Party Politics of the Late Antebellum North." *Journal of the Civil War Era* 9.4 (December 2019): 546–68.

Gellner, Ernest. *Nations and Nationalism.* Ithaca, NY: Cornell University Press, 2008.

Glickstein, Jonathan. *American Exceptionalism, American Anxiety: Wages, Competition, and Degraded Labor in the Antebellum United States.* Charlottesville: University of Virginia Press, 2002.

Gobat, Michel. *Empire by Invitation: William Walker and Manifest Destiny in Central America*. Cambridge, MA: Harvard University Press, 2018.

———. "The Invention of Latin America: A Transnational History of Anti-Imperialism, Democracy and Race." *American Historical Review* 118.5 (December 2013): 1345–75.

Grant, Susan-Mary. *North over South: Northern Nationalism and American Identity in the Antebellum Era*. Lawrence: University Press of Kansas, 2000.

Gray, John. *Liberalism*. Minneapolis: University of Minnesota Press, 1983.

Greenberg, Amy. *Manifest Manhood and the Antebellum American America*. Cambridge, UK: Cambridge University Press, 2010.

Greene, Jennifer, and Patrick Kirkwood. "Reframing the Antebellum Democratic Mainstream: Transatlantic Diplomacy and the Career of Pierre Soulé." *Civil War History* 61.3 (September 2015): 212–51.

Grenville, J. A. S. *Europe Reshaped, 1848–1978*. London: Fontana, 1986.

Grinspan, Jon. *The Virgin Vote: How Young Americans Made Democracy Social, Politics Personal, and Voting Popular in the Nineteenth Century*. Chapel Hill: University of North Carolina Press, 2016.

Grow, Matthew. *"Liberty to the Downtrodden": Thomas L. Kane, Romantic Reformer*. New Haven, CT: Yale University Press, 2009.

Guyatt, Nicholas. "America's Conservatory: Race, Reconstruction and the Santo Domingo Debate." *Journal of American History* 97.4 (March 2011): 974–1000.

———. *Bind Us Apart: How Enlightened Americans Invented Racial Segregation*. New York: Basic Books, 2016.

Hatter, Lawrence. *Citizens of Convenience: The Imperial Origins of American Nationhood on the U.S.-Canadian Border*. Charlottesville: University of Virginia Press, 2016.

Haynes, Sam, and Chris Morris, eds. *Manifest Destiny and Empire: American Antebellum Expansionism*. College Station: Texas A&M University Press, 2008.

———. *Unfinished Revolution: The Early American Republic in a British World*. Charlottesville: University of Virginia Press, 2000.

Heath, Andrew. "'The producers on the one side and the capitalists on the other': Labor Reform, Slavery, and the Career of a Transatlantic Radical." *American Nineteenth Century History* 13.2 (August 2012): 199–227.

Hendrickson, David. *Union, Nation, or Empire: The American Debate over International Relations, 1789–1941*. Lexington: University Press of Kentucky, 2008.

Hietala, Thomas. *Manifest Design: American Exceptionalism and Empire*. Ithaca, NY: Cornell University Press, 2003.

Hobsbawm, Eric. *Nations and Nationalism since 1780: Program, Myth, Reality*. Cambridge, UK: Cambridge University Press, 1992.

Holt, Michael. *The Political Crisis of the 1850s*. London: Norton, 1983.

Honeck, Mischa. "'Freemen of All Nations, Bestir Yourselves,': Felice Orsini's Transnational Afterlife and the Radicalization of America." *Journal of the Early Republic* 30.4 (Winter 2010): 587–615.

Horsman, Reginald. *Race and Manifest Destiny: The Origins of American Racial Anglo-Saxonism.* Cambridge, MA: Harvard University Press, 1986.

Howe, David W. *Political Culture of the American Whigs.* Chicago: University of Chicago Press, 1984.

Innes, Joanna, and Mark Phillips, eds. *Re-imagining Democracy in an Age of Revolutions: America, France, Britain, Ireland, 1750–1850.* Oxford: Oxford University Press, 2015.

"Interchange: Nationalism and Internationalism in the Era of the Civil War." *Journal of American History* 98.2 (September 2011): 455–89.

Iurlaro, F. "Vattel's Doctrine of the Customary Law of Nations between Sovereign Interests and the Principles of Natural Law." In *The Law of Nations and Natural Law,* edited by Simone Zurbuchen, n.p. Leiden: Brill, 2019.

Jaffa, Harry. *A Crisis of the House Divided: An Interpretation of the Issues in the Lincoln-Douglas Debates.* Chicago: University of Chicago Press, 1999.

———. *A New Birth of Freedom: Abraham Lincoln and the Coming of the Civil War.* London: Rowman and Littlefield, 2004.

Johannsen, Robert. *The Frontier, the Union and Stephen A. Douglas.* Chicago: University of Illinois Press, 1989.

———. "Stephen A. Douglas, 'Harper's Magazine,' and Popular Sovereignty." *Mississippi Valley Historical Review* 45.4 (March 1959): 606–31.

———. *Stephen A. Douglas.* Urbana: University of Illinois Press, 1973.

Johnson, Donald B., and Kirk H. Porter, eds. *National Party Platforms, 1840–1972.* Urbana: University of Illinois Press, 1973.

Johnson, Walter. *River of Dark Dreams: Slavery and Empire in the Cotton Kingdom.* Cambridge, MA: Harvard University Press, 2013.

Kaplan, Amy. "Manifest Domesticity." *American Literature* 70.3 (September 1998): 581–606.

Karp, Matthew. "The People's Revolution of 1856: Antislavery Populism, National Politics, and the Emergence of the Republican Party." *Journal of the Civil War Era* 9.4 (December 2019): 524–45.

———. *This Vast Southern Empire: Slaveholders at the Helm of American Foreign Policy.* Cambridge, MA: Harvard University Press, 2016.

Kelley, Patrick. "The European Revolutions of 1848 and the Transnational Turn in Civil War History." *Journal of the Civil War Era* 4.3 (September 2014): 431–43.

Kelley, Robert. *The Transatlantic Persuasion: Liberal-Democratic Mind in the Age of Gladstone.* Abingdon, UK: Routledge, 1990.

Kelly Gray, Elizabeth, et al. "Roundtable: 'Distant Revolutions: 1848 and the Challenge to American Exceptionalism.'" *H-Diplo Roundtable Review* 12 (2011).

Kerrigan, William T. "Review: E. Widmer, *Young America: The Flowering of Democracy in New York City.*" *H-SHEAR* (November 1999).

———. "'Young America!' Romantic Nationalism in Literature and Politics, 1843–1861." PhD diss., University of Michigan, Ann Arbor, 1997.

Kinealy, Christine. *Repeal and Revolution: 1848 in Ireland.* Manchester, UK: Manchester University Press, 2009.

Kirk, Russell. *The Conservative Mind from Burke to Eliot.* Channel Islands: Gateway, 2001.

Klein, Philip. *President James Buchanan: A Biography.* University Park: Pennsylvania State University Press, 1962.

Kloppenberg, James T. *Toward Democracy: The Struggle for Self-Rule in European and American Thought.* Oxford: Oxford University Press, 2016.

Klunder, Willard. "Lewis Cass and Slavery Expansion: 'The Father of Popular Sovereignty' and ideological infanticide." *Civil War History* 32.4 (December 1986): 293–317.

Kramer, Lloyd. *Nationalism in Europe and America: Politics, Cultures, and Identities since 1775.* Chapel Hill: University of North Carolina Press, 2011.

Lamb, Robert. *Thomas Paine and the Idea of Human Rights.* Cambridge, UK: Cambridge University Press, 2015.

Landis, Michael T. *Northern Men with Southern Loyalties: The Democratic Party and the Sectional Crisis.* Ithaca, NY: Cornell University Press, 2015.

Lause, Mark. *Young America: Land, Labor, and the Republican Community.* Chicago: University of Illinois Press, 2005.

Lueger, Michael. "Henry Wikoff and the Development of Theatrical Publicity in America." MA thesis, Tufts University, 2011.

Lynn, Joshua. "From the Money Power to the Antislavery Power: Jacksonian Democracy and White Supremacy after Jackson." *Tennessee Historical Quarterly* 76.3 (Fall 2017): 276–92.

———. *Preserving the White Man's Republic: Jacksonian Democracy, Race, and the Transformation of American Conservatism.* Charlottesville: University of Virginia Press, 2019.

Maizlish, Stephen. *A Strife of Tongues: The Compromise of 1850 and the Ideological Foundations of the American Civil War.* Charlottesville: University of Virginia Press, 2018.

Malavasic, Alice. *The F Street Mess: How Southern Senators Rewrote the Kansas-Nebraska Act.* Chapel Hill: University of North Carolina Press, 2017.

Mannheim, Karl. "The Problem of Generations." In *Karl Mannheim: Essays,* edited by Paul Kecskemeti, 276–322. Abingdon, UK: Routledge, 1952.

Mason, Matthew. *Apostle of Union: A Political Biography of Edward Everett.* Chapel Hill: University of North Carolina Press, 2016.

———. "'In an Evil Hour This Pandora's Box of Slavery was Again Opened': Emotional Partisan Divisions in the Late Antebellum North.'" *Journal of Civil War History* 66.3 (September 2020): 256–71.

May, Robert E. *Manifest Destiny's Underworld: Filibustering in Antebellum America.* Chapel Hill: University of North Carolina Press, 2002.

———. *Slavery, Race, and Conquest in the Tropics: Lincoln, Douglas, and the Future of Latin America.* Cambridge, UK: Cambridge University Press, 2013.

———. *The Southern Dream of a Caribbean Empire, 1854–1861*. Gainesville: University Press of Florida, 2002.

McDaniel, Caleb. *The Problem of Democracy in the Age of Slavery: Garrisonian Abolitionists and Transatlantic Reform*. Baton Rouge: Louisiana State University Press, 2015.

McPherson, James. *Battle Cry of Freedom: The Civil War Era*. Oxford: Oxford University Press, 1988.

Mead, Walter Russell. "Donald Trump's Jacksonian Revolt." *Wall Street Journal*, September 9, 2014.

———. "The Jacksonian Tradition and American Foreign Policy." *National Interest* 58 (Winter 1999/2000): 5–29.

Mehta, U. S. *Liberalism and Empire: A Study in Nineteenth-Century British Liberal Thought*. Chicago: University of Chicago Press, 1999.

Merk, Frederick. *Manifest Destiny and Mission in American History*. Cambridge, MA: Harvard University Press, 1963.

Miller, Perry. *Nature's Nation*. Cambridge, MA: Belknap Press of Harvard University Press, 1967.

———. *The Raven and the Whale: The War of Words and Wits in the Era of Poe and Melville*. New York: Harcourt, Brace and World, 1956.

Morgan, Edmund. *Inventing the People: The Rise of Popular Sovereignty in England and America*. New York: Norton, 1989.

Morrison, Michael. "American Reaction to European Revolutions, 1848–1852: Sectionalism, Memory, and Revolutionary Heritage." *Civil War History* 49.2 (June 2003): 111–32.

Murphy, Gretchen. *Hemispheric Imaginings: The Monroe Doctrine and Narratives of US Empire*. Chapel Hill, NC: Duke University Press, 2005.

Murrin, John. "A Roof without Walls: The Dilemma of American National Identity." In *Beyond Confederation: Origins of the Constitution and American Identity*, edited by R. Beemen, S. Botein, and E. C. Carter II, 333–48. Chapel Hill: University of North Carolina Press, 1987.

Myers, Marvin. *The Jacksonian Persuasion: Politics and Belief*. Stanford, CA: Stanford University Press, 1957.

Neely, Mark, Jr. "The Kansas-Nebraska Act in American Political Culture: The Road to Bladensburg and the *Appeal of the Independent Democrats*." In *The Kansas-Nebraska Act of 1854*, edited by J. R. Wunder and J. M. Ross, 13–46. Lincoln: University of Nebraska Press, 2008.

———. "Lincoln, Slavery, and the Nation." *Journal of American History* 96.2 (September 2009): 456–58.

Nelson, Robert. "Review: T. M. Roberts, 'Distant Revolutions: 1848 and the Challenge to American Exceptionalism.'" *H-SHEAR Review Session* (May 2010).

Nester, William. *The Age of Lincoln and the Age of American Power, 1848–1876*. Lincoln NE: Potomac Books, 2014.

Nevins, Allan. *Ordeal of the Union*. Vol. 2: *A House Dividing, 1852–1857*. New York: Charles Scribner's Sons, 1947.

Nichols, Roy. *Advance Agents of Manifest Destiny.* Philadelphia: University of Pennsylvania Press, 1956.

———. *The Democratic Machine 1850–1854.* New York: Columbia University Press, 1923.

Oakes, James. *Freedom National: The Destruction of Slavery in the United States, 1861–1865.* Norton, 2012.

———. "Natural Rights, Citizenship Rights, States' Rights, and Black Rights: Another Look at Lincoln and Race." In *Our Lincoln: New Perspectives on Lincoln and His World,* edited by Eric Foner, 109–35. New York: Norton, 2008.

———. "Taming the Anti-Slavery Revolution." *Jacobin Magazine* online (December 11, 2017). https://www.jacobinmag.com/2017/12/civil-war-abraham-lincoln-slavery -stormy-present-review.

Ochser, Paul. *The Story of the Smithsonian Institution and Its Leaders.* New York: Henry Schuman, 1949.

Palen, Michael. *The "Conspiracy" of Free Trade: The Anglo-American Struggle over Empire and Economic Globalization.* Cambridge, UK: Cambridge University Press, 2016.

Parish, P. "An Exception to Most of the Rules: What Made American Nationalism Different in the Mid-nineteenth Century?" *Prologue: Quarterly of the National Archives* 27 (Fall 1995): 219–29.

———. *The North and the Nation in the Era of the Civil War.* New York: Fordham University Press, 2003.

Parke, Benjamin E. *American Nationalisms: Imagining Union in the Age of Revolutions, 1783–1833.* Cambridge, UK: Cambridge University Press, 2017.

Paulus, Sarah B. "America's Long Eulogy for Compromise: Henry Clay and American Politics, 1854–1858." *Journal of the Civil War Era* 4.1 (March 2014): 28–52.

Peck, Graham A. "Abraham Lincoln and the Triumph of an Anti-Slavery Nationalism." *Journal of the American Lincoln Association* 28.2 (Summer 2007): 1–27.

———. *Making an Antislavery Nation: Lincoln, Douglas, and the Battle over Freedom.* Champaign: University of Illinois Press, 2017.

———. "Was Stephen Douglas Anti-Slavery?" *Journal of the Abraham Lincoln Association* 26.2 (Summer 2005): 1–21.

Pocock, J. G. A. *The Machiavellian Moment: Florentine Political Thought and the Atlantic Republican Tradition.* Princeton, NJ: Princeton University Press, 2003.

Potter, David. "The Historian's Use of Nationalism and Vice Versa." *American Historical Review* 67.4 (July 1962): 924–50.

———. *The Impending Crisis, 1848–1861.* New York: Harper Perennial, 1997.

Power Smith, Mark. "The Young America Movement, the Koszta Affair of 1853, and the Construction of Nationalism before the Civil War." *Journal of the Early Republic* 41.1 (Spring 2021): 87–114.

Preston Moore, J. "Pierre Soulé: Southern Expansionist and Promoter." *Journal of Southern History* 21.2 (May 1955): 203–23.

Quigley, Paul. "Interchange: Nationalism and Internationalism in the Era of the Civil War." *Journal of American History* 98.2 (September 2011): 455–89.

———. *Shifting Grounds: Nationalism and the American South: 1848–1865*. New York: Oxford University Press, 2011.

Quitt, Martin. *Stephen A. Douglas and Antebellum Democracy*. New York: Cambridge University Press, 2012.

Reynolds, David S. *Walt Whitman's America: A Cultural Biography*. New York: Knopf, 2011.

Richards, Leonard L. *The Slave Power: The Free North and Southern Domination, 1780–1860*. Baton Rouge: Louisiana State University Press, 2000.

Roberts, Timothy. *Distant Revolutions: 1848 and the Challenge to American Exceptionalism*. Charlottesville: University of Virginia Press, 2009.

Ross, Dorothy. "Lincoln and the Ethics of Emancipation: Universalism, Nationalism, Exceptionalism." *Journal of American History* 96.2 (September 2009): 379–99.

———. *The Origins of American Social Science*. Cambridge, UK: Cambridge University Press, 1992.

Ross, J. M., and J. R. Wunder, eds. *The Kansas-Nebraska Act of 1854*. Lincoln: University of Nebraska Press, 2008.

Rossiter, Clinton. *Seedtime of the Republic*. San Diego, CA: Harcourt, Brace and World, 1953.

Sampson, Robert. *John O'Sullivan and His Times*. Kent, OH: Kent State University Press, 2003.

Sawyer, Stephen. "Between Authorship and Agency: George Bancroft's Democracy as History." *Revue Francaise d'etudes americaines* 118 (2008): 49–66.

Schlesinger, Arthur. *The Age of Jackson*. New York: Mentor Books, 1959.

Scholnick, Robert. "Extermination and Democracy: O'Sullivan, the *Democratic Review*, and Empire, 1837–1840." *American Periodicals* 15.2 (2005): 123–41.

———. "'The Ultraism of the Day': Greene's *Boston Post*, Hawthorne, Fuller, Melville, Stowe, and Literary Journalism in Antebellum America." *American Periodicals* 18.2 (2008): 163–91.

———. "Whigs and Democrats, the Past and the Future: The Political Emerson and Whitman's 1855 Preface." *American Periodicals* 26.1 (2016): 70–91.

Schmidt, R. J. "Cultural Nationalism in Herder." *Journal of the History of Ideas* 17.3 (June 1956): 407–17.

Schroeder, John. *Shaping a Maritime Empire: The Commercial and Diplomatic Role of the American Navy, 1829–1861*. Westport, CT: Greenwood Press, 1985.

Sellers, Charles. *The Market Revolution: Jacksonian America, 1815–1846*. Oxford: Oxford University Press, 1994.

Sexton, Jay. *Debtor Diplomacy: Finance and American Foreign Relations in the Civil War Era, 1837–1873*. Oxford, UK: Clarendon Press, 2010.

———. *The Monroe Doctrine: Empire and Nation in Nineteenth Century America*. New York: Hill and Wang, 2012.

———. "Toward a Synthesis of Foreign Relations in the Civil War Era, 1848–1877." *American Nineteenth Century History* 5.3 (2004): 50–73.

Shire, Laura Clarke. "Sentimental Racism and Sympathetic Paternalism: Feeling Like a Jacksonian." *Journal of the Early Republic* 39.1 (Spring 2019): 111–22.

———. *The Threshold of Manifest Destiny: Gender and National Expansion on the Florida Frontier.* Philadelphia: University of Pennsylvania Press, 2016.

Sim, David. "Following the Money: Fenian Bonds, Diasporic Nationalism, and Distant Revolutions in the Mid-Nineteenth-Century United States." *Past and Present* 247.1 (May 2020): 77–112.

———. *A Union Forever: The Irish Question and U.S. Foreign Relations in the Victorian Age.* Ithaca, NY: Cornell University Press 2013.

Sinha, Manisha. *The Slave's Cause: A History of Abolition.* New Haven, CT: Yale University Press, 2016.

Smith, Adam I. P. "The Fortunate Banner: Languages of Democracy in the United States, c. 1848." In *Re-imagining Democracy in the Age of Revolutions: America, France, Britain, Ireland, 1750–1850,* edited by Joanna Innes and Mark Phillips, 28–39. Oxford: Oxford University Press, 2013.

———. *No Party Now: Politics in the Civil War North.* Oxford: Oxford University Press, 2006.

———. *The Stormy Present: Conservatism and the Problem of Slavery in Northern Politics.* Chapel Hill: University of North Carolina Press, 2017.

Smith, Rogers. *Civic Ideals: Conflicting Visions of Citizenship in US History.* New Haven, CT: Yale University Press, 1997.

Smith, Steven. "Abraham Lincoln's Kantian Republic." In *Abraham Lincoln and Liberal Democracy,* edited by Nicholas Buccola, 216–37. Lawrence: University of Kansas Press, 2016.

Spencer, Donald. *Louis Kossuth and Young America, 1848–1852.* Columbia: University of Missouri Press, 1977.

Stephenson, Anders. *American Expansion and the Empire of Right.* New York: Hill and Wang, 1996.

Tocqueville, Alexis, D. *The Ancien Régime and the Revolution.* London: Penguin, 2008.

Towers, Frank. "Looking Past the Lower North: Republicans, Natural Rights, and the Election of 1860." Paper presented for the Historical Society, Baltimore, June 5–8, 2008.

Tuchinsky, Adam. *Horace Greeley's* New York Tribune*: Civil War–Era Socialism and the Crisis of Free Labor.* Ithaca, NY: Cornell University Press, 2009.

Tucker, Anne. *Newest Born of Nations: European Nationalist Movements and the Making of the Confederacy.* Charlottesville: University of Virginia Press, 2020.

Varon, Elizabeth R. *Disunion! The Coming of the American Civil War, 1789–1859.* Chapel Hill: University of North Carolina Press, 2010.

Vecoli, Rudolph. "The Significance of Immigration in the Formation of an American Identity." *History Teacher* 30.1 (1996): 9–27.

Volk, Kyle. *Moral Minorities and the Making of American Democracy.* Oxford: Oxford University Press, 2015.

———. "The Perils of 'Pure Democracy': Minority Rights, Liquor Politics, and Popular Sovereignty in Antebellum America." *Journal of the Early Republic* 29.4 (Winter 2009): 641–79.

Walters, Kerry. *Lincoln, the Rise of the Republicans, and the Coming of the Civil War: A Reference Guide.* Santa Barbara, CA: ABC-CLIO, 2013.

Widmer, Edward. *Young America: The Flowering of Democracy in New York City.* Oxford: Oxford University Press, 1999.

Wiecek, William. "'A Peculiar Conservatism' and the Dorr Rebellion: Constitutional Clash in Jacksonian America." *American Journal of Legal History* 22.3 (1978): 237–53.

Wilentz, Sean. *Chants Democratic: New York City and the Rise of the American Working Class, 1788–1850.* Cambridge, UK: Cambridge University Press, 2004.

Wilson, Major L. *Space, Time and Freedom: The Quest for Nationality and the Irrepressible Conflict, 1815–1861.* London: Greenwood Press, 1974.

Winger, Stewart. *Lincoln, Religion, and Romantic Cultural Politics.* DeKalb: Northern Illinois University Press, 2003.

———. "Lincoln's Economics and the American Dream: A Reappraisal." *Journal of the Abraham Lincoln Association* 22.1 (Winter, 2001): 50–80.

———. "Review: Yonatan Eyal, *Young America and the Transformation of the Democratic Party, 1825–1861.*" *American Historical Review* 113.3 (June 2008): 834–35.

———. "'To the Latest Generations': Lincoln's Use of Time, History, and the End Time, in Historical Context." *Journal of the Abraham Lincoln Association* 23.2 (Summer 2002): 19–36.

Woods, Michael. *Arguing until Doomsday: Stephen Douglas, Jefferson Davis, and the Struggle for American Democracy.* Chapel Hill: University of North Carolina Press, 2020.

———. *Emotional and Sectional Conflict in the Antebellum United States.* Cambridge, UK: Cambridge University Press, 2014.

———. "'Tell Us Something about State Rights': Northern Republicans, States' Rights, and the Coming of the Civil War." *Journal of the Civil War Era* 7.2 (June 2017): 242–68.

Zagarri, R. "The Rights of Man and Woman in Post-Revolutionary America." *William and Mary Quarterly* 55.2 (April 1998) 203–30.

Zakaras, Alex. "Nature, Religion, and the Market in Jacksonian Political Thought." *Journal of the Early Republic* 39.1 (Spring 2019) 123–33.

Zelnik, E. "Self-Evident Walls: Reckoning with Recent Histories of Race and Nation." *Journal of the Early Republic* 41.1 (March 2021) 1–38.

Zuckert, Michael P. *Natural Rights and the New Republicanism.* Princeton, NJ: Princeton University Press, 1994.

Zurbuchen, Simone. *The Law of Nations and Natural Law.* Leiden: Brill, 2019.

Index

popular sovereignty in, 169; Revolution (1789), 32–33, 98, 194; Revolution (1848), 57, 81, 83–84, 172; voting rights in, 156
Freehling, William, 69
Free-Soil Party: Campbell and, 186; Cuban annexation and, 125–26, 127–28, 144; election of 1852 and, 91–92, 134; election of 1856 and, 164; Kane and, 184; Kansas-Nebraska Act and, 144; natural rights and, 19; O'Sullivan and, 72, 185, 186; race and, 23; slavery and, 144–45, 184; territorial expansion and, 125–29; Van Buren and, 133; Whitman and, 127–28
free trade: Belmont and, 181; Cushing and, 205n25, 231n30; Douglas and, 213n67; European revolutionary movements and, 103–6; Henry and, 189; Pierce and, 139; tariffs and, 103–4, 205n25, 231n30; territorial expansion and, 113
Frémont, John C., 128, 137, 155, 163
French, Parker H., 110
Fritz, Christian, 26, 210n50, 216n5, 216n7
Fugitive Slave Law, 92, 134, 135, 178

Gadsden Purchase, 139
Geiss, John, 9
Geller, Ernest, 208n40
generational consciousness, 211n57
Georgia, 151
German state, revolutionary movement in, 84, 85
Giddings, Joshua, 144
Gilpin, Henry, 4, 30–31, 70, 105, 122
Glickstein, Jonathan, 234n97
Gobat, Michael, 222n1
Godwin, Parke, 126–27
Goepp, Charles: on Great Exhibition of 1851, 104, 188; nationalism and, 89; *The New Rome*, 96, 104, 106; popular sovereignty and, 171; on race, 215n78; scientism and, 31; *The United States of the World*, 166
Gollovin, Ivor, 102, 228n84
Gordon, Thomas, 208n41
Grandin, William, 90

Great Exhibition of 1851 (London), 104, 188
Greeley, Horace, 127, 130, 166, 233n74
Greenberg, Amy, 222n1
Greene, James Gordon, 39
Grenville, J. A. S., 156
Grinspan, Jon, 155
Grotius, Hugo, 76
Grow, Galusha, 107, 142, 154, 203n1, 228n78
Grow, Matthew, 115
Guizot, François, 78, 84, 116
Guyatt, Nicholas, 232n61, 244n71
Gwin, William, 173

Hale, John P., 92, 125, 232n61
Hapsburg Empire, 85, 100
Harper's Weekly on plot to assassinate Douglas, 174
Harris, Wiley, 145
Harrison, William H., 69
Haskin, John B., 165, 166, 167
Hawaii, 111
Hawthorne, Nathaniel, 15, 38, 40–44, 96–97; *The Blithedale Romance*, 211n62; "The Celestial Railroad," 43; "The Earth's Holocaust," 43; *Life of Franklin Pierce*, 41–42; *Scarlet Letter*, 41
Haynes, Samuel, 230n115
Henningsen, Charles, 102, 228n80
Henry, Caleb S., 151–52, 188–91, 200
Herder, John Gottfried, 11, 209n45
Hiester, I. E., 145
Hobbes, Thomas, 33, 75
Hobsbawm, Eric, 208n40
Holt, Michael, 144, 191, 212n65, 236n21
Homestead Act of 1849, 233n74
Horsman, Reginald, 219n79
Howe, Daniel, 196, 209n47, 225n10
Hugo, Victor, 4, 194–95; *Les Misérables*, 195
Hulsemann, Baron, 100
Humboldt, Alexander von, 74–75, 223nn18–19
Hungary: Kossuth and, 81–82; revolution (1848) in, 84, 85–86, 100, 167
Hunter, Robert M. T., 159

sovereignty and, 146; rise of, 152–63; slavery and, 125, 187–91; Whig Party and, 18; Young America movement and, 7–8, 9, 21

Rhode Island, 52–55, 63, 66

Richards, Leonard, 234n97

Richardson, William, 7, 90, 128, 136, 203n1, 239n95

Roberts, Timothy, 224nn3–4

Robertson, William H., 118

Romanticism, 11

Ross, Dorothy, 10, 29, 154, 198–99, 206n37, 209n48, 210n55, 216–17n10

Rossiter, Clinton, 208n41

Russia: Crimean War and, 106, 107, 156; Hungarian revolution (1848) and, 86

Sampson, Robert, 219nn78–79

Sand, George, 32

Sanders, Anna, 228nn80–81, 244n66

Sanders, George: on colonization of Africa, 183–84; conservative shift of Young America and, 159; Cuban annexation and, 117, 120; *Democratic Review* and, 3, 55, 89–90; diplomatic role of, 96, 227n62; Douglas and, 7, 9, 90, 91, 203n1, 239n96; election of 1852 and, 9; election of 1856 and, 205n32; election of 1860 and, 243n63; European politics and, 98; Gollovin and, 228n84; sectional conflicts and, 93; slavery and, 118, 146, 181; Society for Universal Democratic Republicanism and, 102; territorial expansion and, 110, 124, 186

Savage, Jon, 84, 94

Sawyer, Stephen, 210n55

Scholnick, Robert, 34

Schurz, Carl, 125

scientism, 27–28, 29, 31, 32, 74, 186

Scott, Winfield, 92

Second Bank of the United States, 1–2

Second Great Reform Act of 1867 (Britain), 156

self-government: Cuban annexation and, 115–16; Dorr Rebellion and, 56, 61;

natural rights and, 26, 56, 61; O'Sullivan on, 221n17. *See also* popular sovereignty

Seward, William, 18, 86, 87–88, 128, 158–59

Sexton, Jay, 230n115

Shields, James, 2, 136

Shire, Laura Clarke, 210n53

Sickles, Daniel, 96

Silver Greys, 150

Simms, William Gilmore: *Progress in America*, 129

slavery: Compromise of 1850 and, 92, 134–37, 145, 147, 236n16; conservative transformation of Young America movement and, 155–63; Cuban annexation and, 118–32, 185, 230n2, 234n97; Jacksonian ideology and, 16–17, 22, 167–68, 171, 174; Kansas-Nebraska Act of 1854 and, 17, 20, 101, 109, 137–47, 236n21; natural rights and, 18–19, 133–63; popular sovereignty and, 22, 164–92; Republican Party and, 125, 187–91; territorial expansion and, 67, 72, 118–32; Whig Party and, 144, 149–55; Young America movement and, 22–23, 181–87

Slidell, John, 73, 174

Smith, Adam, 33

Smith, Adam I. P., 15, 54, 234n97, 240n107

Smith, Caleb Blood, 60–61

Smith, Gerrit, 125–26, 144, 232n61

Smith, Rogers, 219n83

Smith, Steven, 209n43

Smith, William R., 100

Smyth, Thomas, 49

social contract theory, 11–12, 29

Society for Universal Democratic Republicanism, 101–2

Soulé, Pierre: conservative shift of Young America and, 157–58; Cuban annexation and, 14, 111, 227n69; diplomatic role of, 96, 98–100; Douglas and, 7, 203n1, 239n96; dueling by, 174; European revolutions and, 87, 108; Ostend Manifesto and, 119, 227n69; slavery and, 118; territorial expansion and, 110, 226n61, 227nn69–70

*Lincoln's Dilemma: Blair, Sumner, and the Republican Struggle
over Racism and Equality in the Civil War Era*
PAUL D. ESCOTT

*Slavery and War in the Americas: Race, Citizenship, and State
Building in the United States and Brazil, 1861–1870*
VITOR IZECKSOHN

Marching Masters: Slavery, Race, and the Confederate Army during the Civil War
COLIN EDWARD WOODWARD

*Confederate Visions: Nationalism, Symbolism, and
the Imagined South in the Civil War*
IAN BINNINGTON

Frederick Douglass: A Life in Documents
L. DIANE BARNES, EDITOR

Reconstructing the Campus: Higher Education and the American Civil War
MICHAEL DAVID COHEN

Worth a Dozen Men: Women and Nursing in the Civil War South
LIBRA R. HILDE

*Civil War Talks: Further Reminiscences of George
S. Bernard and His Fellow Veterans*
HAMPTON NEWSOME, JOHN HORN, AND JOHN G. SELBY, EDITORS

The Enemy Within: Fears of Corruption in the Civil War North
MICHAEL THOMAS SMITH

*The Big House after Slavery: Virginia Plantation
Families and Their Postbellum Experiment*
AMY FEELY MORSMAN

Take Care of the Living: Reconstructing Confederate Veteran Families in Virginia
JEFFREY W. MCCLURKEN

Civil War Petersburg: Confederate City in the Crucible of War
A. WILSON GREENE

A Separate Civil War: Communities in Conflict in the Mountain South
JONATHAN DEAN SARRIS

Lincoln's Tragic Admiral: The Life of Samuel Francis Du Pont
KEVIN J. WEDDLE

The War Hits Home: The Civil War in Southeastern Virginia
BRIAN STEEL WILLS

Ashe County's Civil War: Community and Society in the Appalachian South
MARTIN CRAWFORD